"Too Much for ⸺⸺⸺ Endurance"

The George Spangler Farm Hospitals and the Battle of Gettysburg

Ronald D. Kirkwood

Savas Beatie
California

Library of Congress Cataloging-in-Publication Data

Names: Kirkwood, Ronald D., author.
Title: "Too Much for Human Endurance": The George Spangler Farm Hospitals and the Battle of Gettysburg / by Ronald D. Kirkwood.
Description: First edition. | El Dorado Hills, California: Savas Beatie, [2019] | Includes bibliographical references.
Identifiers: LCCN 2019005827| ISBN 9781611214512 (hardcover: alk. paper) | ISBN 9781611214529 (ebk.)
Subjects: LCSH: Gettysburg, Battle of, Gettysburg, Pa., 1863. | United States—History—Civil War, 1861-1865—Hospitals. | United States—History—Civil War, 1861-1865—Medical care. | United States. Army of the Potomac. Corps, 11th. | Military hospitals—Pennsylvania—Gettysburg Region—History—19th century. | Farms—Pennsylvania—Gettysburg Region—History—19th century. | Spangler family.
Classification: LCC E475.53 .K57 2019 | DDC 973.7/349—dc23
LC record available at https://lccn.loc.gov/2019005827

First paperback edition, first printing
ISBN-13: 978-1-61121-531-1

SB

Savas Beatie
989 Governor Drive, Suite 102
El Dorado Hills, CA 95762
Phone: 916-941-6896
(web) www.savasbeatie.com
(E-mail) sales@savasbeatie.com

Our titles are available at special discounts for bulk purchases. For more details, contact us at sales@savasbeatie.com.

Proudly printed in the United States of America.

Maps by Derek Wachter

For the Gettysburg Foundation,
who saved the Spangler farm and its stories.

"IS MY LEG OFF?"

"We were hurriedly carried to the ambulances and driven to a field-hospital established in a large barn a mile or more from Gettysburg. In and around that barn were gathered about fifteen hundred wounded soldiers, Union and Confederate. They were begrimed, swollen, and bloody, as brought in from the field, and, for the most part, had received as yet but little surgical treatment. Some were barely alive, others had just died, and many were in a state of indescribable misery. In the centre of the barn stood an amputating table, around which two or three surgeons were busily performing their dreadful offices.

"A handsome young German captain, whose leg had been shattered by a musket-ball, was placed upon the table and chloroformed. After the operation of removing his injured limb was complete, he was brought to where I lay and placed beside me. The pallor of his face betokened great loss of blood and extreme weakness. After some minutes, he opened his eyes, and, turning languidly toward me, inquired, 'Is my leg off?' Being told that it was, he gazed intently at his hand, and, observing that a ring had been removed from his finger, he remarked, 'I would not care for this, were it not for a little friend I have down there at Philadelphia.' He could not say much more, for his remaining vitality was fast ebbing away. In a few hours it was gone."

— Capt. Alfred E. Lee, 82nd Ohio*

* Alfred E. Lee, "Reminiscences of the Gettysburg Battle," *Lippincott's Magazine of Popular Literature and Science*, vol. 32, GNMP Library, Box V8 (Philadelphia, PA, 1883), 60.

Table of Contents

Table of Contents (continued)

Maps, photos, and illustrations have been interspersed
throughout the manuscript for the convenience of the reader.

Foreword
A Farm Worth Saving

A few months after my October 1993 retirement from the federal government in Washington, D.C., I began my volunteer "career" with the Friends of the National Parks at Gettysburg. The Land Protection Plan for Gettysburg National Military Park was published that same month and year. This plan was based in large part on proposals in the Boundary Study that led to legislation signed into law on August 17, 1990 (P.L. 101-377), and "reflects expanding the park's boundary by 2,050 acres," among other things considered necessary for the proper management of the national military park and its resources. The expanded park boundary would then total 5,733 acres. As a Friends board member, I was provided a copy of the Land Protection Plan and advised to study it carefully and be aware of its value.

The establishment of a new park boundary added 13 resource areas considered significant for preservation and correct interpretation of the battle fought in July 1863 and its landscape, soldiers, and civilians. One of those areas was the George Spangler Farm of 80 acres. The area objective, specified on Page 11 of the Land Protection Plan, was to:

> Maintain the historic woodlands, buildings and pastoral open space of the Spangler Farm and screen modern development along Granite Schoolhouse Lane . . . to: . . . Develop an active interpretive program focusing on the area's use as a major hospital site and supply and artillery park for Union troops on Cemetery ridge [and] maintain a visitor tour route shielded from modern development.

All properties in the newly defined boundary were assigned an acquisition priority of high, medium, or low based on the historic significance. The George Spangler Farm was assigned a high priority, but it was in private ownership known then as an "in-holding." The Andrew family had owned the farm for many years, and part of the family still occupied the house until 2008.

Not until 2006, soon after the merger to become the Gettysburg Foundation (between the Friends and the Gettysburg National Battlefield Museum Foundation), did serious discussions begin about this high-priority item. Then-superintendent John Latschar knew the Andrew family and made introductions for us. Gettysburg Foundation staff member Sally McPherson and I, as a Foundation board member, met with the Andrew family representative to discuss possibilities for acquiring the farm. It was the hope of the family that the farm would one day become part of the park, its buildings be restored, and its history be preserved and told for generations to come.

In April of 2008, the Foundation completed the acquisition of this major piece of land and its structures, and the many phases of saving the buildings began. With gifts from major donors and campaigns with the Friends membership, the reconstruction and/or rehabilitation of the barn, summer kitchen, and smokehouse has been completed. The non-historic structures and vegetation have been removed, and new orchards have been planted. The history is being told and the scene is being preserved.

It is astounding to look back at "what was" and see "what is" at the Spangler farm today. Personally, it was once thought to be nearly impossible to acquire and, even more, to save the farm's original structures. In the 1990s, I was convinced it would be impossible to remove the power lines from the historic fields of battle. Because I remember how the battlefield and the Spangler farm used to look, as opposed to how they now appear, I am proud to have been one of the volunteers during these years of preservation and education.

Thanks to the vision and determination of the National Park Service, Gettysburg Foundation, Andrew family, and others, the George Spangler Farm has been preserved for generations of future visitors. And now thanks to Ron Kirkwood and his important book *"Too Much for Human Endurance": The George Spangler Farm Hospitals and the Battle of Gettysburg*, so have its stories, many of which previously were hidden from history.

Ron's book is a tribute to the Spangler family, the soldiers and surgeons who turned the barn into a field hospital in July 1863, the historians and architects whose input to preservation and education was crucial, and the hundreds of contributors and volunteers, without whom the current site would today be in ruins. Congratulations and thanks to Ron for this enjoyable and educational book.

Barbara J. Finfrock
Vice Chair
Gettysburg Foundation

Introduction

The Spangler story is the rare important Gettysburg tale that has never been told in its entirety.

George and Elizabeth Spangler were living the 1863 dream on a beautiful, peaceful, growing, and thriving farm just south of Gettysburg. The healthy family of six worked hard and had a bounty of loving extended family members in the area. And then, on July 1 as the guns boomed north and west of town, someone from the XI Corps medical staff of the Army of the Potomac guided his horse up their farm lane to announce that their land was being taken over for use as a hospital. Other than in the most general sense, little was known of the horrors that came thereafter.

In an effort to rectify this, *"Too Much for Human Endurance"* emphasizes the family, their farm, the hospitals, the Union medical staff established there, and the people who lived, camped, worked, suffered, and died there. The Spangler farm and land also played a crucially important role in the battle, one that might surprise many veteran readers of Civil War history. Thousands of books and many generations later, there is still uncharted territory about that battle that remains to be shared.

I started as a volunteer guide at the Gettysburg Foundation's George Spangler Farm Civil War Field Hospital Site when it opened in 2013. When I look back now, I realize how embarrassingly little I knew about the farm, its inhabitants, and its role in the battle. I learned more with each new season I served there. Over time, I was able to gain a better understanding of what the Spanglers and their four kids experienced while stuffed together into one bedroom for more than five weeks with the horrors of a Civil War hospital all around them. I studied how the large number of wounded arrived there and how hard the doctors and nurses worked in an effort to heal them, or at least make their last minutes on earth as comfortable as possible. I learned about the Army of the Potomac's Artillery Reserve, with its 106 cannons, hundreds of wagons, some 2,300 men and as many horses parked there, overflowing the property as the artillerists awaited the call to roll to the front.

I couldn't wait to read and learn more about this farm and the people involved. What little was available in the public domain was fascinating, but much of it was stored out of public view. It quickly became obvious there must be many untapped Spangler-related stories waiting to be found and documented. It was then I decided to roll up my sleeves and write a book on the subject.

The wonderful research, stories, and reports already gathered were put together through countless hours of dedicated Spangler work by talented historians Kathleen Georg Harrison, Wayne Motts, Dan Welch, Gettysburg hospital expert Greg Coco, and others. I benefited greatly from their selfless efforts. The now 80 acre Spangler property was purchased by the Gettysburg Foundation in 2008. Help poured in from the National Park Service, the Adams County Historical Society, Keystone Preservation Group Inc., LSC Design Inc., and others that helped uncover the farm's stories. All of this got me started on a Spangler book.

As my research went on, every discovery of the identity of a soldier who spent time on the Spangler property and every piece of new information about members of the Spangler family filled holes in this untold story. I quickly learned the Spangler farm was essentially at the center of a giant logistical wheel through which untold thousands of men, guns, and wagons passed to reach the Union front. The more I researched, the more I realized how little I knew about the outsized impact the Spanglers and their land had on the outcome of the battle.

In addition to all of the work that needed to be done in Gettysburg, research took me all over the East Coast, including Washington, D.C., Cornell University, Philadelphia, West Chester, and York, Pennsylvania, and the US Army War College at Carlisle. I paid many visits to the National Museum of Civil War Medicine in Frederick, Maryland, took a side trip to Sharpsburg, and even traveled to Enterprise, Kansas. I was stunned by how much information was available. Love letters from homesick doctors and soldiers, diaries, a bounty of books by people who were at or crossed the Spangler farm that included a few paragraphs about what they saw and did there, official reports, postwar interviews, and thousands of cards and pension files (and more) housed at the National Archives in Washington. Someone just needed to dig through the archival material and find those items with a Spangler focus.

It is now possible to make the case that the Spangler land was one of the most important in helping determine the battle's outcome, and perhaps the single most important farm. Many others—Rose, Bliss, Codori, Henry Spangler, McPherson,

Brian, Herbst, and Rummel—experienced terrible fighting that ruined their property. The size and central location of the George Spangler farm, however, made it possible for the Army of the Potomac to place sizable artillery and infantry reserves near the front and close to the roads it needed to get the guns and men up in time to be of service. The army also used the Spanglers' Powers Hill to help take back Culp's Hill and protect the crucial Baltimore Pike, which was the army's most important logistical lifeline running immediately behind the Union right flank. No single farm had a greater impact on the battle's outcome than the Spangler farm.

It was important to find a way to convey the suffering of the wounded as well as the doctors and nurses who labored around the clock under horrific conditions. What did they feel and think? What did they smell and see? Many were there because they were wounded or dying, but many others were drawn to the Spangler farm out of a Christian or civic sense of duty to help the unfortunate soldiers.

The suffering these people endured, of course, is impossible for us to fully comprehend today. Thanks to the wealth of firsthand accounts that have now surfaced, however, the men and women themselves are able to tell us what they witnessed and suffered as men screamed and cried and died and ear-splitting cannon blasts reverberated across the expansive property. As is always the case in every human endeavor, recollections, sometimes written long after the war, did not always line up concerning events large and small. I did my best to evaluate the accounts and thread them together in a way that conveyed the full story of this farm and the remarkable people who lived and worked there.

You won't find the Spangler farm and Powers Hill on an official battlefield map. They, together with Granite Schoolhouse and Granite Schoolhouse Lane, are not part of the official battlefield auto tour. As we now know, however, that doesn't mean these places did not play a crucial rule in the outcome of the battle. It's time the important story of the Spanglers, their land, and their neighborhood is told in full, which is what this book attempts to do. It is my hope the personal stories within these pages provide a sense of what the Spanglers and others suffered through and help us understand why this property is so important to the history of our country.

Hopefully, this book fills one of the remaining holes in the story of the battle of Gettysburg.

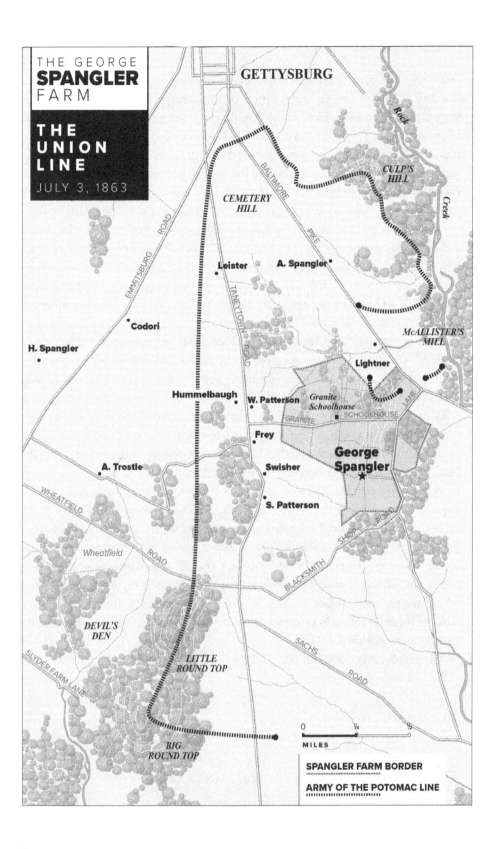

THE GEORGE
SPANGLER
FARM

THE UNION LINE

JULY 3, 1863

GETTYSBURG

BALTIMORE PIKE

CEMETERY HILL

CULP'S HILL

EMMITSBURG ROAD

TANEYTOWN ROAD

Leister

A. Spangler

Codori

McALLISTER'S MILL

H. Spangler

Lightner

Hummelbaugh

W. Patterson

Granite Schoolhouse

GRANITE SCHOOLHOUSE LANE

Frey

George Spangler ★

A. Trostle

Swisher

S. Patterson

WHEATFIELD

Wheatfield

ROAD

BLACKSMITH SHOP ROAD

SLYDER FARM LANE

DEVIL'S DEN

LITTLE ROUND TOP

SACHS ROAD

BIG ROUND TOP

0   ¼   ½
MILES

SPANGLER FARM BORDER

ARMY OF THE POTOMAC LINE

Chapter 1

Our Land, Our Home:
The Spanglers

"This issue is one of preservation or destruction."
— *Pennsylvania governor Andrew G. Curtin, appealing for
troops as the Army of Northern Virginia enters the commonwealth*

June 3, 1863: General Robert E. Lee of the Army of Northern Virginia sends Maj. Gen. Lafayette McLaws' division of Lt. Gen. James Longstreet's I Corps from Fredericksburg, Virginia, toward Culpeper Court House, thus beginning the Gettysburg Campaign and the invasion of the North. More Confederate divisions will follow in the coming days, setting off a panic north of the Mason-Dixon Line. Frightened Pennsylvanians now know that this powerful Southern army and its victorious leader are heading in their direction. But where is he aiming?

June 12: Governor Andrew G. Curtin of Pennsylvania knows Lee's army is approaching and reacts with a proclamation. He writes, in part, "The importance of immediately raising a sufficient force for the defence of the State cannot be overrated." The purpose of the militia corps to be raised, Curtin says, "will be mainly the defence of our own homes, firesides, and property from devastation."[1]

June 15: Brigadier General Albert Jenkins' Confederate cavalry brigade crosses the Potomac River. A day later, he reaches Chambersburg, just 24 miles west of

---

1 William J. Tenney, *The Military and Naval History of the Rebellion in the United States* (New York, NY, 1866), 385-386.

Gettysburg, in the first Confederate incursion of Pennsylvania in the Gettysburg Campaign. Governor Curtin writes: "I now appeal to all the citizens of Pennsylvania, who love liberty and are mindful of the history and traditions of their Revolutionary fathers, and who feel that it is a sacred duty to guard and maintain the free institutions of our country, who hate treason and its abettors, and who are willing to defend their homes and firesides, and do invoke them to rise in their might and rush to the rescue in this hour of peril. This issue is one of preservation or destruction."[2]

June 22: Major General Robert E. Rodes' division of Lt. Gen. Richard Ewell's II Corps enters Greencastle, about 30 miles from Gettysburg, triggering the Confederate infantry invasion of Pennsylvania. "Great excitement prevails," writes Gettysburg resident Sarah Broadhead, "and there is no reliable intelligence . . . and so we are in great suspense."[3]

June 30: Martial law is declared in Baltimore and western Maryland by Maj. Gen. Robert C. Schenck, commander of the Union's VIII Corps. "All peaceful citizens are required to remain quietly at their homes," Schenck declares, adding that "seditious language or mischievous practices tending to the encouragement of the rebellion are especially prohibited, and will be promptly made the subject of observation and treatment. . . . To save the country is paramount to all other considerations."[4]

Defensive works are hurriedly thrown up as far away as Pittsburgh, but on June 26 the picture becomes clear for citizens of the commonwealth as the Confederates begin to settle in throughout south-central Pennsylvania from Chambersburg to York to Wrightsville to Carlisle to just across the Susquehanna River from Harrisburg. On the 26th, local militia man George Washington Sandoe is shot and killed on the Baltimore Pike by Confederates under Maj. Gen. Jubal Early as they capture Gettysburg on their way to York. Governor Curtin raises 25,000 men by June 20, but he issues a late and desperate plea for 60,000 more: "A people who

2 Ibid.

3 Sarah M. Broadhead, *The Diary of a Lady of Gettysburg, Pennsylvania, June 15 to July 15, 1863*, Adams County Historical Society (Gettysburg, PA).

4 Robert C. Schenck, Official Report, June 30, 1863, in *The War of the Rebellion: Official Records of the Union and Confederate Armies* (Washington, D.C., 1971), Series 1, vol. 27, pt. 1, 437-438. Hereafter cited as *OR*. All references are to Series 1 unless otherwise noted.

want the heart to defend their soil, their families, and their firesides, are not worthy to be counted men."[5]

It is too little and too late for the upcoming raids and brawl. Just as Union troops were known to do in the South, the Confederates destroy bridges and property and take horses, cattle, sheep, and goods after crossing the Mason-Dixon Line. Sometimes, residents are paid with Confederate bank notes, which have no worth in Pennsylvania. In the most horrific acts of the raids, former slaves who are now living a life of freedom are seized and sent back to the South into slavery.

The whole of south-central Pennsylvania reaches crisis mode. In Gettysburg, many residents, including entire families, rush out of town. Frightened blacks flee to safety while they can. Many Gettysburg-area residents send their horses and mules more than 40 miles east to safety across the Susquehanna River in Lancaster County. Colonel Isaac Seymour of the 6th Louisiana reported that one Adams County resident tried to hide his horse in the elegant parlor of his large home.[6]

Then, on the cloudy and comfortable 70-degree morning of July 1 and after almost a month of mounting anxiety, the full fury of the Civil War opened on the residents of Gettysburg. "What to do or where to go, I did not know," lamented Sarah Broadhead. "People were running here and there, screaming that the town would be shelled. No one knew where to go or what to do. . . . Our neighbors had all gone away."[7]

Amid this mayhem, George and Elizabeth Spangler and their four children stayed right where they were. This was a decision made within full earshot and view of the Civil War. In fact, the killing of militia man George Washington Sandoe on the Baltimore Pike days earlier took place near their property.

The Spanglers undoubtedly wanted to protect their land and their successful and growing farming operation that they had built from scratch over the previous 15 years. In addition, their German Spangler and Dutch Brinkerhoff roots ran deep in south-central Pennsylvania, and now was certainly not the time—war or no war—to abandon their home and their farm. But they had no way of comprehending the magnitude of what they were about to experience because of their stand.

---

5 Tenney, *The Military and Naval History of the Rebellion in the United States*, 393.

6 William and Isaac Seymour Collection, James S. Schoff Civil War Collection, William L. Clements Library, University of Michigan.

7 Broadhead, *The Diary of a Lady*.

* * *

George Spangler was born in Straban Township, Adams County, on December 19, 1815, making him 47 years old during the battle of Gettysburg. George's mother, Mary Knopp Spangler, died in 1819 at age 24 when George was three years old, and his brother, John, was one. Sometime later, his father, Abraham, married Elizabeth Lady, who provided the siblings with nine half-brothers and half-sisters. Abraham and Elizabeth bought a 205-acre farm on the Baltimore Pike just outside of Gettysburg in 1827. This farm with the now famous Spangler's Spring was occupied by George's half-brother Henry and his wife, Sarah Plank Spangler, during the battle, while Abraham and Elizabeth lived on their second property, a 30-acre farm along the Chambersburg Pike on the west side of town. Nicholas Eckenrode rented Henry and Sarah's Emmitsburg Road farm, a property that on July 2-3 would serve as a launching pad for Army of Northern Virginia charges against the Army of the Potomac. Abraham and Henry's Baltimore Pike farm sits near the current-day intersection with Hunt Avenue at 1118 Baltimore Pike and is marked by a Civil War hospital sign.

In 1841, the 25-year-old George married 22-year-old Elizabeth Brinkerhoff (born September 4, 1818, in Mount Pleasant Township). She was one of about 10 children of Cornelius and Elizabeth Snyder Brinkerhoff. There were many Brinkerhoffs living throughout Gettysburg and Adams County at the time of the battle, especially on farms south of Hunterstown in Straban Township. Brinkerhoff's Ridge on Hanover Road east of town was the site of a July 2 cavalry and infantry fight and was named for Henry Brinkerhoff, a cousin of Elizabeth Spangler and the owner of the farm where the battle took place.[8]

According to tax records, George and Elizabeth didn't own land in the early years of their marriage, though they did own horses and cows. In all likelihood, they lived on and farmed someone else's property. They purchased 80 acres from Henry Bishop in 1848, acreage that marked the beginning of the farm they would own during the battle. This property was at 488 Blacksmith Shop Road, Cumberland Township, just off the Baltimore Pike, just south of Gettysburg, and only a mile by road from Abraham Spangler's farm.

George and Elizabeth spent the next 15 years working hard and building their family, their prosperity, and their farm. First child Harriet Jane was born in 1842

---

8 http://familyharttng.info. 1984-2016 FamilyHart Inc. Accessed November 18, 2016; Ancestry.com. Accessed April 11, 2017; http://bergencountyhistory.org/forums/index.php?topic=1219.0. Accessed April 21, 2017.

George Spangler's son Beniah (center) with wife Sarah and daughter Mary Elizabeth on the family farm circa 1888 around the 25th anniversary of the battle. *William Tipton*

(21 at the time of battle), Sabina Catherine in 1844 (19), Daniel E. in 1845 (17), and Beniah John in 1848 (14). The Spanglers bought their first carriage in 1852.

There wasn't much to the property when they bought it. It is believed that the Spanglers first moved into a small log building in what is now the south end of the house (the side of the house farthest from the barn). While there, they built the northern portion of the building in stone around 1850, and at some point the log cabin portion was removed. The house was 26 feet by 28 feet at the time of the battle. Farming on the property dates to the early 1800s or earlier.

The Spanglers began developing their farm within a year or two of purchasing it, and they did so with a fine attention to detail. The original stone house included six rooms over two stories, with two rooms and a hall on the first floor, with a staircase up to the second floor, which contained the stair hall and two additional rooms. The house also had a fully excavated cellar and an attic. The first-floor rooms, particularly the formal front room, were well-appointed, with a fireplace, deep-paneled window jambs, beaded baseboard and chair rail trim, and carved window and door trim. Similar trim was also in place upstairs.[9]

George and Elizabeth continued to aggressively build and buy, purchasing land from several neighbors. According to the Gettysburg Foundation's Historic Structure Report: ". . . surviving buildings from this development include the small

---

9 The Gettysburg Foundation sponsored a Historic Structure Report (HSR) in 2010-11 conducted by LSC Design Inc. of York, Pennsylvania, and Keystone Preservation Group Inc. of Perkasie, Pennsylvania, with assistance and guidance from the Foundation, the National Park Service, and the Adams County Historical Society. These are the organizations that modern-day fans of The George Spangler Farm Civil War Hospital Site can thank for what we know about the farm of 1863 and the reconstruction that has taken place faithful to historic detail. The work of these organizations saved history and the farm.

The likely appearance of the Spangler house in 1863. *Gettysburg Foundation*

two-story stone house [six rooms], a large stone and frame standard Pennsylvania bank barn, a one-and-a-half story stone summer kitchen, and a small brick and frame smokehouse. It is likely that additional outbuildings—sheds, pens, an outhouse, etc.—were part of the development. The property also included woodland, grain fields, an orchard, and vegetable garden. It is not known if Spangler developed the existing farm on the site of, and to include, earlier buildings." The orchard was south and southwest of the Spangler house.

By 1863, a variety of fencing—post-and-rail, stone, and stone-and-rider fences (wood rails over stone)—crisscrossed the Spangler property, with a more detailed enclosure (such as a picket fence) possibly surrounding the yard. Their beautiful two-story bank barn, 72 by 45 feet, was a work of art and typical of the bank-barn style. Brought to Pennsylvania during the 1700s and 1800s by the Swiss and Germans, it featured a ramped bank on the back leading directly to the top floor to make it easy to load and unload wagons. A forebay, or overhang, extended from the front of the barn and allowed for more storage on the upper level. The bottom floor was for livestock and a root cellar that was built into the bank. As was common with the Linear Mid-Atlantic Farm style, the roof peaks of both the house

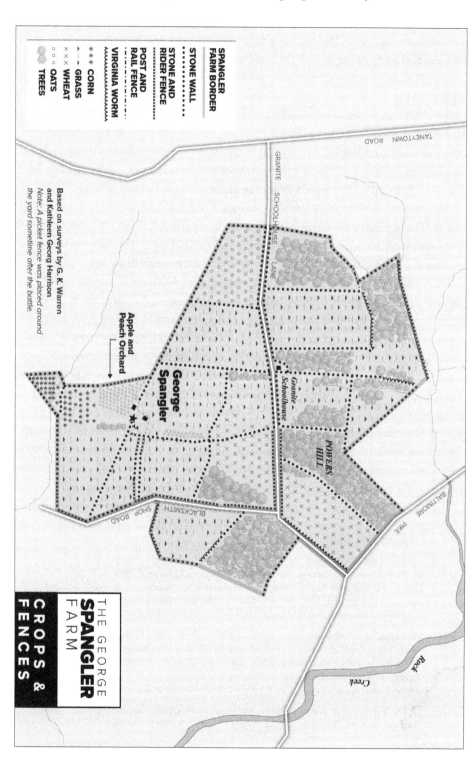

THE GEORGE
SPANGLER FARM
CROPS & FENCES

Based on surveys by G. K. Warren and Kathleen Georg Harrison
Note: A picket fence was placed around the yard sometime after the battle.

Legend:
- SPANGLER FARM BORDER
- STONE WALL
- STONE AND RIDER FENCE
- POST AND RAIL FENCE
- VIRGINIA WORM
- CORN
- GRASS
- WHEAT
- OATS
- TREES

Labels on map: TANEYTOWN ROAD, GRANITE SCHOOLHOUSE LANE, Apple and Peach Orchard, George Spangler, Granite Schoolhouse, POWERS HILL, BLACKSMITH SHOP ROAD, BALTIMORE PIKE, Rock Creek

and the barn aligned. Other outbuildings for storage and processing were built between and around the two main buildings.[10]

The Confederates noticed the large barns and German lifestyles on their march to Gettysburg. "This valley thro' which we have moved is densely populated, being quite unlike in our own country—but what a population!" exclaimed Major Eugene Blackford of the 5th Alabama Sharpshooters. "[A]lmost entirely Dutchmen, with immense barns, and small inconvenient dwelling houses. All drink 'lager' & eat 'sauer-krout,' from one year's end to the other." *Cincinnati Gazette* war reporter Whitelaw Reid called the Pennsylvania bank barns "great horse palaces."[11]

According to the 1850 census, farmer Spangler's property was valued at $2,500. The agricultural census reflects a modestly sized farm of 80 improved and 22 unimproved acres, most of it planted in wheat and oats. The farm produced a significant amount of dairy products, including 200 pounds of butter a year.

According to the Historic Structure Report, by 1860 their real estate value had doubled to $5,000. The farm was "successful and growing." Its livestock, much of which lived in the stable of the bank barn and in the fenced barnyard, included six horses, seven milk cows, five heads of beef, three sheep "that produced 20 lbs of wool," and thirteen pigs. The most recent harvest reflected a wide diversification of crops: 130 bushels of wheat, 600 bushels of corn, 202 bushels of oats, 12 bushels of buckwheat, 25 bushels of Irish [white] potatoes, 12 bushels of sweet potatoes, $20 of market produce, 20 tons of hay, 11 bushels of clover seed, and two bushels of grass seed (some of which would have been stored in the upper story of the barn). The family used its summer kitchen with its large cooking fireplace and ample workspace to prepare their food. The smokehouse, which stood at the southeast corner of the house, was used to cure the meat from the butchered hogs.[12]

In 1861, the Spanglers bought another 65 acres of farm and woodland on the north side of their existing property from Peter Weikert's heirs. This expansion

---

10 Henry Glassie, "Eighteenth Century Cultural Process in Delaware Valley Folk Building," in Dell Upton and John Michael Vlach, eds., *Common Places: Readings in American Vernacular Architecture* (Athens, GA, 1986), 394-422. The Spanglers' beautiful bank barn was rebuilt by the Gettysburg Foundation in 2015-16 with strict attention to historic detail.

11 Eugene Blackford to his mother, June 28, 1863, in Lewis Leigh Collection, 1861-65, US Army Heritage and Education Center (Carlisle, PA); Whitelaw Reid, in Gary W. Gallagher, ed., *Two Witnesses at Gettysburg* (Malden, MA, 2009), 21. These bank barns remain common throughout south-central and eastern Pennsylvania today and are easy to spot. They are all over Adams County and the battlefield and some are in excellent condition.

12 The Spangler barn, summer kitchen, and smokehouse appear today as they did in 1863 thanks to the work, dedication, and fundraising of the Gettysburg Foundation.

swelled the Spangler farm to 166 acres. An advertisement in *The Adams Sentinel* dated September 5, 1860, noted that the land could be divided into four separate properties, but the Spanglers bought all of it in one transaction. The purchase included most of Powers Hill, which would become a key strategic site for the Army of the Potomac in the upcoming battle. As the Spanglers' acreage grew, it is highly likely that they brought on hired help.

From south to north, George and Elizabeth's property extended about three-quarters of a mile from its southernmost to northernmost points. It was about the same from east to west. About 1,000 feet of the Spanglers' northern border met the southern boundary of father Abraham Spangler's property, which sat on both sides of the Baltimore Pike. The eastern portion of today's Gettysburg National Military Park Visitor Center complex sits on what was once Abraham Spangler land. The western part of the complex is on the former Catherine Guinn property. Spangler property dominated that portion of the Union line: It would have been a walk of about 7,250 feet on a straight line starting at George's southernmost boundary and heading north, crossing the boundary from George's property onto Abraham's and continuing until reaching Abraham's northern property line within a couple hundred feet of Evergreen Cemetery.

George Spangler was a well-respected community leader in the Gettysburg area and served on the Cumberland Township School Board. A teacher he hired in 1853 wrote after George's death in 1904 that Spangler "made a lasting impression on my mind as a man of truthfulness and honesty in all things." George's obituary in *The Adams Sentinel* on February 3, 1904, described him as "a life-long Democrat." Northern Democrats were divided during the Civil War, with some supporting President Abraham Lincoln and his policies toward the breakaway South, and the others opposing him. Gettysburg even had three weekly newspapers, with the Democratic *Compiler* expressing mostly Southern views, while the *Sentinel* and the *Star and Banner* favored abolition. The Spanglers appeared to have done a significant amount of business through the *Sentinel*, so it is likely they were Lincoln Democrats.[13]

By 1860, about half of the 89 congregations in the county were Lutheran or Reformed, with most members of German extraction. The Spanglers attended Christ Lutheran Church (today's Grace Lutheran) in Two Taverns, a lengthy ride of some three and one-half miles down the Baltimore Pike, though they likely took a

---

13 William G. Black, "A Memory of George Spangler," in *Gettysburg Compiler*, February 17, 1904.

back-country shortcut. George served for many years as an elder in the church, and son B. J., as Beniah was called, was a deacon.[14]

With the railroad already there and expanding, Gettysburg was a modern town in 1863 with a host of goods readily available for its 2,400 residents. Most in the borough were tradesmen such as leather tanners, printers, carriage makers, businessmen, and other professionals. The town's prosperity created a hunger for the produce of local farms, so the Spanglers made regular trips into town to sell their fruits, vegetables, and dairy products.

Much like their town and the house and barn that they built with a great attention to detail, the Spanglers were a modern 1863 family. They had created a successful farm and lifestyle on a large piece of property through hard work, good vision, and brains. Everything was in order, and undoubtedly, all six Spanglers contributed. On the morning of the first Wednesday of July, however, everything they had—their property, their livelihood, and their lives—came under threat as two large armies totaling some 165,000 men closed in on Gettysburg.

That afternoon on July 1, medical staffers of the Second Division of the Army of the Potomac's XI Corps guided their horses up the Spangler lane (which still exists today) as the sound of gunfire, reverberating like a heavy summer storm a few miles away to the north and northwest, enveloped the farm. George, Daniel, and Beniah were probably out cutting or hauling in wheat or mowing and putting up hay. Elizabeth, Harriet, and Sabina could have been in the garden, house, or summer kitchen. To the surprise and dismay of whoever first heard the news, the medical staff officers announced they were seizing the house, the buildings, and the land for a hospital and everyone needed to leave at once for their own safety.

It probably didn't take the Spanglers long to decide what to do. Even though the sounds of war drew closer with each passing hour, they made the decision to stay put, even when ordered out, their pleas persuading the XI Corps medical staff to grant their request. The six Spanglers would live and sleep shoulder-to-shoulder from July 1 to August 6, 1863, in one upstairs bedroom as their world crumbled around them.

---

14 *History of Adams County Pennsylvania* (reprint of 1886 edition) Adams County Historical Society (Gettysburg, PA); www.achs-pa.org/about-us/history-of-adams-county. Adams County Historical Society. Accessed April 21, 2017.

Spangler Farm Short Story

Two trees on Ancestry.com reveal that Elizabeth Brinkerhoff Spangler was second cousin once removed to Cpl. Henry M. Brinkerhoff, who fought with Lt. Col. George Armstrong Custer as part of the 7th Cavalry at the Little Bighorn in June 1876. Unlike Custer, Brinkerhoff survived the massacre.

Henry Brinkerhoff was born in 1854 in Straban Township, Adams County, near Hunterstown. The member of Company G, 7th Cavalry, was 22 at the Little Bighorn and described by the Army Register of Enlistments as standing five feet six inches with blue eyes, light hair, and a fair complexion. Brinkerhoff fought at the Little Bighorn under Maj. Marcus Reno, where despite being overwhelmed by the more powerful forces of such Sioux and Cheyenne leaders as Sitting Bull and Crazy Horse, the troops retreated up a hill and defended the position until the Indians left two days later. At Reno's order, Brinkerhoff rode away to find Gen. Alfred Terry and his approaching troops and guide them to their location. According to Brinkerhoff, he was the first trooper to see Custer's corpse and the mangled bodies of his dead fighters as he passed them on his way to General Terry. After his military service, Brinkerhoff settled in Los Angeles and died there in 1933 at the age of 78.

The Brinkerhoff-Custer connection goes beyond the Little Bighorn. Both men were in the Gettysburg area during the 1863 battle, Brinkerhoff as a boy of nine and Custer as a 23-year-old brigadier general who staged a daring charge and fought near several Brinkerhoff farms just south of Hunterstown on July 2, including that of Henry's father, John. Custer also fought near Brinkerhoff's Ridge outside Gettysburg on Hanover Road on July 3, where he engaged in another daring charge. As a boy, Brinkerhoff surely heard many stories about the gallant Custer's July 2 Hunterstown fight and narrow escape no more than a couple of miles down the road from his home. Young Henry would have heard the artillery blasts, and might have seen some of the action. He likely explored the battlefield afterward.

It's fascinating to wonder whether Brinkerhoff asked Custer in 1876 about the day outside of Hunterstown in 1863 when he fought next door to so many Brinkerhoff farms. It is even possible that Henry ended up on Reno Hill in 1876 because Custer's actions 13 years earlier in Pennsylvania inspired him to join the United States cavalry.[15]

15 Henry Brinkerhoff, "Sergeant Brinkerhoff Tells New Side of the Most Famous of Indian Fights," in *Helena, MT, Independent Record,* July 1, 1928.

Chapter 2

An Early Start on the Suffering

"The Americans loathe all the Germans and slight them whenever they can."
— *German XI Corps Assistant Surgeon Carl Uterhart, 119th New York*

George Spangler was descended from German immigrants, and coincidentally, the hospital soon to be erected on his property had a decidedly German flair: 15 of the 27 regiments in the Union XI Corps were either all German or comprised of significant German elements. The Germans who made up the bulk of the XI Corps were already hurting in other ways before they suffered another humiliating bloody rout on July 1 north of Gettysburg. Their suffering on the field and in the corps hospital on the Spangler property was only a continuation of their physical and mental anguish.

* * *

The XI Corps had a rather convoluted genesis. Part of the command had fought in the 1862 Shenandoah Valley Campaign, where many of the Germans alienated locals by looting their homes, planted seeds of division with native-born troops, and turned in a less-than-stellar performance at the battle of Cross Keys, where they were routed from the field. Operating in the Mountain Department, they were placed under Maj. Gen. John C. Fremont on June 26, 1862, as part of the new "First Army Corps." A directive that they serve under Maj. Gen. John Pope in his newly formed Army of Virginia, however, did not sit well with General Fremont, who outranked and despised Pope. Fremont promptly resigned.[1]

Major General Franz Sigel, a German native and political general, assumed command of the I Corps three days later. Many of the German troops spoke little English, but managed a slogan—"I fights mit Sigel" ("I'll fight with Sigel")—that still rings with nationalistic pride. The troops fought for two long days under Sigel at Second Bull Run in late August. They suffered heavily, losing nearly 300 killed, 1,400 wounded, and 430 missing.

The name of the corps was changed by General Orders No. 129 on September 12, 1862, to the XI Corps. Because it had been so roughly handled at Second Bull Run, the organization remained in camp around Washington, D.C., to rest and reorganize when Lee's Confederate Army of Northern Virginia invaded Maryland that same month. Fortune remained with the men that fall and winter when they were tasked with picketing the Potomac River fords or acting as a deep reserve during the bloody fiasco at Fredericksburg that December before finally going into winter quarters.[2]

Sigel resigned when demands to enlarge the small XI Corps were rebuffed. Major General Oliver O. Howard was promoted to replace him at the head of the corps. The general who had lost an arm on the Virginia Peninsula the previous spring was something of a religious fanatic, a trait that did not sit well with the anti-clerical Germans in his new command. The appointment of Brig. Gens. Francis Barlow and Charles Devens, both considered to be martinets, did not help matters.[3]

Whatever luck the XI Corps possessed left it that spring when Maj. Gen. Joseph Hooker, the new commander of the Army of the Potomac, opened the Chancellorsville Campaign by moving in late April 1863 against Lee's army in northern Virginia. Howard's three divisions under Carl Schurz and Devens and Adolph von Steinwehr, about 12,000 men, marched west to cross the Rappahannock before swinging around and tramping southeast over the Rapidan. By the time it stopped, the corps was holding the army's far right flank, facing

---

1 James S. Pula, *Under the Crescent Moon with the XI Corps in the Civil War, Vol. 1: From the Defenses of Washington to Chancellorsville, 1862-1863* (Savas Beatie, 2017), 5. Dr. Pula's recent two-volume study is the definitive history of the XI Corps. A majority of his second installment entitled *Under the Crescent Moon with the XI Corps in the Civil War, Vol. 2: From Gettysburg to Victory, 1863-1865* (Savas Beatie, 2018) covers the weeks leading up to Gettysburg and its aftermath.

2 Pula, *Under the Crescent Moon*, vol. 1, 32-54.

3 Ibid., 70, 75-76.

mostly south in a thickly wooded and brushy area known locally as "the Wilderness."

Howard's men were seemingly on an island at Chancellorsville. There were no other Union corps within a mile of the XI's left flank, and its right flank was not anchored on the river or any type of defensible terrain. Howard did little if anything to prepare his position when Hooker alerted him that Confederate troops were moving in his direction. Eight of his regiments had never fired at a Confederate; the balance had fighting experience, but had never participated in a successful battle. Howard's men were sitting ducks.

As a band played and the men of the XI relaxed, dealt cards, and prepared dinner, Lt. Gen. Thomas "Stonewall" Jackson's corps took up a position in the woods to the west. Many of the Union men were aware of enemy activity in the woods beyond their flank, but were unable to convince high-ranking officers of what they had seen. An artillery captain named Hubert Dilger rode to find Hooker, but was refused entry. When he notified Howard of the presence of Confederates off his flank, the corps leader scoffed at the report and assured him the Confederates were moving away in retreat, not preparing an assault.

Jackson's first line of troops advanced at about 5:30 p.m., charging east out of the woods in a giant gray wave. Within a short time nearly 30,000 men were on the move crashing into the exposed XI Corps flank. Outnumbered and out of position, there was little Howard could do to halt what was already underway. The surprise, rout, and retreat were on. Hastily thrown together defensive lines offered a more stubborn effort than many accounts suggest, but the Confederates easily outflanked or pushed their way through each position. A Union hospital was damaged as panicked members of the XI rushed through its tents and equipment.

"The resistance offered was speedily beaten down, there was nothing left but to lay down their arms and surrender, or flee. . . . Arms, knapsacks, clothing, equipage, everything, was thrown aside and left behind," wrote Confederate artillery officer Maj. David Gregg McIntosh. "The camp was in wild confusion. Men lost their heads in terror, the road and the woods on both sides were filled with men, horses and cattle, in one mad flight. The rebel yells added terror to the situation. . . . The XI Corps had been routed and were fleeing to the river like scared sheep."[4]

---

4 Pula, in *Under the Crescent Moon*, vol. 1, dedicates an entire long chapter, "Evening, May 2, 1863," 144-192, to the XI Corps' position, Jackson's attack, and the resistance and final rout of the corps; David Gregg McIntosh, *The Campaign of Chancellorsville* (Richmond, VA, 1915), 36, 39.

Darkness and the natural disorder of combat brought a halt to the surprise offensive, but not before the XI suffered 259 killed, 1,173 wounded, and 994 missing or taken prisoner in less than two hours of fighting and fleeing in the battle of Chancellorsville. The rout created a firestorm of criticism launched in Howard's (and the XI Corps') direction from the public, fellow officers, and his own men. The pious general said he got through it by looking "to the Great Shepherd for his care and guidance."[4]

The collapse of the right flank and eventual loss at Chancellorsville deepened the already-existing prejudice against foreign-born fighters within the Army of the Potomac. Despite the fact that the XI Corps was heavily outnumbered, assigned a difficult position, and surprised on its flank, many within the army and people across the Union believed the corps' soldiers in general and the Germans in particular were poor fighters and even cowards—a label that would stick through Gettysburg and long after the war despite how well they eventually performed. The German wounded and hospital staff heard these criticisms at the Spangler hospital, and they read about it in Northern newspapers. The public and newspapers ridiculed the Germans and XI Corps with such labels as "The Flying Dutchmen" and "Running Half Moons" in reference to the XI Corps' symbol (a crescent moon).[5]

"The Americans loathe all the Germans and slight them whenever they can," explained Carl Uterhart of the 119th New York, a native German and XI Corps assistant surgeon.[6] The commander of the Third Division, Maj. Gen. Carl Schurz, agreed. "The XI Corps, and, by error or malice, especially the Third Division, has been held up to the whole country as a band of cowards," he penned in his official report of battle. "We have been overwhelmed by the army and the press with abuse and insult beyond measure. We have borne as much as human nature can endure. I am . . . far from saying that it would have been quite impossible to do better in the position the corps occupied on May 2; but I have seen with my own eyes troops

4 Oliver Howard, *Autobiography of Oliver Otis Howard, Major General United States Army*, 2 vols. (New York, NY, 1907), vol. 1, 378. Jackson was mortally wounded that night by friendly fire while conducting a reconnaissance of his lines.

5 *Brooklyn Daily Eagle*, June 27, 1863, 1; George Benson Fox to his father, July 4, 1863, in Christine Dee, ed., *Ohio's War, the Civil War in Documents* (Athens, OH, 2006), 116.

6 Carl Uterhart to his mother, May 27, 1863, in Walter D. Kamphoefner and Wolfgang Helbich, eds., *Germans in the Civil War: The Letters They Wrote Home* (Chapel Hill, NC, 2006), 161.

who now effect to look down upon the XI Corps with sovereign contempt behave much worse under circumstances far less trying."[8]

The Chancellorsville debacle convinced the War Department to launch an inquiry into the ethnic makeup of the XI Corps. According to Howard, 11 of his 27 regiments were "all German": 26th Wisconsin, 82nd Illinois, 29th New York (disbanded after Chancellorsville), the 41st, 45th, 54th, 58th, and 68th New York, and the 27th, 74th, and 75th Pennsylvania. Another four, he affirmed, were of mixed nationality, but strongly German: 119th New York, 107th Ohio, and the 73rd and 153rd Pennsylvania. The four regiments unlucky enough to suffer the initial brunt of Jackson's wave assault were strongly or all German, as were a dozen of the 18 XI Corps regiments involved that day.[9]

The manner in which they were led coupled with the disaster and criticism that followed prompted many discouraged and homesick XI Corps officers to quit during the weeks following Chancellorsville. "A great many officers are resigning, at least many in this corps, and quite a number are going home on leaves of absence," future Spangler surgeon Dr. Daniel G. Brinton wrote in a letter to his father on May 24. "Some of the officers give us the reason for resigning that they do not want to remain in a corps that has disgraced itself, but this is nonsense. The din of the last battle still rings in their ears and it is not so melodious as the voices of their wives and children. Quite a number of them talk about going to Oregon."[10]

The XI Corps, and especially the Germans within its ranks, still carried the Chancellorsville baggage on the morning of July 1 when the roughly 9,000 men now affixed with the crescent moon hustled north from Emmitsburg, Maryland, on their way to Gettysburg. The soldiers were happy to be out of Virginia, but morale remained low. Few believed they were being treated fairly, and most were unhappy with their officers. Recent rains, coupled with humidity and deep and muddy roads, only added to their woes.[11]

Like the XI Corps, Dr. Jonathan A. Letterman and the medical department of the Army of the Potomac had problems of their own. The department had

---

8 Carl Schurz, Official Report, May 12, 1863, in *The Miscellaneous Documents of the House of Representatives for the First Session of the Fifty-first Congress, 1889-90* (Washington, D.C., 1891), 658.

9 Howard in "List of German troops in the Eleventh Army Corps," May 21, 1863, in *The Miscellaneous Documents of the House of Representatives*, 660-661.

10 Daniel G. Brinton to his father, May 24, 1863, Dr. Daniel Garrison Brinton papers, 1863-1899. Ms. Coll. 177. Chester County Historical Society Library (West Chester, PA).

11 For a detailed examination of the XI Corps on the morning of July 1, see Pula, *Under the Crescent Moon*, vol. 2, 1-41.

improved in every area after Dr. Letterman took over as the army's medical director in June 1862. His new methods of advanced first aid stations, collection and treatment of wounded, and an improved diet saved untold numbers of men who would have otherwise perished.

On the morning of July 1, however, II Corps commander Maj. Gen. Winfield Scott Hancock ordered Letterman's 25 wagons comprising the hospital supply train to stop just south of the Pennsylvania line at Taneytown, Maryland. The next day, the Army of the Potomac's new commander, Maj. Gen. George. G. Meade, sent the wagons more than 10 miles farther from Gettysburg to the area of Westminster, Maryland. Corps ambulance wagons with dressings, chloroform, and surgical essentials were all that was allowed to roll north with the troops to the vicinity of Gettysburg. Wounded men could be operated on at the Spangler hospital and elsewhere, but they would not have food, hospital clothing, tents, bedpans, and proper beds. Once any buildings were filled with the injured, the remaining wounded would have to be placed outside. "Without proper means," Letterman complained, "the Medical Department can no more take care of the wounded than the army can fight a battle without ammunition." The health and care of his soldiers was important, but it was not General Meade's chief priority. He had a battle to win, and he needed the roads clear so his infantry, artillery, and cavalry could move quickly and arrive where they were most needed. It was a calculated decision that would cause much suffering and cost many lives.[12]

Major General John Reynolds' I Corps reached Gettysburg first, with the XI Corps not far behind. The two corps, together with Maj. Gen. Dan Sickles' III Corps, made up the army's unofficial "left wing" under Reynolds. While the I Corps waged a titanic struggle just west of town, the XI Corps approached Gettysburg via the Emmitsburg and Taneytown roads (just west of the Spangler property). Reynolds was already dead, killed early in the fighting that morning, and Confederates were also approaching from the north. Howard rushed his men through town in front of cheering residents and assumed a position on undulating and mostly open and indefensible ground. His position was too long to hold with the men he had, and, once again, his flanks were "up in the air."[13]

By early that afternoon the XI Corps' First and Third divisions were in position north of Gettysburg. In what turned out to be a prescient and even brilliant

---

12 Jonathan Letterman, *Medical Recollections of the Army of the Potomac* (New York, NY, 1866), 156.

13 Pula, *Under the Crescent Moon*, vol. 2, 33-34.

decision, General Howard had earlier ordered Brig. Gen. Adolph von Steinwehr's Second Division to remain behind to protect Cemetery Hill, a rising piece of ground just southeast of town that Howard had mounted to study the surrounding geography. "This seems to be a good position, Colonel," Howard told Theodore A. Meysenburg, his assistant adjutant general. "It is the only position, General," replied the staff officer. Both men appreciated that the army would desperately need to hold Cemetery Hill in case of a retreat from west and north of town.[14]

Musicians—usually younger teenagers—helped at hospitals during and after battles by providing water to the wounded, cleaning and wrapping wounds, carrying stretchers, helping load ambulances, and doing whatever else the medical staff needed. As the fighting men assumed their places above town, the musicians and others were dispatched to the Spangler farm and other places around town where corps wounded would be rushed for medical care.

Fife player Joseph Gillis of the 82nd Ohio, a 19-year-old shoemaker from Delaware, Ohio, would spend three weeks caring for Confederate wounded at the Spangler hospital. On July 22, 1863, he wrote a letter home to 17-year-old sister Emily describing his ordeal. "We, the 82d, had to march through an open field to a cluster of woods," he began. "We played the tune called 'The Yankees are Coming.' It is a very quick piece and pretty. The Rebs let go solid shot. The first went about three feet from the back drummer, and you ought to have seen him juke. Several came very close before we got to the woods. Then the Regt. was formed. The Col said, 'Musicians to the hospital, March.' I bid goodbye to the boys and left." Gillis' trials were just beginning. "We, the band, went to the town to help with the wounded,

and had not been there long when here comes the Yankees with the Rebs after them. Myself and B. Young, a drummer, stepped out onto the pavements, and the rebs said, 'Halt, halt, you damn yankees.' Then I thought is they could catch me, why all right. Young and I jumped a little fence and into another street. Them after us full tilt. They got Young, but they could not get this chap. I dug out, skipping every other street till I was almost out of town. . . .[15]

---

14 Ibid., 6.

15 Joseph Gillis to his sister, July 22, 1863. Letter provided by Dale and Barbara Smith to Dan Welch of the Gettysburg Foundation in 2013.

Musician Joseph Gillis

Courtesy of Dale and Barbara Smith
and the Gettysburg Foundation

Gillis made it safely to the Spangler XI Corps hospital, though his unit didn't know it. He was officially listed as missing.

Drummer Thaddeus Reynolds, 19, of the 154th New York, was another musician who faced extreme danger that day. Unlike Gillis, however, he didn't get away. The five-foot four-inch Reynolds was struck by enemy lead in the left hand and hip while holding the horse of Assistant Surgeon Dwight W. Day, losing most of his hand. He was knocked out with chloroform in an attempt to ease his anguished screams, and he died July 12 on the Spangler property. In all, 19 XI Corps musicians were killed, wounded, or captured at Gettysburg.[16]

The Confederates who struck Howard's troops belonged primarily to a division under Maj. Gen. Jubal A. Early, with assistance from another division farther west under Maj. Gen. Robert Rodes, both part of Maj. Gen. Richard Ewell's II Corps. Rodes' men kicked off the assault against Oak Ridge from the west and north, where the right flank of the Union I Corps rested, while Early's roughly 5,000 men attacked out of the north against what is now known as Barlow Knoll and the troops aligned in the open ground to its west. Rodes' attack began at about 2:00 p.m., with Early following against the XI Corps at about 3:00. Early's battering attacks heavily pressed Howard's men and collapsed the line on Barlow Knoll. Like it had been at Chancellorsville, the XI Corps was outnumbered and fighting on poor terrain—mostly open ground with few fences or natural defenses. Though

---

16 Travis W. Busey and John W. Busey, *Union Casualties at Gettysburg: A Comprehensive Record*, 3 vols. (Jefferson, NC, 2011), vol. 3, 697, 1,234-1,235.

the men fought hard, for the second time in two months the XI Corps found itself in headlong retreat.

"We met the enemy at Rock Creek. We attacked them immediately, but we had a hard time in moving them," recalled Pvt. George W. Nichols of the 61st Georgia, part of John B. Gordon's brigade. The Rebels advanced with their accustomed yell, but Howard's men "stood firm until we got near them. They then began to retreat in fine order, shooting at us as they retreated. They were harder to drive than we had ever known them before. Men were being mown down in great numbers on both sides." General Gordon agreed with the private's assessment when he reported, "The enemy made a most obstinate resistance."[17]

Most of the XI Corps regiments that fought hard and "made a most obstinate resistance" were all or strongly German, including the 82nd Illinois, 54th, 58th, and 119th New York, 107th Ohio, 26th Wisconsin, and 74th, 75th, and 153rd Pennsylvania. One of the Keystone regiments, Col. Francis Mahler's all-German 75th Pennsylvania, was in the middle of the fighting near the Adams County Almshouse when Mahler was struck in the leg and his mortally wounded horse fell upon him. Mahler managed to squeeze out from under the animal only to be shot again, this time mortally, as he cheered on his men against the advancing Confederates. Mahler fought in uprisings in Germany in the late 1840s with Major General Schurz before escaping to America, where he married and settled in Philadelphia. Schurz rushed to his dying friend's side, writing later, "Now with death on his face he reached out his hand to me on the bloody field of Gettysburg, to bid me a last farewell."[18]

Many of the XI Corps wounded in the Day 1 fight were taken prisoner because of the rapid advance of the Confederates, but Mahler was quickly removed from the field and carried to the Spangler hospital, where he died at age 36 on July 4 or 5. His widow, Jennie, was 31. The Philadelphia City Council honored Mahler later in July with a resolution and paid for his funeral. Mahler's brother, 2nd Lt. Louis Mahler, was killed in the same action that afternoon.[19]

The travails that overtook the all-German 82nd Illinois on July 1 were described by Capt. Matthew Marx to a German-language newspaper in Chicago.

17 G. W. Nichols, *A Soldier's Story of His Regiment (61st Georgia)*, James Verner Scaife Collection, Civil War Literature, Cornell University Library (Ithaca, NY), 116; John B. Gordon, Official Report, August 10, 1863, Gettysburg National Military Park Library & Research Center, Box B-8, Misc. Notes Concerning Gordon's Brigade Folder.

18 Carl Schurz, *The Reminiscences of Carl Schurz*, 3 vols. (New York, NY, 1908), vol. 3, 12.

19 *Philadelphia Inquirer*, July 21, 1863.

The sufferings were typical of what many XI Corps regiments experienced that afternoon:

> Suddenly, I heard a horrible scream, a second and a third, which followed a frightful wail. I raised my head and saw Ernst Fuhrmeister, my sergeant, without any legs. A ball had torn one completely off and smashed the other one to pieces at the knee. The blood ran in streams. . . . Emil Giese lay just behind me with a shattered leg and next to Friedrich [Calmback], who likewise had a shattered leg. Finally, John [Bolken] crawled using his hands and feet; blood streamed from his head and back, and all this happened within 10 minutes. Gustav Giese, my sergeant now, rushed immediately to help his brother, ignoring the terrible rain of bullets. . . . Sergeant[s] Fuhrmeister and [Calmback] died that evening from loss of blood. Emil Giese's leg was amputated above the knee and I hear that he is in good spirits and out of danger. [A. H. Mignell], the bugler, had his already once amputated arm made a bit shorter because a minnie ball smashed it.

A. H. Mignell and Gustav Giese underwent their amputations at the Spangler farm hospital.[20]

The 17th Connecticut, part of Brig. Gen. Adelbert Ames' brigade, was among the first of the XI Corps regiments hit that day. Whitlock brothers Joseph S. (about 20 at Gettysburg) and Nephi (about 18) joined the regiment together as privates a year earlier and were now fighting for their lives. Joseph was hit in the hand and taken to the Spangler property, where what was left was amputated. He died in mid-July at the farm. Nephi survived his wound, so at least one of the two brothers made it home.[21]

Some of the XI Corps men fell back past the almshouse, which was serving as the XI Corps' aid station. The troops tried to find some cover there before taking off for town. Part of the corps was pushed through Pennsylvania College (now Gettysburg College). Nearby was the Second Division's First Brigade under Col. Charles R. Coster, which had rushed up from Cemetery Hill to try to cover the retreat of the XI Corps only to be bloodily repulsed for its bravery. Coster put three

20 Matthew Marx to *Illinois Staats-Zeitung* newspaper, July 8, 1863, in Joseph R. Reinhart, ed., *Yankee Dutchmen Under Fire: Civil War Letters From the 82nd Illinois Infantry* (Kent, OH, 2013), 94.

21 PA Register 554 "Register of the Sick and Wounded" of 1884 from the Office of the United States Surgeon General, and Carded Medical Records Volunteers, Mexican and Civil Wars, 1846-1865, from Records of the Adjutant General's Office, both from the National Archives and Records Administration, Washington, D.C.

of his four regiments at a brickyard on what is now Coster Avenue, and the fourth, the 73rd Pennsylvania, at the train station downtown. Coster's three regiments went up against eight Confederate regiments. The force of numbers made itself felt in the shocking casualty disparity. The 154th New York lost three-quarters of its men, the 134th New York more than half, and the 27th Pennsylvania about one-third.[22]

Coster's outnumbered men stood their ground and poured on their own heavy fire, but the Louisiana and North Carolina brigades under Harry T. Hays and Isaac Avery moved quickly through it. Within minutes, Coster's three regiments were almost surrounded and being hit from multiple directions in a virtual tornado of fire. They had no idea which way to face and fight, a sad fact indicated by the multiple wounds suffered by many men of the 134th New York who were later treated at the Spangler hospital after the Confederates retreated on July 4. It is particularly exemplified by the following three men:

Corporal James Brownlee received seven gunshot wounds at the brickyard, one of which broke four ribs. He also was shot three times through the bowels and in the left thigh, right thigh, and lower back. In addition, he was struck in the knapsack and knocked down by an 18-inch piece of railroad iron fired from a Confederate cannon. Somehow Brownlee, who was treated at both the Spangler hospital and Camp Letterman, survived his wounds and the war.[23]

Corporal John B. Thomas received six gunshot wounds: One in a finger, one in each arm, one in the groin, and one in each leg. He died about three weeks later after being treated for a time at the Spangler hospital.[24]

Private Orlando Sperbeck received three gunshot wounds: One in his right wrist, one in his left arm, and one in his left leg below the knee. He was treated at the Spangler hospital and survived.[25]

22 A mural and monuments depict and honor this fight at its location at present-day Coster Avenue. (39°50'6"N 77°13'42"W).

23 George H. Warner, *Military Records of Schoharie County Veterans of Four Wars* (Ann Arbor, MI, 2002), 326; Tenney, *The Medical and Surgical History of the War of the Rebellion,* 488.

24 Warner, *Military Records of Schoharie County Veterans of Four Wars,* 324.

25 Ibid., 334.

Another soldier treated on the Spangler property was Sergeant John A. Bush of the 154th New York, who was hit in the right arm while fighting at the brickyard. His limb was amputated at the Spangler hospital, and—as many other wounded men did—he kept the shell fragment that was removed as a souvenir.[26]

The sacrifice of most of Coster's brigade helped save the day for the Union by allowing just enough time for the retreating survivors of the XI Corps to flee through the crowded and panicked streets of Gettysburg and stream up Cemetery Hill, the defensive position that would form the strong hinge of Meade's line during the following two days of battle. By the time they reached Cemetery Hill, the XI Corps soldiers who fought for Barlow Knoll and survived covered about two miles during their retreat.[27]

Private Reuben Ruch, 19, of the 153rd Pennsylvania, Col. Leopold von Gilsa's brigade, arrived at the Spangler hospital on July 4. He had been wounded in each leg during the early part of the fight. "I looked to the rear and our men had all fallen back about two rods [11 yards], firing as they retired," recalled the wounded private. "This gave me a good view of those that were left dead on the first line of battle. It presented a regular swath of blue coats, as far as I could see along the line. They were piled up in every shape, some on their backs, some on their faces, and others turned and twisted in every imaginable shape. There was a dead man on each side of me," continued Ruch. "As I stood between those two lines of battle, viewing the windrow of human dead composed of my old comrades, it presented a picture which will never fade from my memory while I remain on earth—a picture which tongue cannot tell nor pen describe."[28]

The lack of ambulances was one of the many problems facing the wounded and dying men of the XI Corps on July 1, as the fighting and quick retreat forced the wagons to escape to safety. The men left behind who were strong enough got out on their own or made it out with the help of comrades. Others unable to get away were captured and taken to Confederate hospitals or left on the field to suffer under the hot sun without food and water until help arrived. Those who survived for days on the battlefield or in Confederate field hospitals were taken to the XI

---

26 John A. Bush to Edwin Dwight Northrup, August 30-31, 1888, in Edwin Dwight Northrup Papers, #4190, Box 35, Division of Rare and Manuscript Collections, Carl A. Kroch Library, Cornell University (Ithaca, NY).

27 For a good account of Coster's brickyard fight, see Pula, *Under the Crescent Moon*, vol. 2, 79-83.

28 William R. Kiefer, *History of the One Hundred and Fifty-Third Regiment Pennsylvania Volunteers Infantry: Which Was Recruited in Northampton County, Pa., 1862-1863* (Easton, PA, 1909), 212-213.

Corps hospital (and elsewhere) July 4-5 after the Army of Northern Virginia retreated. All too many died horrible, agonizing deaths while waiting to be rescued.

Doctor Letterman's use of aid stations—or field dressing stations—during battles saved untold Union lives. These stations were marked by a red flag and established close to the front line, usually behind boulders, trees, or in a depression. Here, assistant surgeons and stewards handed out water and provided initial first aid such as bandages and lint for wounds, tourniquets, whiskey for shock, splints for fractures, and morphine for pain.

Triage determined who was in the most need of immediate help, with the wounded separated by the severity of their wounds. Those whose lives could possibly be saved by surgery were hurried into an ambulance or onto a stretcher and rushed to the division or corps field hospital. The less seriously injured were bandaged and sent back to their regiment or to the field hospital for further care. Those considered mortally wounded—especially with head, chest, and abdomen wounds—were made as comfortable as possible and set aside somewhere out of the way to die or be taken to a field hospital later.

The proximity of these aid stations to the front line helped save lives, but their very nature also created significant danger to XI Corps medical staff. On July 1, when the Rebels broke Howard's line, the aid stations had to pick up and flee during the retreat. The hasty withdrawal left some XI Corps medical staff, among them Assistant Surgeon Corydon C. Rugg of the 154th New York, stuck behind enemy lines as prisoners with no way to reach the Spangler hospital.

The other great danger of these aid stations was that they were often in the line of fire. Assistant Surgeon Jacob Laubli of the 68th New York sustained a severe foot fracture when he was caught in the middle of the fighting. He was discharged that November because of it. He did, however, make it safely to the Spangler hospital for treatment.

Thirty-three-year-old Assistant Surgeon William S. Moore of the 61st Ohio suffered an even worse fate. Doctor Moore was directly behind the Union front line along the Taneytown Road on the morning of July 3 attempting to move wounded men farther away from the firing. He mounted his horse and rode about 20 yards to the rear when "some large projectile," explained 61st Ohio Surgeon Enoch Pearce, hit Moore in the right thigh. Moore was placed on a stretcher and moved into the two-story log cabin of Catherine Guinn. A frantic messenger reached Dr. Pearce about 11:00 a.m. at the XI Corps hospital, explaining that Dr.

Assistant Surgeon William S. Moore
61st Ohio

Gettysburg Foundation

Moore had asked for him personally. Pearce arrived at the Guinn cabin within 15 minutes and found Moore weak and in shock.[29]

"Before he could be removed from the house in which I found him to this Field Corps Hospital in the rear," Pearce wrote in 1864, "the battle which had considerably abated suddenly increased and continued with most dreadful violence for about two hours during which this house was struck by shot and shell eleven times, two balls passing directly through the walls of the upper story." The cannonade preceding Pickett's Charge was under way. "This circumstance I mention because it had a very injurious effect upon the patient, adding to his first shock and prolonging it. . . . As soon as the battle was decided in our favor and it became safe to remove him, he was about 4:00 p.m. carefully transported to the Field Corps Hospital where he received every possible attention. No operation was performed. He died July 6, 1863." Pearce remained with Dr. Moore at the hospital "and gave him special attention and was at his bedside when he died."[30]

Moore was buried in the growing cemetery south of the Spangler house. He left behind Sarah, his 29-year-old wife, a two-year-old daughter named Kate, and one-year-old son named William in Clermont County, Ohio, near Cincinnati. Sarah

29 The cabin, which no longer stands, was in what is now an open area on the east side of the Taneytown Road between both cemeteries and a National Park Service building. It was about 175 yards north of Meade's headquarters, though on the opposite side of the road (39°49'6"N 77°14'6"W).

30 William S. Moore Pension File No. 43488, National Archives and Records Administration (Washington, D.C.).

Moore's brothers William and John Fee arrived at the Spangler hospital not long after Moore died to find and take their brother-in-law's body home to their "broken-hearted sister."

"We soon found the grave of Dr. Moore," William Fee wrote, "and, after obtaining the liberty to transport his remains through the lines, we disinterred them, and had them hermetically sealed in a tin case. We spent nearly two days in passing over the battle-ground. Multitudes of people were there to secure the remains of their departed friends, or to comfort those who were wounded and dying. I passed by many places where near relatives, fathers, mothers, brothers, sisters were disinterring their friends," he continued. "So fearful was the spectacle, it was too much for tears. I never saw a tear shed by any person on that historical battle-field."[31]

Thirteen Army of the Potomac medical officers were wounded at Gettysburg, but Assistant Surgeon Moore, caught at an aid station right behind the front line, was the only fatality.

Sarah Moore never fully recovered from her husband's death. She didn't remarry, and according to the 1870 federal census she and her children were living with her parents, her occupation listed as "Helps mother." She received a monthly $17.00 widow's pension until she died in 1911, plus $2.00 a month for each child until they reached age 16.

Many of the German wounded who reached the Spangler farm faced another obstacle: A language barrier. Many spoke good or at least passable English, but many others who were newer immigrants spoke little or no English or were difficult to understand because of their heavy accent. Sergeant Joseph Charlesworth, 64th New York, II Corps, said simply he "could not understand the Germans."[32]

The language barrier was exacerbated by the fact that XI Corps medical staff at the Spangler hospital had many English-only speaking divisional surgeons. This communications obstacle sometimes delayed time-critical surgeries and hampered understanding of the treatment involved. The inability of staff to understand patients and vice versa led to many names being misspelled in the official hospital records.

---

31 William I. Fee, *Bringing the Sheaves: Gleanings from Harvest Fields in Ohio, Kentucky and West Virginia* (Cincinnati, OH, 1896), 447-448.

32 Joseph Charlesworth to Northrup, February 21, 1893, in Edwin Dwight Northrup Papers, Box 35, Cornell University.

The suffering that began at Chancellorsville and continued through the first day of Gettysburg would continue through two more days of fighting and long afterward for the wounded and dying Germans and others who were now pouring into the XI Corps hospital. Some of these men spent five weeks on the Spangler farm and months in Gettysburg recuperating while others were shipped to hospitals elsewhere. Many never left the Spangler farm. Still others carried the burden of their wounds every day for the rest of their lives. Too many made sacrifices for a country that didn't seem to want them.

Citing the strong feelings held by the rest of the army toward the XI Corps, General Meade recommended after Gettysburg that the organization be broken up. As a result, the XI Corps was reduced in size and merged with the newly formed XX Corps in 1864. It fought bravely and successfully through the end of the war.

Spangler Farm Short Story

Captain Francis Lackner of the all-German 26th Wisconsin limped into a church hospital in Gettysburg after being wounded in the right calf during the July 1 battle. He remained there until he was picked up July 4 and transported to the XI Corps hospital. "We lay for several days among the dead & wounded, while the surgeons were operating and amputating," he explained. "Within a week or so, however, I received a leave of absence & went home; as I limped through East Water Street in Milwaukee I saw a crowd of people before a newspaper office, reading & discussing the list of dead and wounded, my own name on the list; the crowd followed me to the nearby St. Charles Hotel where I held a little reception, but unfortunately could not answer all the questions of the anxious fathers and mothers as to the fate of their sons."

Lackner returned to the 26th Wisconsin later in 1863 and served through the end of the war, earning the rank of brevet lieutenant colonel. He went on to become a noted attorney in Chicago and died at age 88 after moving to Pasadena, California.[33]

---

33 Pula, *Under the Crescent Moon*, vol. 2, 69; Francis Lackner, *Brief History of the 26th*, www.russ scott.com/~rscott/26thwis/frlabref.htm. Accessed December 10, 2017.

Chapter 3

In the Middle of It All:
The Spangler Farm Hospital

"Little sleep fell to our share. Four operating tables were going night and day."

— *Surgeon-in-Chief Dr. Daniel G. Brinton, Second Division, XI Corps*

*A*s it turned out, George and Elizabeth Spangler's farm wasn't an ideal location for a field hospital after all because it was too close to the Army of the Potomac's front line.

The XI Corps medical staffers who selected the Spangler farm on the afternoon of July 1 had no way of knowing that the Union line would eventually extend more than a mile south down Cemetery Ridge, only a few hundred yards west of the Spangler property. Nor could they have known that the northern "fish hook" portion of the line would engulf Culp's Hill and wrap around to near the Baltimore Pike, right behind the Spangler property to the northeast. From nearly every direction but the southeast the newly established XI Corps hospital was much too close to the fighting and almost surrounded by it. And it paid for that location on July 2-3 by taking direct hits from Confederate artillery overshots from Seminary Ridge to the west and Culp's Hill.

On July 1, however, there were few if any places that offered a better spot for a large field hospital. Indeed, the advantages of the Spangler property appeared almost tailor-made for the army's use. The Baltimore Pike, an improved toll road of crushed stone, ran next to the Spangler property to the east and provided ready access to the sprawling farm. The Taneytown Road ran close on the western side, and Granite Schoolhouse Lane, at the time the northernmost road between the farm and Gettysburg, cut through the Spangler property. These roads and the farm's proximity to the fighting would reduce the time it took to get the wounded from the battlefield to the hospital and thus increase substantially the odds of saving many lives.

In addition, the springs and streams on the Spangler farm offered a ready supply of fresh water and Rock Creek was only a short walk away. The upper and lower levels of the big Pennsylvania bank barn presented ample space for a hospital. The barn's forebay, or overhang, which extended seven feet from the front wall, provided protection from the sun and rain and fresh air for surgeons and their patients. Also, the farm's ground was dry and fairly flat.

Medical staff would need a roof over their heads, and the Spangler house offered just that. The house, barn, summer kitchen, and other farm buildings were good places for patients and there was plenty of room for patient and staff tents and a cook-house. Wheat and hay could be used to enhance the comfort of wounded men, and the Spanglers' livestock and growing and stored crops could be utilized for food. In addition, the trees on the property could be cut down and fences torn down to be used for firewood. Unbeknownst to George Spangler, his recent purchase of lumber intended for the building of a hog pen would provide the Union army with a bounty of free wood.[1]

For all these reasons (and undoubtedly others), on July 1 the Spangler farm appeared to be a perfect spot for a hospital in Dr. Jonathan Letterman's still relatively new field hospital system. As noted earlier, Letterman assumed command as medical director of a disorganized and even dangerous Army of the Potomac medical department in June of 1862. The entire organization was badly in need of an overhaul and forward-thinking activists who were anxious to come up with solutions for unnecessary deaths as men waited days for surgery and even longer before being picked up from a battlefield. What the 38-year-old native of Canonsburg, Pennsylvania, accomplished in a single year leading up to Gettysburg dramatically changed how things would be set up at the Spangler hospital compared with how it would have been earlier in the war. The new medical director instituted a number of basic changes that improved the overall health of the Army of the Potomac.

---

1 The cook-house was in the Spangler yard, covered by an open tent or canvas. Part of George Spangler's claim for reimbursement filed after the war to the Quartermaster General's Office in Washington, D.C., included "1200 Shingles used by Hospital" and "1000 feet boards used for beds at Hospital." Spangler Damage Claim R-241, 1876, "George Spangler Farmstead Historic Structure Report," prepared for the Gettysburg Foundation by LSC Design, Inc. and Keystone Preservation Group, Inc. November 7, 2011.

Dr. Jonathan Letterman, seated at left, with his staff. *Library of Congress*

For example, he ordered soldiers to take a bath once a week (twice a week later in the war), and put on clean underwear once a week. He improved their diet by including more fruits and vegetables, and he introduced exercise and more rest. (For example, he suggested that the men should not be drilled more than twice a day.) Letterman ordered the digging of long and deep latrines known as "sinks" and insisted the men use them instead of urinating or emptying their bowels anywhere they pleased. He also instructed that garbage and other refuse be buried and deep wells dug. He ordered more tents because many men were sleeping in the open or with little shelter. He also showed the army how to pick drier, better ground for hospitals and camps and how to use pine branches as bedding to get soldiers off the bare ground. Those basic improvements decreased diseases such as scurvy, malaria, typhoid fever, diarrhea, and dysentery. Letterman's foresight and his relentless fight for improved health made the army a more powerful fighting machine.

Letterman also improved hospital record keeping and made sure medical supplies were always close to the army. His new ambulance system and ambulance wagons saved lives, as did the implementation of battlefield aid stations and better triage. Review boards were established to weed out incompetent surgeons.

The setup and organization of the XI Corps Spangler hospital reflected the changes instituted by Letterman. The director had sent out a circular on October

Dr. Letterman instituted regular training of members of the Army of the Potomac ambulance corps, such as for this Zouave regiment. *Library of Congress*

30, 1862, announcing the replacement of regimental hospitals with division field hospitals. Instead of one hospital for each regiment, with one surgeon per regiment, there would be one hospital for every division (perhaps eight to 10 regiments or more), with the best surgeons overseeing surgical operations. Better and more-carefully selected surgeons meant better results and more lives saved.[2]

The Spangler hospital quickly morphed into an XI Corps hospital made up of three divisions and 26 regiments. By way of comparison, the II Corps' division hospitals remained divided, with the First Division located July 2-3 at the Granite Schoolhouse on the Spangler property and the other two divisions at farms along the Taneytown Road.

Letterman ordered that each division hospital have a surgeon-in-charge with two assistants. The surgeon-in-charge was the division hospital administrator. One of his assistants oversaw the feeding and sheltering of the wounded while the other kept records of the wounded men's name, rank, company, regiment, injury, and treatment. The assistant surgeon in charge of keeping records was also ordered to "see to the proper interment of those who die, and that the grave is marked with a

2 By the summer of 1863, a typical regiment in the field consisted of between 300 to 400 men effective for duty.

head-board, with the name, rank, company, and regiment legibly inscribed upon it."[3]

Three medical officers per division—called operators—performed the actual operations, and each had three assistant surgeons. There also were additional medical officers, hospital stewards who acted as pharmacists, nurses, and orderlies. Even though the Spangler farm was used as the hospital for the entire XI Corps, its medical staff kept a surgeon-in-chief for each of its three divisions. It maintained one surgeon-in-charge/medical director in charge of everything at the sprawling hospital and one assistant medical director/medical inspector under him. Following Letterman's division hospital instructions point-by-point would have placed nine operators and 27 assistant surgeons at the Spangler hospital, though in fact there were more operators than that between July 1-5 and significantly fewer thereafter.[4]

Letterman's division field hospital system cut its teeth at the battle of Fredericksburg in December 1862 and again at Chancellorsville in May 1863 before the Spangler land was confiscated for its third demonstration. It was the Second Division of the XI Corps that claimed the Spangler property for its hospital before it quickly evolved into the corps hospital.

On July 1-3 and thereafter, XI Corps wounded benefited significantly from Letterman's improved ambulance system. "No system had anywhere been devised for their management," explained the medical director. "They were under the control both of Medical officers and Quartermasters, and, as a natural consequence, little care was exercised over them by either. They could not be depended upon for efficient service in time of action or upon a march, and were too often used as if they had been made for the convenience of commanding officers." Before Letterman took over, civilians often drove the ambulances, and many of them refused to ride into danger zones or fled at the first sign of a fight, stranding the wounded for up to a week and virtually guaranteeing their death.[5]

On August 2, 1862, Maj. Gen. George B. McClellan, at that time the commander of the Army of the Potomac, announced that Letterman's proposed ambulance corps would be established. Two-horse ambulances were assigned to each regiment, battery, and corps headquarters, as well as a four-horse ambulance

---

3 Jonathan Letterman, *Medical Recollections of the Army of Potomac with Memoir of Jonathan Letterman* (D. Appleton, NY, 1866), 58-60.

4 Ibid., 59, 61.

5 Ibid., 22-23.

for each regiment—each with two stretchers. The two-horse wagon was the workhorse to quickly get the wounded off the field and to the nearest hospital. The four-horse ambulances at Gettysburg were mainly used for carrying food and wounded men who were well enough to be moved, such as from the Spangler farm and other field hospitals to the train station, where they were taken to general hospitals in Washington, D.C., Annapolis, Philadelphia, Baltimore, York, Pennsylvania, and elsewhere.[6]

Each two-horse ambulance had a driver and two stretcher bearers, each drilled on such matters as the proper method of picking up a stretcher, walking with it, and placing it in and taking it out of an ambulance without further injuring the patient. These matters received little if any attention when ambulances were part of the Quartermaster's Department. Letterman, however, knew small details mattered, including that the front stretcher bearer "steps off with the left foot and the rear man with the right, etc." To do otherwise could result in the tumbling of the wounded man to the ground.

Captain Thomas Livermore, who was in charge of the II Corps ambulances at Gettysburg, delivered wounded soldiers to the Spanglers' Granite Schoolhouse hospital. His ambulance corps, he explained, consisted of "in round numbers, 13 officers, 350-400 men, and 300 or more horses, with a little over 100 ambulances and 10 or 12 forage and forge wagons. . . . Each two-horse ambulance was a stout spring wagon very much like an ordinary express or grocer's wagon. . . . Inside this wagon were two seats the whole length . . . stuffed and covered with leather." The wounded could sit in these ambulances or the wagon could be set up to carry three men lying lengthwise. In the back of the ambulance under each seat was a water keg "containing a faucet, which contained fresh water for the wounded." In the front under the driver's seat "was a supply of beef stock, and I believe bandages and other hospital stores" such as lint, chloroform, whiskey, and even condensed milk. The invaluable canvas-covered stretchers were hung on each side of the ambulance, and the entire wagon was covered "with white canvas on bows." Letterman insisted that the horses and their operators be in good condition, "and the officers were intelligent."[7]

The springs on these ambulance wagons reduced the bouncing and agony of the wounded. Some wounded were given morphine before their ambulance ride, though most arrived at the Spangler farm complex in anguish, screaming or

6 Ibid., 24.

7 Thomas L. Livermore, *Days and Events, 1860-1866* (Boston, MA, 1920), 239-240.

moaning in intense pain. Each ambulance had retractable curtains on the sides, and many had a built-in canvas at the top that could be pulled out and around the wagon and attached to the ground, forming a tent. "The teamsters parked their wagons in the wheat fields, principally, ambulance wagons," wrote George Spangler after the war. "One field of ten acres was nearly white with wagons."

All told, the XI Corps ambulance corps at Gettysburg consisted of 100 ambulances, nine additional wagons, 270 men, and 260 horses.[8]

Letterman created one of the most efficient ambulance systems in the history of war. The Army of the Potomac would no longer rely upon untrained soldiers, musicians, convalescents, or civilians to remove the wounded from the battlefield. His was a trained, professional corps manned by soldiers selected for their character, courage, and intelligence, and who could thus be counted upon to perform well literally under fire. The ambulance drivers and stretcher bearers had a strong incentive to do their work well because they remained with their regiment and when called upon knew they were aiding their friends and even family members. General McClellan, himself an outstanding organizer of men and machines, was impressed by Letterman's achievements and went so far as to claim that he had "never met with his superior in power of organization and executive ability."[9]

Like so many aspects of the Confederate war effort, its ambulance service did not compare favorably with its Union counterpart. Supplies of every kind and readily available manpower were always in short supply, including within its

---

8 Spangler Damage Claim N-1892, 1875, Historic Structure Report; Louis C. Duncan, "The Greatest Battle of the War – Gettysburg," in *The Medical Department of the United States Army in the Civil War*, Cornell University Library, 15.

9 George B. McClellan to Charles H. Crane, February 26, 1883, in *Journal of the Military Service Institution of the United States*, vol. 4 (New York, NY, 1883), 276. Unfortunately for Dr. Letterman, two months before Gettysburg his mentor and superior, William A. Hammond, was being castigated for banning use of unsafe calomel (mercury) within the army on ill soldiers. Hammond's decision was later proved sound. Letterman served as Inspector of Hospitals in the Department of the Susquehanna before resigning from the army in December 1864—four months after Hammond was court-martialed and dismissed. Letterman moved to San Francisco with his wife and worked as a general superintendent of an oil exploration company, but the company went bankrupt a year later. He suffered depression after his wife died, became sick, and died in San Francisco in 1872 and was eventually buried in Arlington National Cemetery. On November 13, 1911, the US Army hospital at the Presidio was named Letterman Army Hospital in his honor. His tombstone reads: Medical Director of the Army of the Potomac, June 23, 1862, to December 30, 1863, who brought order and efficiency into the Medical Service and who was the originator of modern methods of medical organization in armies. He published his memoirs as *Medical Recollections of the Army of the Potomac* (D. Appleton, New York, 1866).

medical service. The North enjoyed numerous major centers of industry, but the more agrarian South lacked the skilled labor, facilities, and materials necessary to construct elaborate ambulances on the order Letterman demanded. Most Confederate-built ambulance wagons were simply converted from army or farm wagons or captured Union rolling stock. Private Justus Silliman of the 17th Connecticut was unfortunate enough to not only be wounded at Gettysburg, but to ride in one of the makeshift Confederate ambulances. He managed to survive the trying experience, but complained that the Southern ambulance "resembled our butcher wagons at home."[10]

System or no system, once the wounded started falling on the first day at Gettysburg, confusion ensued in getting the XI Corps injured quickly to the Spangler farm. If the wounded made it to Cemetery Hill or another ambulance gathering spot, they usually could find a wagon for the 1.6-mile ride to the hospital. Many of the wounded, however, were scattered on the fields north of town or within the town itself, which was rapidly taken over by the victorious Confederates. Private Jacob Smith of the 107th Ohio, part of Brig. Gen. Adelbert Ames' brigade, served as an ambulance driver that July afternoon. "In our retreat through the town and when near our lines we loaded our wagons with wounded who had managed to get back that far," recalled Smith. "We hauled them about a mile to the rear of the battle line out of the reach of immediate danger, and after unloading them started back to the front for another load. We were not long in finding sufficient wounded soldiers to fill our wagons and these we took back to where we had unloaded the first load. The place where we had taken the wounded was alongside of [the] Baltimore pike, close to the point where Rock Creek crosses the road, and just about a mile in the rear of our lines upon Cemetery Hill."[11]

The heavy combat was over late that afternoon with the Confederates in control of most of Gettysburg and the woods and fields north and west of town. The evening hours were consumed with skirmish fire and sharpshooters, which inflicted even more casualties while the generals on both sides analyzed their positions and debated what to do next. Private Israel Spencer of the 136th New York, Col. Orland Smith's brigade, who would himself become a patient at the XI Corps hospital, described the scene on Cemetery Hill once the I Corps and XI

10 National Museum of Civil War Medicine in Frederick, MD; Justus M. Silliman, Edward Marcus, ed., *A New Canaan Private in the Civil War: Letters of Justus M. Silliman, 17th Connecticut Volunteers* (New Canaan, CT: New Canaan Historical Society, 1984), 41-42.

11 Jacob Smith, *Camps and Campaigns of the 107th Regiment Ohio Volunteer Infantry, From August, 1862, to July, 1865* (Navarre, OH, 2000), 88-89.

Corps were routed off the field. The fighting had died down, but the agony was only beginning: "The 1st night after the fighting was over the most awful sounds and noises came from our left and front. For hours all we could hear would be someone cursing or praying or calling for water."[12]

As the fighting wound down, the work of the ambulance drivers and stretcher bearers picked up, the lanterns on the rumbling wagons glowing as they continued their work. There were so many injured men that the ambulances rolled back and forth between the Spangler hospital and the battlefield until well into the night, the route marked by red flags and signs. Hundreds of wounded XI Corps comrades were unreachable, prisoners of war behind the newly established Confederate front.

One of Col. Leopold von Gilsa's men, Pvt. S. C. Romig of the 153rd Pennsylvania, recalled the details of his wound on East Cemetery Hill on the night of July 1 and quick ambulance work that transported him to the Spangler farm. "I was just in the act of firing when I was hit by a ball in my left knee," began the private. "I, of course, ceased firing,

and lay down and took in the situation which was very sorrowful for me and rendered me helpless to move. Lieutenant [Henry R.] Barnes, commander of the Company, at that time came near where I was lying. I told him quickly the condition I was in, as there was no time for a long story. He sent two men to carry me from the field and away from danger, which they did willingly, I suppose to get away themselves. They took me up to Cemetery Hill across the road and laid me down in some grass when my two comrades, which were, so kind to me, vanished. I looked about and learned that I was lying in a grave yard, the old Gettysburg cemetery. Soon, however, an ambulance came along and I was taken up, and the horses driven as fast as they could go, and I was lodged in the XI Corps hospital.[13]

Hospital help was hard to come by and the wounded so numerous that once an ambulance driver—no matter how exhausted—finished his deliveries, he was often assigned to take a turn working overnight at the Spangler hospital. When he finished driving, Private Smith of the 107th Ohio was assigned to provide water to

12 "Letters from Private Israel P. Spencer, Company A," www.russscott.com/~rscott/136thny/ltisrasp.htm. Accessed January 2, 2017.

13 Kiefer, *History of the One Hundred and Fifty-Third Regiment Pennsylvania Volunteers Infantry: Which Was Recruited in Northampton County, Pa., 1862-1863*, 185.

the injured, change a patient's position if needed, and look after their needs from midnight until 2:00 a.m. "As all people are not alike in disposition," Smith explained, "so among the wounded there were different natures encountered; some because of their wounds were murmuring and complaining continually, while others seemed perfectly resigned and cheerful though as badly wounded as the former. One or two of the wounded under our care died during the night."[14]

One Union soldier at the hospital, in particular, attracted Private Smith's attention:

> He had been shot through the mouth, the ball entering one side of his cheek and out the other; in its passage through it had broken out four or five teeth and cut his tongue pretty near off. He was also shot through one of his arms, and a musket ball had struck a small Bible which he carried in a pocket over his left breast, with sufficient force to go entirely through it, lodging and fastening a bunch of eight or ten letters which were in the pocket between the Bible and his body; his escape was truly miraculous, as the ball came with sufficient force to have gone entirely through his body; the Bible in that case proved an effective shield.[15]

The medical staff had rushed to get the hospital organized and as ready as possible to receive the wounded, who began arriving at the Spangler farm about 4:00 p.m. on July 1. Animals had been removed from the yard and ground level of the barn, and cleanup of their waste was probably just getting started. The filthy conditions and smell of the farm seemed anything but conducive for a hospital and place of healing. The grains and other crops and equipment were in the process of being removed from the top level of the barn to make room for patients on its expansive floor.[16]

Four operating tables were set up under the forebay extension of the barn. These "tables" could have been window shutters or doors, a kitchen table, or planks of wood taken from the Spangler property, supported by barrels, stacked wood, or even pieces of farm equipment. If available, a rubber and

---

14 Jacob Smith, *Camps and Campaigns*, 89.

15 Ibid.

16 Hospital flag regulations were not firm in July 1863, but a yellow or red flag was likely hung from the Spangler barn or in front of it to mark the location as an army field hospital. It wasn't until 1864 that the Union regulated that the official field hospital flag be yellow with a large green "H" in the center.

Ambulances and troops (above and facing page) cut through the Spangler property on Granite Schoolhouse Lane next to Powers Hill in this 1863 drawing by Edwin Forbes. The Baltimore Pike is shown mainly on p. 39. NPS and John Bachelder maps and soldier comments indicate there were more trees below the lane in 1863 than shown here. *Library of Congress*

moisture-resistant "gum blanket" was placed on the operating tables. These gum blankets were used by soldiers for protection against the weather or as a ground cover for sleeping. The operating tables ran parallel to the barn under the forebay with the surgeons' backs to the wall, thus providing the most light during daylight hours while being somewhat protected from the weather.

An initial triage took place at battlefield aid stations, but not every soldier went through it. Some were taken straight to the hospital by comrades while others managed to reach the place on their own. Even if a wounded soldier was triaged, a second triage usually took place just outside the Spangler barn. Those in urgent need of a life-saving amputation or other procedure were placed on the ground floor of the barn, not far from the operating tables. Later, as the amputations wound down, the most seriously wounded men were placed on the stable floor. Those less seriously wounded or whom doctors believed could wait longer for their

surgeries were placed upstairs in the barn or out in the open; they would move to the tables when it was their turn.

Because the corps ambulance wagons jammed with medicine, dressings, chloroform, and other essentials had been allowed to reach the Gettysburg area, operators could conduct amputations and other surgeries immediately. What they couldn't get ready were tents, food, hospital clothing, and other essential supplies needed for the care, safety, and healing of the wounded after their initial treatments and surgeries were completed. These supplies, it will be recalled, were still more than 20 miles away in Westminster, Maryland. Once the trickle of wounded became a steady stream and then turned into a raging flood, doctors knew they were going to run out of protected space and many other things they surely needed. The result was that many of the unfortunate wounded had to sleep on the bare ground, unprotected from flying and crawling insects and the July sun and rain.

Doctor Daniel G. Brinton, who played a large role in the Spangler farm hospital story, took in the early part of the battle on Cemetery Hill. Unlike today, with the view blocked by trees and other impediments, he had a clear line of sight of the movements of the respective armies in that sector and the first day of fighting on the far side of town. The surgeon-in-chief of the Second Division, XI Corps, turned his horse about and rode to the Spangler property to begin the gruesome but life-saving work he knew was about to come his way. The experienced doctor knew his tortuous work would be days of nearly unending, backbreaking labor.

"During the day the medical officers were busily engaged in choosing and arranging a hospital," Brinton wrote in his diary. "Its location was altered twice owing to the approaching fire of the enemy, but finally it was definitely established in a large barn 1 mile back from the cemetery. The wounded soon began to pour in, giving us such sufficient occupation that from the 1st of July till the afternoon of the fifth, I was not absent from the hospital more than once and then but for an hour or two. Very hard work it was, too, & little sleep fell to our share. Four operating tables were going night and day."[17]

It only took a single day to nearly ruin the farm. According to a US quartermaster's report from a damage claim filed by George Spangler, "On the 1st of July, Union troops encamped in his wheat field and in other parts of his farm in large numbers, large numbers of wounded were brought to the buildings during the battle.... The land was greatly injured and damaged by driving and trespassing over it. The barn was shattered and boards destroyed by the use of the hospital."[18]

Neighbor Nathaniel Lightner shared both ownership of Powers Hill with the Spanglers and their wartime nightmare. "Under an apple tree I found the surgeons with a man stretched out on our dining room table and cutting and sawing a leg off, and on the grass there lay a pile of limbs," recalled Lightner, who discovered that a hospital had been established on his property while he was away in town. "I went around to the kitchen door and looked in. Horror of horrors! The floor was covered with wounded men. The stove was red hot, and the men were baking and the men were taking and cooking up everything in the house that was edible. They had taken full possession."

Lightner sought out a surgeon and asked him what he should do, given the circumstances that had befallen him. "Do you live here?" asked the doctor. "Is this your place?" When Lightner told him it was, the surgeon waved him off with grim advice: "Go back, go back; take your family and go [to] the rear; that is all I can tell you." With that, the bloodstained man of medicine returned to his work. The

---

17 Daniel G. Brinton, "From Chancellorsville to Gettysburg, a Doctor's Diary," in *The Pennsylvania Magazine of History and Biography*, vol. 89, no. 3 (Harrisburg, PA, 1965), 313.

18 Spangler Damage Claim N-1892, 1875, Historic Structure Report.

landowner was not quite ready to capitulate. "Can't I get some clothing at least out of the house?" he asked. "Yes, if you can find any," shot back the doctor. Lightner entered his own home "by his permission, but could not find a thing that had not been torn up and put to use—not even a dress of my wife's. We set out with the children, six in number, and made our way back on foot as well as we could, among the oncoming troops and trains, four miles to a relative, where I left them, and returned about midnight to the neighborhood."[19]

Unlike their neighbor, the six-member Spangler family stayed through all of it, banished to a single upstairs bedroom in their small home. Two parents and four children, ages 14 to 21, crammed into a broiling hot and humid space. If they wanted to stay, they had no choice as to accommodations, because as a member of the medical staff told them, everything else on the property was needed to treat the wounded. From July 1 until August 6, the Spanglers experienced a Civil War nightmare of blood, amputated limbs, agony, screams, death, and nauseating smells firsthand, all while their belongings were stolen and their property was under siege. Matters would only get worse for them on the second day of their voluntary captivity, when enemy artillery rounds screamed out of the sky and fell about them. Like many of the patients, their lives would be in danger.

Spangler Farm Short Story

Spangler neighbor Jacob Hummelbaugh "Went to Spanglers house and remained there at times during the battle" and "was back and forth often during the battle," according to a report filed years after the Civil War. That's because as horrible and crowded and overrun and frightening as things were at George Spangler's farm, starting on July 2 it was worse at Hummelbaugh's. The property of the shoemaker and farmer sat at what is today the intersection of Pleasanton Avenue and Taneytown Road, less than a mile house-to-house from the Spangler property and directly behind the Union line. The property was used as a temporary II Corps aid station and field hospital during the battle and received almost constant artillery and infantry overshots. It also was where the mortally wounded Confederate Brig. Gen. William Barksdale was treated and first buried. After the war, Hummelbaugh talked about the scene on the Spangler farm in support of their damage claims, as described by the US quartermaster: "Union troops were

---

19 "Horrors of Battle," an interview with Nathaniel Lightner by "A. F. C.", *Washington* (D.C.) *Evening Star*, November 4, 1893.

encamped on his farm during the battle, and many of them about the house and barn, some were encamped on his wheat field. The wheat crop was entirely destroyed, also the oats, grass, and potatoes. The house and barn were occupied as a hospital by the 11th Army Corps for five weeks and upwards. His fences were destroyed, wood injured, barn greatly injured by the use of the hospital. Saw the soldiers use up boards for coffins etc."

Hummelbaugh's small house still stands and looks as it did in 1863 thanks to restoration by the National Park Service. Jacob Hummelbaugh, who was a widower in 1863, and his wife, Sarah, are buried next to the Spanglers in Evergreen Cemetery in Gettysburg.[20]

20 Spangler Damage Claim N-1892, 1875, Historic Structure Report.

Chapter 4

Restless Nights

"I buried my head in my pillow to shut out the sounds that reached us."

— *A Union field hospital nurse*

Almost no one in or near Gettysburg got much sleep on the night of July 1-2, especially hospital workers and the wounded soldiers who had found their way to the Spangler farm. Even as the clock edged past midnight and into the early morning of July 2, Gettysburg and the surrounding area bustled with activity after one of the most horrific days ever suffered by an American town.

The generals had little time for rest. On the opposite side of the battlefield, Gen. Robert E. Lee was awake reading reports, talking with various officers, and pondering his strategy for the upcoming day. His Army of Northern Virginia had wrecked two of the seven Union infantry corps in Maj. Gen. George Meade's Army of the Potomac and driven them into and through Gettysburg. The high ground (Cemetery Hill) that he hoped to capture on the evening of July 1, however, remained in Union hands. Most of his army was up, but part of General Longstreet's I Corps was still on the road. Was the rest of Meade's command strung out and hustling to reach the field or already up and waiting? Lee, who was always unwilling to let the initiative pass to his opponent, intended to attack. The only question was where he would do so.

Closer to the Spangler property at about the same hour, a group of officers, some mounted and others on foot, were gathered in and near the arched gatehouse that prominently marked Evergreen Cemetery on the Baltimore Pike. General Meade reached Cemetery Hill about 1:00 a.m. after a long ride through the darkness, where he immediately began conversing with several generals assembled there, including the XI Corps' Howard and the army's chief of artillery, Brig. Gen. Henry Hunt. It was difficult to evaluate the Union line without much light, but the officers explained the day's events, the lay of the land, and how the army was holding strong, defensible terrain. "There was a bright moon, so the dawn of day crept upon us unawares," Howard later explained. "Before sunrise I rode with General Meade along our lines to the left. . . . He sat upon his horse as the sun was rising, and with his field glass took a survey of the Cemetery Ridge and its environments."[1]

As the officers talked, rode, and walked the Union line, ambulances full of injured men rolled past on their way to the various hospitals. Other soldiers were busy digging trenches or building breastworks. Some managed to find sleep even in these troubled times.

The bulk of Meade's army (II, III, V, and VI Corps) was still approaching the battlefield and would reach it that night or early the next day. Major General Henry Slocum's XII Corps had arrived late on the afternoon of July 1 and divided, with one division moving to occupy Culp's Hill and the other tramping a couple miles south to anchor the line near the Round Tops. Slocum would reunite his corps on Culp's Hill the following morning. The survivors of the defeated I Corps were in position on Culp's Hill on Slocum's left, and what remained of the XI Corps had gathered on and around Cemetery Hill.

As Meade learned during his briefing and exploration, the Union line was anchored on its right that early morning on wooded and rocky Culp's Hill southeast of Gettysburg. From there, the line ran northwest onto Cemetery Hill just below town, and then due south before petering out on upper Cemetery Ridge. The Confederates as best as Meade could figure held a line roughly parallel to his own about one mile distant on upper Seminary Ridge that ran through the town itself and ended at some point opposite Culp's Hill. This formation gave Meade some hope, for his line was on good ground and was shorter and easier to reinforce than his opponent's, who held a longer exterior front that would be more difficult to manage.

The commander of the II Corps, Maj. Gen. Winfield Hancock, reached the field on July 1 well ahead of his men. When Meade received word that I Corps commander John Reynolds was dead, he ordered Hancock to ride ahead and take command of the chaotic field. Meade anticipated pushback because XI Corps

1 Howard, *Autobiography of Oliver Otis Howard*, 424.

commander Howard outranked Hancock, so Meade provided him with written orders. To his credit, Howard cooperated and the generals divided their responsibilities, with Howard assuming control of the line east of the Baltimore Pike, which included East Cemetery Hill and Culp's Hill. The II Corps reached the field early on July 2 and extended the Union line from Howard's left flank south down Cemetery Ridge.[2]

Major General Dan Sickles' III Corps trickled onto the field in several pieces, the first on the afternoon of July 1 and the balance during the night and the next morning. The corps camped along lower Cemetery Ridge on Hancock's left flank.

The V Corps under Maj. Gen. George Sykes spent most of the night marching to Gettysburg and arrived on the army's right before Meade shifted it south behind the army. Sykes' men arrived on the Spangler, Musser, and Bucher farms later that morning and bivouacked on the southwest side of the 1863 intersection of the Baltimore Pike and Granite Schoolhouse Lane (a few yards south of where it is today). Meade knew the VI Corps under Maj. Gen. John Sedgwick would not arrive anytime soon. It had the farthest to march and would do so all that night and most of the next day. By the time it ended, the VI Corps' forced march covered some 34 miles and ended in the same place the V Corps had been—the Spangler and other nearby properties—before being moved to join the fighting on the army's left flank.[3]

The men of the XI Corps slept as best they could the night of July 1-2 under and around artillery pieces, along stone walls, and in the open air on Cemetery Hill and East Cemetery Hill. Some used gravestones for pillows. "We slept in the cemetery last night," wrote musician and stretcher bearer Pvt. Henry Henney of the 55th Ohio. "The moon shone most of the night and the Union troops were concentrating there, on south of Gettysburg. All night could be heard the rumble of cannons and artillery, moving into position along Cemetery Ridge. We could hear the shouting of the men as they rode their horses over the soft ground. Fences were being leveled," he continued, "and everything was gotten into shape for the struggle which seemed imminent on the following day."[4]

2 Pula, *Under the Crescent Moon*, vol. 2, 108-112.

3 Larry Tagg, *The Generals of Gettysburg: The Leaders of America's Greatest Battle* (Savas Publishing, 1998), 34, 63, 82, 105, 123-124, 144.

4 Henry Henney, Diary and Letters, February 3, 1862-January 7, 1865. Civil War Times Illustrated Collection, Hem-I, Box 15, US Army Heritage and Education Center.

*   *   *

With wagons and horses frantically coming and going and the screams and cries of the wounded and the dying rising from their barn and surrounding grounds, it is doubtful the Spanglers slept much during the first night of the occupation of their farm, especially with all six family members crammed into one bedroom. The sounds must have been horrific and something that haunts you for as long as you live. A nurse working at another hospital admitted she buried her head in her pillow to "shut out the sounds which reached us."[5]

XI Corps ambulance drivers wanted to get all of the corps' wounded to the hospital on the Spangler property, but it was an impossible task. Many of the XI's wounded were in hospitals behind Confederate lines or still on the battlefield behind the enemy front, unable to move much and in anguish, in and out of consciousness, covered by biting insects, and crying for water and home. Other wounded and dying men from the XI Corps were prisoners at impromptu hospitals set up in and around town in churches, schools, warehouses, businesses, homes, and sheds. Regimental surgeons and assistant surgeons on both sides treated soldiers in town regardless of the color of their uniform, while civilians cleaned and bandaged wounds and attempted to soothe and feed the soldiers as best they could in places where no doctor was present.

"As the afternoon [of July 1] wore away the churches and warehouses on Chambersburg, Carlisle and York streets nearest the line of battle, were filled with wounded," related Gettysburg resident Daniel Skelly, who was 18 at the time. "Then the court house, as well as the Catholic, Presbyterian and Reformed churches and the school house on High street received the injured soldiers, until those places had reached their capacity, when private homes were utilized, citizens volunteering to take them in and care for them." Skelly carried buckets of water into the courthouse and did his best to slake the thirst of the men inside. "Some of them were so frightfully wounded that a lady could not go near them," he recalled. "These I gave water to, while she cared for those who were not so severely wounded. Quite a number of our townspeople were there doing everything they could in the relief work as the wounded were carried in."[6]

---

5 Mrs. Edmund A. Souder, *Leaves From the Battle-field of Gettysburg. A Series of Letters From a Field Hospital and National Poems* (Philadelphia, PA, 1864), 23.

6 Daniel Alexander Skelly, *A Boy's Experiences During the Battles of Gettysburg* (Ann Arbor, MI, 1973), 15.

Brigadier General Francis Barlow, one of the two new generals recently appointed by Howard and in command of the First Division, would end up at the Spangler hospital after the battle. Late on the afternoon of July 1, however, found him at the Josiah Benner house on Harrisburg Road north of town. The general had been shot three times while leading his men in the defense of a hill now known as Barlow Knoll. A Confederate doctor examined him. The prognosis was less than favorable, admitted Barlow, who was advised a bullet had lodged in his pelvic area and "there was little chance for my life." Believing the wound mortal, the Southern doctor gave him morphine for comfort.

Adjutant and 1st Lt. Theodore Ayrault Dodge fought with the 119th New York, part of Col. Wladimir Krzyzanowski's Second Brigade of Schurz's Third Division. The officer, who had been shot in the ankle, shared the Benner house with Barlow. "His chance of survival seemed very slim," wrote Dodge, "but, like a brave man, he resolved he would not die, unless it was an absolute consequence; and as a reward for his valor in health and in sickness, he subsequently got well." Dodge said he knew firsthand of recoveries "from sheer force of will; and I have known men with slight wounds that ought not to have kept them on their sick-list three weeks, worry themselves into the grave, for fear they were going to die." General Barlow was moved on July 2 a short distance down Harrisburg Road to the John S. Crawford house, where he joined Capt. Alfred E. Lee of the 82nd Ohio, another wounded man from Schurz's division destined for the Spangler hospital.[7]

Other temporary pre-Spangler hospitals housing XI Corps wounded on July 1 included the Adams County Almshouse on Barlow Knoll, the Trinity German Reformed Church and a school (both on East High Street), the College Edifice on the current Gettysburg College campus, the Lutheran Theological Seminary, the Elizabeth Culp house on York Street, and many more. The almshouse was so full of XI Corps and Confederate wounded that many had to be placed outside until someone died and a bed became available. Many buildings used for hospitals had a red flag hung on the outside to discourage disturbance by either army. The XI Corps regimental doctors working in and around town at these hospitals worked through the night of July 1-2 just as the doctors did at Spangler, but they had the added stress of doing it behind Confederate lines as prisoners of war.

"I was captured between the Poor House and the town," recalled 31-year-old Dr. Abraham Stout of the 153rd Pennsylvania, one of Col. von Gilsa's brigade

7 Pula, *Under the Crescent Moon*, vol. 2, 56-60, 62-64; Tagg, *The Generals of Gettysburg*, 127; Theodore Ayrault Dodge, "Left Wounded on the Field," in *Putnam's Magazine*, vol. 4, July-December, 1869 (New York, NY), 323.

doctors. "Colonel D. B. [David B.] Penn, of the 7th Regiment of the [Louisiana] Tigers, saw me and dismounted. He walked by my side and asked me who I was and then told me I was his prisoner, taking me to the German Reformed Church, when he said to me: 'You ought to take this church for a Hospital.' I said, 'Yes, if it is not locked,' 'Well,' said the Colonel, 'if it is we can soon open it.' But we found the doors unlocked, and took possession. In less than half an hour it was filled with wounded men, mostly Union men."[8]

Private Justus Silliman of the 17th Connecticut was knocked out by a shot to the head on the first day of battle and awoke to find himself surrounded by Confederates. His was a meandering journey to the Spangler farm. Silliman was first taken to the Confederate hospital at the Elizabeth Weible farm east of town near the York Pike and transferred the next day to the Trinity German Reformed Church in town. He was then shipped to the school on East High Street and moved a fourth and final time to the Spangler XI Corps hospital once the battle was over.[9]

Private James B. Rowe fought with the 134th New York on the right side of Col. Coster's doomed infantry line in the brickyard on the first afternoon of the battle. He would have been taken prisoner behind enemy lines in town if not for the help of a quick-thinking Union surgeon. Rowe slipped into a house being used as a temporary hospital and dropped to the floor with a group of severely wounded men. When Confederates examined the house looking for Union soldiers, the surgeon gestured toward the collection of injured and replied, "Those are my severest cases." Rowe rejoined his regiment several days later after the Confederates evacuated the town.[10]

The surgeons at George and Elizabeth Spangler's farm found no sleep at all that first night of the battle. Somehow, their bodies and brains kept functioning under the weight of it all. The arrival of their medical wagons allowed them to perform operations and treat the wounded, but like it was at the aid stations earlier elsewhere on the field, food, tents, clothing, and bedding had yet to arrive. Many of the wounded remained exposed to the chilly overnight air lying on bare ground, and that wasn't going to change any time soon.

The exhausting and uncomfortable nights were just getting started.

---

8 Kiefer, *History of the One Hundred and Fifty-Third Regiment*, 131-132. Doctor Stout served in the church during the battle then at a school close to it on East High Street for the next three weeks. He mustered out of the army with his regiment at the end of that July.

9 Justus M. Silliman to mother, July 3, 1863, in Marcus, ed., *A New Canaan Private*, 41-42.

10 Warner, Military Records of Schoharie County Veterans of Four Wars, 295-296.

Spangler Farm Short Story

Private Israel P. Spencer of the 136th New York, Col. Orland Smith's brigade, Maj. Gen. von Steinwehr's division, was a blue-eyed 19-year-old that July. The young six-foot one-inch farmer from western New York was wounded on the skirmish line west of the Taneytown Road on July 2, prompting a trip to Spangler. "J. A. Mead, Mart Finch and Lon Crandall were slightly wounded, as well as myself, with a scratch across my left should," he wrote in a letter home. "This being the real first battle that we had been in I saw things and heard of others I never ever dreamed of before. Men at the hospital hit in every conceivable place. . . . I helped another fellow who was helping a man who was shot through his mouth, and the blood was running so he could not talk. Well, we got over to the [Spangler] field hospital and my shoulder smarting very badly," he continued. "I pulled off my jacket and looked at the wound a minute and said to [some] of the fellows, 'I am going back,' and so I did." Private Spencer is not listed among the wounded because he returned immediately to his unit.[11]

Ruch Report No. 1

Private Reuben F. Ruch of Lehigh County, Pennsylvania, was 19 when he left home in 1862 to join the 153rd Pennsylvania. A wartime photo shows a dapper, clean-shaven Ruch with hair neatly combed from left to right and an open coat over a vest. Ruch spent a month in a hospital in the spring of 1863 with typhoid fever, and although he had recovered enough to rejoin his unit, he was not fully recovered when the long trek north into Pennsylvania began. He was wounded in each knee defending Barlow Knoll on the first day of fighting and ended up at the Spangler hospital after the battle. He wrote extensively about his time in Gettysburg and at the Spangler farm. This is the first segment of his story, in his own words, as we follow him to and at Spangler. More reports will follow in later chapters:

> I saw a red flag on a church on the southeast corner of the town [The Trinity German Reformed Church at East High and Stratton streets on July 1] . . . I found the house full. I saw a sight which I will never forget. I should call it a slaughter-house. There must have been ten or twelve amputation tables in this room . . . they were all busy . . . the doctors had their sleeves rolled up to their shoulders and were covered with blood. I saw

11 "Letters from Private Israel P. Spencer," www.russscott.com/~rscott/136thny/ ltisrasp. htm. Accessed January 2, 2017.

Pvt. Reuben F. Ruch

History of the 153rd Regiment P.A. Vol. Inf.

all I wanted to of this part, and I climbed the stairs to the floor above. I found an empty pew . . . an old doctor came through the church and told us all who could travel should get out of the church . . . that our line was breaking again . . . I saw there was no chance for a cripple to get out of the church so I went back to my pew and waited for service to commence. . . . A guard came through and relieved me of my gun.

. . . I saw nothing to eat until the morning of the 4th, which made it just three days on an empty stomach. . . .

. . . The man in the pew in front of me had a flesh wound in the hip. He belonged to the 134th N.Y. This man's whole conversation was about home. If he were only at home. I got very tired of his talk and told him they were getting along at home without him. I tried every way I could to draw his mind from home, but he was the worst homesick man I ever saw. I think it was on the second day he got sort of childish. He wanted me to hold his hands, and I gave him some short answer. He turned around and laid his arm on the rail of the pew in front of him as if he were going to sleep. I thought he had gone to sleep, having been quiet for half an hour, when a doctor came through the aisle and asked us if there was anything he could do for us. I told him to look at the New York man, for he had not said anything for half an hour, and that I thought he was dead. The doctor looked at him and found him dead and stiff.[12]

12 Kiefer, *History of the One Hundred and Fifty-Third Regiment*, 216-218.

Chapter 5

Love and Madness: The Hovey Family

"I have had a good deal of care of him and called him my Soldier Boy and tried to take the place of Mother Sister & Friend. I think I never had such a trial parting with one that I had no more acquaintance with."

— Nurse Marilla Hovey, in a letter to the family of a soldier who died at the Spangler XI Corps hospital

A medical officer and his family serving together at a field hospital during the Civil War was not only rare, but nearly unheard of. "I've not seen reference to any other medical officer having his family with them and I can't imagine a field hospital being a suitable place to bring his family into," notes one historian. The sole exception labored together on the sprawling XI Corps Spangler farm hospital. When word spread that a new three-year infantry regiment would be recruited from Allegany, Livingston, and Wyoming counties in western New York, it was only natural that Dr. Bleecker Lansing Hovey would join it.[1]

The 44-year-old Hovey enlisted on August 19, 1862, at Albany and mustered in with the balance of the men of the 136th New York the following month at Portage. Many of the regiment's enlistees had grown up in the small village of Dansville and knew Hovey as their physician. He had visited their homes and was close to them, their parents, and even their grandparents. That's how it worked for small-town doctors. He had taken care of these men as children, and now that they

---

1 John Heiser, Historian, Division of Interpretation, National Park Service, Gettysburg National Military Park, via email, Dec. 23, 2016.

Dr. Bleecker Lansing Hovey

New York State Military Museum

were adults and about to go off to war he would continue doing so in the field—something that was common for regimental surgeons in both armies.[2]

Marilla Hovey worked alongside her husband for 20 years as a nurse, so she knew the young men almost as well as he did. She had no desire to send her husband or the local lads off to war alone. As a result, she, together with the Hoveys' only child, 17-year-old son Frank, decided to join him in the field, where they continued that comfortable personal and professional relationship. Little did they know, though, what was in store for the fresh young regiment. By the time the command mustered out in June of 1865, it had served in nearly 20 battles, beginning at Chancellorsville in May 1862 and ending in North Carolina at Bentonville, and countless smaller actions, skirmishes, and other operations; participated in the March to the Sea under William T. Sherman; and taken part in the Grand Review in the nation's capital. Nearly 80 men and officers would be killed or mortally wounded during its arduous service, hundreds more would be wounded, and nearly 100 others would perish from disease.[3]

Three months after Dr. Hovey left with the regiment, Mrs. Hovey joined her husband in December 1862 in central Virginia outside Fredericksburg. Her presence there confused Dr. Henry Van Aernam of the 154th New York:

When I first used to call at Surg. Hovey's quarters, Mrs. Hovey seemed to be occupying them with the Dr. as his wife with no appearance of Hospital

2 Frederick H. Dyer, *A Compendium of the War of the Rebellion* (Des Moines, IA, 1908), 197.

3 Ibid, 1,457.

arrangements, but later on when the 11th A.C. had gone into winter quarters . . . I visited Surg. Hovey's quarters, and found in their vicinity a well organized Brigade Hospital in which Mrs. Hovey was serving as a nurse. The place looked tidy and inviting and she seemed to have a good supply of Sanitary stores at command. If I gave any thought to the matter of her employment at that time, I supposed she was employed by either the Sanitary or Christian Commissions, as the nurses in the Brigade field hospitals were generally enlisted men, convalescents or 'light duty' men, detailed by reason of having an aptitude for hospital service. This Hospital was kept under Mrs. Hovey's care until the Spring campaign.[4]

Dr. Hovey, wife Marilla, and son Frank were present for each march, battle, and encampment. They experienced the same hardships as the soldiers, including the bad food, unhealthful sanitation, fluctuations in weather, and gruesome hospital scenes. Dr. Hovey knew he could trust and rely on them both.

*   *   *

Most female nurses worked at well-established brick-and-mortar Civil War hospitals or helped at field hospitals once a battle ended. One such nurse was Cornelia Hancock, who left behind vivid letters to family members about her time as a nurse in Civil War hospitals. She was the first female nurse to reach the II Corps' division hospitals after the battle of Gettysburg. "I was in that corps all day, not another woman within a half mile . . . women are needed very badly."[5]

Marilla Hovey and Frank were working at the Spangler hospital on the afternoon of July 1—the first day of Gettysburg—so she was there days before Cornelia Hancock arrived at the II Corps division hospital. Working as an orderly at the hospital, young Frank gathered firewood and kept the fires going, helped carry the wounded, rolled bandages, wrapped wounds, fetched and provided water, and assisted the cooks. It is possible and even likely he was enlisted at times to hold down patients who squirmed and moved while under anesthesia, and he might have even been trained to administer it. With his mother and father, he was right in the middle of the nightmarish sights, sounds, and smells of the battlefield hospital.

4 Henry Van Aernam letter in support of the pension application of Marilla Hovey, October 24, 1893. Letter provided by Rex Hovey, great-nephew of Mrs. Hovey.

5 Henrietta Stratton Jaquette, ed., *Letters of a Civil War Nurse: Cornelia Hancock, 1863-1865* (Lincoln, NE, 1998), 7.

Mrs. Hovey cared for a soldier's spiritual and physical well-being. She wrote numerous letters to families while patients healed or just before or after they died. Field hospital nurses were so taxed during the day that most sacrificed sleep to write these letters at night. Mrs. Hovey was often the first person to break the unbearable news to loved ones. While working on the Spangler farm, she wrote to the family of 24-year-old Cpl. Lucien J. Smith of the 136th New York:

Dear Friends of Mr. Smith,

Although a stranger I take my pen to share the sad [news] of the death of Lucien J. Smith who departed this life July 14 at half past two o'clock. He was wounded by a ball through his lung that came out of his back. And another in his foot.

I have had a good deal of care of him and called him my Soldier Boy and tried to take the place of Mother Sister & Friend. I think I never had such a trial parting with one that I had no more acquaintance with. He was beloved by all that knew him. I have not seen as many tears shed by the bedside of death as by His.

But my dear friends there are many things for your comfort. His wounds were received while doing his duty in defence of our glorious union—Surrounded by eight of his regiment who mourned as for a Brother—and Better than all He left a clear & bright evidence that he was fully prepared to join the heavenly throng who have washed their robes & made them white in the blood of the Lamb.

I talked to him about dying. He loved to talk about it. In answer to the question, "Do you love the Lord Jesus Christ?" "Oh yes. I love him." "Have you made a public profession of that Love?" "When I was seventeen years old." "Do you still trust him?" "Yes though he slay me yet will I trust in him."

At another time he said I had the greatest dreams. I thought I could fly right home to my savior. . . . While on his breast I lean my head and breathe my life out sweetly there. . . . He made a motion that he wanted something. I gave him a pencil. He wrote "Sing." I sang Oh sing to me of heaven when I am called to die sing songs of holy ecstasy to waft my soul on high there will be no more sorrows there. In heaven above, where all is love, there will be no more sorrows there & another. Tho often here were weary, there is sweet rest above. A rest that is eternal where all is peace and love. There is sweet rest in heaven. He clapped his hands and pointed his finger toward heaven & tried to say home. He said many other things which I hope I may see someone to tell but I am taking time to write from others that are dying.

He wished I should have his money & see that he was embalmed & sent home. I have had him Embalmed, paid 25 cents. I got a government coffin & have him buried here & his grave marked so you can get him any time. I could not come with his body or I would. I sent a telegraft to you & hope to see you before I leave. He had 37 cents. I will keep the balance while I stay here unless I see someone to send it. Then when I get ready to leave I will send it by mail to you. His other things will be sent to you. I have nothing to do with them.

Be assured you have my warmest sympathy in this deep affliction for so noble a son and Brother. I can testify that everything has been done for his comfort & restoration that could be under the circumstances & We all feel his loss deeply....

Yours Truly, Mrs. B.L. Hovey[6]

On July 13, one day before he died, Smith dictated a letter to his parents which suggests he did not know his wound was mortal. "[I]f a possible thing I wish that my brother Byron or Allen soon will come down here," he explained,

My wounds are getting along probably as well as can be expected. The ball is not yet out of my foot, but the Doctor thinks that it will come out before long. It is sloughing off coming out of the hole it went in at. It has been very painfull but Christ has sustained me in all things. I find his arms around and about me at all times. O! Pray for me that I may be so happy as to meet you once more in the family circle. Should it be the providence of God that I should be taken away I hope we will meet again in heaven.

With love to all. I am dear parents your same loving son.

Lucien Smith[7]

6 Letter, Marilla Hovey to Dear Friends of Mr. Smith, courtesy of Rex Hovey.

7 Lucien Smith to parents, letter provided to author by Rex Hovey.

Grateful family members, both of the deceased and of the wounded, often wrote back to Mrs. Hovey to thank her for her kindness. She received the following letter after informing the family of Pvt. William T. Levey (134th New York) that he had been wounded at Dug Gap, Georgia, in 1864:

Mrs. B. L. Hovey,

Dear Friend:

We have just received the sad news of our dear brother's condition. Our hearts are filled with grief and sorrow at the thought of never more beholding our dear brother's face in this world. Tell him, if he still lives, that if it were possible we would willingly fly to his bedside to receive one parting kiss before he goes away forever. Oh how we will miss him at home, but our parting will be for only a short time and then we hope to meet in heaven, where parting shall be no more.

Dear brother, cast yourself upon the Lord and he will have mercy upon you, and upon our God he will abundantly pardon. Be assured, dear brother, we will not forget to pray for you.

Dear Mrs. Hovey, we feel very thankful to you for the interest you have taken in our dear brother. I hope you will continue to be kind to him and do all you can to comfort and prepare his soul for heaven and God will reward and bless you. I wish you would cut off a lock of my brother's hair and send it home and you will oblige. Farewell dear brother until we meet again.

From your affectionate sister, Jennette Bradt[8]

Private Levey, age 24 at the time of his wounding, survived and was discharged for disability on July 17, 1865. He married and lived a long life, dying at age 80.[9]

Like all of the surgeons at the XI Corps hospital, Dr. Hovey performed countless amputations. He also was personally involved in the treatment of Confederate Brig. Gen. Lewis Armistead, who arrived at the Spangler hospital after

---

8 Letter from Jennette Bradt to Marilla Hovey, no date, courtesy of Rex Hovey.

9 Pension File No. 72.297 on Fold3, Ancestry.com, accessed December 20, 2016.

being mortally wounded during Pickett's Charge on July 3. The Virginia officer lingered for two days before dying on July 5.

Hovey had experience treating Civil War wounded a year before he performed surgery in the field at Chancellorsville and Gettysburg. In July 1862, while still a private citizen, word reached western New York that soldiers from the 13th New York from Rochester, Dansville, and Brockport were being mistreated at one of the hospitals that had sprouted up around Washington, D.C. According to the July 17 edition of *The Dansville* [NY] *Advertiser*, "Dr. Hovey was dispatched by our citizens to ascertain and transmit to us their true condition, which the Doctor not only expressed his willingness and anxiety to do so but told us that as long as he could be of service to the boys, he would remain there and devote himself to their welfare."[10]

Not surprisingly given what would take place later that same year, Mrs. Hovey accompanied her husband. Together, they reported that the rumors of poor care were true. There were simply not enough doctors or nurses, medicine, or proper beds for the men. Some were even lying in the halls of the Justice Department, the Supreme Court, the Capitol, and elsewhere. Once he joined the 136th New York and the regiment reported to Washington, Dr. Hovey moved to the front of the food line to inspect what the government was feeding the new soldiers. Disgusted by what he discovered, he instructed the men to not eat the meat, which was discolored, rancid, and bug-infested.[11]

The man who would work so hard to save so many lives almost didn't make it to the Spangler farm. In a March 1863 column in *The Dansville Advertiser* (to which he was a frequent contributor), he voiced what he described as the displeasure of the regiment and the army with the Lincoln administration's recently enacted Emancipation Proclamation. "The administration policy on the slavery question is not looked upon with favor by any class in the army," he wrote. "Men entered the field to sustain the constitution as it was, not that any new question should be brought in. There are none but desire to see the country rid of the curse, yet there are few who are willing to sacrifice their lives to free a class of inferior beings, who perhaps would be worse off in their new condition, than they are now. A restoration of the country as it was," he continued, "is the desire of the soldier, and

10 *The Dansville Advertiser*, July 17, 1862.

11 Ibid., and phone interview with Rex Hovey, Sept. 22, 2016.

not to subvert the institutions of any state." The opinion he expressed in the article resulted in Dr. Hovey's court-martial.[12]

Dr. Hovey was placed under house arrest in April, but was released in May to help with the flood of casualties at Chancellorsville. Afterward, he was found guilty but avoided incarceration by apologizing to his peers and his regiment. Within weeks the Army of the Potomac was fighting in Pennsylvania and the 45-year-old doctor was at the Spangler farm.

The Hoveys worked tirelessly at the Spangler hospital the entire time it was open, from July 1 to August 6. Once the last man was gone, Dr. Hovey was given a 20-day furlough and the family headed home to Dansville to rest and probably attempt to process the life-changing event that they had just been through at Spangler. Their return was important enough for *The Dansville Advertiser* to write about it:

The Surgeon's Return

Surgeon Hovey, wife and son returned from the army on Saturday last. The Surgeon has a furlough of 20 days, and we expect to hear considerable of his personal experience. Mrs. Hovey has spent the greater portion of her time in the hospitals, and we hear much of the good she has accomplished among the sick and wounded. She is eminently fitted for such duties, and it is to be regretted that we have not many like her.[13]

While home, the tireless Mrs. Hovey was enlisted to raise funds by the New York Soldiers' Relief Association. J. N. Granger, chairman of the state-run association, wrote a letter dated August 14, 1863, to the "Patriotic Ladies and Gentlemen of the State of N. York." Less than a week after she had left the XI Corps hospital, Mrs. Hovey, who "has been engaged earnestly in relieving our wounded soldiers at Gettysburg, and who has received to my knowledge the warmest praise and commendation by the operating surgeons there, for her

---

12 *The Dansville Advertiser*, March 12, 1863. The Emancipation Proclamation, issued on the heels of the Union victory over the Army of Northern Virginia at Antietam in September 1862, freed all slaves in states that were still engaged in rebellion. Implementing the doctrine, in a practical sense, was impossible, but the declaration shifted the war from one to save the nation into a crusade against the institution of slavery. Lincoln issued the Emancipation Proclamation on September 22, 1862, and it went into effect on January 1, 1863.

13 The *Dansville Advertiser*, August 1863.

devoted sympathy and efficiency. . . . will represent to you our wants, or rather the necessities of the soldiers, and from that you will infer the wants of our society. We hope she will be successful in aiding us and know that at least she will be kindly received by you."[14]

* * *

In recognition and thanks for his service, Dr. Hovey received a brevet promotion to lieutenant colonel on August 9, 1865, and was mustered out the next day. He returned to private practice after the war in Rochester, New York, becoming one of the city's most admired residents. He died at age 89 in 1906 and was remembered as "a most distinguished representative of the medical fraternity, a man who through the long years of an active practice has kept in constant touch with the advancement and progress being made in the profession and has therefore made his service of the greatest possible value to his fellow men."[15]

Mrs. Hovey continued in the field with her husband after Gettysburg until 1864, when she teamed with well-known Union nurses Dorothea Dix and Annie Wittenmyer to establish and superintend numerous special-diet kitchens in large general hospitals in the South. These kitchens provided higher-quality meals as prescribed by the surgeons for patients with special needs caused by disease or their specific condition. With the sponsorship of the US Christian Commission, the Sanitary Commission, and the government, this program improved the overall low quality of hospital food. Mrs. Hovey and her special-diet kitchens often returned patients to good health faster than medication.

Marilla received no pay for her years of tireless, tender, and sympathetic service in Civil War field hospitals and special-diet kitchens. However, Congress passed a law in 1892 granting a monthly pension to any nurse who faithfully performed her duties during the Civil War for at least six months. Starting in August 1893, she earned a military pension of $12 a month before dying seven years before her husband, age 81, in 1899.

"Her disposition was mild and affectionate, her nature strong and brave, so that she seemed to see the bright and beautiful in life and overlooked the dark side," eulogized the *Rochester Democrat and Chronicle*. "She was generous to the poor,

14 Ibid.

15 *The Biographical Record of the City of Rochester and Monroe County, New York* (New York, NY, 1902), 36.

and up to the time health failed she was a daily visitor to the sick and needy, always giving a cheerful word and frequently a prayer. She had a record of nearly two hundred sick and dying soldiers who came under her special care. . . . That work lay so near her heart that her interest in it never waned, and she never tired of talking of army scenes and life."[16]

Frank Hovey received a commendation for his wartime service, but the only child of Bleecker and Marilla did not do well later in life. He never married, switched jobs often, suffered from alcohol abuse, and engaged in fistfights as an adult. According to a descendant, Frank "was in and out of insane asylums." The following story appeared in a New York newspaper on January 7, 1898:

FRANK HOVEY INSANE
Once Prominent in Monroe County Politics

Frank Hovey, the son of Dr. Bleecker Hovey, one of the wealthiest and most influential citizens of Rochester, was today committed to Bellevue to be examined as to his sanity. Hovey has been residing with his father for many years at No. 34 North Fitzhugh Street, Rochester.

Six years ago, after a paralytic stroke, Hovey was confined in an insane asylum for two years. Since his release from the asylum Hovey has been acting sanely and living quietly at his home in Rochester, until about ten days ago, when he disappeared.

Three or four days after his disappearance the banks in Rochester began to receive checks signed by Hovey from a hotel in this city. Dr. Willard D. Becker of Rochester and a detective succeeded in arresting Hovey here last night. He is 52 years old. Some years ago he was rather prominent in Monroe County politics and was Under Sheriff. Dr. Becker said that he would have Hovey transferred from Bellevue to an institution in Rochester.[17]

Frank died in 1898 while his parents were still alive. Perhaps Frank's travails were the result of the horrors he had witnessed as a teenager at Spangler and other

---

16 *Rochester Democrat and Chronicle*, February 13, 1899.

17 Edwin Dwight Northrup Papers, Box 16, Carl A. Kroch Library, Cornell University.

hospitals. Interestingly, Dr. Hovey devoted "much time [to] the subject of insanity" after the war.[18]

Spangler Farm Short Story

Another nurse who traveled with her husband and the troops and made it onto the Gettysburg battlefield before most other nurses was Elmina Spencer, a teacher and the wife of Cpl. Robert H. Spencer of the 147th New York (Brig. Gen. Lysander Cutler's brigade, Brig. Gen. James Wadsworth's division, I Corps). Corporal Spencer worked as ward master in charge of hospital supplies in August 1862, and Elmina went most places he did. The Spencers arrived in Gettysburg on the morning of July 1 and set up in a barn at an unknown location near the battlefield, where she served tea, coffee, and crackers to wounded XI Corps soldiers. This was one of two early XI Corps aid stations or field hospitals overrun and abandoned before the corps hospital was established on the Spangler property.

After the early hospital was broken up, Elmina founded the 147th's I Corps First Division hospital at Mark's German Reformed Church (known locally as "White Church") on the Baltimore Pike. This church (39°47'32"N 77°11'33"W) was about a half-mile on the right past the modern-day Outlet Shoppes at Gettysburg heading south out of town. The original church building no longer stands.

Elmina, about 40 years old during her time in Gettysburg, worked at the White Church hospital for three weeks before being appointed agent for the state of New York to care for its sick and wounded in the field through the end of the war. In that role, she worked at the Camp Letterman general hospital outside Gettysburg until mid-November 1863. According to a US Christian Commission report, "Those belonging to the First Division of this corps, who lay in White Church, were fortunate in having the attention of Mrs. Spencer, from New York."[19]

---

18 *The Biographical Record of the City of Rochester and Monroe County, New York*, 37.

19 Linus Pierpoint Brockett and Mary C. Vaughan, *Woman's Work in the Civil War: A Record of Heroism, Patriotism and Patience* (Philadelphia, PA, 1867), 404-415; "United States Christian Commission for the Army and Navy, for the Year 1863, Second Annual Report" (Philadelphia, PA, 1864), 73.

Chapter 6

Medicine, Sanitation, and Survival

"One day cured me of a hospital. Give me the picket line every time in place of a hospital!!!"
— *Capt. Matthew B. Cheney, 154th New York*

horrific scenes that Maj. Gen. Carl Schurz witnessed at the Spangler hospital on July 4, 1863, remained vivid to him years later. The former Third Division commander of the XI Corps described what he witnessed in his memoir *The Reminiscences of Carl Schurz*. "Most of the operating tables were placed in the open where the light was best, some of them partially protected against the rain by tarpaulins or blankets stretched upon poles," he began. "There stood the surgeons,

> their sleeves rolled up to the elbows, their bare arms as well as their linen aprons smeared with blood … around them pools of blood and amputated arms or legs in heaps, sometimes more than man-high. Antiseptic methods were still unknown at that time. As a wounded man was lifted on the table, often shrieking with pain as the attendants handled him, the surgeon quickly examined the wound and resolved upon cutting off the injured limb. Some ether was administered and the body put in position in a moment. The surgeon snatched his knife . . . and the cutting began. The operation accomplished, the surgeon would look around with a deep sigh, and then—'Next!'

The process went on hour after hour, wrote the retired general, "while the number of expectant patients seemed hardly to diminish." On occasion, a

Maj. Gen. Carl Schurz

Library of Congress

wounded man would call out the fact that "his neighbor lying on the ground had given up the ghost while waiting for his turn, and the dead body was then quietly removed." Now and again an exhausted surgeon, having reached the outside limits of his capacity, "would put down his knife, exclaiming that his hand had grown unsteady, and that this was too much for human endurance—not seldom hysterical tears streaming down his face."[1]

Depending on the limb, a good Civil War surgeon who had not yet reached the point where "his hand had grown unsteady" could perform an amputation in five to 15 minutes. The death rate doubled when an amputation was delayed more than 48 hours after the soldier was wounded because by that time blood poisoning, bone infection, or gangrene had usually set in. The backlog of soldiers waiting for surgery, coupled with the fact that some had been left untreated for days on or around the battlefield before being recovered, increased the frequency of these problems at the Spangler hospital. And many of these fatal issues were the result of an invention by a French army officer.[2]

The barrels of Civil War rifled muskets were lined with spiral grooves. The soft lead bullet fired from these weapons was invented by Claude-Étienne Minié, and was responsible for most of the wounds suffered during the war. The hollow base of the cone-shaped lead round, which weighed about an ounce, expanded to fill the rifling and spin the projectile. This made the "Minie ball," as it was called by the

---

1 Schurz, *The Reminiscences of Carl Schurz*, vol. 2, 38-40.

2 National Museum of Civil War Medicine, Frederick, Maryland.

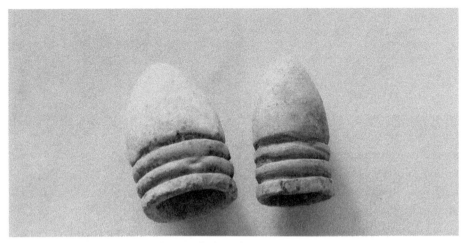

Lead Minie balls, fired from rifled muskets. *National Museum of Civil War Medicine*

soldiers, more accurate and faster than a round musket ball fired from a smoothbore musket.

Although Minie balls traveled faster than round balls, most remained inside the body. Because it was made of lead, the Minie ball expanded or flattened when it hit its target. The result was often devastating. The projectile splintered large sections of bone into smaller pieces and could destroy surrounding soft tissue. The bullet was so destructive it was banned worldwide in the late 1800s.

The widespread damage created by Minie balls dramatically increased deadly infections. Statistics consistently demonstrated that a soldier stood a much better chance of survival if his bone-shattered arm or leg was amputated—the sooner the better. Civil War surgeons knew this, so their goal was to perform an amputation within 24 hours of receipt of the wound. Contrary to many popular misconceptions, the doctors were not hacks performing amputations because they were unqualified to treat injured men. They performed the gruesome task because they knew it saved lives and was the best treatment option available.[3]

Who was a candidate for amputation depended upon the nature of the wound. Amputations could be avoided if the bone and joint were not severely injured and there wasn't a large amount of tissue damage. If the arm or leg bone or joint was badly broken or shattered and could not be cleanly set—wounds that were often accompanied by significant tissue damage that could cause an infection—the limb

3 Ibid.

Amputations and surgeries took place under the forebay of the Spangler barn.
The posts on the right were not present in 1863. *Ron Kirkwood*

had to come off or the patient would eventually perish. A soldier's health played a role in his ability to survive an amputation. A mentally strong, disease-free, and well-fed man had a much better chance of survival than a worn-down, hungry, and ill soldier, though unfortunately the latter scenario was more likely.

Civil War surgeons, called "operators," did not know about bacteria. The operators moved freely from one amputation to the next without washing their hands or knives or simply washing with water and not using soap while remaining in the same blood-soaked apron. Soldiers sometimes went weeks without bathing or washing their uniform, so germs and filth were often carried from their body or clothing into the wound by a bullet or artillery fragment. Doctors introduced germs by probing wounds with instruments that had not been properly sterilized or wiggling in a filthy finger. On the Spangler property, amputations took place next to the barnyard and stable and their manure piles.

There were a few antiseptics and disinfectants available during the Civil War, but how they worked and how to properly use them was not fully understood.

Antiseptics were usually used to treat an infection after it was well along instead of cleaning the wound or a knife to prevent an infection from developing in the first place. Infection rates dropped later in the war and after the war's end as the relationship between antiseptics and disinfectants and infections became better understood.

Latrines—or sinks, as they were called—contributed to infections and the spreading of disease. Long trenches a couple of feet wide and several feet deep were likely dug some distance from the Spangler house, barn, streams, and wells, and usually near trees or bushes to accommodate some level of privacy. Boards with holes were placed over the trenches for the men to sit on. Army of the Potomac instructions required that six inches of dirt be put in daily to cover what was left behind until the trench was filled to within two feet of the surface, at which point it was completely filled in and a new latrine dug.

Doctors, officers, and female nurses likely used the Spangler outhouse instead of a sink. Bedpans were available for patients who could not move. The Spanglers likely had chamber pots to use in the house as well as their outhouse. While their farm was occupied, they probably walked a few hundred yards to bathe in Rock Creek or used a pan of water in their bedroom.

The tendency of soldiers to ignore the sinks and relieve themselves wherever they pleased frustrated Medical Director Dr. Jonathan Letterman. The widespread practice contributed to the spreading of disease, as did digging latrines too close to a water supply. It is therefore no surprise that the filthy field hospitals and encampments made diarrhea the number one killer in the Civil War. Diarrhea was even deadlier than the Minie ball.[4]

Weather permitting, operators preferred to perform amputations outside, which is why they worked whenever possible under the 7-foot overhang on the front of the Spangler barn. The light and ventilation there were significantly better. Plus, they were away from the smells and sounds of the wounded inside the barn.

Three men worked at a Civil War amputation table. One was the operator, who was in charge. The second person administered anesthesia, which was usually chloroform. This was administered by putting it on a cloth or towel and placing that over the patient's nose and mouth. Sometimes it was dropped onto a sponge in a funnel placed over the patient's nose and mouth. The person administering it might be a hospital steward, an orderly, or an assistant surgeon. In desperate cases in the field, it might even be a civilian. The person administering the anesthetic

---

4 Letterman, *Medical Recollections of the Army of the Potomac*, 14.

Chloroform was administered via a towel, cloth or funnel with a sponge in it.

Ron Kirkwood

sometimes had no training other than quick instructions by the operator. They learned as they went, accidentally killing some patients along the way until they eventually became good at it. Lieutenant Colonel Freeman McGilvery's batteries performed outstanding work at Gettysburg while based on Spangler property as part of the Army of the Potomac Artillery Reserve, but he died in 1864 from the effects of chloroform while undergoing a simple finger amputation.[5]

The third person at the table—again an orderly or steward—helped hold the patient in place. Patients were given just enough chloroform to put them to sleep and make them insensitive to pain. Each patient was unique, their body chemistry and requirements different. Sometimes they convulsed, moaned, or screamed during the early stages of administering the anesthetic, thus requiring the third person at the table. These reactions conveyed to other wounded men the frightening but false impression that their comrade could feel the amputation being performed. In fact, the convulsions and utterances normally took place before the amputation itself had begun. This is called the "excitement phase" of the surgery. Sometimes, unfortunately, overworked Civil War operators facing a backlog of injured men awaiting amputation did not wait until the end of the excitement phase to begin cutting, the result being inaccurate incisions. Patients occasionally awoke during surgery and had to be put under again.[6]

Ninety-five percent of surgeries in the Civil War were performed with anesthesia. Contrary to a common Civil War myth, wounded men about to

---

5 Ether was also used, but it was less popular than chloroform. Ether was highly flammable, which meant it could not be used at night around lanterns, and could be easily inhaled by medical staff members. *New York Daily Herald*, September 7, 1864.

6 Gettysburg National Military Park Licensed Battlefield Guides Rick Schroeder, MD, and Fran Feyock, CRNA, both of Conemaugh Memorial Medical Center, Johnstown, PA, at "A Surgical Case Review Conference," October 7, 2017, Gettysburg, PA.

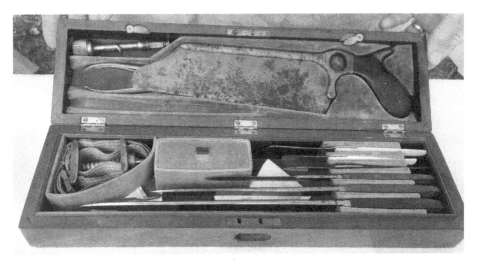

A surgeon's kit. *Ron Kirkwood*

undergo an amputation were not given a leather strap, bullet, or piece of wood to bite on while the surgeon hacked away a limb until the patient screamed or passed out from the pain.[7]

Before the amputation began, a tourniquet was placed on the limb to prevent bleeding and the operator examined inside the wound with his finger or an instrument to find where the splintered bone ended and the good bone began. Once that was determined, the doctor started the cut about one-half inch or more above the shattered bone. A double-sided catlin knife was used to begin the amputation if flaps of skin were being cut upward on the limb for later use with a prosthesis. Otherwise, a Liston knife, with a one-sided blade, cut down through muscle and tissue. This was a circular cut, not a direct cut straight to the bone. Operators cut around the front of the limb and then cut around the back. They were usually at the bone with just two swipes. Then they pulled the muscles out of the way and used the bone saw to complete the cutting part of the amputation. A

---

7 National Museum of Civil War Medicine. By way of comparison, amputations were performed without anesthesia during the American Revolution. Officers sometimes received alcohol before their amputation, but enlisted men usually clamped down on a piece of leather or a stick. With at least two men holding the patient down on the table and a tourniquet applied, the surgeon cut through the skin and muscle directly to the bone. This was called a "guillotine amputation." The muscle was pulled out of the way and the surgeon sawed through the bone. Bleeding veins and arteries were cauterized with boiling pine pitch, after which the tourniquet was removed. Most patients went into shock during this procedure and did not survive. Interview of Dr. Spencer Annabel, internist, Hornell, NY, on July 2, 2016, in Gettysburg.

good surgeon could get through the bone with just three cuts. Debris and projecting pieces of bone were found and removed.

Once the end of the bone was smoothed and any bone dust cleaned off, the surgeon searched for veins and arteries that needed to be tied. The assistant loosened the tourniquet to discover any bleeding (veins oozed blood, while arteries spurted it). Each vein and artery was found and tied off one by one. Find a bleeder, retighten the tourniquet, tie off the vein or artery, loosen the tourniquet, find the next bleeder, tie it, and so on. Each one was tied with unsanitized silk (the Confederate army often used horse hair). A little hook called a tenaculum was used to grab and pull back arteries that had retracted during cutting.

Flap amputations were sometimes utilized so the wound could be closed with hanging tissue and skin. The wound was loosely sutured so that pus could drain after the almost inevitable post-op infection set in. The operator checked on the healing process three or four days later to determine whether additional surgery was needed to retie bleeding veins or arteries. Sometimes, more of the limb had to be taken off in a second surgery because of gangrene, which spread easily at Spangler because patients were placed so close to one another in the crowded conditions. It was not uncommon at the Spangler facility for a soldier to die from a disease contracted at the hospital rather than from his battle wound. The wound was dressed post-surgery with a wet cloth or gauze called "water dressing" that might or might not be clean, but certainly wasn't sanitized. Dressings were sometimes reused or kept on for days because of the volume of wounded men who needed attention.

All of this was completed within 15 minutes or less and then it was on to the next patient. On the Spangler property, this procedure continued for days with minimal rest for the operators.

During the battle and before the wagons carrying the bedding and tents were allowed into the area, post-surgery patients at the XI Corps hospital were given morphine powder on the wound for pain, awakened, and then likely placed somewhere in the barn or under a tree in the orchard behind the Spangler house. Or, with inside space no longer available, some were placed in the open on a layer of hay, though they soon ran out of hay and men had to lie on bare ground. Civil War hospital tents, which typically held eight to 10 men, gradually arrived after the battle and covered the fields around the Spangler barn.

For the duration of the battle and for a time afterward, patients remained in their same filthy uniforms or were stripped down because the wagons with hospital clothing were not being allowed in to keep the roads clear for faster troop movement. There also was a severe food shortage at the XI Corps hospital at this time.[8]

Once a pile of limbs grew large enough, someone would be assigned to load the severed arms, legs, feet, and fingers into a wagon and haul them away. What they did with all of those limbs piled high outside the Spangler barn remains unknown. In all likelihood, they were carted to a distant spot on the property and buried.

A strong odor and insect problem developed in and around wounds and as piles of amputated limbs grew. The harassment by hordes of incessant flies was a constant source of suffering and complaint by the hospital staff and wounded. Infected wounds exuded a putrid odor, with the worst cases of infection detectable several feet away. It was not uncommon during the Civil War to hang pine branches on tents in an attempt to fight the smell.

Amputation survival rates depended on where on the body the amputation took place. The most common amputation sites on the body were the hand, thigh, lower leg, and upper arm. Amputations of the hand or fingers were the least likely to cause death, with mortality rates running at just 2.9%. The loss of a foot or a toe was 5.7%; an elbow joint, 7.6%; wrist joint, 10.4%; forearm, 14%; upper arm, 23.8%; ankle joint, 25.1%; shoulder joint, 29.1%; lower leg, 33.2%; thigh, 54.2%; knee joint 57.5%; and hip joint, 83.3%.[9]

As the memoirs of General Schurz and others make abundantly clear, many surgeons could not handle the stress and strain of the deaths and amputations while working day after day with little or no rest. Large numbers over the course of the conflict either quit or were removed. Breakdowns were common. Most of these medical men were country doctors, and the wounds they were forced to treat were not something they were trained to handle physically and mentally.[10]

Medical school in the mid-nineteenth century usually consisted of just six months of lectures, three months of interning with a local doctor, six more months of listening to the same lectures again, and another three months under a doctor's tutelage. Students paid for every lecture they attended, which is how the professors earned their salaries. As surprising as it might be today, some Civil War doctors had very little or no medical training. Although Army medical exams were given, some

---

8 Letterman, *Medical Recollections*, 155-157.

9 *The Medical and Surgical History of the Civil War*, 15 vols. (Wilmington, NC: 1990), vol. 12, 877-878.

10 Annabel interview.

men who were not qualified to practice medicine were passed through because of the dire need for doctors.[11]

Both armies published manuals of how to perform every operation, be it a finger, foot, arm, or leg. If you could watch someone else do it or if you could read instructions, you could learn. After awhile, the operators who rose to the top had proved their worth and were transferred to the division hospitals or a corps hospital such as the one on Spangler property. "These officers were engaged assiduously, day and night, with little rest, until [July] 6th . . . in attendance upon the wounded," wrote Doctor Letterman of the surgeons at Gettysburg. "The labor performed by these officers was immense. Some of them fainted from exhaustion, induced by over-exertion, and others became ill from the same cause. The skill and devotion shown by the medical officers of this army were worthy of all commendation; they could not be surpassed."[12]

Fear of the operators among the wounded and the thought of losing a limb was all too real. Many badly damaged men had to be pushed by comrades to see the surgeon, and some asked a friend to feel out a doctor about the necessity of amputations. Many weren't convinced an amputation was an absolute necessity until they were told that bones had been splintered and they would die unless the limb came off. Sometimes, even that wasn't enough to convince them.

Civil War surgeons took their craft seriously and made many advancements. They often sent reports on special cases to the surgeon general to share and for further review. Head, chest, and abdomen wounds were almost always fatal, despite the best efforts of the doctors. Experience taught them to give those unfortunate patients something to make them comfortable before placing them out of the way to die. There are exceptions to every rule, and one of them ended up at the Spangler farm hospital in the form of Pvt. William Furlong of the 153rd Pennsylvania.

Furlong was about 30 years old at Gettysburg. The immigrant from County Cork, Ireland, was living in Northampton County, Pennsylvania, when he enlisted in the 153rd. He was big and strong for the 1860s at five feet 10 inches and 175 pounds.[13]

11 Ibid.

12 Letterman, "Report on Medical Operations at Gettysburg," October 3, 1863.

13 Joseph K. Barnes, surgeon general, *Medical and Surgical History of the War of the Rebellion*, vol. 2, 241; William Furlong Pension File No. 778974, National Archives.

Furlong survived the terror and flying lead when he and his regiment were overrun on July 1 on Barlow Knoll and managed to make it through Gettysburg to East Cemetery Hill. There, while he and his comrades were hunkering behind a stone wall to avoid Confederate sharpshooters firing from town and artillery fire from nearby hills, a shell fragment struck the Irish immigrant in the head. The wound, which smashed the bones above his left eye and exposed his brain through a hole an inch-and-a-half wide and four inches long extending all the way to his left temple, knocked him unconscious.

"Two of our men were ordered to carry him to the rear," Pvt. Stryker A. Wallace of the 153rd recalled after the war, "which they were doing when a general riding by said to the men, 'Don't you see that the man is dead?' They laid him down. In the meantime the battle was raging all along the line . . ." Furlong remained unattended, explained Wallace, until he was picked up two days later by the ambulance corps and taken to the Spangler farm. Once the surgeons realized the nature and extent of his wound and decided that survival was not possible, they had him carried out of the barn. Private Wallace found Furlong on July 5 "at the corner of the barn [likely the northeast corner, which would be the side of the barn farthest from the house but nearest the driveway] with a big flat stone for a pillow, his overcoat having been folded and placed under his head." Someone threw a blanket over him, but soon thereafter he "lost his coat out from under his head, and his blanket had slipped from him. Blood was running from the wound and from his eyes and nose," recalled his comrade. "His lips were so swollen he could not speak. He was conscious, recognizing my voice, and by prying open his mouth with a spoon I fed him some soup. The first food he had taken since he entered the battle four days before."[14]

Wallace continued:

I went to the chief surgeon, told him of this man, that it had been supposed he would die, but that he had not died, and that he ought to have medical attention. He went out with me and looked at him and said, 'That is a very interesting case; he is a big, strong fellow, he can pull through. . . . He sent an assistant surgeon to dress his wound. While the poor fellow had been lying there, without food, drink or shelter, it had rained, and the cavity in his head was half full of water. Dr. Neff afterwards said that probably the rain had saved his life, as it kept down inflammation. I asked the Chief Surgeon what I should do with the man. He

---

14 Kiefer, *History of the One Hundred and Fifty-Third Regiment*, 240-241.

replied, 'Put him wherever you can.' That meant a great deal or it meant nothing, as every place was full. I got a stretcher and another soldier, and seeing a large tent going up about one hundred yards away, I remarked to my comrade, that I suppose is a regimental tent, but the surgeon says we shall put him wherever we can. We will take him right in and lay him down. He is too badly hurt for them to throw him out. If they protest we will tell our orders. And so we did, there being a sort of protest, but the condition of the patient and the order of the surgeon prevailed.[15]

Furlong was transferred to the Cotton Factory Hospital in Harrisburg on July 16, where bone fragments were removed from his wound. On August 10, "the patient was cheerful" and "the intellect was unimpaired."[16] Private Wallace happily reported that Furlong "was restored to his family with a hole in his head and the loss of an eye. . . . When I afterwards saw him in Pennsylvania he suddenly grabbed me and drew me to his bosom and lifted me clear off my feet for joy."[17]

Once the war ended Furlong settled near Binghamton, New York, married, and had children. He received $8.00 a month as an invalid pension, which was increased to $15.00 in 1866, $18.00 in 1872, and $24.00 in 1883. He worked a bit on the railroad as his wound allowed, but his applications for pension increases outline the extent of the suffering he experienced through the rest of his life. In one report, the examining doctor wrote that he had "a hole in the forehead that is never closed. Severe pain in the head. Sight in right eye being affected by the injury & at times he is almost blind. He has to be led by his little girl. He cannot see to work." According to another application, "The cavity of the skull still remains exposing to view the membrane of the brain." And another: "The most perfect recovery possible will make him three fourths disabled."[18]

Despite the horrific nature of his "fatal" wound, Furlong lived until 1912. His wife, Catherine, applied for a widow's pension, but was denied.

Another Spangler Farm case reported in *The Medical and Surgical History of the War of the Rebellion* involved the ancient art of drawing blood to cure disease or reduce a patient's amount of blood if he or she was thought to have an excess

15 Ibid.

16 *The Medical and Surgical History of the War of the Rebellion*, vol. 2, pt. 1, 241.

17 Kiefer, *History of the One Hundred and Fifty-Third Regiment*, 241.

18 Furlong pension file, National Archives.

amount, which many considered to be a cause of illness. Could venesection (bloodletting), the medical guide wondered, reduce hemorrhaging and limit inflammation in penetrating chest wounds? Cited as an example for the affirmative was the curious case of Pvt. Richard Phelps of the 25th Ohio, General Ames' brigade, Barlow's division. The 19-year-old, who was hit by a shell fragment on July 1 that fractured a rib and entered his lung, was treated at the XI Corps Spangler hospital. "The patient stated that on the reception of the injury he bled so profusely that the vein of the left arm was opened," explained the medical journal, "with the effect of soon checking the internal hemorrhages. He spat up blood, however, until the 10th, but no secondary hemorrhage set in." Phelps eventually regained his strength and was returned to duty that September.[19]

In addition, it was common in the Civil War for surgeons to use leeches to drain blood and fight infections, so surgeons at Spangler probably sent hospital workers to local waterways to gather them.

Spangler Farm Short Story

Lockjaw, more commonly known today as tetanus, was frequently cited as a cause of death at the XI Corps field hospital. Lockjaw was an infection caused by a bacterium that entered the body through wounds. Lockjaw got its name from one of its symptoms, i.e., stiffness of the lower jaw and neck. A patient with lockjaw died an agonizing death with convulsions and windpipe spasms that cut off breathing. Sergeant William R. Kiefer of the 153rd Pennsylvania, writing about comrade Sgt. John Seiple, observed that he "was in the ward of the barn and died near where I was in attendance. He suffered intensely from lockjaw, and when I saw that he could not live I thought death was preferable as I witnessed him breathing his last." One soldier suffering from lockjaw at Spangler is known to have been given chloroform to allow him to die in peace.

Today, tetanus can be prevented with a shot and treated with antibiotics, but only about one in 10 Civil War patients with lockjaw survived.[20]

---

19 *The Medical and Surgical History of the War of the Rebellion,* vol. 2, 644-645.

20 Kiefer, *History of the One Hundred and Fifty-Third Regiment,* 191; www.vermontcivilwar.org/medic/medicine3.php. Accessed April 24, 2017.

Chapter 7

A Sunrise Walk

"Next we stretched ourselves on the ground to make up lost sleep, and rest our feet after a twenty-four hours scarcely broken march, and get our heads level for the coming test."

— *Col. Joshua Lawrence Chamberlain, 20th Maine, on the V Corps' arrival at Gettysburg*

Balmy weather ushered in July 2, 1863. The thermometer would barely touch 80 degrees, and the gentle breeze that caressed the southern Pennsylvania countryside kept down the humidity. Large, fluffy, cumulus clouds broke up the direct rays of the sun that had taken such a toll on the soldiers of both sides the previous day. It was not uncommon for Gettysburg weather in July and August to climb into the 90s with high humidity for days or weeks on end, so the locals found the July 2 conditions comfortable. But there was little else to celebrate because by midnight some 15,000 men would be killed or wounded in what was one of the bloodiest days in American history.[1]

The sun that rose at 4:47 a.m. that day exposed an XI Corps hospital that had not changed much since the last sunset. Vanishing shadows gave way to exhausted surgeons, assistant surgeons, stewards, and nurses still working by the dancing light of lanterns in a desperate attempt to save shattered lives. The ambulance corps was only then finishing its last deliveries, and many of these men were now helping tend the injured.

1 Michael Jacobs, "Meteorology of the Battle," www.gdg.org/Research/Other%20 Documents/Newspaper%20Clippings/v6pt1l.html. Accessed January 11, 2017.

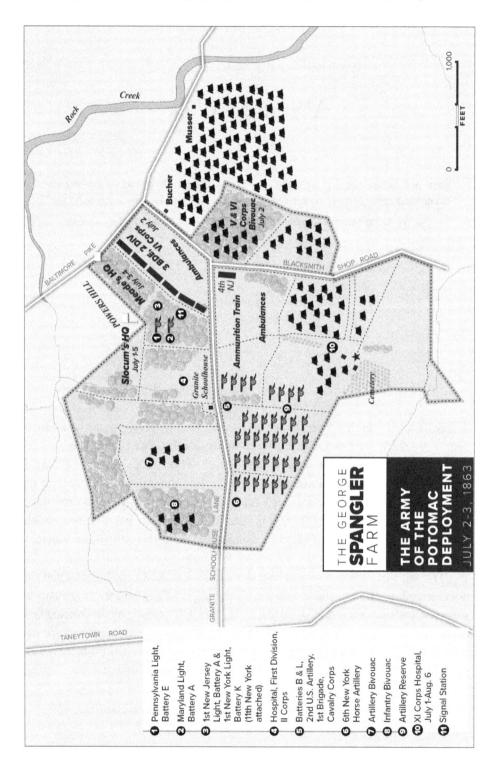

Rock Creek

Musser

Bucher

V & VI Corps Bivouac July 2

Ambulances

BALTIMORE PIKE

3 BDE 2 DIV VI Corps July 2

Meade's HQ July 3-4

POWERS HILL

Slocum's HQ July 1-5

BLACKSMITH   SHOP   ROAD

4th NJ

Ammunition Train

Ambulances

Granite Schoolhouse

Cemetery

SCHOOLHOUSE LANE

GRANITE   SCHOOLHOUSE   LANE

TANEYTOWN   ROAD

1,000

FEET

0

THE GEORGE **SPANGLER** FARM

THE ARMY OF THE POTOMAC DEPLOYMENT

JULY 2-3, 1863

1 Pennsylvania Light, Battery E

2 Maryland Light, Battery A

3 1st New Jersey Light, Battery A & 1st New York Light, Battery K (11th New York attached)

4 Hospital, First Division, II Corps

5 Batteries B & L, 2nd U.S. Artillery, 1st Brigade, Cavalry Corps

6 6th New York Horse Artillery

7 Artillery Bivouac

8 Infantry Bivouac

9 Artillery Reserve

10 XI Corps Hospital, July 1-Aug. 6

11 Signal Station

We don't know what George Spangler was seeing or thinking that morning, but it is likely he was up early, assuming he had gone to bed at all. Being a man of the land, he would have been up and outside, checking on his once-picturesque farm now overrun with crying and dying men, stacks of human limbs, and horses, mules, wagons, and strangers visible in every direction. Just getting out of his own home meant squeezing around and stepping over strangers. The constant motion and hum of activity would have been sights and sounds unfamiliar to him, as would the putrid smell of blood, infection, death, and sewage.

As George would have quickly discovered, every building on his property was being used in some medical capacity, including the ground level of his house, summer kitchen, barn, and any other outbuildings there at the time. If his livestock and produce had not yet completely vanished, it soon would. Thousands of people were jammed on the property with no food wagons to fill their bellies. The result was a foregone conclusion. "As to the potatoes, sheep, hogs, and garden vegetables," lamented George, "the troops helped themselves to them." The "skins of the sheep and hogs" were haphazardly tossed about, but the landowner never did see the blue-clad soldiers take and slaughter the stock. Any meat curing in his smokehouse was already long gone.[2]

The well just outside the summer kitchen a few yards from his house was a congregating point. The hospital needed water for its work, as did every person and animal on the property. The well was deep and productive, but was sorely tested that July.[3]

The yard, already crowded, would become even more so in the coming days because of the lack of tents, the arrival of additional wounded, and the absence of supplies to set up the hospital cook-house. A few tents for the hospital staff might have made it in with the medical essentials, but none of the staff would have had time to use them yet. The tents would eventually be set up near the barn. Once tents for the patients arrived, they went up all around the Spangler buildings and in the fields. The tents were erected in rows in the fields, with "streets" between them. Freshly cut pine branches were hung on the tents to combat the nausea-inducing smells.

Once the general sense of being overrun had sunk in, George—and any member of the Spangler family who ventured outdoors—would have quickly

2 Spangler Damage Claim N-1892, 1875, Historic Structure Report.

3 Another well found in the Spangler yard in recent years is believed to have been added after the Civil War.

spotted the amputations and surgeries taking place under the forebay of their barn. Wounded and dying men might have reached out to George, begging for help, asking for water, or just wanting to talk. A good man, leader in his church and community, and president of the Cumberland Township School Board, George was all about caring and helping. He would have joined the hospital workers and helped any way he could.

Wounded men waiting to be processed still littered the muddy and waste-filled yard in front of the barn, and the lane was busy with men, horses, and wagons coming and going. Guards posted around the barn kept out the stragglers and shirkers who routinely congregated at hospitals.

If George walked south from his house, he would have discovered that wounded men were resting in his apple and peach orchard, lying under the trees or propped up against the trunks. Beyond was a corn field and low grasslands through which ran the best stream on the Spangler land, though just a couple feet wide and a handful of inches deep. Men and horses were there, bathing and drinking in the sweet, strong-flowing water.

The confusion and general chaos of an army spilled off the Spangler property that early morning. Just beyond and inside the western border of the Spangler land and along the Taneytown Road, various II Corps brigades had begun to gather for much-needed rest after days of arduous marching. Within an hour or two, they would move out once more, beginning about 7:00 a.m., to deploy along Cemetery Ridge. One II Corps regiment there was the 64th New York, which included Capt. Henry Van Aernam Fuller. Henry was the nephew and namesake of XI Corps surgeon Henry Van Aernam of the 154th New York, who was working on the Spangler property while his nephew rested just a short distance away.[4]

North of the Spangler house ran Granite Schoolhouse Lane, a dirt farm road that children used to walk through the heart of Spangler property to Granite Schoolhouse, which sat upon land donated by the Spanglers. Union troops and supplies were rushing back and forth even at this early hour on what was the main transportation link of the Army of the Potomac from Baltimore Pike to Taneytown Road. The army's commander, Maj. Gen. George G. Meade, rode back and forth across and around the Spangler land during his sleepless first night at Gettysburg. Within a few hours, the Spangler fields and woods around the one-room

---

4 Unknown author, Company F, 64th New York. Unpublished memoir. Manuscripts Department, Lilly Library, Indiana University. Copy in File Folder #V6-NY64: 64th New York Infantry. Vertical files, GNMP Library.

George Spangler was paid $75 in 1889 for a plot of land along Granite Schoolhouse Lane for this monument to Batteries B and L, 2nd US Artillery, 1st Brigade, Cavalry Corps. *Ron Kirkwood*

schoolhouse would be packed with wounded from the First Division of General Hancock's II Corps.

Artillery in the form of Batteries B and L, 2nd US Artillery (First Brigade, Cavalry Corps) arrived on the far side of the lane from the schoolhouse about 5:30 a.m. The batteries rolled into place and remained in reserve there for most of the next two days, coming under fire on July 3 from Confederate guns in the grand cannonade preceding Pickett's Charge.[5]

A little farther east across the lane, the Spanglers owned about three-fourths of Powers Hill, which was also a hub of activity that morning. XII Corps commander Maj. Gen. Henry W. Slocum was awake and actively directing troop movements. Slocum set up his headquarters at the top and bottom of the hill on Spangler and

5 Historic Structure Report, Gettysburg Foundation, page 920. A quarter-century after the end of the war the US Army's Chief of Engineers, Brig. Gen. John M. Wilson, contacted George in a letter dated February 5, 1889. Wilson, a former member of the horse artillery unit that had spent time during the battle on the Spangler property, was inquiring about a 25-by-25-foot piece of ground across Granite Schoolhouse Lane and "45 ft." from the school. "Will you sell this small piece of land to the government?" for a monument to the batteries, he asked. "If so, at what price?" George agreed, responding on March 2, "I will sell the ground if you give me seventy-five dollars you can have the twenty-five feet square." Papers were signed in January 1890. The monument is there today.

Powers Hill today. The area at the bottom of the hill was one of George Spangler's wheat fields in 1863 and was used as an ambulance park. *Ron Kirkwood*

Nathanial Lightner property as soon as he arrived near Gettysburg on the late afternoon of July 1 and kept his headquarters there throughout and after the battle. It was from Powers Hill (called Slocum's Hill during the battle) that Slocum directed the XII's defense and assault of Culp's Hill and from which he would pull his First Division on the afternoon of July 2 and send down Granite Schoolhouse Lane for a successful just-in-time rescue of members of the Artillery Reserve, whose III Corps infantry support had been routed from the army's left.[6]

Some 900 men from the XII Corps' 2nd Brigade, part of Geary's division, served as a line of defense around "Slocum's Hill" on July 2 to help protect the army's supply line to Westminster should a disastrous retreat down the Baltimore Pike from Cemetery Hill transpire. Also in that neighborhood below Powers Hill, as well as across the lane, were some of the 100 XI Corps ambulances and the hundreds of horses and men needed to operate them. Ambulance corpsmen not busy helping in the hospital by this time were sleeping in or under their wagons after an exhausting night of hauling in the wounded, or perhaps they were unable to

6 John Bachelder Day 2 map.

sleep and were sitting around smoky early-morning campfires made from wood taken from Spangler land. Some of the wounded men who managed to get themselves to the Spangler hospital on their own sacked out in ambulances from sheer exhaustion.

Other Spangler fields also hosted spillover portions of the ambulance parks for the II Corps and XII Corps, placed there to take advantage of the central location to the expanding Army of the Potomac line of battle. The XII Corps ambulances were probably already present, with the II Corps wagons set to arrive there and on other properties along the Taneytown Road a little later that morning.

The Spangler, Musser, and Bucher land east of Blacksmith Shop Road and south of Granite Schoolhouse Lane played host to a powerful but weary force later that morning with the arrival of Maj. Gen. George Sykes' 10,900-man V Corps, which marched most of the night from Hanover to reach the battlefield.

Later that day, Sykes' corps would play one of the most important roles in the battle on and below the Round Tops. Until then, its soldiers were held in reserve after crossing in the morning from Hanover Road to the Powers Hill area. They rested in the early afternoon on and around the Spangler property on the southwest side of the intersection of Granite Schoolhouse Lane and the Baltimore Pike.[7]

According to a letter by Lt. Robert G. Welles of the 10th US, Col. Sidney Burbank's brigade of Brig. Gen. Romeyn Ayres' division, the V Corps was squarely on Spangler property that morning. The brigade, explained Welles, rested "in the shade of a large oak grove" at the junction of Granite and Blacksmith Shop roads. "In front [at the Spangler farm] was a cornfield and a large barn at the left used as a Hospital. On the right of the field, a road or lane [Granite Schoolhouse Lane] led directly to the front—another road [Blacksmith Shop Road] running at right angles, in front of us."[8]

Joshua Lawrence Chamberlain was promoted to colonel of the 20th Maine that June, a command in Strong Vincent's brigade, Brig. Gen. James Barnes' division, V Corps. The former professor was not well known when he arrived on the Spangler farm about midday, but his intersection with history would begin later that day when his regiment ended up holding the army's far left flank on Little Round Top against determined enemy attacks. Chamberlain fell with a horrific wound in the

7 This 1863 intersection was about 200 feet south of where it stands today, having been moved north in the 1930s by the Civilian Conservation Corps and the Pennsylvania Department of Transportation.

8 Robert G. Welles to Isaac M. Fisher, August 23, 1863, Catalog 42247, in Gettysburg National Military Park Collections.

Col. Joshua Lawrence Chamberlain

Courtesy of Theodore J. Chamberlain

early days of the Petersburg Campaign but returned during the war's final months and played a prominent role in the surrender of General Lee's Army of Northern Virginia at Appomattox. Fame and his war record united long after the war, the bulk of it after his death when writers of books and newspaper articles and producers of film and television focused on his work that late afternoon of July 2.

"Told to rest awhile, we first resumed the homely repast so sharply interrupted the evening before," wrote Chamberlain in his memoirs as he described the situation once the V Corps arrived outside of Gettysburg and before Vincent's brigade stopped at and then rushed through the Spangler farm to the southern end of the battlefield. "Next we stretched ourselves on the ground to make up lost sleep," he continued,

and rest our feet after a twenty-four hours scarcely broken march, and get our heads level for the coming test. We knew that a great battle was soon to be fought, a desperate and momentous one. But what much more impressed my mind was the great calm, the uncertainty of overture, and seeming lack of tactical plan for the tremendous issue. We were aware that other troops were coming up, on one side and the other; but we had no means of knowing or judging which side would take the offensive and which the defensive, or where the battle would begin. All the forenoon we had no other intimation as to this, than the order given in an impressive tone to hold ourselves ready to take part in an attack . . . but whether to be begun by us or the enemy, we neither knew, nor could guess.[9]

9 Joshua Lawrence Chamberlain, "Through Blood and Fire at Gettysburg," in *Hearst's Magazine*, vol. 23, January 1913.

V Corps commander Sykes spent part of the afternoon on Powers Hill with Slocum as his corps rested in the Spangler neighborhood before it went into action. Powers Hill was less wooded in 1863 than it is today, which made it a good spot for Slocum and Sykes to view the evolving battlefield in several directions. That view also made Powers Hill a good spot for a Union signal station, which had been positioned there the day before and remained there throughout and after the battle. The station sent messages from the Spangler and Lightner properties via waving flags and couriers and was where General Meade retreated when his headquarters on the Taneytown Road in the Widow Leister house on Cemetery Ridge was shelled prior to Pickett's Charge.[10]

The Spanglers had no way of knowing during those early-morning hours of July 2 that the V and later VI corps were not the only large organizations that would arrive that day to rest among their crops, woods, grasses, and orchard. Rumbling its way from Taneytown on the west side of their property on the Taneytown Road was the miles-long Artillery Reserve and its ammunition train, a loud, slow parade of more than 100 artillery pieces, hundreds of wagons, and thousands of men, horses, and mules. The train, which carried thousands of rounds of fixed ammunition, wouldn't complete its hours-long landing on the Spangler property until that afternoon. By that time, George and Elizabeth's farm was jammed from corner to corner with men, animals, and nearly every military implement imaginable.

At 2:00 p.m. on the afternoon of July 2, the 166-acre Spangler farm had at least three times more people on it than Gettysburg's entire population of 2,400. And that's not counting the II Corps First Division hospital that was about to be flooded with wounded and dying at Granite Schoolhouse.

Spangler Farm Short Story

A friend described 22-year-old Capt. Henry Van Aernam Fuller of the 64th New York as tall, dark, and handsome—a superior mental force and manly person with an intellectual face who stood six feet tall, erect, and dignified. Fuller was of pleasing address, an interesting and forcible writer, and an engaging conversationalist and speaker. He began as a private in 1861 and was soon

10 OR 27, pt. 1, 592, and Gettysburg National Military Park Ranger Troy D. Harman, in "In Defense of Henry Slocum on July 1," Page 68, http://npshistory.com/series/symposia/gettys burg_seminars/9/essay3.pdf. Accessed March 26, 2019.

Capt. Henry Van Aernam Fuller,
64th New York

US Army Heritage and Education Center

promoted to all the way to captain. Fuller, explained the 64th's Maj. L. W. Bradley, "distinguished himself . . . in every action in which the regiment had been engaged."

Captain Fuller's II Corps regiment, part of Col. John Brooke's brigade, Brig. Gen. John Caldwell's division, rested with other units of the II Corps on and near the Spangler farm on the morning of July 2, though he never managed to meet up with his uncle, Dr. Henry Van Aernam, who was working at the Spangler hospital when Fuller was resting nearby. When the call came, Fuller and the rest of the New Yorkers and others in Caldwell's division tramped late that afternoon to confront the massive Confederate assault launched by James Longstreet's First Corps against the left end of Meade's Federal army. The III Corps holding that part of the field was collapsing and reinforcements were badly needed to stabilize the chaotic front.

The 64th New York moved onto the Rose Farm and plunged into the Rose Woods, where Caldwell's command hit Confederates from Maj. Gen. John Bell Hood's division. Captain Fuller was shot and killed in the woods between the Wheatfield and Devil's Den. He left behind his wife of two years, Adelaide, and one-year-old son Henry.

Dr. Van Aernam did not know of his nephew's and namesake's nearby death when he wrote to his wife, Amy Melissa, on July 15. "I have heard nothing from Henry Fuller since I left Gettysburg," he lamented. He wrote a very different letter two weeks later after he learned the sad news. "He was really the 'bravest of the brave,'" Van Aernam penned to his wife. "In his short life he won a name and established a character that any man of hoary years might well be proud of! But will the bauble of fame or recital of heroic deeds nobly performed 'soothe the dull cold ear of death'? Or restore him to his family or friends?"

Captain Fuller died just a mile and a half from where his uncle was working in the Spangler hospital. His body remained behind Confederate lines where he fell until it could be retrieved on July 4. He was made brevet-colonel after his death.

Today, a small monument (39°47'43" N 77°14'43" W) just off the former trolley line path marks where Fuller died.[11]

11 L. H. Everts, *History of Cattaraugus County, New York* (Philadelphia, PA, 1879), 276; OR 27, pt. 1, 409; Henry Van Aernam letter to his wife, July 15, 1863, in Henry Van Aernam Papers, Box 1 of 1, Henry Van Aernam Correspondence (Originals), 1862-1864, US Army Heritage and Education Center; Van Aernam letter to his wife, July 30, 1863, in Henry Van Aernam Papers, Henry Van Aernam Correspondence (Transcripts), 1862-1864.

Chapter 8

The Artillery Reserve to the Rescue

"The 'Reserve' formed an imposing column . . . exciting the wonder of the inhabitants, who
gathered at every cross-road to gaze on the strange and warlike spectacle."

— *Capt. James F. Huntington, commander of the Artillery Reserve's Third Volunteer Brigade*

An occupant of one of the gas-filled balloons that the armies
occasionally used for reconnaissance during the Civil War
would have beheld a breathtaking sight outside Gettysburg on July 2, 1863. Several
hundred feet below, a serpent-like form comprised of many hundreds of soldiers,
wagons, horses, mules, and cannons moved fitfully along the muddy Taneytown
Road toward Gettysburg.

The long mass of humanity, animals, and equipment bent and twisted with
each turn in the little country road. The rattling of equipment, the yelling of the
artillerymen and teamsters, would have been clearly audible to the balloonist.
Those civilians on the ground watching would have felt the movement, and the
power the column represented would have been rather frightening.

This slithering column was so long and so strong that its tail—still many miles
away, was nowhere to be seen. If he was a Union man, the balloonist would have
rejoiced at the grand sight because the Army of the Potomac's Artillery Reserve
was arriving and was about to save the day.

It required a monumental effort on July 2 to move the Army of the Potomac's
Artillery Reserve and ammunition train from Maryland to its landing spot on the
Spangler farm outside of Gettysburg. The Artillery Reserve was comprised of five
artillery brigades—19 batteries totaling 106 guns at Gettysburg. Each battery had
six tubes (at full strength), with each gun requiring eight to 10 men to properly load,

This is part of one artillery battery. There were 19 Artillery Reserve batteries on the Spanglers' farm for a while on the afternoon of July 2. *Library of Congress*

fire, and move it back into position before repeating the process. Six horses pulled each cannon and the attached two-wheeled limber containing ammunition. Another six horses pulled the accompanying four-wheeled caisson filled with more ammunition and other accouterments required by the gunners. Additional horses, mules, and men were needed to pull and operate wagons needed for repairs, baggage, rations, and a multitude of other needs. All told, the Artillery Reserve comprised about 2,375 officers and men and a similar number of horses and mules.[1]

Each of the seven Union infantry corps at Gettysburg had its own artillery brigade composed of four to as many as eight batteries for a total of about 200 available guns. These artillery brigades moved with their respective corps. The Artillery Reserve, however, wasn't attached to any single organization but to the army itself. The genius behind this organizational arrangement was that the guns

---

1 Gettysburg National Military Park Commission, and John W. Busey and David G. Martin in *Regimental Strengths and Losses at Gettysburg* (Hightstown, NJ, 2005), 116. According to Brig. Gen. Henry J. Hunt, there were 108 cannons in the Artillery Reserve at Gettysburg. OR 27, pt. 1, 241.

Chief of Artillery Brig. Gen. Henry J. Hunt

Library of Congress

could be broken out and sent where they were most needed. The Artillery Reserve could be tapped to enter the battle whenever and wherever its firepower was required.

The artillery brigade attachment to each corps was installed after Chancellorsville, replacing a more confused attachment to divisions. This gave more control to Chief of Artillery Brig. Gen. Henry J. Hunt, the top artilleryman of his day. The Artillery Reserve was also beefed up with more cannons after Chancellorsville and put under the command of Brig. Gen. Robert O. Tyler, who, like Hunt, was a leading artillery mind of the era. That meant the batteries gathering on the Spangler farm would have the leadership, power, and proximity to the line to be a difference maker at Gettysburg.

General Meade was still in the Taneytown area early in the evening of July 1 when he ordered "about eight" of the 19 Artillery Reserve light batteries to be sent to Gettysburg as soon as possible. Tyler left at sundown with the First Regular and Fourth Volunteer brigades, arriving for the night a few miles outside of Gettysburg "on the Taneytown Road, near the cross-road leading to Two Taverns." Those batteries reached Spangler property by 8:00 a.m. the next day, setting up "behind the line of battle of the III Corps, about one-and-a-half miles from Gettysburg."[2]

The other 11 batteries making up three brigades had a 3:00 a.m. reveille and left Taneytown at "early dawn," arriving at the Spangler farm between 10:00 a.m. and early afternoon. Following those 11 batteries to the Spangler property was the

2 OR 27, pt. 1, 872.

Brig. Gen. Robert O. Tyler

Library of Congress

artillery ammunition train of about 100 wagons and more than 600 additional horses and mules, making that powerful miles-long parade that morning of cannons, horses, men, and ammunition wagons. "The 'Reserve' formed an imposing column . . . exciting the wonder of the inhabitants, who gathered at every cross-road to gaze on the strange and warlike spectacle," said Capt. James F. Huntington, commander of the Reserve's Third Volunteer Brigade.[2]

"Keeping steadily in motion, we pass Round Top, on the Taneytown road, about noon," recalled Pvt. William E. Parmelee of the 1st Ohio Light Artillery Battery H, Huntington's brigade. "Hot and tired, we are glad to go into park in an open field to the right of the pike on which we have been marching. . . . [I]n front of us is Power Hill, with signal station and batteries in position. To our right is the Baltimore pike, to our left and front is the slight ridge extending from the village cemetery to Round Top."[3]

Captain John Bigelow's 9th Massachusetts Battery of Lt. Col. Freeman McGilvery's First Volunteer Brigade would see heavy work in the hours ahead. Before it ended up fighting for its life on the Trostle farm, it went into park on George Spangler's property. "[We] turned to the right [Granite Schoolhouse Lane], through those narrow and rough roads, and again to the right, into a field west of Spangler's barn, going in park before noon," recalled Sgt. Levi W. Baker. "We were

2 Ibid.; James Freeman Huntington, "Notes of Service With a Light Artillery at Chancellorsville and Gettysburg," *Marietta* (OH) *Sunday Observer*, August 4, 1918.

3 William E. Parmelee, "At Gettysburg," in Richard Sauers, ed., "Fighting Them Over: How the Veterans Remembered Gettysburg in the Pages of *The National Tribune*" (Baltimore, MD, 1998), 407-408.

one half mile east of the Taneytown road. Spangler's barn was taken for a hospital, and a large number of Rebel wounded were there; some of the boys went there and saw them. Our teams were watered. We were soon fed, and dinner eaten, and we watched the increasing artillery fire. Thus passed the time till about 4 p.m. Our place in the park was on the left and rear, and in the southwest corner of the field." The guns and wagons of Bigelow's 9th Massachusetts stopped directly behind and close to the Spangler barn.[5]

"The Artillery Reserve and its large trains," explained General Hunt, "were parked in a central position on a crossroad [Granite Schoolhouse Lane] from the Baltimore pike to the Taneytown road."[6] The 4th New Jersey was assigned to guard the ammunition train and arrived with it. Its companies B, D, E, F, G, I, and K, together with the ammunition wagons, settled in on the Spangler property on the southwest side of the intersection of Granite Schoolhouse Lane and Blacksmith Shop Road. Union infantry and artillery would later be placed across the lane from them on Powers Hill to not only move against Culp's Hill, but to protect the ammunition train and the army from an attack around its right flank and rear.

The mass of men, animals, wagons, and equipment was parked on the Spangler property mainly because of the farm's location, accessibility, and size. Here was a farm big enough to handle what the army needed that was close to the evolving front line and fed by a good road system comprised of the Taneytown Road, Granite Schoolhouse Lane, Blacksmith Shop Road, and the Baltimore Pike. This would make it especially convenient to rush cannons and ammunition pretty much anywhere along the front as needed.

The farm's rolling landscape was surrounded by hills and ridges and patches of timber and thus provided a bit of a hiding place from the Confederates (though some officers worried about the ammunition train being overrun if there was a breakthrough in the line at Culp's Hill or Cemetery Ridge). In addition, there was wood for fires and a good water supply for the high demands of the men and animals. The Spanglers had good well water (two if you count the one by the Granite Schoolhouse), plus a steady stream running through the southwest corner of the property and another smaller stream that started near Granite Schoolhouse Lane and ran under Powers Hill. The substantially larger Rock Creek was within

5 Levi Wood Baker, *History of the Ninth Massachusetts Battery* (Fort Mitchell, KY, 1996), 55-56.

6 Henry J. Hunt, "The Second Day at Gettysburg," in Robert Johnson Underwood and Clarence Clough Buel, eds., *Battles and Leaders of the Civil War*, 4 vols. (New York, NY, 1888), vol. 3, 296.

walking distance. The value of a good central location and the Artillery Reserve's speed and power would be proven time and again on July 2-3 and play a crucial role in the Union victory. But these advantages for the Army of the Potomac that helped win Gettysburg proved devastating for the Spangler family and their once pristine property.

Ordnance officer Lt. Cornelius Gillett, 1st Connecticut Heavy Artillery, commanded the Artillery Reserve ammunition train, which carried with it 23,883 fixed rounds. As soon as the train of wagons reached the Spangler farm, Gillett "immediately commenced supplying ammunition to the batteries both of this command, and by General Hunt's direction, to those of other corps." Thousands of rounds were parsed out to the various corps' artillery brigades, as needed. By the time the battle ended, the ammunition train had just 4,694 rounds left.[7]

The artillery park and general congestion was an impressive sight, recalled Maj. Charles F. Morse of the 2nd Massachusetts, XII Corps. Morse had an expansive view of the Spangler land from his perch near Culp's Hill. "In the open fields west of the Baltimore pike, in rear of our lines, were the parks of ammunition trains and headquarters wagons with their hundreds of mules and attendants of all kinds that always gather about a wagon camp. Near this camp was the park of the artillery reserve."[8]

General Tyler, the Artillery Reserve's commander, spent a lot of time at the Spangler farm while General Hunt rode back and forth from the farm and his headquarters on the Taneytown Road and along the front lines, personally organizing and overseeing the artillery on the battlefield. Neither man knew it yet, but they were about to turn in one of the finest team performances of the war at Gettysburg.

Born in 1819 in what was then the frontier post of Detroit, Henry Jackson Hunt was 43 at Gettysburg. He graduated from West Point in 1839 and went directly into the artillery, serving in the Mexican War and in the West. Hunt, together with two other officers, penned The Instructions for Field Artillery manual, a consequential publication published by the War Department in 1861. It was widely considered the "bible" for Union artillerists during the war. Hunt was an early proponent of an organizational doctrine that shifted batteries once assigned to divisions and corps to a central reserve controlled at the army level. He

7   OR 27, pt. 1, 878.

8   Charles F. Morse, "The Twelfth Corps at Gettysburg" in Papers of the Military Historical Society of Massachusetts, vol. 14, read before the society March 6, 1917, 26.

was a major in the Regular Army when the Civil War started, and as a staff officer under Maj. Gen. George McClellan organized and trained the Artillery Reserve. His massing and handling of scores of guns at Malvern Hill on July 1, 1862, devastated General Lee's infantry attack—a tactic Hunt was about to repeat with a similar outcome on the last day at Gettysburg.

The Artillery Reserve's size and success prior to Gettysburg depended to a large degree on who was commanding the army and how they wanted to use the extra artillery. Hunt proposed a fast, mobile, versatile Artillery Reserve that could be called upon anywhere on a battlefield in a variety of roles. Now, in George G. Meade, Hunt finally had a commanding officer who shared his vision and trusted him implicitly. Meade appreciated Hunt's instincts, leadership ability, and artillery and strategic skills, and gave him full control at Gettysburg to move artillery as he pleased. Meade's decision paid continuous dividends on the final two days of the fight.[9]

Artillery Reserve commander Robert Tyler was 31 at Gettysburg, another West Point graduate (class of 1853) who also went into the artillery after graduation and served in Utah Territory. He and Hunt had worked together during the first two years of the war, understood each other, and agreed on the potential of the Artillery Reserve to turn the tide of a battle. After the Pennsylvania victory, Hunt said of Tyler, "I knew he would not fail me."[10]

Hunt and Tyler went right to work at Spangler on the morning of July 2, sending the 1st New York Light Battery K and the attached 11th New York, as well as the 1st New Jersey Light Battery A, and the First Maryland Light Battery A across Granite Schoolhouse Lane to Powers Hill, where they were personally placed in position by Meade and Hunt. The rest of the Artillery Reserve, like the infantry of the V Corps was already doing, enjoyed a well-deserved break at the Spanglers' expense.[11]

---

9 https://warfarehistorynetwork.com/daily/the-artillery-reserve-of-the-army-of-the-potom ac/. Accessed Jan. 7, 2019.

10 Hunt to William T. Sherman, February 1882, in David L. and Audrey J. Ladd, eds., *The Bachelder Papers: Gettysburg in Their Own Words, April 12, 1886 to December 22, 1894*, 3 vols. (Dayton, OH, 1995), vol. 2, 813. Tyler's military service was well known, and when he was buried in 1874 in Hartford, CT, the city's flags flew at half-staff, public offices were closed for the day, and the National Guard served as a funeral escort. "Robert Ogden Tyler: A Memorial" (Philadelphia, PA, 1878), 19.

11 OR 27, pt. 1, 872.

This drawing by battery bugler Charles W. Reed depicts the 9th Massachusetts rushing past General Dan Sickles' headquarters near the Trostle house on its way to the area of the Peach Orchard after leaving the Spangler farm on July 2, 1863. The tree on the right remains today.
Library of Congress

But any break, deserved or otherwise, was about to end. Major General Daniel Sickles, commander of the III Corps, held the left flank of the army and without orders to do so moved out from his assigned position on lower Cemetery Ridge, where he was firmly on Hancock's left flank, forward to the Emmitsburg Road. Sickles' line ran from Devil's Den northwest to the Peach Orchard and then due north along the Emmitsburg Road until it petered out with nothing on his right flank. His alignment left a large gap between his right and Hancock's left and an isolated III Corps. Sickles' front formed a triangular-tipped salient around the Peach Orchard that could be attacked on its front and sides, and overshots aimed at one part of his line could miss entirely but strike the flanks or back of men manning another part of his line. His convoluted front was poorly formed and too long to hold against a determined attack. And that was precisely what was coming his way.

Two divisions of James Longstreet's First Corps had marched south behind Seminary Ridge to take up a position to strike Sickles' new position. When it was discovered that Confederates were massing in the woods opposite Sickles, it was too late to retreat to a better position. "I shall need more artillery," Sickles told Meade as Confederate shells began flying in and around his men and guns. "Send for all you want to the Artillery Reserve," replied an upset Meade. A short time later, Longstreet's divisions, one after the other, slammed into the III Corps, prompting a mass exodus at Spangler.[12]

"Colonel McGilvery gave us orders," recalled Capt. John Bigelow of the 9th Massachusetts Battery. "'Assembly' was blown; drivers mounted and within five minutes we were off at a lively trot, following our leader to the left, where the firing was getting to be the heaviest." And so Bigelow's guns departed the Spangler fields for their rendezvous with destiny on the Trostle farm. His was but one of many that would roll out, for Sickles' trauma was the problem Hunt's nimble and powerful Artillery Reserve was created to fix. For the next twenty-four hours, Hunt and Tyler would move guns parked on the Spangler land to precisely where they were needed. Hour after hour, George Spangler's farm served not only as a hospital, but as a staging area for the Artillery Reserve, an ammunition supplier for the army's other artillery batteries, and Meade's "Main Street" to funnel troops and equipment to the front in time to save the line and the day.[13]

Beginning about 3:30 p.m. on July 2, Tyler said he began dispatching units to where they were most needed. The 15th New York Light Battery, Pennsylvania Batteries C and F, 5th Massachusetts Light Battery E (10th New York attached), 9th Massachusetts Light, 2nd Connecticut Light, and 1st New York Light Battery G. The guns lined up in and near the Peach Orchard, adding 34 cannons to the III Corps' line. Hunt was there to personally place the batteries. As the artillery officer told Capt. Patrick Hart of the 15th New York, "Sacrifice everything before you give up that position."[14]

At 4:00 p.m., Tyler ordered more batteries to roll, this time to Cemetery Ridge and Cemetery Hill. Out from Spangler moved the 1st US Battery H, Third US Batteries F and K, 4th US Battery C, 5th US Battery C, 1st Ohio Light Battery H, First Pennsylvania Light Batteries F and G, 1st New Hampshire Light, West Virginia Light Battery C, and 5th New York Light. Tyler delivered some of these in person. "As the battle went on, batteries were frequently detached [from the

12 George Gordon Meade, *The Life and Letters of George Gordon Meade*, 2 vols. (New York, NY, 1913), vol. 2, 327.

13 John Bigelow, *The Peach Orchard at Gettysburg* (Minneapolis, MN, 1910), 52.

14 OR 27, pt. 1, 872; Patrick Hart letter, January 24, 1891, in *The Bachelder Papers*, vol. 3, 1,789. See Appendix 4 for a discussion of the role played by the 2nd Connecticut Light Artillery at Gettysburg.

Artillery Reserve] and went bounding away to the support of the fighting line, with their horses at full run," reported Major Morse of the 2nd Massachusetts.[15]

Many would play a central role in the defense of the XI Corps and East Cemetery Hill that evening—and suffer accordingly—during a sunset charge by elements of Early's division. The 3rd US Batteries F and K and 5th US Battery C wound up in the heart of the action on the Emmitsburg Road, with F and K on the west side of the road from the Henry Spangler farm and the 5th US Battery C on the Nicholas Codori farm before they were finally pushed back onto Cemetery Ridge.

Although the ammunition train remained, within a few hours the Spangler fields were clear of most of the Artillery Reserve cannons, with the 6th Maine Battery saying it was the only one left behind. The Maine gunners were anything but pleased with this, for Confederate artillery overshots rained around them without the ability to reply. "Nearer and nearer came the Enemy's shells, until some of them exploded in the field where the Battery was," Lt. Edwin B. Dow explained. We "remained in restless inactivity, until late in the afternoon, and until every other Battery was called away. . . . Just as they were growing desperate under the enforced idleness, an Aid dashed up." It was about 6:00 p.m., and the order Dow and his men so desperately wanted had finally arrived. Sickles' III Corps front was collapsing and the guns were desperately needed. The staffer, reported Dow, "gave the long looked for orders. With a cheer the Battery dashed to the front, and went into position just in time to save [Capt. John] Bigelow's 9th Mass. Battery [at the Trostle house] from being captured by the Enemy."[16]

Just before Dow's battery rolled out, Meade ordered Sykes' V Corps to move forward in an attempt to save his collapsing flank. The V Corps' First Division under Brig. Gen. James Barnes moved around 5:00 p.m. from the northeast corner of the Spangler, Bucher, and Musser farms near the intersection of the Baltimore Pike and Granite Schoolhouse Lane down the lane to its intersection with Blacksmith Shop Road. After passing the schoolhouse where the lane bears right, Barnes tramped his command left into the fields, crossing the northwest corner of the Spangler property as well as the Jacob Swisher and Sarah Patterson farms. Colonel Vincent's Third Brigade, comprised of the 16th Michigan, 44th New York, 83rd Pennsylvania, and 20th Maine, held the advance and was directed away from

15 Morse, *Papers of the Military Historical Society of Massachusetts*, 26.

16 Edwin B. Dow manuscript, Records of the Adjutant General of Maine, Box 110 (2202-0402), Maine State Archives, copy in Box B-1, GNMP Library.

the rest of the division to the top of the mostly unprotected Little Round Top, where it would soon make history with one of the outstanding defensive efforts of the war. The other brigades, meanwhile, continued west for the Wheatfield area.

Sykes' Second Division under General Ayres followed the same route across Spangler land, and, like the First Division, broke off one brigade to help hold Little Round Top while the remaining pair moved farther west.

The V Corps' Third Division under Brig. Gen. Samuel W. Crawford moved out last. Crawford pushed his men down Blacksmith Shop Road, which ran directly east through the Spangler property close to the farm's southern boundary. If not for unexpected traffic congestion on and around their property, it might have been a faster and more direct route to the Round Tops than that taken by the other two V Corps divisions. "As we advanced we began to meet wounded men returning," wrote a 12th Pennsylvania Reserves veteran serving in one of Crawford's brigades, and "soon the road was so encumbered with wounded walking to the rear, and ambulances going the same way, we had to take to the woods."[17]

By this time, Maj. Gen. John Sedgwick's VI Corps was arriving after a grueling overnight march of more than 30 miles. The corps uncoiled itself on the Spangler, Bucher, and Musser properties recently evacuated by the V Corps. Soon after, Major Thomas W. Hyde of the 7th Maine, part of Sedgwick's VI Corps, arrived on the field. "Two of us had purchased some cherry-pies of a very freckled face girl at a neighboring farmhouse, and had just joined the rest of the staff, who were in the shadiest place they could find upon the banks of Rock Creek," recalled Hyde after the battle. "[W]e were all listening with suppressed excitement to a tremendous outburst of cannon and musketry over the hills to the left." Orders to move arrived soon thereafter: Move to the heavy firing. Two brigades of Brig. Gen. Frank Wheaton's Third Division and one brigade of Brig. Gen. Horatio Wright's First Division marched, like the V Corps, through the Spangler, Swisher, and Patterson farms. "In an instant every man was on his feet," Major Hyde recalled. "The fences were broken down and the heads of the brigades broke off into the fields and began ascending the long slopes toward the Round Tops, nearly a mile away." The fences Hyde recalled breaking down were on the Spangler farm, stone walls crisscrossed their fields, and stone-and-rider fences—stone walls with wooden rails placed over and next to the stones to keep animals in and out—lined parts of Granite

17 John P. Nicholson, ed., *Pennsylvania at Gettysburg* (Harrisburg, PA), 294-295.

Schoolhouse Lane. The VI Corps troops finally stopped to fight on the right front of Little Round Top.[18]

Meade now had another problem to deal with and he needed immediate help to do it, including again from the Spanglers' land. The collapse of Sickles' long and winding III Corps' front left hundreds of men running rearward for their lives through advancing infantry reinforcements and across the Taneytown Road. The collapse meant that some of the Artillery Reserve batteries sent from Spangler to Sickles' aid were alone, exposed without infantry support, and in some cases almost surrounded and in grave danger of being captured or destroyed. A dangerous gap in the line directly behind the batteries on Cemetery Ridge yawned wide, and brigades from A. P. Hill's Third Corps were attacking off Seminary Ridge into that very chasm. The assault threatened to cleave the Union army in two.

"The fire grew more furious from minute to minute, and about half after six, the roar of the battle actually seemed to indicate that our line was yielding," said Maj. Gen. Carl Schurz, Third Division, XI Corps. "A moment later Captain [Hubert] Dilger [1st Ohio Light Artillery Battery I] of my artillery, who had gone to the ammunition train to get a new supply, came galloping up Cemetery Hill in great agitation with the report that the enemy had overwhelmed the Third Corps in the peach orchard and pressing after our flying troops had pierced our left center; that his musket balls were already falling into our ammunition train, and that unless the rebels were beaten back at once," continued Schurz, "they would attack us in the rear and take us prisoners in half an hour. It was a moment of most anxious suspense."[19]

Enter the XII Corps. General Meade instructed Maj. Gen. Henry Slocum to pull his entire XII Corps off Culp's Hill on the far right of the hooked Union line and send it to fill the gap in the line created when Sickles moved forward to the Emmitsburg Road; the breach now existed between Sykes' V Corps and Hancock's II Corps. Slocum decided on his own to leave one brigade on Culp's Hill to hold the valuable high ground and move out with the balance of his command. Slocum's decision allowed the Union to maintain some of its grip on Culp's Hill. The First Division under Brig. Gen. Alpheus Williams moved quickly off the high ground and through the heart of the Spangler property along Granite Schoolhouse Lane,

---

18 Thomas W. Hyde, *Following the Greek Cross Or, Memories of the Sixth Army* Corps (New York, NY, 1894), 148-149.

19 Schurz, *The Reminiscences of Carl Schurz,* 23.

Granite Schoolhouse Lane looked like this for decades after it was officially made a road in the 1880s. In 1863 it was little more than a farm path when Union troops used it to rush to the front. *Center for Civil War Photography*

but two brigades of the Second Division under Brig. Gen. John Geary got lost on the Baltimore Pike and did not play a role in the battle that evening.

Colonel William P. Maulsby of the 1st Maryland Potomac Home Brigade (part of Brig. Gen. Henry Lockwood's independent brigade) recalled how Williams' division moved along Granite Schoolhouse Lane "in a quick step, breaking at times into a double-quick, over the small wagon road leading from the Baltimore Pike to the Taneytown Road, under a broiling sun, the men with no incumbrances but their guns, full cartridge boxes, and blankets rolled and swung over their shoulders." The narrow road was filled with men from Sickles' command "seeking hospitals, and bearing every conceivable kind of ghastly wounds, some with one leg shot off, some with one arm shot away, carried and helped along by their less wounded comrades, and all covered with blood, sweat, and the black grimy smoke and dust and dirt of the battle." The colonel admitted that when he and his officers "first met this spectacle . . . we turned in our saddles to watch the effect on our men; whether it unnerved them . . . the sight we met was of every man unhitching his blanket, throwing it away in the road, and breaking into a quicker step."[20]

20 William P. Maulsby, "Final Report on the Battlefield of Gettysburg" (Albany, NY, 1902), 1,042.

By the time Williams' division met up with McGilvery, who commanded the Artillery Reserve's First Volunteer Brigade and desperately needed infantry support, the sun was beginning to set behind the South Mountain range. The head of the XII Corps reinforcements pushed back the exhausted and depleted ranks of the Confederates from their advanced and threatening position. Some members charged all the way to the Trostle house and helped retrieve Bigelow's abandoned 9th Massachusetts cannons. Williams' division, in combination with heavy II Corps reinforcements that had rushed south off upper Cemetery Ridge, stabilized the left flank of Meade's army.

"If they had broken our lines," admitted Capt. Frederick Winkler of the 26th Wisconsin, "all would have been lost, and sometimes they came so very near, but our Generals were watchful and whenever our lines were closely pressed, wherever they were giving way, there, just before the critical moment arrived, we would see the serried ranks of the reserve march up and re-enforce our lines and drive the rebels back."[21]

Lieutenant Colonel McGilvery's artillery—5th Massachusetts Battery E (10th New York attached), 9th Massachusetts, Pennsylvania Batteries C and F, and 15th New York—had joined the fight after rushing to Sickles' aid near the Peach Orchard, which put these guns and their artillerists in the thick of the fighting. The crews worked their guns magnificently, but Longstreet's heavy infantry assaults hit many commands on their flanks and front, forcing them back about a quarter of a mile to near the Trostle barn and house. "It is a mystery to me that they were not all hit by the enemy's fire, as they were surrounded and fired upon from almost every direction," McGilvery wrote in his official report.[22]

Out of ammunition, the 1st New York Light Battery G of the Fourth Volunteer Brigade and the 15th New York of McGilvery's brigade retired, as did McGilvery's other batteries. Bigelow's 9th Massachusetts, the last Union battery in the area of the Peach Orchard, suffered so many lost horses that it was forced to retire by prolong (using rope and the recoil of its guns), kicking back about four to five yards each time with the men pulling a lanyard timed with each shot, always under withering fire.

With Sickles' corps broken and rushing off the field and no direct infantry support, McGilvery's remaining batteries near the Trostle house fought bravely

21 Frederick C. Winkler letter, July 8, 1863, www.russscott.com/~rscott/26thwis/26pgwk63. htm. Accessed March 30, 2017.

22 Freeman McGilvery, in OR 27, pt. 1, 882.

under an incessant and deadly fire. McGilvery ordered Pennsylvania Batteries C and F and the 5th Massachusetts to withdraw to Cemetery Ridge, but he discovered a wide undefended area in the Union line just north of Little Round Top and knew it needed to be defended. "Col. McGilvery dashed up and announced, 'Captain Bigelow, there is not an infantryman back of you along the whole line from which Sickles moved out," recalled Captain Bigelow of the 9th Massachusetts, who was 22 at the time and a recent Harvard student. "[Y]ou must remain where you are and hold your position at all hazards, and sacrifice your battery, if need be, until at least I can find some batteries to put in position and cover you. The enemy are coming down on you now.' " With bullets and shells flying all around them and Confederates firing into them and some jumping on 9th Massachusetts limbers, the battery held out for about half an hour.[23]

"The enemy opened a fearful musketry fire, men and horses were falling like hail," recalled Bigelow after the war. "The enemy crowded to the very muzzles . . . but were blown away by the canister. Sergeant after Sergt. was struck down, horses were plunging and laying about all around, bullets now came in on all sides for the enemy had turned my flanks. The air was dark with smoke. A Rebel battery had opened on our position and their shells were going over and among us," he continued. "The enemy were yelling like demons, yet my men kept up a rapid fire." Charles W. Reed, a bugler with the 9th Massachusetts, wrote in a letter home: "Congratulate me on passing through the severest fought battle of the war in perfect safety. [S]uch a shrieking, hissing, seathing I never dreamed was imagineable. It seemed as though it must be the work of the very devil himself." McGilvery added: "Justice demands that I should state Captain Bigelow did hold his position and execute his firing with a deliberation and destructive effect upon the enemy in a manner such as only a brave and skillful officer could."[24]

Bigelow's sacrifice bought time for McGilvery to cobble together a collection of guns to fill the hole in the line left by the III Corps. The "Plum Run Line" along lower Cemetery Ridge consisted mainly of cannons from Artillery Reserve batteries, and all played a significant role in driving back the charging Confederate

---

23 Ibid.; Baker, *History of the Ninth Massachusetts Battery*, 60.

24 OR 27, pt. 1, 882; Bigelow to Bachelder, *The Bachelder Papers*, vol. 1, 174; Charles Wellington Reed letter home, July 6, 1863, in Eric A. Campbell, ed., *A Grand Terrible Dramma: From Gettysburg to Petersburg: The Civil War Letters of Charles Wellington Reed* (New York, NY, 2000), 113.

infantry.[25] Bigelow and his battery paid a high price. By the time they finally escaped near dark, the command had suffered eight dead, 17 wounded, and two captured, plus 45 horses killed and 15 wounded. The 9th Massachusetts lost more men in a single day than any other Artillery Reserve battery lost in two days of fighting at Gettysburg.[26]

All artillerists from the four First Volunteer Brigade batteries retired with their remaining guns to the Spangler property. "The night of the 2d was devoted in great part to repairing damages, replenishing the ammunition chests, and reducing and reorganizing such batteries as had lost so many men and horses as to be unable efficiently to work the full number of guns," reported General Hunt. Seventy wagons of artillery ammunition were loaded for the Army of the Potomac on the Spangler property that night. Empty wagons were withdrawn from the Spangler fields and sent farther to the rear on the morning of July 3.[27]

*   *   *

Such was the heroic work of the Artillery Reserve's First Volunteer Brigade on July 2 that, after the war, three members were awarded the Medal of Honor, the highest military honor bestowed by the United States:

Private Casper R. Carlisle, Pennsylvania Battery F: The 22-year-old Pittsburgh native "saved a gun of his battery under heavy musketry fire, most of the horses being killed and the drivers wounded" during the retreat from Wheatfield Road to the Trostle house.[28]

Second Lieutenant Edward M. Knox, 15th New York Light Battery: The 21-year-old New York City native "held his ground with the battery after the

---

25 Today, McGilvery Artillery Avenue, which runs next to the Peach Orchard, is named in honor of Colonel McGilvery. Bigelow was shot twice in his gallant effort, but was picked up and helped onto his horse by bugler Reed, who walked him to the rear as the fire of both lines pierced the air above and around them. Reed had twice defied orders to retreat, and Bigelow thanked him years later by successfully nominating him for a Medal of Honor for his bravery. Bigelow recovered from his wounds and returned to command in August.

26 OR 27, pt. 1, 878.

27 Ibid., 237, 873.

28 www.history.army.mil/html/moh/civwaral.html. Accessed January 27, 2017.

other batteries had fallen back until compelled to draw his piece off by hand; he was severely wounded."[29]

Bugler Charles W. Reed, 9th Massachusetts Battery: The 21-year-old Boston native defied orders to abandon the field, and instead "rescued his wounded captain from between the lines."[30]

Despite its horrific and heroic day on July 2, the Artillery Reserve wasn't done with Spangler land, which would be greatly needed again on July 3.

Spangler Farm Short Story

In 1884, Capt. John Bigelow and Medal of Honor recipient Charles W. Reed of the 9th Massachusetts, together with former battery members Sgt. Levi W. Baker and Pvt. Richard Holland, stopped on George and Elizabeth Spangler's farm when they returned to Gettysburg as part of a contingent to determine the sites for three monuments to their battery.

"Having already secured the services of Mr. Holtsworth [W. D. Holtzworth] the well known guide, we started for Spangler's field, where the reserve artillery went in park in the morning of the 2d of July, 1863," wrote Baker. "Arriving at the house," he continued,

we dismissed our carriage and proceeded on foot to find the field and the spot of our stay there; then followed the way we went to Trostle's field, all of which we identified . . . selecting the position of our several guns. . . . We were well satisfied that we were on the right spot. . . . After spending some time in surveying the field and fixing a spot for our monument, we returned to our hotel. In the evening we met the officers of The Gettysburg Battlefield Association. . . . We were promised a piece of land twenty by forty feet on the road as a monument site, they to fence it and care for it forever. The committee decided to obtain a shaft of Quincy granite, and a general design was suggested by Maj. Bigelow, C.W. Reed and J.K. Norwood, which was finally adopted. . . .

29 Ibid.

30 Ibid.

Also an ammunition chest for the rear of Trostle's field, and stone with an ammunition haversack cut on it to be put on Cemetery Hill [the July 3 location of the 9th].

All three monuments remain today. In addition to selecting accurate monument sites, the 1884 trip allowed the men of the 9th Massachusetts to contemplate how they had fought and somehow survived 21 years earlier. While stopped on the Spangler property, Holland—an accomplished artist—made pencil drawings of the Spangler farm and Granite Schoolhouse that appear in this book. The men retraced their 1863 steps from Spangler to their deployment, as shown in the accompanying map. Bugler and Medal of Honor recipient Reed was also an accomplished artist, and his work also appears in this chapter.[31]

31 Baker, *History of the Ninth Massachusetts Battery*, 208-209.

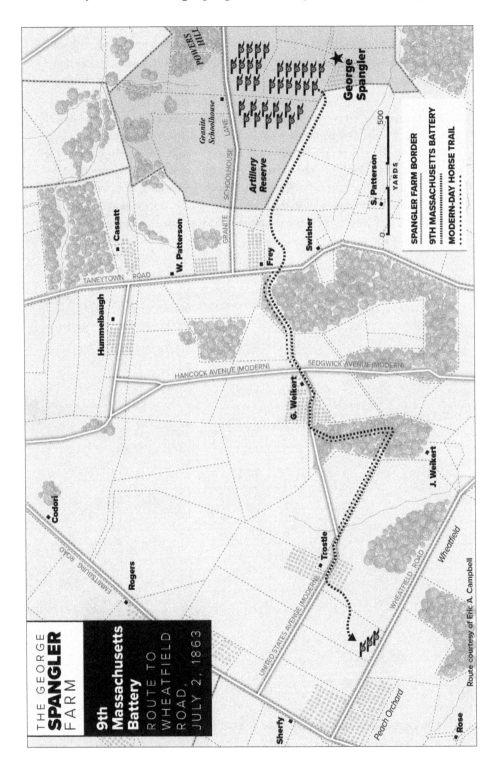

POWERS HILL

★ George Spangler

Granite Schoolhouse

LANE

SCHOOLHOUSE

Artillery Reserve

GRANITE

YARDS

500

S. Patterson

0

SPANGLER FARM BORDER

9TH MASSACHUSETTS BATTERY

MODERN-DAY HORSE TRAIL

Cassatt

W. Patterson

Frey

Swisher

TANEYTOWN   ROAD

Hummelbaugh

HANCOCK AVENUE (MODERN)

SEDGWICK AVENUE (MODERN)

G. Weikert

J. Weikert

Codori

EMMITSBURG ROAD

Rogers

Trostle

Wheatfield

WHEATFIELD ROAD

Route courtesy of Eric A. Campbell

THE GEORGE

SPANGLER

FARM

9th Massachusetts Battery

ROUTE TO WHEATFIELD ROAD, JULY 2, 1863

UNITED STATES AVENUE (MODERN)

Peach Orchard

Sherfy

Rose

How the 9th Massachusetts Traveled from Its Base on the Spangler Farm in 1863 and 1884 (facing map)

1: The 9th Massachusetts left Spangler and cut directly across the Swisher and Frey fields south of Granite Schoolhouse Lane (all private property today) until it reached Taneytown Road. Sergeant Levi W. Baker: "At the order 'Attention,' we all sprang to our places and cleared our guns of grain, for action, and immediately filed out of the [Spangler] field at the corner nearest to us."

2: The battery crossed the Taneytown Road and traveled down the George Weikert farm lane (which today is a horse trail) to the intersection of today's Hancock and United States avenues, and continued down the lane (today a private driveway) and past the Weikert house;

3: Once past the house, the 9th Massachusetts returned to what is now United States Avenue before turning sharply left into Weikert Woods;

4: The horse trail winds south through Weikert Woods before turning left (or west) on United States Avenue to the Trostle house. Baker: "We skirted fields, followed by-roads, and halted in a field southeast of Trostle's house."

5: The battery passed through the gate across the road from the Trostle house and went through the field to its position along Wheatfield Road. Baker: "Soon the order was 'Forward,' and we filed into a lane by Trostle's house, then turned to the left through a gateway. ... The order rang out; 'Forward into line, left oblique. Trot!' and before the left piece was in line, 'Action front!' The distance across the field is about 300 yards, up a gradual slope to a road so little traveled as to be marked by fence more than anything else [the busy Wheatfield Road today]."[32]

32 Ibid., 56-57. Special thanks to Ranger Eric A. Campbell of the Cedar Creek & Belle Grove National Historical Park in Middletown, VA. Campbell wrote about the 9th Massachusetts route in a 1991 issue of *Gettysburg Magazine* while he was stationed in Gettysburg. The route is supplemented by comments from Sgt. Levi W. Baker, 9th Massachusetts.

Chapter 9

For Family and Country:
Private George Nixon III

"During the night, we could hear the cries of hundreds of wounded and dying men on the field. . . . It was the most distressful wail we ever listened to."

— *Bvt. Brig. Gen. Samuel H. Hurst*

George Nixon III was 40 when he enlisted in the Union army in November 1861—much older than the average age of 25 for a Civil War soldier. Nixon and wife Margaret Ann lived in Elk Township, Vinton County, Ohio, just outside of McArthur and south of Columbus. According to the 1860 census, they owned livestock and a few pieces of farm equipment, but no real estate. In all likelihood, he rented the small piece of land he farmed. The Nixons were poor, with a personal estate valued at $110.00. Providing for nine children under those circumstances must have been overwhelming for George and Margaret Ann.

In late 1861, Union enlistee privates received $13.00 a month and a $100.00 enlistment bounty, which would be worth a little under $2,000 in 2018 dollars. (In all likelihood, he received only $25.00 of the bounty when he enlisted, the rest to come later). That kind of money could make a difference for a large family. Perhaps it was patriotism that drove George to enlist, but it is more likely, given his age and

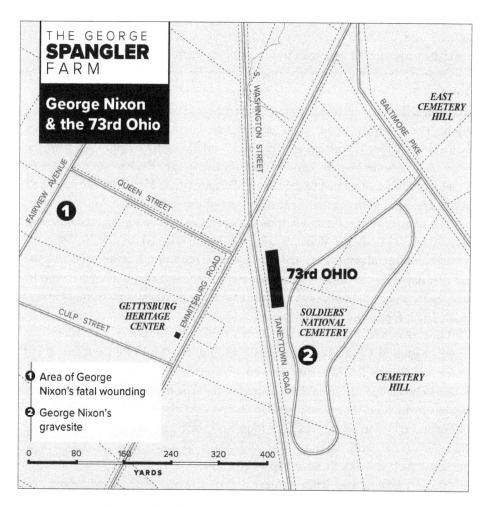

circumstances, that he joined up to support his family during difficult economic times.[1]

The five-foot six-inch heavily bearded enlistee sported brown hair and sad eyes, if his enlistment photo is an indication of how he looked on any given day. Leaving your wife and family to go to war at his age was almost certainly not something he looked forward to doing, so his sad countenance might well indicate his feeling on the day he sat for his photograph. However he felt, saying goodbye to

1 www.in2013dollars.com/1861-dollars-in-2018. Accessed January 4, 2018.

his wife and children must have been gut-wrenching for the father of nine, especially with such an uncertain future awaiting them all.[2]

George's hard life got even tougher once he joined up. He ended up in Company B, 73rd Ohio Volunteer Infantry, which was raised mostly in Ross County and the rural environs around Chillicothe and organized under Col. Orland Smith. The regiment spent time in western Virginia before fighting in the Shenandoah Valley Campaign at McDowell and Cross Keys, and then with the Army of Virginia in Pope's Second Bull Run Campaign. Back in the defenses of Washington, it was attached to the Second Brigade of the First Division of the XI Corps. The 73rd Ohio was now officially part of the Army of the Potomac.

The hardships of military life took a toll on George, and he battled illness as often as he fought the Confederates. He was in the hospital on July 30, 1862, for ophthalmia (eye inflammation), and then again the next month at the end of August and first day of September to be treated for a dislocated arm bone. Two months later, November 15-18, he was being treated for diarrhea, and from February 13-21, 1863, for chronic rheumatism.[3]

Long marches, infectious diseases, and the whipping they had taken two months earlier at Chancellorsville left Nixon and the 73rd Ohio exhausted and somewhat dispirited when they arrived in Gettysburg at mid-day on July 1. Fortunately for the Ohioans, for surely that is what many of them would have thought at the time, they were placed in reserve on Cemetery Hill with the rest of the Second Division of the XI Corps to protect the high ground in case the other elements of the army fighting west and north of town were forced back in retreat—which was exactly what happened.

The 73rd Ohio was deployed near the intersection of the Emmitsburg and Taneytown roads. At the time, no one knew the position would be one of extreme hazard through most of the rest of the battle. After capturing the town of Gettysburg on the afternoon of July 1, the Southern troops used the advantage of the cover offered by its homes and businesses to pour an incessant small arms fire onto Cemetery Hill. In addition, artillery from other points lobbed shells onto the

---

2 Nixon family notes and "From James to Richard: The Nixon Line," by Raymond Martin Bell (Washington & Jefferson College, Washington, PA, 1957), Herbert Wescoat Memorial Library, McArthur, OH. The names and approximate ages of Nixon's wife and children were as follows: Wife Margaret Ann (35), Martha (17), David (15), Samuel (14), Margaret (12), Sarah (11), William (7), Boston (5), Hiram (3), and Elihu (1).

3 Carded Medical Records Volunteers, Mexican, and Civil Wars, 1846-1865, Records of the Adjutant General's Office, RG 94, Entry 534, 73 Ohio, Justice D., to Parson C., Box 2744, National Archives and Records Administration, Washington, D.C.

high ground. The men of the 73rd Ohio were at the front of the Union line on the hill—sitting ducks as one of the closest units to town and unable to return an effective fire.

By the time the battle ended, the 73rd Ohio suffered 145 casualties out of just 338 men (21 killed outright, another 120 mortally wounded or wounded, and four captured or missing) while helping protect the hill so coveted by the Confederates. Its losses were the highest in Orland's brigade at Gettysburg. Among the severely injured was George Nixon III.[4]

On the early evening of July 2 during a small but ferocious firefight between skirmishers, Nixon's Company B advanced several hundred feet west of the Emmitsburg Road and Cemetery Hill. Both sides were attempting to assert control over what was then farmland along a small ridge and fence line. A Confederate division under Maj. Gen. Robert E. Rodes was moving fitfully eastward in what would be a failed quest to take Cemetery Hill. Portions of the XI Corps' Second Division, meanwhile, including Nixon's Company B, were doing all they could to suppress the deadly enemy fire that was taking out one man after another.

"The fire now became heavier in our immediate front," recalled the 73rd Ohio's Major Samuel H. Hurst long after the war. "Their skirmishers had been heavily reinforced. They had gained a fence on a low-lying ridge, from which they could not only annoy our skirmish and battle lines, but also our gunners on the hill. It became necessary to drive them back, in order to protect our batteries. Accordingly," he continued, "our whole brigade line of skirmishers charged and drove them from the ridge; but, going too far, and the enemy being reinforced, they in turn, charged and drove back our line again, with heavy loss." According to Hurst and other sources, the withdrawal of the main Confederate effort didn't lessen the fighting, and "from this time until the close of the battle, there was a most cruel fire of skirmishers and sharp-shooters all along the center." The firing "sometimes amounted almost to the fire of a line of battle, and was especially deadly from its deliberateness of aim."[5]

At some point during this fighting on the evening of July 2, two balls struck George, one in his right hip and the other in his right side. The rounds knocked him to the ground, where he remained bleeding and stuck between the two lines. He remained there well into the night for hours writhing in pain and crying for help

---

4 OR 27, pt. 1, 183.

5 Samuel H. Hurst, *Journal-history of the Seventy-third Ohio Volunteer Infantry* (Chillicothe, OH, 1866), 70.

George Nixon III

Vinton County Historical Society

along with the many other wounded men around him. "During the night, we could hear the cries of hundreds of wounded and dying men on the field," recalled Hurst. "It was the most distressful wail we ever listened to. Thousands of sufferers upon the field, and hundreds lying between the two skirmish lines, who could not be cared for, through the night were groaning and wailing or crying out in their depth of suffering and pain. They were the mingled cries of friend and foe that were borne to us on the night breeze, as a sad, wailing, painful cry for help."[6]

Unfortunately, there was no way for an XI Corps ambulance to roll in and collect these men for medical care. Corporal Richard Enderlin, a musician in Company B who was probably fairly close to the skirmish line, was charged with bringing off any wounded he could reach. After listening to the pitiful wails for hours, he finally could no longer stand the sound of the suffering. So the 20-year-old native of Germany put his own life at risk and crawled out into the darkness. He came upon George within a handful of yards of the Confederate line and dragged and carried him to safety. Enderlin's courage earned him both a promotion to sergeant and the awarding of a Medal of Honor because he "voluntarily and at his own imminent peril went into the enemy's lines at night and, under a sharp fire, rescued a wounded comrade."[7]

George was placed in a wagon and taken with other wounded to the Spangler farm hospital sometime during the early hours of July 3. Little is known of what happened to him once he arrived, though surgeons there wrote on his Carded

6 Ibid., 72-73.

7 www.history.army.mil/html/moh/civwaral.html. Accessed January 27, 2017.

Medical Record (now at the National Archives) that he suffered two flesh wounds and was treated with "water dressing." He lingered for a week before dying of infection on July 10. His age, coupled with the frequent illnesses and wear and tear he had suffered, might also have played a role in his death. He was buried on the property in a rough coffin under a head marker, both made of wood from the Spangler property. His remains were exhumed months later and reburied in the Ohio section of Soldiers' National Cemetery in Gettysburg on the same hill he was defending, not far from where he was mortally wounded and just a few yards from where President Abraham Lincoln delivered the Gettysburg Address.

Private Nixon was 42 when he died on George Spangler's farm. He left a widow and nine children on their own. It was only one of many tragedies and times of grief that the ancestors of future President Richard M. Nixon would bear in the mid-1800s:

— George Nixon, Jr., died on July 3, 1863, one day after his son George III was mortally wounded near that fence line in Gettysburg;

— George III and Margaret Ann's son William (age 8 or 9) died that August, just one month after his father died;

— In 1865, Margaret Ann died at age 38 and was buried in Old McArthur Cemetery in McArthur, Ohio. The eight remaining children were divided among relatives;

— George and Margaret Ann's son Samuel was 17 when his mother died. He was President Nixon's grandfather. Samuel married and had five children, but his wife, Sarah—Richard Nixon's grandmother—died in 1886 at age 33. Samuel's children were dispersed for a time among family members.

Samuel's son and George's grandson, Francis, was born in 1878. Francis lived to see his son Richard become vice president of the United States before dying in 1956. In July 1953, Vice President Nixon visited Gettysburg and placed flowers on the grave of his great-grandfather, George Nixon III.

* * *

George Nixon III's death at Gettysburg entitled Margaret Ann to receive a federal pension of $8.00 a month starting on July 10, 1863. She also received $2.00 per month for each child under age 16. Seven of the Nixons' nine children qualified for the additional pension at the time of their father's death. If George left his wife

Vice President Richard M. Nixon (second from right) placed flowers on the Gettysburg grave of his great-grandfather, George Nixon III, in July 1953. *Gettysburg National Military Park*

and children to join the army with the intention of supporting them, it was an unselfish personal sacrifice that paid off both before and after his death.

The Nixons' oldest daughter, Martha, was married in Vinton County, Ohio, on August 30, 1862, on the same day her father's 73rd Ohio was fighting in Second Bull Run in Virginia. George was in a hospital in neighboring Gallipolis, Ohio, with a dislocated arm at the time. One hopes he made it home for the wedding.[8]

8 Marriage records, Vinton County, OH, 1859-1869, Vinton County Historical and Genealogical Society.

*   *   *

After the war, Bvt. Brig. Gen. Samuel H. Hurst (who had fought as a major in the 73rd Ohio at Gettysburg), returned and placed this fighting that had mortally wounded Nixon around a fence line on the ridge that today is Fairview Avenue. Nixon was shot on or near Fairview Avenue between modern-day Queen and Culp streets, a couple of blocks west of the Gettysburg Heritage Center. Fairview Avenue today is a quiet residential street in the Colt Park subdivision, which is named for the World War I tank training site on the nearby battlefield that was commanded by newly graduated West Pointer Dwight D. Eisenhower in 1917-18. The south portion of the street ends at the battlefield and the former Bliss farm, and the northern end halts at Gettysburg's hospital. A few businesses sit among the houses today, but Fairview Avenue is mainly residential and away from the busy main roads and most of Gettysburg's tourist traffic.

Spangler Farm Short Story

Sergeant Isaac Willis and his brother-in-law, Pvt. Elisha L. Leake, fought in the 73rd Ohio with George Nixon III. Both Willis and Leake were great-great-uncles of future Gettysburg Licensed Battlefield Guide (LBG) Stuart R. Dempsey. Willis and Leake were shot on the skirmish line west of the Emmitsburg Road on the morning of July 2, not far from where Nixon was mortally wounded later that day. Willis, 21, was killed, while Leake, 34, suffered a horrific wound that fractured his jaw and destroyed his mouth and right eye. He was taken to the Spangler hospital and died there on July 8, which meant that Mary Willis Leake lost her husband (Elisha) and brother (Isaac) at Gettysburg. Leake left behind three children.

Leake and Willis were in Company G, which suffered 22 casualties out of 36 men in this July 2 fight. Willis was initially buried where he fell, while Leake was buried on the Spangler farm. Both now rest in Soldiers' National Cemetery in Gettysburg. LBG Dempsey has taken a personal interest in his ancestors and is considered an expert on the XI Corps.[9]

---

9 Information provided by Gettysburg Licensed Battlefield Guide Stuart R. Dempsey.

Chapter 10

Flood Tide:
Day Two at the XI Corps Hospital

"At the doorway I saw a huge stack of amputated arms and legs, a stack as high as my head!
The most horrible thing I ever saw in my life! I wish I had never seen it! I sickened."

— *Pvt. William Southerton of the 75th Ohio*

Medical staffers of the XI Corps were still busy caring for the hundreds of men who were wounded on July 1 when more poured in early the next day. The steady skirmishing and sharpshooting that would consume that entire Thursday, the second day of the battle, guaranteed a steady flow of mangled and suffering men onto the Spangler farm.

The regiments on and below Cemetery Hill took a beating from Confederate sharpshooters hidden in and about town. New Yorkers, Pennsylvanians, and Ohioans alike did their best to keep their heads down and bodies shielded behind any cover they could find near the intersection of the Taneytown and Emmitsburg roads, where the 134th, 136th, and 154th New York, 55th and 73rd Ohio, and 27th Pennsylvania found themselves when dawn broke. Some of the regiments would be involved in fighting that evening a few hundred yards farther west (in what is now the Colt Park subdivision), a sharp and often overlooked affair that sent more wounded soldiers long after dark to the XI Corps hospital. The balance of the XI Corps was positioned farther up the hill or facing north and northeast on and under East Cemetery Hill.

About 4:00 p.m. on July 2, Confederate gunners on Benner's Hill east of Gettysburg and elsewhere opened fire on Cemetery Hill. Batteries from the Army of the Potomac's Artillery Reserve, I Corps, and XI Corps fired back in a bitter duel that lasted some two hours. XI Corps Artillery Brigade components included the First New York Light Battery I, New York Light 13th Battery, First Ohio Light Battery I, First Ohio Light Battery K, and 4th United States Battery G.

"The ground was strewn with broken carriages, dead horses and dead and dying men," recalled Sgt. Samuel Cooper of the First New Hampshire Light Artillery. "And to crown it all, and make the picture still more hideous, every few minutes a shell from the enemy would come tearing through the ground and knocking down the headstones would scatter the broken stone, the sand, earth and bones of the deceased among the living adding stench horror and sacrilege to the rest of the awful scene."[1]

Private John Edmonds of the First Ohio Light Artillery Battery H of the Artillery Reserve was one of the men hit in the iron barrage when a shell almost took off his left foot not far from the rostrum in the present-day Soldiers' National Cemetery. Someone applied a makeshift tourniquet and placed Edmonds on a stretcher. "Boys," he announced despite the intense pain he was suffering, "that was a pretty tough pull on me, wasn't it?"[2]

Edmonds was a 23-year-old teacher from near Toledo, Ohio, when he enlisted in October 1861. He sported brown hair and gray eyes, stood five feet eight inches, and had not yet married, and now he was in a fight for his life. He was carried on the stretcher to the Evergreen Cemetery gate house on the Baltimore Pike, placed in an ambulance, and transported to the XI Corps hospital on the Spangler farm. On July 4, Lt. William A. Ewing of Battery H reported in a letter to his mother that Edmonds was "doing well" after his dangling foot was amputated. His condition declined, however, and he was forced to undergo another amputation. After almost two weeks of suffering, Edmonds died on July 15. The attendants placed his corpse in a wooden casket made at the XI Corps hospital and buried the Ohioan in the makeshift cemetery in the orchard next to the Spanglers' house.[3]

Private Justus M. Silliman of the 17th Connecticut was a patient behind Confederate lines in town when Edmonds was wounded on July 2. The lightly wounded Silliman served as a hospital attendant at the Spangler farm after the battle and got to know Edmonds. "One poor fellow who occupied this tent has left

1 Duane E. Shaffer, *Men of Granite: New Hampshire's Soldiers in the Civil War* (Columbia, SC, 2008), 152.

2 "Letter From Huntington's Battery," *Toledo* (OH) *Blade*, July 18, 1863.

3 William A. Ewing, "News From Battery H," *Toledo Blade*, July 11, 1863.

this world of suffering and gone to Jesus in whom he trusted," Silliman wrote his mother in a letter on the day Edmonds died. "He was a fine intelligent man, was superintendent of the sabbath school in the town at which he had enlisted, his name is John Edmonds. . . . He leaves a mother and sisters. . . . He had his leg amputated twice." Edmonds' body was exhumed and reburied in Soldiers' National Cemetery in Gettysburg. His grave is marked "John Edmunds." He is buried mere steps from where he received his mortal wound.[4]

The July 2 artillery battle over control of Cemetery Hill ended at about 6:00 p.m. The long-arm battle was winding down, but more death and destruction was about to fall upon Cemetery and East Cemetery hills, and the XI Corps would be in the middle of it once more.

Lined up at the base of East Cemetery Hill, from south to north, were regiments from every brigade in the first two divisions of the XI Corps: 33rd Massachusetts, 41st New York, 153rd Pennsylvania, 68th New York, 54th New York, 17th Connecticut, and 75th Ohio, with the 25th Ohio and 107th Ohio bending into an L-shape to face the town itself. About 8:45 p.m., with darkness engulfing the battlefield, three North Carolina regiments from Brig. Gen. Robert Hoke's brigade (under Col. Isaac Avery) and five more Louisiana regiments under Brig. Gen. Harry T. Hays, about 2,500 men, moved out of the gloom and quickly up the slope.

In the face of punishing Union canister fire, the Confederates pushed the 153rd Pennsylvania, 68th New York, and 54th New York up the slope and penetrated a breach that opened in the line. At the top, they hopped over earthen lunettes thrown up in front of the cannons and engaged in desperate hand-to-hand combat with artillerymen from Pennsylvania Batteries C and F of the Artillery Reserve and First New York Battery I of the XI Corps.

"Such hand-to-hand fighting," marveled Pvt. William Southerton of the 75th Ohio. "Johnnies, pushing, crowding, gained our first epaulements in spite of our efforts to block the way." By this time "It was almost impossible to distinguish who were Union, who were Confederate; to shoot and not kill our own men. Artillerists fought with ramrods, wielding them like ballbats."[5]

---

4 Silliman to his mother, July 15, 1863, *A New Canaan Private in the Civil War*, 45. Edmonds' real last name was "Edwards." Someone had spelled it "Edmonds" on the muster roll when he enlisted.

5 "Reminiscences of William B. Southerton" as told to Marie W. Higgins, in William B. Southerton Papers, Ohio Historical Society, Columbus, 1935.

The Confederates drove off Union defenders and seized some of the guns. For a few precious minutes, a portion of East Cemetery Hill was in Southern hands. But rushing over Cemetery Hill through the darkness from the west were reinforcements from the II Corps and the 73rd Pennsylvania and 119th New York from the XI Corps determined to drive away the attackers. The Louisianans and North Carolinians waited anxiously for their own reinforcements to arrive, to no avail. Another attack from the west in the form of Rodes' division against Cemetery Hill miscarried. Without support, the Confederates were unable to hold the valuable high ground and withdrew down the hill to their own lines. Cemetery and East Cemetery Hill remained just out of General Lee's grasp.

East Cemetery Hill was in Union hands once more, but the sacrifice of both sides was evident after the battle. "General [Brig. Gen. Adelbert] Ames reformed his lines and extended aid to the hundreds of rebel soldiers lying wounded inside our lines," explained Lt. Edward C. Culp of the 25th Ohio. "It was a ghastly battlefield."[6] On the other side of the lines, the returning Confederates reached their jump-off point. "The rebels returned again to our street at ten p.m.," recorded Pennsylvania College mathematics professor Michael Jacobs. "Some of them expressed their most earnest indignation at the foreigners—the Dutchmen—for having shot down so many of their men."[7]

About the same time, the XI Corps' 82nd Illinois, 45th New York, 157th New York, and 61st Ohio were rushed farther east to Culp's Hill to reinforce the lone XII Corps brigade that had been left behind by General Slocum. Brigadier General George Greene's brigade was being pushed hard by Maj. Gen. Edward Johnson's Confederate division, and the right side of his line was buckling. The four regiments helped stabilize the line, some of the fighting taking place well after nightfall.[8]

The horrific fighting of July 2 was finally over, but the struggle to save shattered lives was still well underway. "The ground was covered with the groanings and moanings of the wounded," recalled XI Corps commander Howard in a description of the area on and around Cemetery Hill. "While the soldiers were sleeping, the medical men with their ambulances, their lanterns, and their stretchers

6 Edward C. Culp, in Tom J. Edwards, ed., *Raising the Banner of Freedom: The 25th Ohio Volunteer Infantry in the War of the Union* (Bloomington, IN, 2003), 91.

7 Jacobs, *Notes on the Rebel Invasion of Maryland and Pennsylvania and the Battle of Gettysburg* (Philadelphia, PA, 1864), 38.

8 Bachelder, Day 2 map.

. . . were going from point to point to do what little they could for the multitude of sufferers."⁹

East Cemetery Hill became the main ambulance pickup point for the wounded and dying XI Corps men, most of whom ended up at George and Elizabeth Spangler's farm. Many of the wounded were placed in and outside the packed Evergreen Cemetery gatehouse, where they were picked up later by the ambulances and transported to the XI Corps hospital. Those who died waiting for medical attention were buried in temporary graves in and near the cemetery.¹⁰

With help or on their own accord, some of the wounded walked from Cemetery Hill to the Spangler property. Private Southerton of the 75th Ohio, just 19 years old that July, helped Pvt. Norman Brooks, 22, make it to the hospital after Brooks was shot in the face during the night-time fight. "Holding against his face a piece of pants leg he had torn from his own uniform, Norman bent forward as he walked," Southerton recalled years later. "As he adjusted the cloth I saw that a part of his jaw was shot away, many of his front teeth were gone. We made our way behind our battery, and were fairly safe." But getting to the hospital was difficult. "Such a line of wounded men! Many on stretchers, many hobbling trying to make it under their own power," explained Southerton. "To join the procession," he continued,

Norman and I had to cross a corner of the cemetery. Fences and monuments were blown to bits. A shell hissed past my cheek. Some little distance beyond Culp's Hill we came to a stone barn. The hospital, Dr. Wilson, was working frantically near a wide open doorway. He recognized us as I led Norman to him. If any one could help us, Dr. Wilson could. Other surgeons were working just as frantically. All by the light of a few lanterns hung on the walls. Hay was strewn about on the floor for beds for the wounded. At the doorway I saw a huge stack of amputated arms and legs, a stack as high as my head! The most horrible thing I ever saw in my life! I wish I had never seen it! I sickened. I hurried outside, kept out of the way of the stream of wounded that flowed to the hospital.¹¹

9 Howard, *Autobiography of Oliver Otis Howard*, 431.

10 Kiefer, *History of the One Hundred and Fifty-Third Regiment*, 169.

11 "Reminiscences of William B. Southerton." The wounded Confederates left on the hill after this fight were taken to several hospitals, including the XI Corps Spangler hospital.

Brooks survived his disfiguring wound and was transferred the following year to the Veteran Reserve Corps, which used disabled and chronically ill soldiers to perform light service such as guard duty and kitchen and hospital work. Southerton also survived Gettysburg and is believed to have lived to almost 100. Doctor Wilson, whom Brooks and Southerton sought on the Spangler farm, was surgeon Charles L. Wilson of the 75th Ohio. Wilson resigned from the army that October.[12]

Two Confederate privates died on George Spangler's property, both of whom were mortally wounded on East Cemetery Hill on the evening of July 2. North Carolinian James Russel was a 21-year-old farmer when he enlisted in 1861 in Charlotte. He was wounded at Sharpsburg (Antietam) on September 17, 1862, but rejoined the 6th North Carolina in time for the march north to Gettysburg. Russel was shot twice—once in his right knee and again in the upper forearm. When he died at the XI Corps hospital remains unknown. Thomas McCarty of the 8th Louisiana belonged to the tough and famous Louisiana Tigers. He was a native of Ireland and 38 years old at the time of his enlistment in 1861 in New Orleans. McCarty was wounded at the battle of Ox Hill on September 1, 1862, and captured near Fredericksburg, Virginia, in May 1863. He was soon paroled and made the march north into Pennsylvania. Like Russel, the date of McCarty's death passed unregistered. Both sets of remains were later exhumed and reburied somewhere in the South in the 1870s.[13]

Other Confederates found their way to the Spangler property. Private Silliman of the 17th Connecticut mentioned Pvt. Mark A. Hubert of Company K, 5th Texas Infantry, in a letter to his mother on July 15. "We also have two Confederates one from Texas, a fine intelligent man shot through the leg," penned Silliman from the Spangler property. "His name is Mark Hubert [Robertson's] brigade, Hood division Longstreet corps. The other is one of a Va. regt. struck in breast by a shell. I have doubts of his recovery."[14]

Private Hubert was wounded during the assault of the 5th Texas up the rocky slope of Little Round Top. The Texas regiment suffered 211 casualties out of 409 men taken into action that day. The "fine intelligent" Hubert, who was born in 1837, left the Spangler hospital on July 24 and, according to a diary he kept on the

---

12 www.civilwardata.com/active/hdsquery.dll?SoldierHistory?U&385010. Accessed March 1, 2017.

13 From notes prepared for the Gettysburg Foundation by Gettysburg Licensed Battlefield Guide Wayne Motts, formerly of the Adams County Historical Society and now chief executive officer of the Civil War Museum in Harrisburg, Pennsylvania.

14 Silliman, *A New Canaan Private in the Civil War*, 45.

Sgt. Nelson W. Jones

Collections of Maine Historical Society

blank pages of a New Testament, arrived at a prison hospital in Baltimore the following day. "I will be truly glad when my time comes to be exchanged," he admitted on July 27. "The Yanks treat us as well as I could expect, but I prefer Dixie's hospitality."[15]

Of his time at the XI Corps hospital, he wrote, "For three weeks after I was wounded I had nothing but a shirt." Hubert was still suffering from leg and foot pain, swelling, drainage issues, and bleeding when he left the Spangler farm, symptoms that would continue for months thereafter. "This morning," he penned while in Baltimore on September 24, "I took a knife and cut it open it runs mostly blood." Hubert was paroled and put on a steamship bound for Richmond on September 26, his 27th birthday. His wound eventually healed and he lived to age 70.[16]

Given the bloody chaos on a sprawling battlefield like Gettysburg, it is not surprising that many wounded never made it to their assigned division or corps hospital. One example was Sgt. Nelson W. Jones of the 3rd Maine, Brig. Gen. Hobart Ward's brigade, Maj. Gen. David Birney's division, Sickles' III Corps. Jones, who was 18 at the time of his enlistment in 1861, was fighting in the Peach

---

15 M. A. Hubert, diary, 1863, Dolph Briscoe Center for American History, Univ. of Texas at Austin.

16 www.findagrave.com/memorial/44015126/mark-anthony-hubert. Accessed March 1, 2017.

Orchard on July 2 when he was hit. He was taken to the Spangler hospital, probably by someone from the Artillery Reserve because the 3rd Maine was fighting alongside Reserve batteries that had been parked on the Spangler farm.

Jones was a good soldier and promoted from private to sergeant in 1862. He also was a good son, taking time to write letters home while worrying about his parents and their farm work in Palermo, Maine. "[I]t is so lonsome here that I do wish I was at home or some where else for a spell but I don't wory any only I am afraid you will get out of health doing your work alone," he wrote to his parents on August 7, 1861. I sometimes think I ought to have staid at home and helped you instead of inlisting and come out here to fight. . . . Father please write me how your health is and if it is hard work for you to do the work all alone and if you can do your falls work without hired help if you cant I will try and help you all I can." Jones never made it home to help his parents on the farm. He died at the XI Corps hospital and was buried there before being exhumed months later. He rests today in the Maine plot of Soldiers' National Cemetery.[17]

Corpsmen spent the night of July 2-3 under lantern light searching for, picking up, and delivering a stream of the latest mass of wounded. "About eleven at night the ambulances were busy collecting and carrying to the rear great loads of mangled and dying humanity," recalled V Corps surgeon Joseph Thomas of the 118th Pennsylvania. "The wagon trains, with tents and supplies, had not yet arrived, and the wounded were deposited on the ground. . . . As they were removed from the ambulances they were placed in long rows, with no reference to the nature or gravity of their injuries, nor condition or rank. Friend and foe alike, as they had been picked up promiscuously, were there laid side by side. Soon the ambulances ceased their visits," he continued, "as they had gathered up all that were accessible, or could be found in the darkness. . . . Opiates were administered to alleviate pain and water supplied to appease their thirst."[18]

Jacob Smith of the XI Corps' 107th Ohio, helped carry the wounded to the ambulance wagons. "The last comrade we took back in the evening, we had to carry to the hospital [on a stretcher], a distance of more than a mile," he said, "the wagons having been driven away before we came. After hunting up our wagons we passed the night in them."[19]

17 www.soldierstudies.org/index.php?action=view_letter&Letter=1499, March 1, 2017.

18 Samuel Cecil Stanton, ed., *The Military Surgeon: Journal of the Association of Military Surgeons of the United States*, vol. 32 (Chicago, IL, 1913), 405.

19 Smith, *Camps and Campaigns*, 103.

The size of the XI Corps hospital staff of stewards, nurses, and orderlies increased throughout the battle to handle the overflow crowd of wounded. Corporal John Irvin of the 154th New York recorded that 12 to 14 men from his regiment alone were detailed to the Spangler hospital on July 2.[20]

Pvt. James R. Middlebrook, age 30, was a lawyer and farmer in the 17th Connecticut. He arrived to help in the hospital on the 2nd after losing all his gear in the Barlow Knoll fight on July 1. He worked almost three weeks at Spangler. "When I came here I thought to do something for the soldiers & I am now doing all I can for them – Dressing wounds, giving them water & waiting on them to make them as comfortable as we can," he wrote to his wife, Frances. "Our hospital is a large barn & is full some 200 on the first floor where I am & under as many more & lots of them in Tents around outside then are some 80 men in the barn with legs & arms off & it is enough to make ones heart bleed to witness the amputations . . . it my duty to do all I can for them . . . [and] shall stay as long as I can stand it."[21]

While the medical personnel worked as best they could, General Meade called together his top generals for a council of war in the tiny Lydia Leister house on the Taneytown Road. He asked them: Should we stay in our present position or retire? If we remain, shall we attack or await an attack of the enemy? If we wait, how long?

The overwhelming decision was to "stay and fight it out," as General Slocum advised, and that the army remain on the defensive and let the Confederates attack. If General Lee didn't attack, the Army of the Potomac could then choose the right time and place to attack him.[22]

The army would stay put. The hospitals could expect another day of horrific arrivals.

Spangler Farm Short Story

Lieutenant Gulian V. Weir, Battery C, 5th US Artillery, arrived on the Spangler property early on July 2 with the First Regular Brigade of the Artillery Reserve. The son of a West Point professor was a respected artilleryman who had served since almost the beginning of the war and had earned many accolades. His reputation

---

20 Edwin Dwight Northrup Papers. Box 16, Carl A. Kroch Library, Cornell University.

21 Middlebrook, Louis F Scrapbook, 1897-1906, Box MS 73139. Connecticut State Historical Society, Hartford, CT. Letter written July 9 at Spangler.

22 Minutes of war council, July 2, 1863, *OR*, 27, pt. 1, 73.

Lt. Gulian V. Weir
Weir Farm National Historic Site

would take a hit several hours after he left the Spangler farm.

The 5th US was placed just east of the Emmitsburg Road on the Codori farm. There, under artillery and infantry fire and out of canister, it was nearly captured by Colonel Lang's Floridians about 7:30 p.m. Weir and his horse were shot. In his report, he noted that everything after his wounding "seemed to be very much confused." He ordered his guns to withdraw, but lost three guns to the enemy. General Hancock charged Weir with cowardice. Weir returned to the Spangler farm that night with what was left of his battery. He remained there until July 3, when his heavily damaged battery played a key role beating back Pickett's Charge near the Bloody Angle. Despite this success, Weir never got over his forced retreat and embarrassing reprimand from Hancock.

Weir returned to Gettysburg in 1885 and relieved the trauma by walking the Codori property where his battery had been swept away. The return to Gettysburg, he admitted, made him "a broken man." Weir wrote several anguished letters to Hancock practically begging him for a grant of forgiveness that would never come. "All I am working for now General is that where Gettysburg is shown I may have my place with Battery 'C' a clear conscience and record, to be able to talk about Gettysburg or any other battle that I was in, nothing more. . . . And, that you will, if you can to your entire satisfaction, in course of time, give me a few lines as to my work at Gettysburg." When he did not hear back Weir wrote again five days later: "I fear I may have expressed myself so bitterly as to incur your displeasure." He wrote three more letters within as many weeks, the last one claiming "There is much in my letters of November 15 and 25th which now, looking at in a calmer mood, I would rather had been left unsaid—I wrote too much as I felt, and regret very much having done so—I thought I had lived down all bitter feeling on the subject." It is believed Hancock never answered Weir's letters.

The former artillery commander lived an emotionally tortured year after his 1885 visit to Gettysburg before putting a gun against his chest in July 1886 and pulling the trigger. He was 48. Weir left behind a wife and six children.[23]

23 OR 27, pt. 1, 880; https://unionveterans.wordpress.com/2012/04/03/haunted-by-gettys burg/. Accessed March 3, 2017; Weir letter to Winfield Scott Hancock, November 25, 1885, in

Ruch Report No. 2

His Path to Spangler
Pvt. Reuben F. Ruch, Company F, 153rd Pennsylvania

"The morning of the 2d of July I got downstairs [at Trinity German Reformed Church] to see what was going on. Here I met a Johnnie on guard. He belonged to a North Carolina regiment and as he seemed to be a nice kind of a Reb I struck up a conversation with him. . . . He said there was no use fighting in the North, for he had never seen such a rich country as Pennsylvania, and that our towns were yet full of men, in fact a fellow would not miss those that were in the army. I told him that he had better stay north when the Rebel army retreated south, which they would in a day or two. That our people would not kill him and that he should stay north till the war was over. He told me that the old flag was good enough for him, that he lived in a rented house, and never owned a negro, that he would take my advice and stay north but for one thing. He had a wife and two children . . . and if he did stay north, and the Rebels found it out they would use his family meaner than dogs.

"I went back upstairs . . . and I had a grand view of the greater part of the battlefield. . . . A little before sundown I saw a stir and a moving about of the Rebs under the window where I was sitting, as if they were getting ready for some kind of a move. I also saw them drinking out of a barrel. The head of the barrel was knocked in. One would get a tin cup full and three or four would drink out of the same cup before it was empty. . . . It was straight whiskey, and they were getting ready to charge the Eleventh Corps [on East Cemetery Hill].

"It was between sundown and dark when they started in three lines of battle. . . . Every man took his place, giving the Rebel yell, by this time our grape and canister began to plow gaps through their ranks. . . . To see grape and canister cut gaps through ranks looks rough. I could see heads, arms, and legs flying amid the dust and smoke . . . it reminded me much of a wagon load of pumpkins drawn up a hill and the end gate coming out, and the pumpkins rolling and bounding down the hill. The only fault I found with this charge was that it got dark too soon, and I could not see the end of it. . . . The slaughter was terrible."[24]

Bachelder Papers, vol. 2, 1,153; Weir to Hancock, November 30, 1885, in *Bachelder Papers*, vol. 2, 1,154; Weir letter to Hancock, December 15, 1885, in *The Bachelder Papers*, vol. 2, 1,161.

24 Kiefer, *History of the One Hundred and Fifty-Third Regiment*, 218-220.

Chapter 11

The Granite Schoolhouse Hospital

"Here under the shelter of some boulders lay a large number of our wounded and dead who had been brought from the field. They lay upon the ground covered with their blankets, and the living were nearly all silent, having fallen asleep from fatigue."

— *Capt. Thomas Livermore, II Corps ambulance commander*

The Spanglers were hosting enough of the battle of Gettysburg already and paying a fearful price for the privilege, but on July 2 the Union army heaped even more misery upon them. Because on this day, members of the medical staff of Brig. Gen. John Caldwell's First Division of General Hancock's II Corps concluded the Granite Schoolhouse and fields around it were exactly what they needed and claimed the area as a hospital.

Some II Corps doctors from Caldwell's division had set up shop that morning on the William Patterson farm on the Taneytown Road. The Patterson property was on the north side of the Taneytown Road's intersection with Granite Schoolhouse Lane and bordered the northwest end of George Spangler's land.

Wounded skirmishers filtered into the Patterson farm throughout the morning, but not enough to discourage Surgeon-in-Charge Dr. William Warren Potter, 57th New York, from taking a ride or walk up the Taneytown Road to General Meade's headquarters. The casual atmosphere of the small hospital changed at about 3:00 p.m. when the Confederates opened their assault against Sickles' III Corps on the army's left and their artillery overshots pelted the Patterson farm, making it an untenable place to stay.

Dr. Potter recalled "arriving at the place where I had left the hospital [and] not a person was to be found, and no traces of it could be discovered." The surgeon set

Private Richard Holland of the 9th Massachusetts drew this image of the Granite Schoolhouse when members of the battery returned to the Spangler farm in 1884. *Gettysburg National Military Park*

out in search of the missing hospital and "soon found its new location near a stream protected by a ridge from great danger of shells, though we were somewhat nearer the lines than before. It seems that, during my absence, the hospital was literally shelled out of its first position, and this new place was sought out as a necessity." His description "somewhat nearer the lines than before" described the hospital's proximity to Culp's Hill just across the Baltimore Pike to the east.[1]

"The hospital was moved hastily," said 28-year-old chaplain John Henry Wilbrand Stuckenberg of the 145th Pennsylvania. "I moved my horse, took him farther back to the side of a hill under cover of some high rocks. Leaving my horse there in charge of some of our regiment, I went to assist the wounded." Justin Dwinelle, surgeon-in-charge of the II Corps hospitals at Gettysburg, described the First Division's hospital setting as "in the edge of the woods near the stone School house."[2]

1 William Warren Potter, "Three Years with the Army of the Potomac: A Personal Military History," *Buffalo Medical Journal*, vol. 67 (August 1911 to July 1912), 438.

2 David T. Hedrick and Gordon Barry Davis, Jr., eds., *I'm Surrounded by Methodists: Diary of John H. W. Stuckenberg Chaplain of the 145th Pennsylvania Volunteer Infantry* (Gettysburg, PA, 1995), 78; "Report of Surgeon Justin Dwinelle, Surgeon in Charge of the Second Corps Hospital at the Battle of Gettysburg," GNMP Library, Vertical File V5-Dwinelle, Justin. Report provided by Scott Dwinelle, Woodbridge, VA.

Chaplain John H. W. Stuckenberg

Hedrick and Davis, "I'm Surrounded by Methodists"

As a result of the move, the Spanglers now had two major hospitals on their property, one with all three divisions of the XI Corps in their house, barn, other buildings, and fields, and the II Corps' First Division hospital just a quarter-mile northwest of their house in the middle of their land. In addition, the II Corps medical staff claimed the schoolhouse as its headquarters. Granite Schoolhouse Lane was the primary artery used by the Army of the Potomac to shift troops and artillery to and from the battlefield and was almost dead center in the Spangler property. It was going to be even more congested on that little farm lane with frantic drivers and their horses pulling ambulances jammed with wounded men. At times late in the afternoon and early evening, ambulances going east on the lane to the hospital had to crawl through troops rushing down the path to the front line to the west.[3]

The woods in and around the schoolhouse location are continuous today, but that was not the case in 1863. During the battle, the land east and west of the school was mainly open fields mixed with patches of trees (including between the school and Powers Hill). The easternmost field hosted the bulk of the wounded. One of the Spangler wheat fields below Powers Hill touched the eastern field, and their other wheat field was across the lane from this open area. The only solid woods in the area in 1863 were behind the school, and wounded also were placed there.[4]

3 The schoolhouse is long gone, having been torn down in 1921. It sat across Granite Schoolhouse Lane from the 2nd US Artillery Batteries B and L monument a few yards to the west (39°48'17"N 77°13'22"W).

4 Solomon Powers operated a quarry for years directly under the hill that would someday bear his name.

Union infantry and artillery units used open spaces west of the school for bivouacs. Boulders that offered the wounded and dying some protection from the elements remain, as does the stream in the valley between the schoolhouse and Powers Hill. This stream runs under Granite Schoolhouse Lane (though it is normally dry at the road today). Both the school and hospital thus had ready access to this source of water and a spring in the area that might have been behind the school.

Before the afternoon of July 2 was over, Granite Schoolhouse doctors already had more wounded than they could handle. Hancock had shuttled thousands of II Corps troops south down Cemetery Ridge in an effort to keep the army's left from collapsing. The troops battled there in the Wheatfield and on the Rose farm, with the fighting moving north all along Cemetery Ridge to Cemetery Hill. By the time the battle ended on the afternoon of July 3, the II Corps had lost nearly 800 killed, 3,200 wounded, and almost 400 missing out of fewer than 10,500 engaged—the highest number in each category of any corps in the Army of the Potomac. "The first Division caught the heaviest of the blow," explained Dr. Potter, "many killed and wounded were the result, and the latter were now being brought to the hospital in great numbers."[5]

Tall, good-looking, confident, caring, and devoted to his religion, Chaplain Stuckenberg was a native of Germany and a Lutheran pastor in Erie when he joined the 145th Pennsylvania (Col. John Brooke's brigade) as its chaplain in 1862. Now he was back in Pennsylvania, praying with the soldiers before they entered battle and ministering to and treating the wounded and the dying on and around the Spangler property.

On the afternoon of July 2, the Rev. Father William Corby, the future president of the University of Notre Dame, granted general absolution to hundreds of men in Col. Patrick Kelly's (Irish) Second Brigade, Caldwell's division, forgiving them of their sins before the imminent deadly action. With sounds of the battle looming closer and louder, the men listened as Father Corby climbed on a boulder for all to see and explained what he was about to do. Then, as he began to grant absolution in Latin, the men—even the Protestants—dropped on their right knee with heads bowed and hat in hand to receive forgiveness. General Hancock and other mounted officers nearby also took a moment from battle preparations to remove

5   OR 27, pt. 1,177; Busey and Busey, *Union Casualties at Gettysburg*, report II Corps losses as 726 killed, 3,461 wounded, 40 wounded and captured, one wounded and missing, 182 captured, and 99 missing, for 4,509 total casualties, or 40.1%, 1,183; Potter, "Three Years with the Army of the Potomac," 438.

their hats and bow their heads. Many of these men in the Irish Brigade would be dead or seriously wounded within half an hour.

Chaplain Stuckenberg witnessed this solemn event and it so moved him that he asked for and received permission to conduct a brief service for Col. Hiram Loomis Brown's 145th Pennsylvania. After he spoke a few words and said a prayer, the Keystone soldiers marched into battle, where many of them, too, would soon die or be horribly mangled. Stuckenberg shuttled back and forth between the hospital and the wounded on the battlefield, helping anywhere he could for as long as he could.[6]

"Our hospital was at the foot of the hill," Stuckenberg wrote in his diary of Granite Schoolhouse and the field next to it below Powers Hill. "[O]ne of the first wounded men I saw was Col Brown, wounded in the right arm above the elbow. I led his horse to the hospital, where his wound was examined and the cheerful announcement was made that his arm need not be amputated. As Dr. Potter put his fingers in the wound to discover the extent of the injury," he continued, "Col B was writhing in pain—his sufferings evidently being intense. About the same time Col [Brig. Gen. Samuel K.] Zook was carried to the hospital on a stretcher, mortally wounded." Zook was hit between 5:30 and 6:00 p.m. while mounted and leading his brigade in the Wheatfield.[7]

"We were enveloped in smoke and fire, not only in front, but on our left, and even at times on the right," Lt. Josiah M. Favill, Zook's aide de camp, wrote in his journal. "Our men fired promiscuously, steadily pressing forward, but the fighting was so mixed, rebel and union lines so close together, and in some cases intermingled, that a clear idea of what was going on was not readily obtainable. I rode over to him [Zook] instantly, when he looked up with an expression I shall never forget, and said: 'It's all up with me, Favill.'"[8]

Like many soldiers do, General Zook portended his own death and mentioned as much to Dr. Potter on July 1 when the II Corps was marching toward

---

6 Hedrick and Davis, Jr., *I'm Surrounded by Methodists*, 77. A statue of the Rev. Father William Corby stands today on Hancock Avenue near the Pennsylvania monument (39°48'12"N 77°14'4"W).

7 Chaplain John H. W. Stuckenberg, diary, GNMP Library, Gregory A. Coco Collection, Box B-70, Folder 72b. Colonel Brown returned to the 145th Pennsylvania and was captured at Spotsylvania in May of 1864. He was breveted brigadier general that September and resigned in early 1865.

8 Josiah Marshall Favill, *The Diary of a Young Officer Serving with the Armies of the United States During the War of the Rebellion* (Chicago, IL, 1909), 246.

Brig. Gen. Samuel K. Zook

Library of Congress

Gettysburg. "We halted for a rest between eleven and twelve o'clock, and I sat down upon a haycock in a field along the roadside, to rest and graze my horse," Dr. Potter recalled. "General Zook soon joined us, sitting on the hay beside me, and we entered into conversation about the importance of the work before us. . . . The general had bought a horse in Maryland that day, for which he paid $250.00. It was a handsome animal, and he said it was a good purchase if he lived through the impending

battle: but if he should be killed, in that eve, he desired the horse sold. I inferred that he felt apprehensive for his own welfare, and that he might not survive," continued the doctor, "so I cheered him with a few encouraging words, reminding him of his previous good fortune in battle, etc. Alas! in less than a day he had received his mortal hurt."[9]

Lieutenant Favill and another aide, Lt. Charles Broom, transported General Zook to the Granite Schoolhouse, where he was examined by First Division Chief Operator Charles S. Wood of the 66th New York. Wood pronounced the wound mortal. "There being no shelter here, and the enemy's shot frequently reaching the spot," continued Favill, "we took the general on a stretcher, and carried him to a small house some distance in the rear on the Baltimore road, close to a bridge crossing a small creek." Although the aide might not have known it, they had taken the grievously wounded Zook to the G. Flemming Hoke toll house, where Dr. Potter soon examined him. Potter "discovered at once that he was fatally shot, a shell having torn open his left shoulder and chest, exposing the heart-beats to observation. I remained with the General until about eleven o'clock P.M.,"

---

9 Potter, "Three Years with the Army of the Potomac," 436-437.

Col. Edward E. Cross

Library of Congress

continued Potter, "and left word with Lieutenant Favill, of Zook's staff, that I would come again in the morning should he survive the night, which now looked very improbable."[10]

Favill and Broom shifted the general once more, this time to another house farther behind the line. The 42-year-old officer died there on July 3. "Thus ended the career of a brilliant officer, an estimable gentleman, and a faithful friend," Favill lamented. "His death interrupts all our plans for the future, and our interest in military affairs seems to have entirely evaporated. What a blank in our lives his death will cause." General Hancock mourned Zook's loss and described him as "a gallant officer."[11]

The next highest-ranking First Division officer of the II Corps after Zook treated at Granite Schoolhouse on July 2 was brigade commander Col. Edward E. Cross. "We shan't want any of your dead carts here to-day!" he had jokingly told II Corps ambulance chief Lt. Thomas Livermore just minutes before the fight began. He was sadly mistaken. The former newspaperman with a penchant for things military was 31 when a Confederate bullet found his abdomen as he led his men into the woods east/southeast of the Wheatfield. The hard-fighting Cross was on the opposite side of that large bloody field from where Zook was mortally

10 Favill, *The Diary of a Young Officer*, 247; Potter, "Three Years with the Army of the Potomac," 438.

11 Favill, *The Diary of a Young Officer*, 248-249; OR 27, pt. 1, 367. General Zook is honored with a monument (39°47'50"N 77°14'43"W) near the spot where he fell in the Wheatfield and received a posthumous promotion to major general. Thousands visited his casket while on public display at City Hall in New York City. Lieutenant Favill, age 22 at Gettysburg, was more fortunate than his commanding officer. He was promoted to captain in November 1863 and mustered out in August 1864.

wounded, near the present-day intersection of Ayres and Sickles avenues. A monument today marks the spot.[12]

Cross was taken in an ambulance to the vicinity of the school and placed on a bed of wheat made for him by his staff and men, reported 5th New Hampshire Assistant Surgeon William Child. "The gloom of a deep darkness covered all," Child said. "Now and then a shell went screeching across the sky, bursting with a sudden flash and stunning report. Many of his regiment, men who had followed him in a score of battles, were around. . . . All faces were sad, all hearts were sorrowful."[13]

Ambulance chief Livermore finished gathering the wounded about midnight and rushed to Cross' side at the Granite Schoolhouse after learning the officer had requested to see him. "I rode to the spot where he lay. It was a little dell, possibly one through which a little stream ran, between the Taneytown road and the Baltimore road, and from a quarter to half a mile from my park going toward Gettysburg," he recalled after the war. Livermore's ambulance park was along the Taneytown Road near the Spangler fields, with some wagons probably spilling onto Spangler property.[14]

Livermore continued:

Here under the shelter of some boulders lay a large number of our wounded and dead who had been brought from the field. They lay upon the ground covered with their blankets, and the living were nearly all silent, having fallen asleep from fatigue. I picked my way among their prostrate forms to the spot where the colonel lay, and inquiring of an officer of my regiment, whom I saw, which was the colonel, he pointed him out to me, indicating that he was dead. The moonlight or starlight enabled me to see his features distinctly. They were placid and exceedingly lifelike, and it was hard to persuade myself that the flush of life had gone from them. His lofty forehead was smooth, his long, silky beard lay upon his breast disheveled, and he looked more as he would if he slept than seemed possible. I was told that he had called those of his regiment who were about him and told them that he did not regret death, except that he had hoped to see the rebellion suppressed; that he hoped they would be good soldiers and keep up the

12 Livermore, *Days and Events, 1860-1866*, 247.

13 William Child, *History of the 5th New Hampshire Volunteers* (Bristol, NH, 1893), 211-212.

14 Livermore, *Days and Events, 1860-1866*, 254.

discipline and good conduct of the regiment. He sent for various members of the regiment, myself included . . .

Sitting next to Cross' corpse at the schoolhouse, "listening to what the officer told me about him at midnight, surrounded by many wounded," concluded Livermore, "was a sad experience and one which can never forsake my memory."[15]

Colonel Cross was considered a hero in his home state of New Hampshire. He had seen service in most of the major battles in the Eastern Theater and absorbed and survived enemy lead at Seven Pines and Antietam. Former II Corps Chief of Staff C. H. Morgan described Colonel Cross as "a very eccentric character, but an invaluable officer. He was a rigid disciplinarian. . . . If Colonel Cross ever knew fear, no one ever discovered it."[16]

Not everyone viewed the colonel as a hero or invaluable officer, though. Cross' hard-driving, critical personality came with a matching temper that alienated many of his men and officers. Sergeant Thomas P. Meyer of the 148th Pennsylvania, part of Cross' brigade, used the word "tyrant" to describe him. Meyer and some of his comrades in his 10-man Pioneer Corps so disliked him that they refused to bury Cross at Gettysburg.[17]

Livermore also recalled a mortally wounded man named "Patch" from the 2nd New Hampshire at this Spangler hospital. The unfortunate soldier was Sgt. Charles W. Patch, 33, of Sickles' III Corps. Somehow he ended up at a II Corps hospital surrounded by strangers and died of a body wound a few days later. "It was a mournful thing to think of his dying there," lamented Livermore, "not only away from home, but away from those of his own regiment who might have cared for him." Colonel Cross and Sergeant Patch are both buried in New Hampshire. Cross Avenue, which runs south of the Wheatfield, is named after the fallen colonel.[18]

Chaplain Stuckenberg was at the schoolhouse when Colonel Brown of the 145th Pennsylvania, who had been shot in the right arm above the elbow, asked him to find his 21-year-old adjutant named John D. Black, whom Brown believed had been seriously wounded and taken to a hospital. Stuckenberg didn't have to go

15 Ibid., 254-255.

16 C. H. Morgan, "Narrative of the Operations of the Second Army Corps," in Almira Hancock, *Reminiscences of Winfield Scott Hancock by His Wife* (New York, NY, 1887), 203.

17 Thomas P. Meyer, "The Pioneer's Story," in J. W. Muffly, ed., *The Story of Our Regiment: A History of the 148th Pennsylvania Volunteers* (Des Moines, IA, 1904), 461.

18 Livermore, *Days and Events, 1860-1866*, 255.

far. After a short walk from the schoolhouse across one of their fields, he found Black at the Spangler barn. "At the 11th Corps hospital I found Adj. Black wounded through the breast, mortally Dr. [Assistant Surgeon John S. Whildin of the 145th Pennsylvania] thought. He looked very feeble, said little and that in a voice scarcely audible. He thought himself that he could scarcely live till morning," continued the chaplain, "said he suffered greatly, was willing & ready to die & longing for death to relieve him. I asked him whether he had any words for his parents? 'Tell them,' he replied, 'that I fell in a noble cause. I have been a bad boy,' he said, 'but God is merciful.' He was calm & seemed perfectly resigned to his fate. Some effects about his person & his sword he requested me to send home to his parents."[19]

Black surprised himself, his doctors, and his parents by surviving his Gettysburg wound. He returned to action and was wounded in the chest once again during the early stage of the Petersburg fighting in June 1864, was promoted to brevet major in 1865, and died at age 82 in 1923.

Captain John W. Reynolds, who had assumed command of the 145th Pennsylvania when Colonel Brown went down, was also at this hospital, "wounded on the left side of the head," recalled Chaplain Stuckenberg. "He was much excited–elated because our regt. had done so well & had driven the rebels before them. I found many more here of the wounded of our regt. As many as could easily be moved I directed to be taken to our corps hospital, others were made as comfortable as possible." Reynolds was later promoted to major, survived the war, and like Black lived a long life before dying in 1925.[20]

Chaplain Stuckenberg spent much of the long night searching for his regiment's wounded. He returned to the Granite Schoolhouse hospital early on July 3, first to get a little sleep, and then to care for the wounded once more. "I found the doctors and [nurses] busily engaged with the wounded, scattered around in all directions, some lying on blankets, some on straw, a few on stretchers, others on the bare ground," explained the exhausted chaplain. "[Pvt.] E[rastus] Allen of Co G, shot through [the] abdomen suffered terribly. Some of the intestines protruded through the wound and some of their contents would occasionally flow out, producing a horrible stench. Adj Black was much easier and looked much better. The Col [Brown] was walking about, doing well, he started for Baltimore this day. It was very evident that our regiment had again suffered severely, though

19 Stuckenberg, diary, GNMP Library.

20 Ibid.

the extent of our loss was not yet known–many of our wounded men being still missing."[21]

Artillery fire on the right side of the Union army opened at about 4:00 a.m. that July 3 on Powers Hill, almost directly above the Granite Schoolhouse hospital. Slocum's XII Corps was launching a spoiling attack against Culp's Hill to regain control of the entrenchments lost the previous evening to Maj. Gen. Edward Johnson's Confederate division. Chaplain Stuckenberg climbed Powers Hill and watched General Slocum "in person directing the fire" in the dawn artillery bombardment. The attack caught the Confederates off guard and triggered a lengthy action that ended at 11:00 a.m. with complete Union control of the hill.[22]

Just like the XI Corps hospital in and around the Spangler house and barn, the II Corps' First Division hospital at the schoolhouse didn't have everything it needed to handle the flood of wounded and dying. There was a shortage of tents, blankets, food, cooking utensils, medical supplies, and shovels for digging latrines and graves. Most of the wounded would have to rest in the open before and after treatment.

"Our cooking department was early extemporised, we having to rely almost entirely for cooking utensils on the Farmers in the immediate vicinity [including the Spanglers]," explained II Corps surgeon-in-charge Dwinelle. "It was impossible to obtain rations from the Commissary Department, but by taking possession of the contents of a number of unclaimed haversacks and an ox in an adjoining field with some beef stock furnished from the ambulances and small lots of provisions from several other sources, we were able to provide Tea & Coffee and Beef soup for all the wounded as fast as they arrived." Dr. Potter also commented on the logistical situation. "It appears that General Meade had given strict orders that no wagons should go to the front," he wrote. "Thus it came about that during the greatest battle of the war—certainly a pivotal battle—the wounded were subjected to

21 Hedrick and Davis, Jr., *I'm Surrounded by Methodists*, 79.

22 Ibid., 80. Chaplain Stuckenberg was discharged in October 1863 and returned to his church in Erie for a short time. Over the following decades he taught college, traveled to Germany, studied, lectured, and authored books, and eventually settled in Cambridge, MA. He died in London in 1903 at age 68. Stuckenberg left a collection of papers to Pennsylvania College in Gettysburg (the John Henry Wilbrand Stuckenberg Papers). He also donated thousands of dollars, his personal library of 2,500 volumes, and two historic desks to the college. Stuckenberg's wife, Mary Gingrich, settled in Gettysburg after her husband's death and became a leader at the college. Both are buried in Soldiers' National Cemetery in Gettysburg (39°49'17"N 77°13'55"W).

Lt. Charles Fuller

US Army Heritage and Education Center

greater privations in many respects, than when we were fighting on the soil, which, by common consent, was designated the enemy's country."[23]

Lieutenant Charles Fuller, 21, of the 61st New York, part of Colonel Cross' brigade, was wounded in the shoulder and left leg during the heavy seesaw action in the Wheatfield on July 2. Although seriously wounded, the officer left an outstanding description of his journey to the Granite Schoolhouse, the situation there, and his medical treatment that deserves to be reproduced here at length. "When the ambulance started it went anywhere but a good road," he observed. "As it bumped over logs and boulders, my broken leg would thresh about like a mauler of a flail. I found it necessary to keep it in place by putting the other one over it. At last we stopped and were unloaded." Doctors at the schoolhouse were so overwhelmed that Lieutenant Fuller had to wait until the next day to be examined. "In due time light broke in the East [on July 3]," he continued,

> and a little later I could roll my head and take in some of the surroundings. Most of the wounded of the regiment had been gathered at this place, and we made by far the largest part of it. . . . After a time two of our regimental doctors appeared. They cut open my trousers leg, found where the bullet went in, and they did the same with the shoulder. It was clear to my mind that the leg, at least, must come off. I expressed my opinion and said, I thought it would be better to do it at once, than to wait till inflammation set in. At my earnest request they promised me that they would see to it that I should be among the first operated on. . . .

23 "Report of Surgeon Justin Dwinelle," GNMP Library; Potter, "Field Hospital Service with the Army of the Potomac," 16.

After a time the division operating table was set up in the edge of a piece of timber not very far away. I was on the watch, expecting every minute to be taken out, but I waited and waited and no one came for me. I became quite impatient at this delay. I saw one after another brought on, carried up, and taken away, and I was not called for. This aroused my stock of impatience, of which, I naturally always had quite enough. At last I asked my friend Porter E. Whitney and another man to take me down to the table. I made up my mind, if the mountain did not go to Mahomet, the next best thing was for the prophet to go to the mountain.

The men set me down as nearly under the noses of the doctors as could be, and, if something hadn't happened, I presume in a few minutes that heretofore good left leg would have made one of the fast growing pile; but about that interesting moment for me, the enemy began to drop shells that exploded in and about the locality. It was not a fit place to pursue surgical operations. The doctors knew it, so they hastily gathered up their knives and saws, and moved to a place where the projectiles did not drop [near McAllister's Mill on the Baltimore Pike]. The two friends who had taken me there, picked up my stretcher and started for a like place. We had to move several times before the greatest artillery duel of the War began.[24]

Fuller was moved at 10:00 p.m. July 3 to the newly established II Corps First Division hospital at the Jacob Schwartz farm on Rock Creek. His leg was amputated upon arrival. He remained in Gettysburg a couple of weeks before being shipped home via train to Unadilla, New York. There, a local doctor operated on his shoulder and found and removed a bullet in his remaining leg that was missed by the doctors at Gettysburg. He was discharged in December 1863 and lived to age 75.[25]

All three II Corps hospitals—especially the Second and Third divisions at farms on the Taneytown Road—were too close to the Union front line. The Second and Third divisions were at most but a quarter-mile from the line, and the First Division no more than half a mile. The First Division facility was also troubled by Confederate artillery rounds during the morning of July 3. And, just as with the XI Corps facility, at about 1:00 p.m. on July 3 the Confederate overshots

24 Charles A. Fuller, *Personal Recollections of the War of 1861* (Sherburne, NY, 1906), 98-100.

25 The Jacob Schwartz farm on Rock Creek was across modern-day US Route 15 near The Outlet Shoppes.

during the cannonade leading up to Pickett's Charge showered the hospital. Surgeon Dwinelle: "We have almost invariably had occasion to regret having established our Hospitals too near to the line of battle. They should be located two or two and a half miles from the expected Battlefield."[26]

All three II Corps hospitals put plans in motion to load the wounded that could be moved onto wagons, with First Division medical director Dr. R. C. Stiles leading the effort at the schoolhouse on July 3. Those whose lives would be endangered by a wagon ride or who were already near death were to be left at the school. The plan went quickly awry when hordes of men and animals rushed down the road trying to escape the cannonade and fighting on Cemetery Ridge.

"To add to our other difficulties," explained a frustrated Dr. Dwinelle, "for a while we were seriously threatened to be run down by a stampede of pack mules, saddle horses, Army wagons, prisoners & stragglers. It required great exertions to render this stampede less dangerous to the helpless wounded than the shells of the evening." Thankfully, continued Dwinelle, ". . . nearly all of the three divisions [had been moved to safety] by night."[27]

Lieutenant George A. Woodruff, the commander of Battery I, 1st US Artillery, II Corps Artillery Brigade, spent his last hours at the Granite Schoolhouse. The 23-year-old native of Michigan and graduate of West Point led his battery on July 3 at Ziegler's Grove during Pickett's Charge. He was a capable and caring leader, and his men fondly referred to him as "Little Dad." Woodruff was "perfectly cool . . . and seemed to inspire his men," wrote Col. Francis E. Pierce of the nearby 108th New York after watching Woodruff direct his gunners during the pre-Pickett's Charge bombardment.[28]

After the war, Lt. Tully McCrea of the same battery wrote about how his beloved commander met his fate. "He was mortally wounded with a musket ball through his back as he faced and directed his men near the time the Confederates were being forced to retreat from Cemetery Ridge," remembered McCrea. "Woodruff had been wounded and disabled and the men had placed him behind a tree to protect him from being further wounded. It was a sad sight for us to see his life coming to this untimely end, for we knew it was the end from the nature of the

---

26 "Report of Surgeon Justin Dwinelle," GNMP Library.

27 Ibid.

28 Francis E. Pierce, in "The History of the First Regiment of Artillery From its Organization in 1821, to January 1st, 1876," compiled by William L. Haskin (Portland, ME, 1879), 170, Folder 6-US1-ART-I, First US Artillery, Battery I, GNMP Library.

wound. We removed him to the little stone school-house in rear of the line of battle," he continued, "where he remained until he died the next day. Everything was done that could be done with our limited means to make him as comfortable as possible. He died on July fourth, was buried behind the school-house, and his grave so marked that it could be identified. His suffering, from the nature of the wound, must have been great," concluded McCrea, "but not a murmur or groan escaped him. His nerve and courage continued to the end." Before he died, Woodruff told his friends that he regretted that he happened to be shot in the back, asking "that it should be no reflection upon his reputation."[29]

It makes sense that Woodruff was taken to Granite Schoolhouse because his battery was part of the II Corps. As Dr. Dwinelle noted, this hospital was mostly disbanded on July 3, but Woodruff could have been taken there and left overnight because of his dire condition and how much anguish a bumpy wagon ride to a new hospital would have caused him. Burial maps do not show any graves at Granite Schoolhouse, but if Woodruff was buried there, an out-of-the-way grave or graves could have been easily missed on a battlefield littered with them.

Judge George Woodruff traveled to Gettysburg to retrieve his son's body and rebury him at Oakridge Cemetery in Marshall, Michigan. The judge would lose another son a year later when Lt. William S. Woodruff of the First Michigan was mortally wounded in June 1864 at Petersburg. William is buried in Arlington National Cemetery in Virginia.[30]

This little schoolhouse tucked away in the woods received one final important guest after Pickett's Charge and the end of the battle: Maj. Gen. Winfield Scott Hancock. The highly respected commander of the II Corps who had done so much to help win the battle was severely wounded near the end of the charge when a bullet struck the pommel of his saddle and penetrated his inner right thigh, together with small fragments of wood and a bent nail. The stunned officer was assisted off his mount by a pair of aides and someone applied a tourniquet to help stem the blood flow. Hancock examined the wound and withdrew the nail himself. "They [the Confederates] must be hard up for ammunition when they throw such shot as that," he said, not fully realizing the manner in which he had been wounded.

---

29 Bachelder, 1875, "Notes on the Services of Troops at the Battle of Gettysburg," in the John P. Nicholson Collection, Huntington Library (San Marino, CA); Tully McCrea, "Reminiscences About Gettysburg," March 30, 1904, Folder 6-US1-ART-I, First US Artillery, Battery I, GNMP Library.

30 http://arlingtoncemetery.net/wtwoodruff.htm. Accessed January 20, 2019.

Hancock insisted that he remain on the battlefield until the Confederates had retreated and any necessary orders had been issued.

When he was satisfied that the threat had fully passed, Hancock granted permission to be placed in an ambulance. The wagon stopped at Granite Schoolhouse, possibly for further examination of Hancock, but more likely so he could pen what he considered important communications. The wounded II Corps commander was hauled to the II Corps hospitals being set up well behind the lines and departed the next day for a larger and better equipped hospital in Philadelphia. He continued in command of his II Corps into November 1864, when he left active field service. Hancock's wound bothered him for the rest of his life.[31]

Even though the XI Corps hospital and First Division II Corps hospital shared Spangler land, the former was a fraction of a mile farther back from the firing from the west, which might have been just enough to make a difference in direct hits. So while the Spangler field west of their barn was being pounded by artillery fire on the afternoon of July 3, other hospitals were being moved, and Granite Schoolhouse Lane was flooded with those trying to get out of harm's way, the XI Corps hospital stayed put. It then became the closest to the front line of any of the seven Army of the Potomac's infantry division/corps hospitals.

The First Division, II Corps, lost 187 killed, 880 wounded, and 208 missing or captured for 1,275 casualties at Gettysburg, almost entirely on Day 2. Most of the division's wounded on July 2—including a brigadier general, two colonels, and at least two lieutenants—were treated at the little schoolhouse on that little lane on George and Elizabeth Spangler property across the field from the larger XI Corps hospital.[32]

Today, the National Park Service owns the historic patch of land upon which the II Corps division hospital once sat. The southeast corner of what little is left of the school's foundation is about 24 feet from the road and across Granite Schoolhouse Lane from the monument to Batteries B and L, 2nd US Artillery,

---

31 Glenn Tucker, *Hancock the Superb* (Bobbs-Merrill Company, NY, 1960), 155-156. A monument where the George Spangler farm lane meets Blacksmith Shop Road honors Hancock and his good friend Confederate Brig. Gen. Lewis A. Armistead, who was mortally wounded during Pickett's Charge about the same time Hancock suffered his upper thigh wound. Armistead was taken down this lane to the Spangler farm for medical attention. This monument recognizes their friendship and their proximity on Spangler-owned property after the battle ended. See Chapter 13 for more information on Armistead and his medical treatment and death.

32 OR 27, pt. 1, 112; Caldwell's First Division, II Corps monument at Gettysburg. *Union Casualties at Gettysburg* lists 1,310 First Division casualties.

though a few feet to the west. The foundation, roughly 26 by 30 feet of mostly flat rocks, can be seen with some effort in the winter, though it is getting more difficult with every passing year as the stones become more overgrown with thorns, poison ivy, and underbrush.

The modern Gettysburg area is dotted with signs for division hospitals, but no sign or marker exists denoting the site of the major II Corps First Division hospital at the Granite Schoolhouse. Nor is there a place to park and walk in to honor this sacred ground.

Spangler Farm Short Story

The one-room Granite Schoolhouse opened for the 1862-63 school year after the Spanglers provided the land for it. It was placed on 25 perches, or less than one-fifth of an acre. Adams County, Cumberland Township, and the National Park Service are unsure when, exactly, Granite Schoolhouse Lane opened. The Weikert family had advertised many physical features of the area when it sold 65 acres north of the current lane to the Spanglers in 1861, but there was no mention of a road in the advertisement or in any after-sale records. There could have been a path there as early as 1800 that was improved into a lane through the heart of the Spangler land after their purchase and at about the time of the school's opening to make it easier for children to get to and from the school.

George Spangler was president of the Cumberland Township School Board at the time, so it's not surprising that he gave up part of his property for children and education. The fact that the lane was there at all was a surprise to some in the Army of the Potomac because many in the higher echelons of command were utilizing an 1858 Adams County map during the Gettysburg operation. In a letter to historian John Bachelder in 1864, Brig. Gen. Alpheus Williams of Slocum's XII Corps described his confusion about the lane that he had used to rush troops from Culp's Hill southwest to Cemetery Ridge on July 2. "I do not find any road in the maps, but there certainly is one or was made perhaps by our wagons and artillery. My impressions are that it was a regular formed road. At any rate," continued Williams, "I followed this road and path until I struck the Taneytown Road." The land was upgraded to an actual road during the mid-1880s.

Granite Schoolhouse was condemned and closed by the Pennsylvania Department of Health in 1920 because it did not meet sanitary requirements. George Rosensteel purchased the school and its contents for $109.26 in 1921 and demolished the old building. A bit of the school, however, lived on for decades when Rosensteel used a large flat stone from it in the Gettysburg National Museum that he opened on the Taneytown Road in 1921. That museum became the National Park Service visitor center in 1971, which was torn down and replaced in 2008.

The Rosensteels kept their Granite Schoolhouse stone.[33]

33 Alpheus Williams to Bachelder, April 21, 1864, in *The Bachelder Papers*, vol. 1, 163; *The Gettysburg Times*, June 17, 1920, and August 27, 1921.

Chapter 12

Danger from Every Direction:
Day Three at the XI Corps Hospital

"If a sadder task can be found on this earth than that of searching through
field hospitals after a great battle, I know not what it is."

— *Capt. James F. Huntington, Third Volunteer Brigade, Artillery Reserve*

The last day of fighting at Gettysburg began before dawn on July
3, 1863, and it opened on the George Spangler farm. A little
after 4:00 a.m., artillery units on Nathaniel Lightner property and the northeast
corner of the Spangler property on Powers Hill opened on Edward Johnson's
Confederate division hugging Culp's Hill. Most of Slocum's XII Corps had been
hurried off the eminence late the previous afternoon and rushed across Spangler
land to help save the collapsing Union left flank. Determined enemy attacks seized
some entrenchments on the high rocky wooded terrain, a lodgment that threatened
the army's key logistical line along the Baltimore Pike. It was imperative to put the
high ground back under Union control, and the dawn spoiling attack, followed by
infantry fighting, was designed to achieve just that by taking the initiative away
from the enemy.

The booming artillery was heard and felt by most of the occupants of the
Spangler farm, so everyone there but the heavily drugged or the unconscious were
shocked awake to witness the sunrise. The shattering lethal rumbling so early in the
morning was especially unnerving, for it portended yet another day of heavy
bloodshed.

XI Corps commander Howard was resting in Evergreen Cemetery on Cemetery Hill with a tombstone for a pillow when the bombardment opened. "The roaring of the cannon seemed like thunder," he recalled, "and the musketry may be compared to hail striking a flat roof, growing louder as the storm increases, or lessening as it subsides." According to Gettysburg resident Jane Smith, the artillery fire was loud even on the far side of town. "May I never again be roused to the consciousness of a new-born day by such fearful sounds! It seemed almost like the crashing of worlds."[1]

The flow of wounded into and out of the ad hoc medical facility blanketing a large swath of the Spangler farm had slowed before the thunderous artillery fire opened the day. Ambulances delivered the last load of mangled bodies in need of medical care, and their drivers washed the gore from their wagons before collapsing next to them in exhaustion. The medical staff found little rest, for their talents were still sorely needed, and the cries and moans of their patients filled the air of the dark early morning hours in and around the Spangler barn.

Artillery units up and down the Army of the Potomac's hooked-shaped front were nearly finished resupplying their limbers from the ammunition train parked on the Spangler field along Granite Schoolhouse Lane. The arduous task had consumed much of the night, for many batteries had fired all of their ammunition during the intense combat of July 2. The chaotic flow of men, wagons, horses, and equipment on and off the farm was finally petering out. And then the artillery opened.

The Confederates responded to the XII Corps guns with artillery fire of their own. Their overshots landed directly on the Spangler farm, putting everyone and everything there in danger. The 2nd Connecticut Light Battery scrambled to reach Cemetery Ridge in the early light. The battery was hustling to leave the Spangler field when debris from a nearby exploding shell struck Pvt. Eldridge B. Platt, forcing him to the hospital and out of the July 3 fight. "I tell you that was a hot place for a few minutes," recalled Platt, "hotter than it was in the front but I tell you we did not stay there long."[2]

The Confederates would spend hours trying to solidify their uneasy hold on the slopes of Culp's Hill to no avail until the fighting ended about 11:00 a.m. The

---

1 Howard, *Autobiography of Oliver Otis Howard*, 433; Jane Smith, diary, published July 2, 1913, in the *Gettysburg Star and Sentinel*, GNMP Library, File V-8, Civilian Accounts Crawford.

2 Platt to his parents, July 11, 1863, in Eldridge B. Platt Papers, 1862-1866.

XII Corps got its entrenchments back, and the Baltimore Pike lifeline and Meade's right flank were once again safe.[3]

Several Artillery Reserve batteries had returned from their July 2 work to spend the night at their base on Spangler property, including the entire First Volunteer Brigade of the 5th Massachusetts Battery E (10th New York attached), 9th Massachusetts Light, 15th New York Light, and Pennsylvania Batteries C and F. The guns had been in the middle of the heaviest fighting at the Peach Orchard and on the Trostle farm and had suffered accordingly. Lieutenant Colonel Freeman McGilvery, who had calmly and bravely directed those units under intense fire and thus helped plug gaping holes in the collapsing front, found what was left of his units during the night at the Spangler farm.[4]

At daylight, with the pounding of Culp's Hill underway, most of the First Volunteer Brigade was up and sent immediately to Cemetery Ridge. Any Artillery Reserve unit not sent from Spangler then would be in place by the time of Pickett's Charge.

Lieutenant Gulian V. Weir, 5th US, Battery C, spent the night on Spangler property after losing three guns to the Confederates during a retreat from the Codori farm the previous day. The captured cannons, much to Weir's delight, were retaken by infantry from the 13th Vermont and 19th Maine and returned during the night to Weir, who set eyes on them once more when he awoke on the 3rd. (Captain John Lonergan of the 13th Vermont was awarded a Medal of Honor for his gallantry in recapturing those guns and for capturing two Confederate pieces and taking enemy prisoners.) Weir's battery remained on the Spangler farm until early that afternoon, when it rolled into action and performed well by helping repulse Confederate infantry near the Copse of Trees at the height of Pickett's Charge. Many other Artillery Reserve batteries, however, had spent an uneasy night along the front line on Cemetery Hill, Cemetery Ridge, and Powers Hill.

Sergeant Luther B. Mesnard, a member of Company D, 55th Ohio (Orland Smith's brigade) found his way to the XI Corps hospital sometime that morning. The 25-year-old had been shot in the arm the previous day on Cemetery Hill and was initially treated at another hospital. Thankfully for him, the wound was not

---

3 The Army of the Potomac's cannons that took part in this early-morning bombardment stretched from Powers Hill to today's Hunt Avenue next to the Gettysburg National Military Park Museum & Visitor Center. For an outstanding study of the Culp's Hill fighting throughout the battle, see Harry Pfanz, *Gettysburg: Culp's Hill and Cemetery Hill* (Chapel Hill, 1993).

4 OR 27, pt. 1883.

life-threatening. By the time he arrived, the Spangler hospital was in full motion. "I found some thirty or fourty boys from our regiment, and thousands from the corps," he recalled before continuing:

> I spent several hours helping comrades and watching the surgeons at the operating tables. . . . I had started after several canteens full of fresh water, as I noticed a bright boy some 18 years of age standing near one of the tables. One Doctor was looking at his bandaged head, another at his bloody pants leg as the boy's 'Oh the trouble is here,' pointing to his right arm hanging limp at his side. 'I hope you won't have to take it off.' As he took his place on the table, I started on after the water. When I came back with the water he was just coming to, from chloroform. He soon turned and sat on the edge of the table looking around in a dazed sort of a way and rose to his feet and looked at the stump of his arm, and such a look! It seemed to move his very soul.[5]

Some time later, Sergeant Mesnard recalled watching Artillery Reserve batteries bump and roll their way off the farm in a hurry. The curious Buckeye followed the guns and came upon a stunning view. "Our line looked very strong, in the fastness of the rocks and stone walls, the artillery massed on every hill top," he wrote in a letter long after the war describing the situation on Cemetery Ridge. Soon thereafter, "[T]he storm broke forth [and] cannon shook the earth and filled the air with death. I felt that the fate of our country was at stake. Soon orders came for all that could walk to go to the rear as the shells came screeching through the air." The Ohioan was witnessing the beginning of the grand cannonade preceding Pickett's Charge.[6]

On the far side of the field, General Lee had concluded that a powerful attack against what was roughly the center of the Army of the Potomac's front on Cemetery Ridge would break open the line and drive away Meade's army in defeat. Lee had attacked both ends of Meade's line with some success and now it was time to crack the center. Lee organized between 150 to 170 artillery pieces, arrayed in a large crescent, to soften the Union position, demoralize the defenders, and drive away or silence the enemy guns. Once the artillery had done its work, three infantry

---

5 Luther B. Mesnard to his son, Howard, May 6, 1901, in *Reminiscences of the Civil War*, CW/VFM-144, Civil War Vertical File Manuscripts, Special Collections & College Archives, Musselman Library, Gettysburg College.

6 Ibid.

divisions, together with two brigades on their right, would step off Seminary Ridge, tramp across the roughly mile-wide open plain, move up the slope, and carry Cemetery Ridge.[7]

The firing of two Southern guns near the Sherfy house served as the signal for the opening of the cannonade. Within a few moments the Confederate barrage sparked its way along the nearly two-mile line of guns stretching from the Peach Orchard in the south northward roughly parallel to the Emmitsburg Road. General Hunt was setting up Union artillery on the far left of the Union line when the barrage started. Almost immediately he rode to the Artillery Reserve on the Spangler farm and ordered the batteries still there to move to the front once the cannonade ceased. Hunt suspected that infantry would follow on the heels of the bombardment and he wanted his batteries in place to decimate the assault. Later, when Capt. James F. Huntington of the Third Volunteer Brigade rode from Cemetery Hill southeast to the Spangler farm in search of more help, he was informed that every battery was actively engaged and unavailable.[8]

The Confederate artillery barrage was hampered from the start by a combination of ineffectual leadership, defective fuses and equipment, overshots, and a lack of concentrated fire. Still, the flying shells proved lethal and destructive along certain points of the line. A burst of rounds struck the XI Corps position on Cemetery Hill and south along the face of Cemetery Ridge. "In one of my regiments twenty-seven fell at a single shot," reported General Howard, the XI Corps commander. General Schurz, one of Howard's division commanders, was on Cemetery Hill when the guns opened. "The roar was so incessant and at times so deafening," he recalled, "that when I wished to give an order to one of my officers, I had to put my hands to my mouth as a speaking trumpet and shout my words into his ear."[9]

The heat and humidity from the 87-degree day held much of the gun smoke low over the battlefield, which made it difficult and in some cases impossible for the Confederate gunners to figure out how to reposition their pieces after each gun finished its recoil. As a result, many of their shots were flying well over the Union

---

7 For the most detailed and up-to-date study of Pickett's Charge (or Longstreet's Assault), see James A. Hessler and Wayne Motts, *Pickett's Charge at Gettysburg: A Guide to the Most Famous Attack in American History* (Savas Beatie, 2015).

8 Henry Hunt to Bachelder, January 20, 1873, *The Bachelder Papers*, vol. 1, 430; James Freeman Huntington, "Notes of Service With a Light Artillery at Chancellorsville and Gettysburg," in *Marietta Sunday Observer*, August 1918, Ohio Historical Society.

9 Howard, *Autobiography of Oliver Otis Howard*, 436; Schurz, *The Reminiscences of Carl Schurz*, 28.

line and landing on George Spangler's and other properties, causing death, destruction, and fear far behind the front.

"A mule in one of the teams was struck by a solid shot and killed," reported Lt. Cornelius Gillett, commander of the Artillery Reserve ammunition train parked on Spangler property. "[M]any of the animals became so unmanageable that there was danger of a stampede." Teamsters and others took off on a stampede of their own from the Spangler property, prompting fear among the wounded in the orchard and fields "that they would be trampled to death," believed Pvt. Edson Ames of the 154th New York.[10]

When the Confederate bombardment started, Cpt. Andrew Cowan's 1st New York Battery of Sedgwick's VI Corps was in reserve first on Granite Schoolhouse Lane and then in an opening in the West Spangler Woods just behind William Patterson's property off the Taneytown Road. "There was a fine grove of large trees at our backs affording us welcome shade, for it was very hot," Cowan recalled decades later. "[The] air was immediately full of screeching shot and bursting shell. Their aim was far too high, so that the limbs of the trees far over our heads suffered most. Many of my men, however, scattered like partridges at the first burst and the deluge of limbs falling from the tree tops."[11]

Cowan's battery was called to the front and placed just south of the Copse of Trees, where it unlimbered and fired double canister as the Confederate infantry closed within killing distance and climbed the wall. The First New York Battery suffered four men killed, eight wounded, and 14 horses lost during that short but brutal contest.[12]

Surgeon-in-Chief Dr. Daniel G. Brinton of the Second Division, XI Corps, reported that the Spangler barn held about 500 wounded men when the cannonade began, which meant they were squeezed in almost shoulder-to-shoulder. Now the wounded men were under fire yet again, unable to escape or fight back. "On the afternoon of the 3rd we were exposed to a sharp fire of shells," explained Dr. Brinton. "Several horses & one man were killed close to the hospital. Shells fell within 20 ft of the room where we were, and we were much in fear that the barn would blaze, which would have been an unspeakably frightful casualty. Fortunately

10 Gillett, Official Report, August 23, 1863, in *OR* 27, pt. 1, 879; Northrup interview of Edson Ames, September 4, 1890, in Edwin Dwight Northrup Papers, Box 35, Carl A. Kroch Library, Cornell University.

11 Andrew Cowan, "When Cowan's Battery Withstood Pickett's Charge," in *New York Herald*, July 2, 1911.

12 Battlefield monument; *OR* 27, pt. 1, 183.

we did not have this to record. . . . That day was the most terrific fighting ever known in this war."[13]

The threshing floor in the Spangler barn is at the top of the ramp at the back of the barn. The floor had a partition in the middle so the Spanglers could thresh their wheat on either or both floors. Wounded men were placed with their head against the middle partition and feet on each side facing out toward each end of the barn. One of the soldiers lying there was 17-year-old Pvt. Stephen C. Romig of Company F, 153rd Pennsylvania. The lad had been struck by a ball in the left knee on East Cemetery Hill on the evening of July 1.

"I was laid on the threshing floor of the barn used for a hospital, and laid down near the big door. There I had a fine view of the bursting shells coming in our direction," Romig explained. "There were at one time six explosions of shells in one moment. It was a grand sight indeed, but the danger was becoming so great that every man was removed excepting myself and an old German, who expressed himself in something like the words 'Och du lieber Gud was gebds nuch.' (Very loosely translated: 'Oh, dear God, what else?') The surgeon who had been in shortly before looking at my wound ran for his life, his coat tail standing straight out. As he passed the door he called out to me, 'Get out of there as soon as you can,' the same time knowing that I could not move. He soon sent two men to carry me away, which they did."[14]

General Meade was behind the Union line at his headquarters at the Leister house on the Taneytown Road—ground zero for the Confederate overshots. The iron rounds pummeled his headquarters, horses, and men including Chief of Staff Daniel Butterfield, who was wounded. In a move he clearly was not pleased about having to make, Meade and his staff hustled down Granite Schoolhouse Lane and eventually joined General Slocum on Spangler and Lightner property at Powers Hill. There, with a signal station in operation on top, Meade could see, communicate, and command from a safer distance.

Union men, meanwhile, hustled down Granite Schoolhouse Lane to escape the flying shells. What they might not have considered is that troops were in the rear policing the area, including the 4th New Jersey Infantry on Spangler property at the intersection of Blacksmith Shop Road and Granite Schoolhouse Lane guarding the ammunition train and serving as provost guards. Also in the Spangler

---

13 Brinton, "From Chancellorsville to Gettysburg, a Doctor's Diary," 313; Brinton letter to his mother, July 9, 1863, in Dr. Daniel Garrison Brinton Papers.

14 Kiefer, *History of the One Hundred and Fifty-Third Regiment*, 185-186.

The 4th New Jersey Infantry marker rests at the intersection of Blacksmith Shop Road and Granite Schoolhouse Lane, where the infantry guarded the ammunition train on Spangler land. The buildings in the background no longer stand. *Ron Kirkwood*

neighborhood working crowd control was the XI Corps' 157th New York, which had moved there from Cemetery Hill after the morning bombardment ended on Culp's Hill. Brigadier General Thomas Neill's VI Corps brigade was on Powers Hill a day earlier, but the entire command except the 77th New York had been moved across Rock Creek to prevent the Confederates from circling behind Culp's Hill and attacking beyond the Union right flank.[15]

Once the cannonade began, "Fugitives from the field began to rush toward the rear upon the road upon which I was stationed," reported Maj. Charles Ewing of the 4th New Jersey in a calm and clinical manner. "I immediately deployed across

15 William Saxton, diary, in *A Regiment Remembered: The 157th New York Volunteers*, 1996, Cortland County Historical Society, 83.

the road and into the woods on my right flank with fixed bayonets, where I stopped and reorganized between 400 and 500 men, whom I turned over to [Provost Marshal General Marsena] Patrick. As soon as the panic subsided, I resumed my former duty with the ammunition train, which was not again interrupted during the battle." General Patrick happened to be on George Spangler property at that time picking up stragglers, collecting and guarding Confederate prisoners, and overseeing important provost duties. "I had my hands full with those that broke to the rear," observed Patrick after monitoring Granite Schoolhouse Lane, "but we succeeded in checking the disorder & organized a guard of Stragglers to keep nearly 2000 Prisoners all safe."[16]

As he had been doing since the first day of the battle, surgeon Henry Van Aernam of the 154th New York was performing an amputation outside the Spangler barn when the Confederate cannons opened. He stopped his work as shells exploded near the building. "Boys, we may as well suspend," he said with obvious reluctance. "The decisive moment has come." Van Aernam and other medical staff took refuge along the back wall of the barn in and next to the underground root cellar. "All nearly skedaddled," observed Pvt. Emory Sweetland of the 154th New York.[17]

Private John Wheeler of the same 154th regiment was working as a cook at the XI Corps hospital when he vanished during the barrage and did not show up again until that evening. When he returned, Dr. Van Aernam asked where he had been. When Wheeler replied that he was taking a nap in the bushes, Van Aernam scoffed, retorting that if he could sleep during the last three hours, he would be able to sleep in the Day of Judgment "when Gabriel blew his trumpet & said that Heaven & Earth had come together with great noise." The chastised but apparently not embarrassed Wheeler replied, "Say Dr! There is one man in the town of Humphrey that if he should be killed, no one could fill his place & that is myself, & as long as my name is John Wheeler I intend to have my legs take care of my body." Wheeler had pulled a similar two-hour vanishing act two months earlier at Chancellorsville. On that occasion, he claimed to have been "down to the river to get a wash," an

16 OR 27, pt. 1, 902; David S. Sparks, ed., *Inside Lincoln's Army: The Diary of Marsena Rudolph Patrick, Provost Marshal General, Army of the Potomac* (New York, NY, 1964), 267.

17 Emory Sweetland to Northrup, February 18, 1891, in Edwin Dwight Northrup Papers, Box 35, Carl A. Kroch Library, Cornell University.

excuse that drew much laughter from his comrades. "You may laugh & stay there & be shot," Wheeler spat back, "but I'm going to look out for John Wheeler."[18]

An eerie silence fell over the battlefield once the scores of artillery tubes stopped firing. A short time later, artillery fire broke out anew, clearly audible to those occupying Spangler land. An interval after that, the firing of thousands of rifles reached their ears. What none of them knew was that the thousands of Confederate infantry approaching Cemetery Ridge—more popularly known as Pickett's Charge—would be one of the most famous military assaults in history.

According to Private Sweetland, the elevation of the Spangler property provided him with "a plain view" of the massive infantry attack once the Confederates reached the Union line on Cemetery Ridge. "Two or three lines of Union troops were formed at the hospital to receive the charge if the Rebs should break through & come on," he recalled, adding that cannons were placed in position at the barn. Unlike today, the Spangler back fields were cleared of trees, so Sweetland could indeed have witnessed Pickett's Charge from a rise in those fields or from the top level of the barn.[19]

Private William J. March of Company D, Col. Francis V. Randall's 13th Vermont (Brig. Gen. George Stannard's brigade, John Reynolds' I Corps), offers a good example of the many wounded non-XI Corps soldiers taken to the Spangler farm on the third day of the battle because of the proximity of the hospital to the Union front. Once the cannonade started, all other major hospitals began the process of moving farther from the line.

March was one of perhaps as many as 40,000 men from Canada—not yet a country, but a series of provinces known then as British North America—who crossed the border to fight for one of the armies (mostly Union). Private March was only 18 years old when he fought at Gettysburg. He was working as a carpenter building a church in Colchester, Vermont, when he enlisted with the nine-month 13th Vermont in September 1862. March's widowed mother was home in Quebec, awaiting word on her son and counting the days to when his enlistment would end.

March was only three weeks from being mustered out with the rest of the 13th Vermont when he found himself on the front line on Cemetery Ridge south of the famous Copse of Trees. The brigade would do magnificent work that afternoon when Brig. Gen. James Kemper's Confederate infantry veered north during the final stage of the assault. General Stannard, on his own accord, pushed his large

---

18 Ibid; Wheeler survived the war and mustered out with Company D in June 1865.

19 Ibid.

regiments forward off the line, turned them right, and fired deadly blasts into Kemper's flank and rear. March was not with his comrades for that spectacular tactical event, for he had already been hit in both legs below the knees by a cannon ball. The private made tourniquets as he lay on the field that likely prolonged his life, but the damage had already been done. His comrades carried him to the nearby Spangler farm, where he died soon thereafter.

Writing in the third person years later, Sgt. John Hovey Lyon, a fellow member of the 13th Vermont, recalled talking to March's mother about her son's death. "The writer well remembers, after this long lapse of years, a sad and pathetic interview with this bereaved mother a few weeks after our term expired when she called on him to make inquiry regarding the circumstances of her son's death," recalled Lyon. He continued:

She was told the story as follows: Your son was a good and faithful soldier in the field. He kept well and had been able to cheerfully perform all of the duties of a soldier. He marched to Gettysburg with the regiment and during the terrific battle remained at his post until carried off wounded. In the afternoon of the third during the great artillery duel—now celebrated in history—he was wounded in both legs below the knees by cannon shot. He unaided placed tourniquets above the wounds and was carried off the field to a large barn used for a hospital. There he died in an hour. The next morning after the close of the battle, Orderly Sergeant Marrs E. J. Tyler, J. B. Beauchemin (the latter one of those who carried him off the field) and the writer procured spades and a blanket and went to the hospital to bury him, when we arrived were told that he had been buried that morning with other dead.

March was exhumed from his Spangler grave within the following months and reburied in Soldiers' National Cemetery. The mortally wounded private arrived at the hospital with $20.00, and a surgeon recorded his mother's address and promised to send it to her. It never arrived.[20]

Staff officer Cpt. Frederick Stowe was on Cemetery Hill when he was hit on the right side of the head by a Confederate shell fragment. The wounded officer

20 Ralph Orson Sturtevant and Carmi Lathrop Marsh, *History of the 13th Vermont Regiment Volunteers* (privately published, 1910), 538. Lyon's remembrance of March is in the chapter about Company D. That chapter was written in March's honor and includes the following inscription: "Dedicated to the loving memory of our brave hero, William March, slain in the Battle of Gettysburg, July 3rd, 1863."

Capt. Frederick Stowe

Harriet Beecher Stowe Center

was the assistant adjutant general to Brig. Gen. Adolph von Steinwehr (Second Division, XI Corps) and the son of Harriet Beecher Stowe, who wrote the bestselling anti-slavery book *Uncle Tom's Cabin.* Stowe's duties included writing and distributing the general's orders, overseeing camps and marching, record keeping, and generally helping any way he could. Stowe, age 23, was rushed to the XI Corps hospital for treatment. As both an officer and the son of a well-known author, his lot would not be in the barn or out in the open. According to Dr. Van Aernam, he was placed in a corner of a "little bed room." Neither of the Spanglers' two upstairs bedrooms were "little," so it is highly likely that he was put in the summer kitchen, a separate building close to the main house used for cooking, canning, and other chores. According to Doctor Brinton in a letter home, Stowe was hit "in the parastoid process of the temporal bone, by a fragment of shell which I extracted on July 3." The doctor added, "Though I left him doing well, I am not without anxiety as to the result."[21]

Stowe's parents waited anxiously for nearly two long weeks before learning of the fate of their son. They had not received word from him after the great battle ended and had no idea whether he was alive, dead, a prisoner, or lying wounded in a hospital. A letter dated July 11, 1863, addressed to Stowe's mother arrived from the XI Corps hospital written by the Rev. J. M. Crowell, a Christian Commission delegate visiting the Spangler hospital from Philadelphia. "Among the thousands of wounded and dying men on this war-scarred field, I have just met with your son,

---

21 Northrup interview of Van Aernam, August 28, 1893, in Edwin Dwight Northrup Papers, Box 35, Carl A. Kroch Library, Cornell University; Brinton, "From Chancellorsville to Gettysburg, a Doctor's Diary," 313; Brinton to his mother, July 9, 1863, in Dr. Daniel Garrison Brinton Papers.

Captain Stowe," confirmed the reverend. "If you have not already heard from him, it may cheer your heart to know that he is in the hands of good, kind friends. He was struck by a fragment of a shell, which entered his right ear. He is quiet and cheerful, longs to see some member of his family, and is, above all, anxious that they should hear from him as soon as possible. I assured him I would write at once," he added, "and though I am wearied by a week's labor here among scenes of terrible suffering, I know that, to a mother's anxious heart, even a hasty scrawl about her boy will be more than welcome."[22]

Captain Stowe left Gettysburg via train in mid-July with other wounded men and was admitted to a military hospital in New York City to complete his long and painful rehabilitation. He survived the wound and the war, but when he returned home he resumed a long-time struggle with his addiction to alcohol. Severe headaches, chronic inflammation, and the loss of hearing in his injured ear only exacerbated this abuse. In 1870, Stowe boarded a ship in Florida and sailed around South America to California. He arrived safely in San Francisco, but to the anguish of his family he disappeared and was never heard from again.[23]

The complete repulse of Pickett's Charge ended the main fighting at Gettysburg. For the time being the armies remained mostly in place, the generals sorting through the chaos to plan their next move. And just as they had during the first two days of the battle, the Spangler fields and roads once again served the Army of the Potomac well.

For a third straight day, wounded and dying men flooded into the hospitals. There simply was not enough medical staff to handle this much trauma. "The wounded came in rapidly so by the next day we had over a thousand to attend to," recalled Dr. Brinton. "Many of them were hurt in the most shocking manner by shells. My experience at Chancellorsville was nothing compared to this & and I never wish to see such another sight."[24]

"If a sadder task can be found on this earth than that of searching through field hospitals after a great battle, I know not what it is," confessed Captain Huntington of the Artillery Reserve years after the war. "In matters of this sort," he continued,

---

22 Charles Edward Stowe and Harriet Beecher Stowe, *Life of Harriet Beecher Stowe: Compiled From Her Letters and Journals* (London, 1889), 372.

23 www.harrietbeecherstowecenter.org/hbs/stowe_family.shtml. Accessed March 23, 2017; Stowe Pension Application No. 69920, National Archives.

24 Brinton to his mother, July 9, 1863, Dr. Daniel Garrison Brinton Papers.

figures convey no adequate idea. One can talk or write glibly enough, about eight or ten thousand wounded men. Who realizes the fearful sum of human sufferings these figures are vainly intended to represent? Those huge Pennsylvania barns covered with the mangled bodies of men thick as they could lie, many among them destined never to see the light of another day, presented a spectacle that time can not efface from the memory of those whom duty called to witness the saddest of mortal sights. . . . We were only able to find a part of our men; these we saw were as well cared for as circumstances admitted. A grassy couch was never more welcome than on that night. The mental and physical strain of such a prolonged conflict is excessive. I do not remember ever feeling more utterly used up in my life, than on the last night of Gettysburg. I went to sleep, thankful that I could. . . .[25]

The time on the Spangler fields for Huntington and his Artillery Reserve had come to an end. The ammunition train pulled out during the cannonade in search of a safer locale along the Baltimore Pike, and the reserve batteries that had taken up positions along the line remained there. The Artillery Reserve had performed brilliantly during its two days using the convenient Spangler property as its base, rolling out batteries and restocking ammunition wherever needed. It paid a frightful price for its efficiency by suffering 42 killed, 187 wounded, and 13 missing along with 316 horses killed. "The artillery of the reserve proved all that could be expected or even asked of it," confirmed Maj. Thomas W. Osborn, commander of the XI Corps' Artillery Brigade. "[W]ithout their assistance I do not conceive how I could have maintained the position we held. I feel most thankful for their assistance, and the very willing and cordial manner in which it was rendered."[26]

At the Spangler hospital, meanwhile, an important and newsworthy evening delivery arrived in the form of a wounded Confederate general who fell only after he and some of his men had pierced the Union line atop Cemetery Ridge. Captain Frederick Stowe was about to get a roommate.

---

25 Huntington, "Notes of Service With a Light Artillery at Chancellorsville and Gettysburg."

26 OR 27, pt. 1, 878; Thomas W. Osborn, Official Report dated July 29, 1863, in *The Miscellaneous Documents of the House of Representatives*, 750-751.

Spangler Farm Short Story

The Artillery Reserve and ammunition train horses and mules on the Spangler farm suffered just like the men of both armies. They were hungry, thirsty, and beaten down by long marches and frightening artillery rounds that landed around them. Many suffered from disease and injuries. "The mules stood in harness, without feed or water for three days and two nights of the battle, ready to move at a moment's notice," neighbor Nathaniel Lightner observed of the Spanglers' farm. "The mules and drivers were more like dead than living things." Horses were supposed to receive a daily ration of 14 pounds of hay and 12 pounds of oats or corn, but the wagons carrying their food were banished to Maryland. The Spangler crops and grasses offered a small saving grace for the animals.

The Spangler property was also used to provide a portion of the 15 gallons of water each animal needed each day. Rain was plentiful in the Gettysburg area in June and July 1863, so a stream flowing next to and through the southern and western ends of the Spangler property provided water. There also was a smaller stream that cut between Powers Hill and Granite Schoolhouse in addition to a deep and strong well next to the Spangler summer kitchen and a well somewhere near the school. The larger Rock Creek was a short walk or ride away. Every source of water around Gettysburg, however, soon suffered from overuse and contamination from dead and wounded men and animals and human and animal waste.

With the enormous weight of the cannons and ammunition, each artillery horse pulled an average of 700 pounds. Those physical demands, hunger, disease, and the danger of battle gave artillery horses a life span of just eight months.[27]

Ruch Report No. 3

His Path to Spangler
Pvt. Reuben F. Ruch, Company F, 153rd Pennsylvania Infantry

"I woke up before daylight [on July 3]. The cannonading commenced. . . . As soon as I could see I saw long lines of Rebel infantry moving around Culp's Hill on the Union right. There the battle opened just at the break of day. . . .

"I retired upstairs. . . . After the infantry fighting on the right things were very quiet until . . . a sulphuric tornado of shells broke loose. The Rebels opened the ball

27 "Horrors of Battle," an interview with National Lightner; National Museum of Civil War Medicine.

with a hundred and fifty cannon and the Union replied with nearly one hundred. The brick church was rocking and the windows rattling as though there was an earthquake. . . . I saw lots of men turn pale. . . . The church was not a very safe place, for we did not know what minute some of these shells would come down through the roof . . . but when the end came another grand view came. This was Picketts' charge . . . I had a good view of this. . . .

This was the end of the heavy fighting at Gettysburg. It was not long after this till we received a call from a Rebel doctor and Major requesting all those who could walk to get out and start for Richmond . . . the old doctor pronounced me unable to travel, and they made out a parole for me. . . . The Rebel army left during the night. . . . I was not sorry when they were gone."[28]

---

28 Kiefer, *History of the One Hundred and Fifty-Third Regiment*, 220-222.

Chapter 13

The Death of
Brigadier General Lewis A. Armistead

"Armistead lingered through the 4th and died on the 5th, leaving an example of patriotism, heroism and devotion to duty which ought to be handed down through the ages."

— *Col. Rawley Martin, 53rd Virginia*

officer ordered his men to their feet and aligned his ranks. Lewis A. Armistead's brigade had not reached the battlefield until the evening of July 2, so it missed the heavy fighting during those first two days. Indeed, many of the men worried that they would not see combat at all in Pennsylvania in what they were confident would be another striking Confederate victory. But on the afternoon of July 3, Armistead's Virginians found themselves positioned behind the brigades of Brig. Gens. Richard Garnett and James Kemper, all three comprising a division led by Maj. Gen. George Pickett. The grand cannonade was over and it was now the infantry's turn. Armistead's turn.

At 46, the Confederate general with a wiry frame and thinning gray hair was one of the oldest officers on the field. He would grow no older.

* * *

According to Dr. Henry Van Aernam of the 154th New York, the ambulance carrying Brig. Gen. Lewis Addison Armistead reached the George and Elizabeth Spangler farm at dusk on July 3, 1863. Dusk would have been about 8:00

Brig. Gen. Lewis Armistead

Gettysburg National Military Park

p.m.—more than four hours after he was mortally wounded leading his men in what would become one of the most famous charges in history.[1]

The injured general was removed on a stretcher and placed next to the ambulance near the barn. XI Corps hospital workers Pvt. Emory Sweetland and Pvt. Edson Ames of the 154th New York described Armistead's appearance, respectively, as "pretty bloody" and "covered with blood." According to Sweetland, Armistead announced, "You have a man here that is not afraid to die."[2]

The Spangler hospital was a shoulder-to-shoulder mass of confusion and agony when Armistead arrived. Hundreds of men wounded in the large-scale cannonade and infantry attack that followed were pouring in as understaffed and overwhelmed surgeons desperately sorted through the broken bodies in an attempt to find those who could be saved with immediate attention. The arrival of the Confederate general, however, turned heads. Likely none of the hospital staffers or wounded had any idea of Armistead's historic courage that day, but they were still drawn to him. A large crowd of workers and gawkers formed around the newly arrived officer. The crowd was eventually broken up when Dr. Van Aernam arrived at Armistead's side and ordered that he be carried away.[3]

1 Northrup interview of Van Aernam, August 4, 1890, Edwin Dwight Northrup Papers, Box 35, Carl A. Kroch Library, Cornell University.

2 Northrup interview of Sweetland, September 11, 1893, and interview of Edson Ames, September 4, 1890, Edwin Dwight Northrup Papers, Box 35, Carl A. Kroch Library, Cornell University.

3 Northrup interview of Sweetland, Edwin Dwight Northrup Papers, Box 35, Carl A. Kroch Library, Cornell University.

Doctor Daniel G. Brinton of the XI Corps' Second Division was one of the first surgeons to examine Armistead. The general "was brought to my hospital and myself & Dr. Harvey [Dr. Bleecker Lansing Hovey, 136th New York] late of Rochester N.Y. examined & dressed his wounds. They were two in number, neither of them of a serious character, apparently," he recalled. "The one was in the fleshy part of the arm, the other a little below the knee in the leg of the opposite side. . . . Both were by rifle balls, and no bone, or leading artery or nerve was injured by either. . . . His prospects of recovery seemed good."[4]

Armistead died on the Spangler farm two days later.

* * *

Armistead's extraordinary exertions on July 3, 1863, in the face of artillery and infantry fire became the stuff of legend across the South, and indeed, much of the country. Walking across a mile of open ground under a hot summer sun at his age was no simple task in itself. Armistead crossed that open suicidal field in a heavy uniform with the constant threat of death or dismemberment flying all around him. At some point beyond the Emmitsburg Road he placed his hat on the tip of his sword and, together with perhaps a few score of fellow Virginians, surged up and over the low stone wall and into Union lines. "Follow me, boys!" he cried. "Give them the cold steel!" He reportedly put his hand on one of Lt. Alonzo Cushing's guns of the 4th US Artillery only to be shot down.

For decades after the Civil War, Confederate veterans described the fallen general with words such as "noble" and "gallant." They said his name and described his actions with awe and reverence. "Brave Armistead," they would say. Robert E. Lee, Stonewall Jackson, Lewis Armistead. In the view of those in the South, this was the honored company he kept—brilliant heroes who gave their all and regularly whipped a more powerful enemy in what turned out to be a lost cause and lost war.

Even the passage of six decades failed to dampen the ardor of those mesmerized by the drama and pathos of the moment. "And there in the Bloody Angle our heroic chief, grasping a captured cannon to turn it on the foe, fell among his devoted men, pierced with mortal wounds and sealing with his heart's blood the high-water mark of the Confederate cause," lamented Mrs. H. F. Lewis of Bristol, Tennessee, in an article for *Confederate Veteran* magazine. Armistead died two days

---

4 Brinton to Henry H. Bingham, March 22, 1869, in *The Bachelder Papers*, vol. 1, 358.

Sergeant Drewry B. Easley, 14th Virginia: "We went up to the second line of artillery, and just before reaching those guns a squad of from twenty-five to fifty Yankees around a stand of colors to our left fired a volley back at Armistead and he fell forward, his sword and hat almost striking a gun." *Alfred R. Waud, courtesy New York Public Library*

later, she continued, "leaving an example of patriotic ardor, of heroism, and devotion to duty which ought to be handed down through the ages. None died on that field with greater glory than he, though many died whose names we hold in deathless honor. The heart of Virginia was wrung with anguish. Her stately head was bowed in grief. The flower of her chivalry fell in that fatal charge. But none so lamented as Armistead," she concluded, "none crowned with glory like his. Many another had done valiantly, but he surpassed them all."[5]

Armistead was also the subject of poetry:

A thousand fell where Kemper led;
A thousand died where Garnett bled;

5 Mrs. H. F. Lewis, "General Armistead at Gettysburg," *Confederate Veteran*, 40 vols. (Nashville, TN, 1893-1932), vol. 28, 406.

In blinding flame and strangling smoke,
The remnant through the batteries broke,
And crossed the works with Armistead.[6]

Despite the fact that Armistead was so well known and his fate so well documented, mystery lingers surrounding his final hours at the XI Corps hospital. Armistead did indeed die, surprising Dr. Brinton and others, but the nature of his wounds and cause of death are still under debate. Many firsthand witnesses claim he was shot three times, not twice as Brinton indicated. Was he eventually placed in the Spangler house, as some suggest, or in the summer kitchen, as others report? Even the simple fact of where on the Spangler land he was buried raises questions.

We might not ever know for sure unless an unknown document or letter comes out of nowhere and surprises historians. There are even two sides still today on non-Spangler Armistead facts. Did he say "I am the son of a widow," the Masonic sign for help, after being shot? Who talked to him after he was shot? What did Armistead say?

Many people around the world first learned of Armistead thanks to the wonderful Pulitzer Prize-winning book *The Killer Angels* and the movie based on it, "Gettysburg." Armistead's career and incredibly brave charge up Cemetery Ridge are exploits that have attracted deep interest. Many of Armistead's conversations and actions in the book and movie, however, were fictionalized to further the story. Enough real evidence exists, however, to give us a good idea of Armistead's final days, movements, and words getting to and at the Spangler hospital.

Here is what we know with certainty: Armistead came from a proud military family heritage. His father, Walker Keith Armistead, together with four uncles, served in the War of 1812. The elder Armistead served for more than four decades as a commissioned officer. Lewis' uncle, Maj. George Armistead, commanded Fort McHenry in Baltimore during the shelling by the British that inspired Francis Scott Key to write "The Star-Spangled Banner."

Armistead was admitted to the United States Military Academy at West Point, but a fight with future Confederate general Jubal Early, during which he broke a plate over Early's head, coupled with poor grades ended his tenure there. Armistead still managed a successful military career, primarily because his father managed to obtain for him a second lieutenant's commission in the 6th US Infantry. He was wounded and received a pair of brevet promotions during the

---

6 Will H. Thompson, from the poem "High Tide at Gettysburg," *Confederate Veteran*, vol. 3, 140.

Mexican War and served throughout the West prior to the Civil War. He became close friends with future Union general Winfield Scott Hancock and future Confederate general Henry Heth. "Armistead, Hancock and I were messmates," Heth recalled in his memoirs, "and never was a mess happier than ours. . . . Armistead was a good-natured man, and I am afraid we teased him too much."[7]

Armistead married Cecelia Lee Love in 1844 and had a son, Walker Keith, later that year. A daughter named Flora Lee followed in 1847. Flora died in 1850, and Cecelia died eight months later. In 1852, more grief arrived when the Armistead family home in Virginia was lost to a fire while he was stationed on the Iowa prairie at Fort Dodge. Armistead married Cornelia Jamison in 1853 and they had one son, Lewis B. Armistead, who died as an infant in 1854. Cornelia died one year later.[8]

Armistead, called "Lo" for Lothario by his friends, was stationed in San Diego with Hancock when the Civil War broke out. Hancock's wife, Almira, hosted a farewell party during which Armistead gave her his prayer book. Inside was the inscription, "Lewis Armistead. Trust in God and fear nothing." It was a sad affair. "The most crushed of the party," remembered Almira Hancock, "was Major Armistead, who, with tears, which were contagious, streaming down his face, and hands upon Mr. Hancock's shoulders, while looking him steadily in the eye, said, 'Hancock, good-bye; you can never know what this has cost me.'"[9]

The Confederacy welcomed his services and Armistead was soon serving as a colonel of the 57th Virginia. He saw his first real combat of the war at the head of a brigade on the Virginia Peninsula at Seven Pines and then with General Lee's Army of Northern Virginia during the Seven Days' Battles, during which he led the forlorn attack against Malvern Hill. Provost duty during the 1862 Maryland Campaign kept him out of action, and as part of George Pickett's all-Virginia division, he missed heavy combat at Fredericksburg. During the spring of 1863, Armistead took part in the Suffolk Campaign, a large-scale foraging operation in southeastern Virginia, and so missed the fighting at Chancellorsville. By the time Pickett's division arrived at Gettysburg on the evening of July 2, the Virginians were itching to engage the regularly defeated enemy.

He was 46 by the time he stood on Seminary Ridge in the early morning of July 3, 1863, making him older than his two fellow brigade commanders Garnett and Kemper, older than his division commander Pickett, and older than his corps

7 James L. Morrison Jr., ed., *The Memoirs of Henry Heth* (Westport, CT, 1974), 56, 66.

8 Hessler and Motts, *Pickett's Charge at Gettysburg*, 122.

9 Almira Hancock, *Reminiscences of Winfield Scott Hancock by His Wife*, 69.

commander James Longstreet. Armistead might have had a sense of his own mortality that day. Two years earlier, he had given his prayer book to Almira Hancock. On the morning of July 3, he handed off something else of sentimental value. "At early dawn, darkened by the threatening rain, Armistead, Garnett, Kemper and your Soldier held a heart-to-heart powwow," Pickett wrote to his much younger fiancée, Sallie Corbell, on the morning of his famous charge. "All three sent regards to you, and Old Lewis pulled a ring from his little finger and making me take it, said, 'Give this little token, George, please, to her of the sunset eyes, with my love, and tell her the 'old man' says since he could not be the lucky dog he's mighty glad that you are.'"[10]

Armistead and his brigade of the 9th, 14th, 38th, and 53rd Virginia and his former regiment, the 57th Virginia, together with Kemper's and Garnett's brigades, suffered under the Union counter-artillery fire early that afternoon in and around the woods on the farm of Henry Spangler, George Spangler's half-brother. Armistead would begin the final march of his life on one Spangler family member's farm and conclude it in a Union field hospital on another Spangler's land. Many of Armistead's men were hit by iron splinters or falling tree limbs as they lay in and next to Henry Spangler's woods, prompting fear and restlessness. "Lie still, boys," Armistead said as Union shells from the cannonade exploded. "There is no safe place here."[11]

"Doctor, all hell is going to turn loose here within fifteen minutes," Armistead told Dr. Arthur R. Barry, chief surgeon of the 9th Virginia. "My brigade must charge those heights, and the slaughter will be terrible. Go and establish your hospital at some convenient point, and be ready, for you will have much to do."[12] Later, as his brigade rose and gathered for the charge, Armistead shouted in his strong voice, "Men, remember what you are fighting for. Remember your homes, your firesides, your wives, mothers, sisters and your sweethearts."[13] To Garnett, as he took his place in front of his men, Armistead is reported to have said: "The issue is with the Almighty, and we must leave it in His hands."

---

10 www.brotherswar.com/Civil_War_Quotes_4j.htm. Accessed April 7, 2017. The ring was likely a wedding ring from one of his two deceased wives.

11 Benjamin L. Farinholt to John W. Daniel, April 15, 1905, in John Warwick Daniel Papers, University of Virginia, copies at GNMP Library, Box B-8, 53rd Virginia Infantry Folder.

12 Rhea Kuykendall, "Surgeons of the Confederacy," *Confederate Veteran*, vol. 34, 209.

13 Ibid.; Martin to Poindexter, "Armistead at the Battle of Gettysburg," *Southern Historical Society Papers*, vol. 39, 186.

Armistead was an old school Regular Army disciplinarian, which did not always endear him to his men. Still, they respected and trusted him. From their holding place behind the Henry Spangler barn, they marched past the buildings heading northeast into the open fields. It was hot and humid that afternoon, with the thermometer touching 87 degrees. Armistead had led men in several battles in different wars and had buried two wives and two of his three children. His only surviving child, 18-year-old Lt. Walker Keith Armistead was next to him, serving as the general's aide-de-camp. Surely the thought of losing the last of his line crossed the mind of the old soldier as they prepared to participate in a mammoth assault everyone knew would, at best, be a bloody slugfest. The drama of the moment was heightened even more because he knew the Union's II Corps, commanded by good friend Winfield Hancock, was waiting for him on the other side of the fields.[14]

It might not have been all that obvious at the outset, but Pickett's men faced a longer march to the Copse of Trees area on Cemetery Ridge than the two divisions on their left under Maj. Gen. Isaac Trimble (who led two brigades from the wounded Dorsey Pender's division), and Brig. Gen. James Pettigrew (who led the wounded Harry Heth's division). Trimble and Pettigrew had more of a straight line of attack. Pickett, however, would have to readjust his lines and oblique left to close the wide distance between his left and their right and centralize the assault against one segment of the enemy line.[15]

Pickett's division moved out with Garnett's and Kemper's brigades in the front line, left to right, and Armistead and his men in the second line behind Garnett. The Virginians tramped ahead through the grass across rolling land that at times dropped the Confederates out of sight of much of Cemetery Ridge. When artillery rounds knocked holes in the lines, the men pressed together and closed the gaps. By the time they reached the Emmitsburg Road and its stout fencing, heavy

---

14 Jacobs, "Meteorology of the Battle," www.gdg.org/Research/Other%20Documents/Newspaper%20Clippings/v6pt1l.html. Accessed April 4, 2017. Hessler and Motts, *Pickett's Charge at Gettysburg*, 122-23, were the first to discover that Armistead's son served with him at Gettysburg as a staff officer.

15 There is a significant amount of debate regarding the objective of the attack. Gettysburg historian John Bachelder, in the 1880s, cited the famous Copse of Trees as the visual landmark for the assaulting columns. In 1863, however, those trees would have been only about 10 feet tall and mostly invisible or insignificant as a central objective. Many modern historians contend Lee's objective was the more visible Ziegler's Grove on Cemetery Hill about 300 yards north of the more famous Copse of Trees. Longstreet later wrote he intended the "center" of his attack to arrive at the "salient," which implies the area of the Copse of Trees and the "angle" represented by the stone walls. For more, see Hessler and Motts, *Pickett's Charge at Gettysburg*, 10-11.

musketry fire and canister rounds from the Union line on Cemetery Ridge were ripping through their lines. Once the Virginians were over the fence, any organized lines were gone, replaced by a staggering mob of men pressing together as they moved up the slope toward the low stone wall and blazing Union line. It is impossible to know how many men made it past the Emmitsburg Road, let alone to the stone wall. Garnett fell somewhere on the slope outside the wall and was never found. Armistead passed in front of that part of the line where his friend Hancock had just fallen with a severe wound directing his II Corps while it decimated the Confederate assault. Just before climbing over the stone wall, the Virginia general put his hat on his sword and urged his men on. Perhaps 100 to 150 men made the nearly suicidal climb over the stones and into the middle of the Union line.[16]

"This report would fail in completeness and in the rendition of justice to signal valor and heroic behavior were it omitted to notice particularly the gallant conduct of our brigade commander, General L. A. Armistead," reported Col. William R. Aylett of the 53rd Virginia. "Conspicuous to all, 50 yards in advance of his brigade, waving his hat upon his sword, he led his men upon the enemy with a steady bearing which inspired all breasts with enthusiasm and courage, and won the admiration of every beholder. Far in advance of all, he led the attack till he scaled the works of the enemy and fell wounded in their hands, but not until he had driven them from their position and seen his colors planted over the fortifications."[17]

A staff officer with Armistead's 9th Virginia, Lt. James F. Crocker, also left an account of the general's final moments in battle:

The earth trembled under the mighty resound of cannon. The air is darkened with sulphurous clouds. The whole valley is enveloped. The sun, lately so glaring, is itself obscured. Nothing can be seen but the flashing light leaping from the cannon's mouth amidst the surrounding smoke. Gen. Lewis A. Armistead, the commander of our brigade . . . fortune made him the most advanced and conspicuous hero of that great charge. He was to us the very embodiment of a heroic commander. On this memorable day he placed himself on foot . . . and strode in front of his men, calm, self-collected, resolute and fearless. . . . When he

---

16 As a staff officer, it is believed Walker Keith Armistead might have ridden ahead of the lines during the advance, but how far or for how long remains unknown. The younger Armistead survived Gettysburg and the war. Ibid., 123.

17 William R. Aylett, "Report of Colonel William R. Aylett, 53rd VA Infantry, Commanding Armistead's Brigade," in *Miscellaneous Documents of the House of Representatives*, 1,000.

reached the stone wall where others stopped, he did not pause an instant–over it he went and called on all to follow.[18]

Several soldiers, Confederate and Union, left accounts that claim to relate what they witnessed beyond the stone wall. Captain Benjamin Farinholt, 53rd Virginia:

Gen. Armistead claimed the day as ours, and, standing by one of the captured pieces of artillery, where the brave Federal Capt. [Lt. Alonzo H.] Cushing had fallen, with his dead men and horses almost covering the ground, called on us to load and use the captured cannon on the fleeing foe. Just then Hancock's command came forward with full ranks and fresh for the struggle, attacking us with great impetuosity and delivering against our much decimated ranks at close range at least fifty bullets to our five. Gen. Armistead was laid low by three wounds at the first fire.[19]

Sergeant Major Anthony W. McDermott, 69th Pennsylvania:

We poured our fire . . . until Armistead received his mortal wound; he swerved from the way in which he winced, as though he was struck in the stomach, after wincing or bending like a person with [a] cramp, he pressed his left hand on his stomach, his sword and hat . . . fell to the ground. He then made two or three staggering steps, reached out his hands trying to grasp at the muzzle of what was then the 1st piece of Cushing's battery, and fell. I was at the time the nearest person to him. . . . His men threw down their arms, most of them lay down between us and the wall.[20]

Sergeant Drewry B. Easley, 14th Virginia:

I mounted the fence and got one glance up and down the line, while General Armistead mounted it just to my left, with only a . . . cannon between us. I forgot

---

18 James F. Crocker, *Gettysburg: Pickett's Charge and Other War Addresses* (Portsmouth, VA, 1915), 40, 44, 47.

19 Farinholt, in "Battle of Gettysburg—Johnson's Island," *Confederate Veteran*, vol. 5, 469.

20 Anthony W. McDermott to Bachelder, June 2, 1886, in *The Bachelder Papers*, vol. 3, 1,412-1,413.

my company and stepped off the fence with him. We went up to the second line of artillery, and just before reaching those guns a squad of from twenty-five to fifty Yankees around a stand of colors to our left fired a volley back at Armistead and he fell forward, his sword and hat almost striking a gun. I dropped behind the gun and commenced firing back at them till they located me and poured another volley. They shot my ramrod off where it entered the stock. I then ran back to the stone fence to get another gun. General Armistead did not move, groan, or speak while I fired several shots practically over his body; so I thought he had been killed instantly and did not speak to him.[21]

Private Milton Harding, 9th Virginia:

General Armistead evidently received his mortal wound immediately after crossing the stone wall. . . . I was within six feet of him to his left, and observed that he staggered painfully, and could barely keep his feet until he reached the enemy's guns . . . some sixty feet from the wall, although he continued to lead the charge like the hero he was. As he slapped his left hand on the gun he sank to his knees, and then fell full length to his right. I asked him if I could do anything for him. He requested me to get a small flask of brandy from the satchel he had carried by a strap from his shoulder, and from this he drank a swallow or so. I asked where he was wounded. He replied that he was struck in the breast and arm. In answer to my offer to assist him, he advised me to look out for myself. About that time the enemy recaptured the guns, and I, with others, retreated to the stone wall, where I was taken prisoner.[22]

Captain Charles H. Banes, 72nd Pennsylvania:

The distance from the front of the 72nd Regiment, to which Armistead fell was not over thirty-three paces, we measured it on the day of the fight. It was so near that one of the 72nd Regiment men said that he heard a man calling for his

---

21 D. B. Easley, "With Armistead When He Was Killed," *Confederate Veteran*, vol. 20, 379.

22 Milton Harding, "Where General Armistead Fell," *Confederate Veteran*, vol. 19, 371.

mother, who was a widow and I saw them carrying him off the field. Three men of the 72nd Regiment carried him up.[23]

*   *   *

Corporal Thomas H. Presnell of the 1st Minnesota detailed his recollection of what happened with Armistead immediately after he was wounded in an 1890 letter to a friend:

After the battle was over, but while everything was confusion and excitement, I was returning from one of the wheat stacks to which I had assisted one of my comrades, toward the point occupied by Cushing's battery. I met a party carrying a wounded man in a blanket. . . . I immediately saw that the occupant of the blanket was a Confederate officer, and was informed that he was Gen. Armistead. He seemed to be badly wounded in the head but was conscious and was talking, though rather incoherently. Among other things he asked was how Gen. Hancock was, and on being told that he was wounded, said: 'I am sorry; he is a grand man.' I remember he said this: 'We made a good fight, but lost; thank God Virginia did its duty.'[24]

Captain Henry Bingham of Hancock's staff spoke with Armistead as he was being carried away, and wrote about it six years later in a letter to Hancock. "I met Armistead just under the crest of the hill, being carried to the rear by several privates," he began. "I ordered them back, .

but they replied that they had an important prisoner and they designated him as General Longstreet. . . . I dismounted my horse and inquired of the prisoner his

---

23 Charles H. Banes, testimony, April 24, 1890, in *The Bachelder Papers*, vol. 3, 1,705. The call could have been from Armistead, for the Mason's sign for help from a brother Mason is to claim oneself as the son of a widow. Hancock was wounded in the thigh while directing his men on his horse about 560 yards from where Armistead was hit. The timing of their wounds was probably close. Each spot is designated today by a marker: Armistead's 66 yards north (39°48'45"N 77°14'8"W) of the Copse of Trees and Hancock's (39°48'14"N 77°14'4"W) 210 yards northwest of the Pennsylvania monument (though the II Corps commander later questioned the accuracy of his monument's placement).

24 Thomas H. Presnell to Jasper Searles, March 3, 1890, in the *Duluth* (MN) *Herald*. www.1st minnesota.net/#/soldier/324. Accessed April 13, 2017.

Maj. Gen. Winfield Scott Hancock

Library of Congress

name he replied General Armistead of the Confederate Army. Observing that his suffering was very great I said to him, General, I am Captain Bingham of General Hancock's staff, and if you have anything valuable in your possession which you desire taken care of, I will take care of it for you. He then asked me if it was General Winfield S. Hancock and upon my replying in the affirmative, he informed me that you were an old and valued friend of his and he desired for me to say to you, 'Tell General Hancock for me that I have done him and done you all an injury which I shall regret or repent [I forget the exact word] the longest day I live.' I then obtained his spurs, watch chain, seal and pocketbook. I told the men to take him to the rear to one of the hospitals.[25]

Bingham's claim that Armistead expressed regret was attacked in the South after the war as a scandalous lie. Heated denials appeared in Confederate Veteran magazine and other publications. An article in the *Southern Historical Society Papers*, for example, published a Union account in an effort to refute Bingham's letter. "One of my church members, a very reliable gentleman . . . was wounded on the third day and taken to a hospital in the rear," wrote Rev. Theodore Gerrish of the First United Methodist Church in Bangor, Maine. Gerrish, a former member of the 20th Maine, was referring to Pvt. Willard H. Moore of the 97th New York, I Corps. "General Armistead was brought to the same hospital and placed beside him," continued Gerrish. "I asked [Moore] what opinion he formed of the General from what words he heard him utter. He replied that all who saw him there were strongly

25 Bingham letter to Hancock, January 5, 1869, *The Bachelder Papers*, vol. 1, 352.

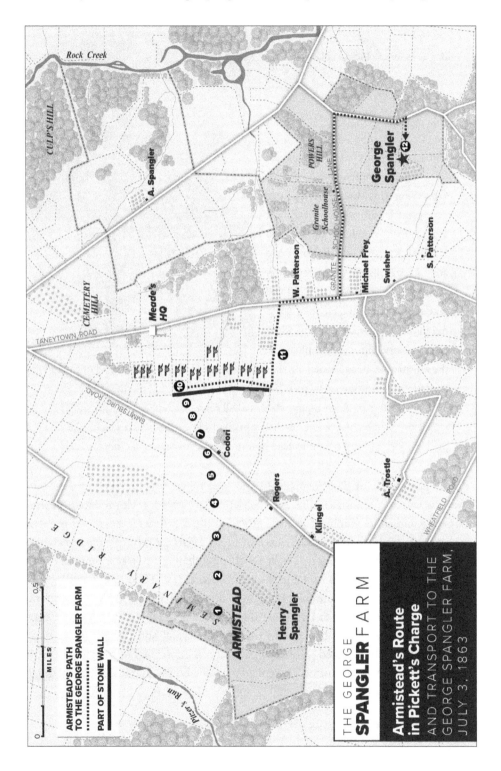

General Armistead's Journey from the Henry Spangler Woods
to the Spangler Farm Hospital

1: Brig. Gen. Lewis A. Armistead's five regiments were posted in and near the "Spangler Woods" behind the buildings on Henry Spangler's property prior to their charge. The weather clear, 87 degrees, and humid. Understanding the deadly mission ahead, Col. Rawley Martin (53rd Virginia) recalled, "None of the usual jokes, common on the eve of battle, were indulged in." No part of the Union line was visible.

2: The first 200 yards of the advance carried the brigade to a rise parallel with and north of the Spangler buildings, where the men could see the top of the Round Tops, Brian house, and roof of the Codori barn.

3: The three Virginia brigades under Pickett continued, angling left (northeast) to a fence and into another swale, blocking out everything but the summit of Big Round Top. Gen. Pickett: "You never saw anything like it. They moved across that field of death as a battalion marches forward in line of battle upon drill, each commander in front of his command, leading and cheering on his men."

4: The ground rose to another fence line 200 more yards farther. The entire Union line was now in sight. Colonel Martin, 53rd Virginia: "The scene was grand and terrible, and well calculated to demoralize the stoutest heart." Now the Confederates can be seen, and the Union artillery opens fire on the Virginians.

5: Another swale dropped them out of sight. Armistead and his men could only see bits and pieces of the Union line as they approached within 100 yards of the Emmitsburg Road and Codori barn, still angling left/northeast. Even though mostly out of view, the Northerners knew where they were and hit them with shells.

6: The Emmitsburg Road was fence-lined on both sides. Now within the final 260 yards, they could see the entire Union line again. Union artillery and infantry fire became more deadly, ripping gaps in the line as they crowded to squeeze through the fence openings.

7: The brigades of Armistead and Richard B. Garnett crossed the Emmitsburg Road to the left (north) of the Codori buildings while James L. Kemper's men advanced on their right (south). (One of Garnett's regiments went to the right of Codori.) Enfilading fire from the 13th & 16th Vermont regiments, whose men had rushed out into the field, devastated them.

8: Yet another swale halfway between the road and the Union line meant Armistead could only see from the Brian house to the Copse of Trees, although powder smoke made seeing much of anything difficult. Armistead ordered a double quick. Rev. James E. Poindexter, former captain, 38th Virginia: "The hiss of bullets was incessant. Men fell at every step; they fell, I thought, like grass before the scythe."

9: Armistead and perhaps as many as 150 men reached and crossed the wall.

10: Armistead was shot down near the site of his marker. He and those who crossed the wall had marched about one mile in about thirty minutes, much of it under fire.

11: Armistead was probably picked up by an ambulance in this vicinity.

12: Armistead arrived in an ambulance at the George Spangler XI Corps hospital. George was the older half-brother of Henry Spangler, on whose property Armistead and his brigade had begun their charge.

impressed upon two points in the General's character: 1. An intense, all-consuming desire for the Confederates to win the battle. 2. To die like a soldier."[26]

Bingham gave Hancock Armistead's personal effects later that evening when he found his wounded superior in an ambulance at "a temporary Hospital in the woods." The ambulance was parked at the Granite Schoolhouse hospital of the First Division of Hancock's II Corps on the Spangler property. The hospital wasn't entirely broken up yet and the general made a brief stop there, likely to issue communications (possibly to General Meade), or to have his wound further examined or treated on his way to the more permanent II Corps division hospitals being organized on the Jacob Schwartz farm.[27]

When Hancock stopped for a short time at the Granite Schoolhouse, he and Armistead were likely on the same Spangler property at the same time. If only the two old friends could have known. Even in their severely wounded conditions, one last reunion of dear friends would have lifted the spirits of both men. Hancock was in Philadelphia the next day, where he began a long and painful rehabilitation.

* * *

Armistead was carried in an ambulance down Taneytown Road to Granite Schoolhouse Lane, then on Blacksmith Shop Road to the Spangler lane until he reached the barn. Dr. Van Aernam timed his arrival at about dusk. That seems late, but it is plausible. The Virginia general lay wounded on the field for some time before he was carried away at the end of the battle. According to the witnesses we know of, the small procession carrying Armistead stopped on more than one occasion for conversations and other reasons. But the biggest problem was finding an ambulance. Hundreds of them were already filled with wounded and rolling away from the front. Even Hancock had to wait for an ambulance, so how much time passed before one was found for a wounded Confederate remains unknown. Regardless of the importance of the injured occupant, the bumpy journey to the

---

26 J. William Jones, *Southern Historical Society Papers*, vol. 11, 285. It remains possible and even likely that Armistead told Bingham that he regrets or repents any injury he caused. Apologizing for harming friends—especially a dear one such as Hancock—while himself seriously and perhaps mortally wounded, does not detract from his love and commitment to Virginia and the Confederacy.

27 Bingham to Hancock, *The Bachelder Papers*, 351. The Jacob Schwartz farm was near the modern-day Outlet Shoppes at Gettysburg.

Spangler hospital was a stop-and-start affair on gridlocked roads and lanes. Given all that, Armistead could indeed have arrived about 8:00 p.m.

However, it is also possible that Dr. Van Aernam misremembered the time when he was interviewed about it 27 years after the event. Fellow Spangler patient Lt. T. C. Holland of the 28th Virginia, Garnett's brigade, claimed he and Armistead were placed "beneath the shade of some trees," which clearly implies it was still at least somewhat sunny when they arrived. Holland also claimed Armistead asked the doctors and staff working around him to "please don't step so close to me." Holland, however, was writing more than five decades after the event in question. Given all that had to be done to get to the farm, it is highly doubtful Armistead made it there before 5:30 p.m. or 6:00 p.m.[28]

Dr. Van Aernam, who described General Armistead as "fine looking," used the words "wild nervous flighty" to describe him, and claimed that he uttered, "war must cease, men of same blood," and that he "could not live." Dr. Van Aernam, like Dr. Brinton, did not believe that Armistead's wounds were fatal and told Armistead as much, and that he would receive the "best of care & would not neglect him."[29]

Hospital workers Cpl. John Irvin and Private Ames, both of the 154th New York, cared for Armistead after his initial examination, but accounts disagree as to where they placed him. "Edson Ames & me carried him into Geo Spanglers house & lade Him on the bed," recalled Irvin. "He had two wounds in the body & one in thigh. I gave Him some liquor." Ames added that Armistead "raised up in bed and shouted, 'Tell my comrades that I died a brave man.'"[30]

Private Justus M. Silliman of the 17th Connecticut reported that Armistead was not on a Spangler bed but "lay in the kitchen," while Dr. Van Aernam recalled Cpt. Frederick Stowe "was in one corner of little bed room & A[rmistead] in other."[31]

28 T. C. Holland, "With Armistead at Gettysburg," *Confederate Veteran*, vol. 29, 62; Northrup interview of Van Aernam, August 4, 1890, Edwin Dwight Northrup Papers, Box 35, Carl A. Kroch Library, Cornell University.

29 Northrup interview of Van Aernam, August 4, 1890.

30 John Irvin to Northrup, in Edwin Dwight Northrup Papers, Box 16, Carl A. Kroch Library, Cornell University; "Presidents Soldiers Statesmen," H. H. Hardesty. Spangler Farmstead file, 1491-92, Adams County Historical Society (Gettysburg, PA).

31 Silliman letter to his mother, July 7, 1863, *A New Canaan Private in the Civil War*, 44; Northrup interview of Van Aernam, August 28, 1893, Edwin Dwight Northrup Papers, Box 35, Carl A. Kroch Library, Cornell University.

Historian William Storrick quoted George Spangler's son Beniah decades after the war as saying that Armistead was "taken to the house, laid on the floor of the kitchen."[32] Architectural studies indicate the Spanglers did not have a way to cook in their house at that time, and that an actual kitchen wasn't installed until the early 1900s. Beniah could only have been speaking of the summer kitchen, which was detached from the house and still stands. Doctor Jay Kling of the 55th Ohio recalled that Armistead "was placed on a bed in the farm cottage, and made as comfortable as possible." Because of this testimony, most historians now believe Armistead was taken to the summer kitchen.[33]

Farmers used separate summer kitchen buildings in the 1800s for cooking, canning, and other chores to keep the heat out of the house and to reduce the risk of a major fire. The Spangler summer kitchen was (and remains) just a few yards from the house. The interior measures 17 by 12 feet, less a few feet for the large fireplace. That was enough room to place important patients such as Stowe and Armistead inside and still allow for the medical staff to treat them. It also provided more privacy for these important individuals. It should also be recalled that the Spangler house was one-third smaller then than it is now and had just two bedrooms. One bedroom was occupied by the six Spanglers while the hospital was operational and the rest of the house was filled with medical staff and wounded.

According to Doctor Kling, Armistead "was suffering intense pain, induced by the wound. Stimulants and anodines [painkillers] were immediately given him." He also reported that Armistead personally described his wounding: "I placed my hand upon one of your cannon, but no live man could remain there. In falling back I received my wound when about two rods distant from the cannon on which I had placed my hand. It was murder to send men to such a place."[34]

Doctor Brinton, who spent time getting to know Armistead, concluded he was "a fine man, intelligent & refined. . . . I had considerable conversation with him & was much pleased with his manners & language." The 17th Connecticut's Private Silliman thought Armistead was "rather past middle aged. He is from Va and one

32 William Storrick, "Armistead and the Battle of Gettysburg," *Gettysburg Times*, March 3, 1939.

33 Jay Kling to Joseph T. Derry, reprinted October 13, 1896, in the *Atlanta Journal-Constitution*. It is possible Ames and Irvin did indeed carry Armistead into the crowded house, and that he was removed to the summer kitchen at a later time.

34 Ibid.

of the reb wounded says he was one of the best disciplinarians in their army." Private Sweetland recalled Armistead's "grey hair & whiskers."[35]

As with so many aspects of Armistead's final hours, the time of his death is also in question. Dr. Van Aernam lists it as 3:00 a.m. on July 5. Armistead, he recalled, "about midnight was rational but great wild." Private Ames remembered that he died between 2:00 and 3:00 a.m. Spangler patient Holland of the 28th Virginia put the time at "about 9 a.m. on July 5 after intense suffering." At Armistead's request, Dr. Van Aernam related that he had the US and Confederate money in the dead general's pockets sent to Almira Hancock.[36]

Doctor Brinton offered a theory six years after treating Armistead of why he died from what so many considered two non-fatal wounds: "In conversation with the General he told me he had suffered much from over-exertion, want of sleep, and mental anxiety within the last few days. His prospects seemed good, and I was astonished to learn of his death. It resulted not from his wounds directly, but from secondary fever & prostration."[37]

Prostration, as Brinton said, meant extreme physical and mental exhaustion. The explanation is plausible. Armistead, who had led an especially grief-filled adult life, had just suffered through a desperate, failed, and traumatic charge that decimated his brigade. He likely had no idea whether his only living child, Walker Keith Armistead, was alive or dead. He knew his friend Hancock had also been seriously wounded, perhaps mortally. The amount of sustenance, including water, the aging general had consumed over the previous several days is also unknown. Almost certainly he was suffering from dehydration even before he touched his hand to a hot cannon, and perhaps sunstroke as well. Perhaps he just considered it his time to die as a brave soldier, and that he had had enough. Captain Bingham, in another letter to General Hancock, described Armistead when he met him on the

---

35 Brinton, "From Chancellorsville to Gettysburg, a Doctor's Diary," *Pennsylvania Magazine of History and Biography*, 313; www.jstor.org/stable/20089816. Accessed April 10, 2017; Brinton to his mother, July 9, 1863, Dr. Daniel Garrison Brinton Papers; Silliman to his mother, July 7, 1863, *A New Canaan Private in the Civil War*, 44; Northrup interview of Sweetland, Edwin Dwight Northrup Papers, Box 35, Carl A. Kroch Library, Cornell University.

36 Northrup interview of Van Aernam, August 4, 1890, Edwin Dwight Northrup Papers, Box 35, Carl A. Kroch Library, Cornell University; Northrup interview of Edwin Ames, September 4, 1890, Edwin Dwight Northrup Papers, Box 35, Carl A. Kroch Library, Cornell University; Holland, "With Armistead at Gettysburg," *Confederate Veteran*, vol. 29, 62; Northrup interview of Van Aernam, Edwin Dwight Northrup Papers, Box 35, Carl A. Kroch Library, Cornell University.

37 Brinton to Bingham, *The Bachelder Papers*, vol. 1, 358-359.

battlefield as "seriously wounded, completely exhausted, and seemingly broken-spirited." Almira Hancock also had a theory: "I as well as my husband, believed that he courted the death that finally came to him at Gettysburg."[38]

Lieutenant Crocker of the 9th Virginia of Armistead's brigade, who was also wounded in Pickett's Charge, was being treated as a prisoner just down the road at the XII Corps hospital on the Bushman farm. His captors trusted him enough to grant the officer permission to visit Armistead and go into Gettysburg. After all, the wounded general was his commanding officer, and Crocker knew the area extremely well because he was valedictorian of his class of 1850 at Pennsylvania (now Gettysburg) College.

"On my way to town I called by the Eleventh Corps Hospital, to which General Armistead had been taken, to see him," Crocker recalled. "I found that he had died. They showed me his freshly made grave. To my inquiries they gave me full information. They told me that his wound was in the leg; that it ought not to have proved mortal; that his proud spirit chafed under his imprisonment and his restlessness aggravated his wound. Brave Armistead! The bravest of all that field of brave heroes! If there be in human hearts a lyre, in human minds a flame divine, that awakens and kindles at the heroic deed of man," he concluded, "then his name will be borne in song and story to distant times."[39]

Today, many doctors and historians who have studied Armistead's death believe it is likely that he died from a pulmonary embolism (blood clot) that moved from his leg to his heart. In that scenario, the embolism would have developed in Armistead's wounded calf as he sat or lay idly at Spangler and moved to his chest and killed him. His symptoms would have included shortness of breath and chest pain. Different witnesses described the general as "wild" and near the end in "intense pain." Not being able to breathe and the pain he would have been suffering from as a result of a pulmonary clot support this conclusion.

In another scenario, a fever (as Dr. Brinton indicates) from an infection could have developed from the two non-fatal wounds, which was not uncommon given the state of medicine in 1863. An infection would not have killed Armistead that quickly, but it could have been a contributing factor with sunstroke, heat exhaustion, dehydration, and blood loss. Armistead had told Dr. Brinton he was in a weakened state when he arrived in Gettysburg. Today, Armistead would have

---

38 Almira Hancock, *Reminiscences of Winfield Scott Hancock by His Wife*, 69; Bingham to Hancock, *Southern Historical Society Papers*, vol. 10, 428.

39 Crocker, *Gettysburg: Pickett's Charge and Other War Addresses*, 54.

been put on an IV as soon as possible after his wound. It is also possible that he had some undiagnosed underlying health issue that contributed to his demise.

Newspaper reports from July 1863 note that Armistead was wounded in the arm and leg, which, coupled with other accounts, make a strong case that he was indeed wounded twice. There is another hypothesis that Armistead was treated for an additional wound in the chest or abdomen, a theory advocated by two doctors, a captain, a sergeant major, and three privates who were with Armistead at some point after he was shot.

Recall that Sgt. Maj. Anthony W. McDermott of the 69th Pennsylvania observed that Armistead "swerved from the way in which he winced, as though he was struck in the stomach, after wincing or bending like a person with [a] cramp, he pressed his left hand on his stomach." Captain Benjamin Farinholt of the 53rd Virginia claimed he saw Armistead fall with three wounds. Hospital worker Cpl. John Irvin personally observed "two wounds in the body & one in thigh," and Private Silliman of the 17th Connecticut noted that he was struck in the "breast and leg." Doctor Kling, who certainly knew what a wound looked like, reported that, "On examination, it was found that a rifle ball had entered his body in the right lumbar region, passing through the kidney and bowels, making its exit in front."[40]

In his 1893 interview, Dr. Van Aernam recalled that he and Dr. Hovey were Armistead's primary caregivers. Dr. Hovey reported that Armistead was shot through the chest—a wound that was found after Dr. Van Aernam had stripped the general of some of his clothing. But Dr. Van Aernam never jumped into the two- or three-wound debate.[41]

Perhaps the most compelling testimony in this regard was offered by Pvt. Milton Harding of the 9th Virginia, who said he rushed to Armistead's aid immediately after he was shot. As quoted earlier in this chapter, when Harding "asked where he was wounded," Armistead "replied that he was struck in the breast and arm."[42]

Some Spangler doctors who were with Armistead cited a chest wound, while others who were with him did not. These different recollections of what should be an obvious, memorable event are frustratingly typical for the Civil War. Ultimately,

40 Irvin to Northrup, Edwin Dwight Northrup Papers, Box 16, Carl A. Kroch Library, Cornell University; Silliman, *A New Canaan Private in the Civil War*, 44; Kling to Derry, *Atlanta Journal-Constitution.*

41 Northrup interview of Van Aernam, Edwin Dwight Northrup Papers, Box 35, Carl A. Kroch Library, Cornell University.

42 Harding, "Where General Armistead Fell," *Confederate Veteran*, vol. 19, 371.

we just don't know. Today's medical experts, historians, and readers will have to decide for themselves what killed the heroic Confederate general.

After he died, hospital attendants wrapped the brigadier general in a blanket and placed his corpse in a homemade casket made of wood appropriated from the Spangler farm. Musician Alfred J. Rider, 23, of the 107th Ohio was one of those responsible for burying Armistead. It was his job to not only inter the dead, but record their names and turn their effects over to Surgeon-in-Charge Dr. James Armstrong of Philadelphia. The Southern general was buried in a marked grave in an orchard south of the Spangler house.[43]

Armistead's burial was significantly better than what most of his Confederate comrades received at Gettysburg. Often days after they died, many of their bloated and disfigured bodies were finally dragged into mass trench graves somewhere on the battlefield close to where they had fallen. Some identified by comrades were individually buried with temporary markers that usually didn't last long when exposed to the Pennsylvania elements. Battlefield graves were shallow, and heavy rains often washed away the top soil to reveal decaying corpses. Family members traveled north in an attempt to locate their lost sons, fathers, and brothers. Thousands were eventually exhumed and shipped south in the early 1870s to be reburied in Richmond's Hollywood Cemetery and elsewhere, usually in mass unknown graves. Even today, we are unsure of the number of men who were buried at the Spangler hospital and their identities.[44]

As good as his burial was, Armistead's tragedy worsened when a doctor took a financial interest in his death. After four summer weeks inside a box on Spangler land, Armistead's body was disinterred in its deteriorating condition and embalmed. "I buried Gen. Armistead and his body was afterward disinterred and embalmed by Dr. Chamberlain of Philadelphia," explained Rider. "Dr Chamberlain told [me] that he thought Armistead's friends would pay a good price for his body."[45]

"Dr. Chamberlain" was probably C. B. Chamberlain of Philadelphia, one of the private enterprise Civil War embalmers who followed the armies and profited from the dead. And he was right. Armistead's family retrieved his remains that October and reburied him at Old St. Paul's Cemetery in Baltimore, where his uncle

---

43 Rider to Bachelder, *The Bachelder Papers*, vol. 2, 1,129.

44 The best book on the treatment of the wounded and burial of the dead is Gregory Coco, *A Strange and Blighted Land: Gettysburg: The Aftermath of a Battle* (Savas Beatie, 2017).

45 Rider to Bachelder, *The Bachelder Papers*, vol. 1, 129.

George, of War of 1812 fame, is buried. Today, the cemetery is surrounded by a high wall and crowded streets in busy downtown Baltimore. The embalmer probably made a couple of hundred dollars off Armistead. After all, he was a brigadier general, and the higher the rank, the more embalmers charged. Many privates, for example, were embalmed for less than a dollar.

Armistead's death ended Walker Keith Armistead's short staff career as his father's aide-de-camp. General Lee offered the young man a position with the army's chief of ordnance, perhaps as a means of protecting him, but he turned it down and returned to the 6th Virginia Cavalry, the unit in which he had originally enlisted. Keith, as he was known because he also had an uncle named Walker Keith, was wounded in 1864, but survived the war. In 1871, Keith married Julia Webster Appleton, granddaughter of Daniel Webster, who had served as secretary of state under three presidents. Keith died in 1896 in Rhode Island at the age of 51. Continuing what seemed to be the Armistead family tradition of tragedy, Keith and Julia's third and youngest child—Walker Keith—died in a hunting accident at age 16.[46]

On March 23, 1939, Gettysburg historian Storrick published a story in *The Gettysburg Times* claiming Beniah Spangler told him Armistead was "buried back of the barn," which would be north or northwest of the house rather than south of it in the hospital cemetery in the orchard. There was another report of his burial in the yard next to the summer kitchen. Musician Rider of the 107th Ohio, however, claims he buried and disinterred Armistead in the Confederate section of the hospital cemetery, and this remains the likeliest scenario.

Spangler Farm Short Story

Lewis A. Armistead is one of the most commemorated participants in the battle of Gettysburg, and two markers note his presence at the George Spangler farm hospital.

The first is a monument at the beginning of the Spangler lane noting the friendship and wounding of Armistead and friend Maj. Gen. Winfield Scott Hancock and the fact that they were both treated on Spangler property. This monument was dedicated by the Armistead Marker Preservation Committee on April 8, 2000. On July 5, 1998, the same committee dedicated a plaque to Armistead

---

46 Hessler and Motts, *Pickett's Charge at Gettysburg*, 123.

on the outer wall of the summer kitchen, where it is believed Armistead died on July 5, 1863. That plaque was moved off the wall and placed on a post next to the summer kitchen by the Gettysburg Foundation during rehabilitation of the farm in 2015-16. A granite monument near the Copse of Trees on Cemetery Ridge, one of the most popular on the field, marks the general location of where Armistead was mortally wounded. It was dedicated July 12, 1887. The Masons dedicated the Friend to Friend Masonic Memorial in the annex of the Soldiers' National Cemetery in Gettysburg in 1993. This monument depicts Union Capt. Henry H. Bingham coming to the aid of fellow Mason Armistead after he was wounded.

Two additional plaques honor Armistead at his grave in Old St. Paul's Cemetery in Baltimore. The first was placed in 1912, but it was stolen at a later date. That plaque was replaced by another in 1949, but it was damaged by vandals in 1972. It was rededicated on July 10, 1988, along with a new plaque provided by the United States Veterans Administration.

Chapter 14

July 4, 1863

"I saw long rows of men lying under the eaves of the buildings, the water
pouring down upon their bodies in streams."

— *Maj. Gen. Carl Schurz, Third Division, XI Corps*

5:00 a.m. Brigadier General Adelbert Ames' brigade, now under Col.
Andrew Harris, together with other regiments of the XI Corps, receives
orders to leave Cemetery Hill and East Cemetery Hill and move into Gettysburg to
secure the town and make sure it's safe for ambulances and other elements of the
army to enter. If they are expecting any sort of a fight, they don't get one.
According to Colonel Harris, there were "but few of the enemy remaining who
were easily made prisoners." Lieutenant Edward Culp of the 25th Ohio from the
same brigade recalled how the residents of York Street "were overwhelmed with
joy at what they called their delivery." Another lieutenant from the 75th Ohio,
Oscar Ladley, confirmed Culp's account: "We went like a set of devils and raining
as hard as it could pour down, and of all the waveing of handkerchiefs and smiling
faces, you never saw the equal."[1]

---

1 Andrew L. Harris to J. M. Brown, April 7, 1864, in *The Bachelder Papers,* vol. 1, 715-716;
Richard A. Baumgartner, *Buckeye Blood: Ohio at Gettysburg* (Huntington, WV, 2003), 168; Oscar
Ladley to his mother and sister, July 9, 1863, in Carl M. Becker and Ritchie Thomas, eds., *Hearth
and Knapsack: The Ladley Letters, 1857-1880* (Athens, OH, 1988), 144.

5:40 a.m. The Army of the Potomac signal station at Pennsylvania College reports that the Army of Northern Virginia has abandoned many of its July 3 positions and pulled back behind Seminary Ridge west of town. About an hour later, Confederate ammunition and ambulance wagons are spotted retreating west along the Chambersburg Pike and southwest down the Fairfield Road.[2]

6:35 a.m. Confederate General Robert E. Lee sends a message to Union Maj. Gen. George G. Meade proposing an exchange of prisoners "to promote the comfort and convenience of the officers and men captured by the opposing armies in the recent engagements." Meade rejects the offer: "[I]t is not in my power to accede to the proposed arrangement."

10:00 a.m., from President Lincoln, through the War Department: "The President announces to the country that news from the Army of the Potomac, up to 10 p.m. on the 3d, is such as to cover that army with the highest honor; to promise a great success to the cause of the Union, and to claim the condolence of all for the many gallant fallen; and that for this he especially desires that on this day, He, whose will, not ours, should ever be done, be everywhere remembered and ever reverenced with profoundest gratitude."[3]

* * *

By early Saturday morning, July 4, General Meade was officially set up for business in a small grove of trees at the base of Powers Hill, his tents spread out on George Spangler and Nathaniel Lightner property along the Baltimore Pike. *Cincinnati Gazette* reporter Whitelaw Reid was there when Meade arrived the previous evening. "General Meade rode up, calm as ever, and called for paper and aides; he had orders already to issue," recalled Reid. "A band came marching in over the hill-side; on the evening air its notes floated out–significant melody–'Hail to the Chief.'" By the morning of the 4th, continued the reporter, "the General had a little wall tent, in which he was dictating orders and receiving dispatches; General Ingalls, the Chief Quartermaster, had his writing-table in the open end of a covered

2 *OR* 27, pt. 3, 203.

3 Ibid., 514, 515.

wagon; the rest, majors, colonels, generals and all, had slept on the ground, and were now standing about the camp-fires."[4]

Army of the Potomac Medical Director Dr. Jonathan A. Letterman spent most of the battle near Meade and was with him on Spangler land that morning. It is possible and even likely Dr. Letterman checked on the XI Corps hospital while he was there. Newspaper reporters from Boston, New York, Philadelphia, and elsewhere flocked to the area, further crowding the scene. Cincinnati reporter Reid (and probably other reporters) had stood atop Powers Hill the previous day to watch Pickett's Charge.

A half-mile southwest of Meade's headquarters at the Spanglers' barn, the overnight rain had added to the misery and increased the suffering of those unfortunate enough to find themselves there. Food, clothing, and hospital shelter tents were on their way, but had still not arrived by the morning of July 4. That meant many wounded and dying men were still out in the open. They were in pain, hungry, still in the same filthy clothing they were wearing when wounded, and now soaking wet. Later, a thunderstorm moved in that was so strong that the soldiers of both armies remembered it for the rest of their lives. The rain also drove Meade from open Spangler land to a farm along the Baltimore Pike. "We were almost drowned out of headquarters, down in the woods," recalled Meade chief of staff Maj. Gen. Daniel Butterfield. Although he didn't know it, Meade would not return to George Spangler's property. This rain continued into the night of July 4.[5]

The XI Corps' General Schurz was at Spangler on July 4 to visit his men. He found the scene unsettling. "A heavy rain set in during the day—the usual rain after a battle—and large numbers had to remain unprotected in the open, there being no room left under roof," he recalled decades later. "I saw long rows of men lying under the eaves of the buildings, the water pouring down upon their bodies in streams." Corporal William R. Kiefer of the 153rd Pennsylvania, a hospital steward at the Spangler facility, penned a short diary entry that day: "Many wounded lying on the ground and not covered, horrible sight here. Many amputations." He recalled and expounded on the sodden misery in his postwar regimental history. "Hundreds were lying with but feeble, or in most cases with no shelter, exposed to a cold incessant rain against the sides of the barn, and in an orchard adjoining the sheds. Their moans were heard in every direction," he continued, "and with a

4 Whitelaw Reid, "The Battles of Gettysburg. Cincinnati Gazette Account," in Frank Moore, ed., *The Rebellion Record: A Diary of American Events*, 11 vols. (New York, NY, 1864), vol. 7, 100.

5 Daniel Butterfield, in Bill Hyde, ed., *The Union Generals Speak* (Baton Rouge, LA, 2003), 259.

lantern I moved about from one to another during the long hours of the night. I . . . searched in vain for blankets to cover the suffering and dying." Dr. Daniel Brinton did his best to explain the wet misery in a letter home to his mother five days later: "To add to the scene a heavy rain came up on the fourth & many of the wounded were drenched to the skin and lay writhing with pain in the mud and barn yard water."[6]

One of those suffering outside was 18-year-old private John Rush, a member of the 153rd Pennsylvania. Rush fell wounded in the left arm and right shoulder on July 1 and was transported to the Spangler farm on the Fourth of July in what he called "the heaviest rain since Noah's Flood." He spent what was perhaps the most uncomfortable night of his young life outside on the seat of an ambulance in a Spangler field.[7]

There still wasn't enough protection from the weather when about half of the hospital supplies, tents, and food that had been held back finally reached Gettysburg. "These . . . accommodated but a small portion of the wounded," complained Assistant Surgeon Dr. Cyrus Bacon of the V Corps while describing a scene typical of all of the corps and division hospitals. "Preference was given to those who had sustained operations, and to the most severely injured. The remainder were but imperfectly protected from the rains, their shelter being only such as could be constructed by means of shelter tents. The straw used for bedding consequently became damp," he added, "and, the rains continuing incessantly, little opportunity was given to dry it for several days."[8]

The Artillery Reserve and ammunition train had left the Spangler property by the morning of July 4. Their departure reduced the horse/mule and artilleryman/ teamster population by a couple of thousand each. Hundreds of wagons, caissons, and limbers went with them. This was the first time the Spanglers could clearly see the destruction that had taken place during the army's sojourn on their land. The Union men and vehicles had leveled or consumed their crops and the vegetable

---

6 Schurz, "The Battle of Gettysburg," in *McClure's Magazine*, vol. 29 (May to October, 1907), 285; Kiefer, *War Diary of William R. Kiefer, Drummer of Co. F., 153rd Regiment, Pennsylvania Volunteers, 1862-63*, Gregory A. Coco Collection, Box B-15, GNMP Library; Kiefer, *History of the One Hundred and Fifty-Third Regiment*, 99; Brinton letter to his mother, July 9, 1863, Dr. Daniel Garrison Brinton Papers.

7 www.civilwardata.com/active/hdsquery.dll?SoldierHistory?U&787209. Accessed January 22, 2018; Kiefer, *History of the One Hundred and Fifty-Third Regiment*, 253.

8 Cyrus Bacon, "Third Extract from a Narrative of his Services in the Medical Staff," in *OR 27*, pt. 3, 147.

garden was destroyed. The livestock, meat in the smokehouse, and grains in the barn—their source of income—were gone. Sections of the stone walls and fences crisscrossing the farm had been torn down by artillery batteries and infantry racing to the front. The fields the family had spent 15 years nurturing were little more than a muddy wasteland of wagon tracks, human and animal waste, and crushed crops. Probably at least two long latrine holes scarred the property. The soldiers, however, often didn't bother using these sinks, and horses and mules had left thousands of pounds of waste in their wake.[9]

At least the shelling of their farm was over. It would be quieter and safer now. The Spangler fields, however, weren't entirely empty. Hospital tents full of wounded were beginning to fill the yard and the fields closest to the house and barn and the orchard. Some 100 wagons attached to the XI Corps ambulance corps, together with hundreds of horses and men assigned to it, were still in need. The ambulance wagons accounted for a steady stream of traffic to and from the Spangler farm. When General Lee abandoned Gettysburg that day, he had little choice but to abandon thousands of captured Army of the Potomac wounded as well as thousands of their own injured men. According to Dr. Letterman, 14,193 Union wounded and 6,802 Confederates were left behind.[10] The ambulance corps had the tall task of finding, collecting, and transporting the wounded to the correct corps and division hospitals in time to save them. Every property in the area surrounding Gettysburg was searched. Some of the wounded remained in hospitals in town, but most were shipped to corps and division field hospitals southeast of Gettysburg.

Ambulances, local resident Annie Young recalled, "covered every field and road, bearing away the wounded." Their work wouldn't finish until July 5, but there was no way to save everyone. Some died while waiting and praying to be picked up and delivered to a hospital while others perished shortly after reaching a medical facility, having remained unattended for too long.[11]

---

9   The Spanglers probably ate military and Christian Commission and Sanitary Commission food after the battle while their property was occupied. Even though the battle was over, it would be another five long weeks before George, Elizabeth, and their children could escape their confinement together in that upstairs bedroom.

10   *OR* 27, pt. 3, 195.

11   Anna Mary Young to her cousin, July 17, 1863, in Catharine Merrill, *The Soldier of Indiana in the War for the Union* (Indianapolis, IN, 1869), 121, copy of letter in GNMP Library, Civilian Accounts Crawford, Box V-8.

"During the two days following the battle, those of us who were in the Ambulance Corps were kept very busy hauling wounded soldiers to the field hospitals where their wounds could be dressed and they be properly cared for," recalled Pvt. Jacob Smith, Company D, 107th Ohio. The Buckeye continued:

The badly wounded of the first day's fight fell into the hands of the enemy when our forces retreated back to the line on Cemetery Hill. They had all been put into buildings, but no care or attention had been given them at all, and their wounds had become badly inflamed and were in a very sore condition. Owing to the hot weather many of their wounds had begun to gangrene, thus rendering their recovery far more doubtful than if attention had been given them when first wounded. The fourth of July we spent in moving those wounded who had fallen into the enemy's hands, and a very busy day we had of it before our work was completed there. To add to the disagreeableness of our task, about noon it began to rain and during the afternoon we had several hard, heavy, violent showers. Indeed for severity and violence the times were few and far separated when there were any rain showed to exceed those of today. In a comparatively short time almost the entire face of the country seemed converted into a raging flood of water, sweeping along the valleys and down the hillside slopes, with rapidity and terrible force. It was a fact, and noticed upon the occasion of every hard fought battle during the war, that rain fell, sometimes in great abundance for two or three days following.[12]

Private Justus M. Silliman of the 17th Connecticut was one of the lucky ones who escaped the travails described by Private Smith. "We had every attention shown us, our wounds promptly attended to and received kind treatment," he wrote home to his mother about his time in Confederate hospitals. "Those who a short time previous had been hurling death at us, now assisted our wounded, bringing them water, crackers etc."[13]

Captain Alfred E. Lee of the 82nd Ohio and XI Corps division commander Francis C. Barlow were among the July 1 wounded being cared for in the John Crawford house at 444 Harrisburg Street north of town when an ambulance corps worker hurried in on the morning of the 4th. The corpsman told them it was time

12 Smith, *Camps and Campaigns*, 123-124.

13 Silliman to his mother, July 3, 1863, *A New Canaan Private in the Civil War*, 41.

Capt. Alfred E. Lee

US Army Heritage and Education Center

to evacuate, for the Confederates had pulled back and were now threatening to bombard the town. The man helped Lee and Barlow into a wagon and drove to the Spangler hospital, where Lee was placed in the upper floor of the barn. Barlow was taken into the Spangler house, where he would have the privacy befitting a general. Both men survived their wounds.

Twenty years later, Captain Lee described his ordeal on the battlefield and how he had arrived at the Crawford home on July 1: "A stalwart young fellow dropped at my side, and cried, 'Oh, help me!' Having taken my hand, he struggled to rise, but could not, and, finding his efforts unavailing, murmured, 'Oh, I'm gone! just leave me here.' A moment or two later," continued Lee, "I felt the sting of a bullet, and fell benumbed with pain. It was an instantaneous metamorphosis from strength and vigor to utter helplessness." The entire field around him "was strewn with the prostrate bodies of men in blue." The officer continued:

> I was interrupted by a rebel battery, which came up at a brisk canter and unlimbered its guns where we lay. They seemed to be about to commence firing on the town, through which our troops were yet retreating. Some of the artillerymen having noticed the danger I was in of being trampled by the horses, two of them very gently removed me to a place of greater safety. Supporting my arms on the friendly shoulders of these men and listening to their rough words of sympathy, I could not but feel that they were, after all, both fellow-men and

fellow-countrymen, and wonder how we could be, or rather have been, such deadly enemies.[14]

That evening, a Confederate cavalryman rode up, dismounted, and began tending to the wounded and dying Army of the Potomac men, called for an ambulance and surgeon, and had Captain Lee taken to the Crawford house.

After he was picked up on July 4 and spent several days at the Spangler hospital, Lee and others "who could be removed were furloughed, placed upon a freight-train, and taken to Baltimore, where some of us had the pleasure of seeing in the papers our names (misspelled) in the lists of the killed," he explained. "A few days later I had the additional satisfaction of reading my obituary notice in our home-paper in Ohio, and of spoiling, by an untimely and inconsiderate reappearance, a certain eloquent funeral-sermon that was about to be preached."[15]

Lieutenant Colonel Hans Boebel was hit twice in the right leg leading the 26th Wisconsin during the July 1 fight north of town, first by a Minie ball and then by a shell fragment. The 26th had advanced into a perfect maelstrom of death on the right side of Krzyzanowski's brigade as Barlow's position collapsed. The ambulances found Boebel untreated and writhing in agony three days later and deposited him at the Spangler farm. As he conveyed to a visiting minister, he had "been four days among the idiots in the County Poor House near Gettysburg." After a portion of his right leg was amputated above the knee, Boebel was discharged and sent home to Wisconsin.[16]

With 217 casualties, the 26th Wisconsin suffered more losses than any of the five regiments in Colonel Krzyzanowski's brigade, Schurz's division. The 45th and 157th New York regiments, both in the same division but in General Schimmelfennig's brigade, suffered 224 and 307 casualties, respectively. The majority of these losses were suffered on July 1 around the Adams County Almshouse—where Boebel suffered inside as a prisoner.[17]

14 A company officer, "Reminiscences of the Gettysburg Battle," in *Lippincott's Magazine of Popular Literature and Science* (Philadelphia, PA, 1883), vol. 32, 56-59.

15 Ibid., 60.

16 F. J. F. Schantz, "Recollections of Visitations at Gettysburg After the Great Battle in July, 1863," in Ralph S. Shay, ed., *Reflections on the Battle of Gettysburg*, vol. 13, no. 6, Lebanon County, PA, Historical Society. "Recollections" is an address written by Schantz in 1890. The manuscript was provided by Agnes S. Haak and Mildred C. Haak, granddaughters of the Rev. Schantz. See also, Pula, *Under the Crescent Moon with the XI Corps in the Civil War*, vol. 2, 60-61.

17 "Return of Casualties in the Union Forces," *OR* 27, pt. 1, 183.

Initially, many of the wounded from the 26th Wisconsin and other regiments of both armies were taken to a church in town behind Confederate lines, where they were attended by Dr. Francis Huebschmann, a prominent German immigrant and politician in Wisconsin and the only surgeon in attendance at this hospital. At one point during the July 1 fight, with his makeshift hospital suffering under Confederate artillery fire, an angry Dr. Huebschmann is said to have risked his life by storming outside in the wide open in his blood-stained surgeon's apron to yell at the troops to stop firing at the wounded and instead aim for healthy soldiers who could defend themselves. Huebschmann left town with the 26th Wisconsin after the battle.[18]

Some of the 26th Wisconsin and other injured men of the XI Corps taken to the Spangler hospital held on in pain for a month or more only to die elsewhere. The 26th's Pvt. Franz Benda and Pvt. Nicholaus Young, for example, died at Camp Letterman, and Pvt. Carl Behling survived long enough to die in Baltimore.

The brunt of the Confederate assault, however, fell upon Barlow's division, comprised of the brigades of Ames and von Gilsa. Fighting with Company H in the 17th Connecticut of Ames' command were two good friends from New Canaan. Both had enlisted the previous summer, and both would be wounded and end up together at George and Elizabeth Spangler's farm.

A ball grazed Pvt. Justus Silliman's head, knocking him unconscious. He spent the first three days of July as a prisoner, wondering and worried about his friend Sam Comstock. Silliman found the seriously wounded sergeant on July 4 at the Spangler farm, and described how he cared for him in letters home from the XI Corps hospital. "I searched for Sam as soon as I arrived here," he explained in a July 7 missive. "It was raining quite hard and I finaly found him lying out in the storm in a puddle of water. I procured a stretcher, and with the assistance of others finaly got him in a comparatively comfortable quarters where he still remains." Comstock had remained on the field all night and part of the next day, when someone transported him to the Almshouse. He remained there until July 4, continued Silliman, "when he was recaptured and sent to this place. The bullet entered his hip just below the back bone and was cut out at the side of his leg. The bone is some splintered but it is believed not broken. He is rather weak but has a good appetite and is in good spirits," he added, "his wound is doing well and pains him scarcely any, and although it will be a long time before he will be able to walk I

18 Story by the Milwaukee County Historical Society, "The Cultured Pioneer and Framer of Our State Constitution," www.russscott.com/~rscott/26thwis/franzhub.htm. Accessed December 10, 2017.

Pvt. Justus M. Silliman

New Canaan (CT) Historical Society

have but little doubt that he will in the end come out all right." On July 15, he observed, "Sam is doing well though is quite weak and tired of lying so long in one position. He is in comfortable quarters and has good attention."

Despite that fact that he believed Comstock would "come out all right," Silliman remained concerned about his friend. Two months after the battle on September 3, Silliman penned another letter home, this one from Camp Letterman outside of Gettysburg. "You have probably received the letter I wrote after the reception of the box. Sam enjoys the wine very much he has regular rations of whisky prescribed but take the wine instead which is much pleasanter and more beneficial. I suppose this will shock certain members of the temperance society to hear of it," he continued with a glint of humor, "but I hope they may survive the offense. Sam appears to be improving very slowly. . . . His leg is still suspended in a sling, and he is obliged to remain in one position, but he is in good spirits though quite weak and thin."

Silliman's letters home, however, took a dark turn near the end of the month. "I have just returned from visiting Sam," he began on September 26, and

> he is failing rapidly and is liable to drop away at any moment. He seemed disinclined to talk and wished to sleep. I have made arrangements so that I can have him embalmed. The cost of embalming will be $15.00, box $5.00, Expressage would cost about $24.00 but I went over to see Gen'l Terry to day and when I wish it I can obtain from him transportation to my regt. with permission to go to New Canaan which he says will give me about four or five days there. He has

no authority to grant furloughs but manage it in that way so as to amount to the same thing. He was very kind to arrange it in that way. So if nothing happens to prevent I shall have Sams body embalmed and will leave with it for home as soon as I can procure sufficient money.

Sergeant Sam Comstock died the next day. He was just 21. Silliman got him home as promised, and he is buried in New Canaan. Silliman rejoined the 17th Connecticut and survived the war.[19]

Silliman and Pvt. James Henry Blakeman, Company D, 17th Connecticut, were hit about the same time north of the almshouse. Blakeman (who preferred to be called Henry because both his grandfather and father were named James) had enlisted with his cousin Selah Blakeman on July 29, 1862, and mustered into the 17th Connecticut a month later on August 28. Like his comrade Silliman, Blakeman was taken to the Spangler farm on July 4. "I was hit the first day before I had time to fire my gun, taken prisoner and kept one day then taken to the city and next day our folk took the town and I was taken to our hospital some three miles back," he wrote his mother on the day he arrived at the field hospital. "Here we have to lie on the ground and last night we had a terrible rain so I am a wet as water can make me but that is good for the wound. I was struck by a rifle ball in the left side between the hip and ribs passing through the flank, he continued. "Dr. says he thinks it did not enter the cavity and if not it will heal soon. Do not worry about me for it will do no good. I don't mind it much can get up and walk around quite spry and have a good appetite." Blakeman evidenced both his doubt and his pride about General Howard's corps when he added, "The 11th Corps did not run much this time as their Cas[ualties] plainly show. . . . Tell them I was hit face towards them no Reb saw my back."[20]

Private Blakeman was sent to Jarvis General Hospital in Baltimore on July 13. In a letter to his sister, he described the conditions he experienced at the Spangler hospital and included words to comfort her. "Before we came here we saw pretty hard times lying on the ground with only a shelter tent for five days," he explained. "I was wet through and had not half enough to eat. I wore the same shirt that I was wounded in all bloody for nine days and half that time it was full of maggots & I

19 Silliman letters to family members, *A New Canaan Private in the Civil War*, 43, 45, 47-48.

20 J. Henry Blakeman letter, July 4, 1863, in Lewis Leigh Collection, Book 40/Box 21. US Army Education and Heritage Center, transcribed by Kathleen Georg Harrison, Gettysburg National Military Park.

wore the same pants till I got here. We have now good beds pleasant nurses and plenty to eat."[21]

Cousin Selah survived Gettysburg without so much as a scratch. Henry recovered from his wounds and rejoined his unit. The Blakemans fought together through the rest of the war and mustered out on July 19, 1865, at Hilton Head, South Carolina. Henry went on to serve in the Connecticut legislature.[22]

Because they were usually out in front carrying large national and state banners, flag bearers presented perfect targets for enemy riflemen. Sergeant Lewis Bishop was the national flag color bearer for the 154th New York, Coster's brigade, in the vicious brickyard fight on July 1. Somehow he had passed through the furious assault by Stonewall Jackson's men at Chancellorsville without injury, though his flag and staff endured more than 20 bullet holes. He wasn't as fortunate on the northeast side of Gettysburg, where he was hit in both legs when the regimental position was overrun. Corporal Albert Mericle, the 19-year-old carrier of the state flag in the same regiment, took a crippling blow in the body. Lieutenant James W. Bird of the 154th picked up Mericle's state flag and made his escape—one of the few able to do so. On July 2, Bird was among a dozen or so men from the 154th New York assigned to duty at the XI Corps hospital.

On July 4, the ambulances picked up Bishop, Mericle, and many others from the Brickyard fight, which also included the 27th Pennsylvania and 134th New York. "I saw corporal M[ericle] . . . at the 11th Corps Hospital" on the operating table, recalled Bird after the war. "When he saw me he said 'you are the man who took the flag when I was shot. The reb Lieutenant ordered his men to fire at you, he said 'shoot that son of a bitch with the flag.'" The wounded man's words were among his last, for as Bird sadly noted, "Corporal Miracle was shot through the bowels, and died in two or three days."[23]

The actions of these brave men did not pass unnoticed or unremembered. A New York state relief agent wrote of the time he had spent at Spangler, recalling, "I saw in one tent three soldiers of the 154th who were shot one after another while holding the colors of their Regiment. These were Albert Mericle, Lewis Bishop and Rickert [Cpl. Gilbert M. Rykert, arm amputated], and I think the name of [Sgt.]

21 Blakeman, July 17, 1863, Lewis Leigh Collection.

22 www.civilwardata.com/active/hdsquery.dll?SoldierHistory?U&642802. Accessed May 3, 2017; George Curtis Waldo Jr., ed., *History of Bridgeport and Vicinity*, 2 vols. (New York, NY, and Chicago, IL, 1917), vol. 2, 608.

23 James W. Bird to Matthew B. Cheney, November 30, 1893, and to Northrup, May 20, 1891, in Edwin Dwight Northrup Papers, Box 35, Carl A. Kroch Library, Cornell University.

Col. Eliakim Sherrill's image is on the monument to the 126th New York on Cemetery Ridge.

Ron Kirkwood

John A. Bush [arm amputated] should be added." The Rev. Franklin J. F. Schantz made two visits to the XI Corps hospital. "I was for some time with Louis Bishop," wrote the Lutheran minister from Lehigh County, Pennsylvania. "He was the bold soldier who would not give up his flag when one of his legs was shot off. He stuck to his flag."[24] Rykert and Bush survived their wounds. Mericle died on July 10. Bishop had one leg amputated and died July 31. Both are buried in the New York section of the Soldiers' National Cemetery. Bishop's older brother George, a sergeant, was killed carrying the colors less than a year later in the battle of Rocky Face Ridge in Georgia.[25]

Colonel Eliakim Sherrill of the 126th New York (Col. George Willard's brigade, Brig. Gen. Alexander Hays' division, Hancock's II Corps), was 50 years old when he died in the Spangler house on July 4 after being wounded in the bowels the day before while defending Ziegler's Grove during Pickett's Charge. Sherrill was beloved in central New York, which he had represented as both a state senator and US congressman before forming the 126th regiment in 1862. On July 15, 1863, the *Geneva* (NY) *Courier* penned a eulogy to the fallen officer. "This sad occasion brought together on Sunday last, one of the largest and saddest assemblages, that ever met in our Village," lamented the editorial. "The demonstration showed both

24 Mark H. Dunkelman, *Brothers, Heroes, Martyrs: The Civil War Service of Lewis and George Bishop, Color Bearers of the 154th New York Volunteer Infantry* (Allegany, NY, 1994), 16; Schantz, "Recollections of Visitations at Gettysburg after the Great Battle in July, 1863," *Reflections on the Battle of Gettysburg*, Lebanon County, PA, Historical Society.

25 Carded Medical Records Volunteers, Mexican, and Civil Wars, 1846-1865, Records of the Adjutant General's Office, RG 94, Entry 534, 154th New York, Box 2744, National Archives and Records Administration, Washington, D.C.; George Bishop, New York Civil War Muster Roll Abstract, Fold3.

the respect that is felt for the memory of the man and the sympathy that pervades the community, for the cause in which he so nobly, so heroically lost his life. . . . So deeply had he endeared himself to all who knew him, that scarcely a man could have been taken from our midst who would have been longer remembered, or whose loss would have been more deeply regretted. . . . The Streets in all directions, were full."[26]

Sherrill, the brigade's senior colonel, was in his first full day of command of the brigade because Colonel Willard had been killed the previous evening. Members of the 39th New York had carried the mortally wounded officer to the XI Corps hospital so quickly that the men in Sherrill's regiment didn't even know about it until word arrived days later that he had died. Colonel Sherrill's image is on the monument to the 126th New York in Ziegler's Grove.

* * *

With the fighting over around Gettysburg except for occasional skirmishing and sharpshooting, the food shortage at the various hospitals finally eased on July 4. With more of the roads clear, wagons arrived with some 30,000 rations, and the Christian and Sanitary commissions were allowed into town in force.[27]

The ambulances wrapped up their battlefield rescue mission on the morning of July 5, with a final few pickups on the west end of town after the Confederates finishing clearing out. According to Capt. Louis C. Duncan of the Army of the Potomac Medical Corps, despite being in the line of fire for three terrible days, not one of the 100 XI Corps ambulances was lost. The II Corps medical teams were almost as fortunate, losing only three wagons while picking up and delivering wounded to the Spangler Granite Schoolhouse and other II Corps hospitals.[28]

On the battlefield, meanwhile, the identification and burial of the dead for both sides began in earnest on the 4th and would continue for weeks after the armies left. One of the burial parties consisted of Sgt. Thomas P. Meyer and his 10-man Pioneer Corps from the 148th Pennsylvania of Col. Edward Cross' brigade—the same Cross who had died on Spangler property at the Granite

---

26 https://dmna.ny.gov/historic/reghist/civil/infantry/126thInf/126thInfCWN.htm. Accessed March 13, 2017.

27 Duncan, "The Greatest Battle of the War—Gettysburg," in Samuel Cecil Stanton, ed., *The Military Surgeon: Journal of the Association of Military Surgeons of the United States*, 96 vols. (Chicago, Il, 1913), vol. 32, 218.

28 Ibid., 267.

Schoolhouse facility. Sergeant Meyer's group was responsible for burying some of the dead killed the day before during Pickett's Charge.

"The field presented a dreadful sight," recalled Meyer. "The dead were already in a terrible state of putrefaction. Faces black as coal and bloated out of all human semblance; eyes, cheeks, forehead and nose all one general level of putrid swelling, twice the normal size with here and there great blisters of putrid water, some the size of a man's fist on face, neck and wrists; while the bodies were bloated to the full capacity of the uniforms that enclosed them." One thing the sergeant never forgot was the "indescribable and suffocating stench." The weather, which included "frequent dreadfully heavy showers of rain" mixed with "the great heat of the sun between showers," made it all the worse, and "Confederate sharpshooters in great numbers hid in the trees beyond the Emmitsburg road kept the bullets whistling about us all the time adding danger to the gruesome job."[29]

Groups from nearly all the front-line regiments participated in the repulsive work. "We returned to Little Round Top, where we buried our dead in the place where we had laid them during the fight, marking each grave by a head-board made of ammunition boxes, with each dead soldiers name cut upon it," wrote Col. Joshua Lawrence Chamberlain of the 20th Maine near the end of his official report. "We also buried 50 of the enemys dead in front of our position of July 2." The 20th Maine had spent time on July 2 resting on or near the Spangler property before moving south to hold the spur on Little Round Top.[30]

The suffering extended to the horses as well. Large numbers of the animals, wounded and starving, were still on the field with some desperately crawling on their knees in search of water. Soldiers cut short the horses' misery with a bullet. The battle left several thousand dead horses behind, most of which were burned. Though fairly removed from the battlefield, the stench was so bad in town that citizens there covered their noses with handkerchiefs to filter out the smell. Human and animal corpses in or near streams fouled the waterways and, combined with human and animal waste, caused even more illness and suffering downstream when desperately thirsty patients and staff at hospitals drank the water. Even with recent rains, many Gettysburg-area wells were fouled.

There were more patients and thus more suffering on the Spangler property on July 4-5 than at any time during or after the battle because the wounded and dying were still arriving and large-scale departures to general hospitals and home had not

29 Thomas P. Meyer, "The Pioneer's Story," 465, 453.

30 OR 27, pt. 1, 626.

begun. The Sanitary Commission estimated that there were 1,900 wounded at the XI Corps hospital on July 5. Shortly afterward, Assistant Surgeon Dwight W. Day of the 154th New York put the number at more than 2,200.[31]

Major General Schurz witnessed that mass of agony when he visited his men at the Spangler farm on July 4. The sights and sounds and suffering never left him, and he wrote about it in depth years later in his memoirs. "Many of the wounded men suffered with silent fortitude, fierce determination in the knitting of their brows and the steady gaze of their bloodshot eyes," he began, continuing,

> Some would even force themselves to a grim jest about their situation or about the 'skedaddling of the rebels,' but there were, too, heart-rending groans and shrill cries of pain piercing the air, and despairing exclamations, 'Oh, Lord! Oh, Lord!' or 'Let me die!' or softer murmurings in which the words 'mother' or 'father' or 'home' were often heard. I saw many of my command among the sufferers, whose faces I well remembered, and who greeted me with a look or even a painful smile of recognition, and usually with the question what I thought of their chances of life, or whether I could do anything for them, sometimes, also, whether I thought the enemy were well beaten. I was sadly conscious that many of the words of cheer and encouragement I gave them were mere hollow sound, but they might be at least some solace for the moment.

Schurz, who saw more than his share of bloodshed during the war, lamented that "There are people who speak lightly of war as a mere heroic sport. They would hardly find it in their hearts to do so," he continued, "had they ever witnessed scenes like these, and thought of the untold miseries connected with them that were spread all over the land. He must be an inhuman brute or a slave of wild, unscrupulous ambition, who, having seen the horrors of war, will not admit that war brought on without the most absolute necessity, is the greatest and most unpardonable of crimes."[32]

In a pounding thunderstorm unleashed by the heavens after dark on July 4, the beaten and battered Army of Northern Virginia infantry, artillery, and cavalrymen slogged away from Gettysburg. Parts of the Army of the Potomac, injured almost

---

31 Report on the Operations of the Sanitary Commission During and After the Battles at Gettysburg (New York, NY, 1863), 24; *Cattaraugus Union*, in Dunkelman's *Brothers One and All*, 144.

32 Schurz, *The Reminiscences of Carl Schurz*, 40.

as severely as its opponent, began following the Confederates the next day. Left behind at the XI Corps hospital, the wounded from both sides began a healing process that, for some, would last a lifetime.

Spangler Farm Short Story

Provost Marshal Brigadier General Marsena R. Patrick had a checkpoint on July 4 on the Baltimore Pike at the base of the Spanglers' Powers Hill near General Meade's former headquarters. As essentially the chief of police for the army, Patrick's duties included handling Confederate prisoners, corralling Union stragglers, reclaiming government property after the fight, preventing pillaging by civilians and soldiers, and much more.[33]

As Confederate prisoners moved south through this checkpoint, Marsena's men stopped those they considered too seriously wounded to travel a couple miles down the road to the prisoner holding area across from what the locals called White Church (at the intersection of the Baltimore Pike and White Church Road). These prisoners were sent across the road from the Spangler property to a hospital at McAllister's Mill. Those who died on McAllister property were buried there.[34]

Ruch Report No. 4

His Path to the Spangler Farm
Private Reuben F. Ruch, Company F, 153rd Pennsylvania, the morning of July 4, 1863

"Before I left [the hospital in town] Dr. Stout filled my pockets with bandages, lint, and sticking plaster," explained the private. "He told me I would find lots of boys who had not yet seen a doctor, and that I could dress a wound as well as

---

33 General Meade's July 3-4 headquarters was on Spangler and Lightner property on the Baltimore Pike near the present-day General Slocum XII Corps headquarters marker (39°48'29"N 77°13'4"W). The National Park Service calls the group of trees there the George Spangler Grove, which is about 140 yards to the north (heading toward Gettysburg) of the present-day Baltimore Pike intersection with Granite Schoolhouse Lane. There is no marker honoring the site.

34 Curt Musselman, "McAllister's Mill and the Underground Railroad," *The Sentinel*, a publication of the National Park Service (Gettysburg, PA, 2013), 7.

anybody, and to keep plenty of water on the wounds. I came to Gettysburg a mere private, and when I left I was a sort of full-fledged doctor. I had two ramrods for canes, and my face had not been washed for four days, my pants were ripped for two feet on the outside seam. . . ."

Ruch continued:

I got back to where Pickett's charge had been repulsed the day before. The sight was horrible. The dead Rebs were hanging on the stone wall and on both sides of the fence it was full of dead men. On the Union side they were being carried into rows. They had three rows started and it reminded me of gathering the sheaves in a harvest field. I took a seat on a large stone near the wall and watched the men at their work for over an hour. Then started on for the rear, and must have gotten back about two miles from the town when I came to a barn. Of course the barn doors were open, and I asked a man where I could find the Eleventh Corps hospital. Just as I spoke I heard voices in the barn which was full of wounded . . . the boys of our regiment who were there cheered for me, and said they had room for me. The reason I had such a reception was that it had been reported that I was killed. This barn was full of wounded men from one end to the other. Where there was room for a man you could find one. The hay mows, the feed room, the cow stable, the horse stable and loft.[35]

Chapter 15

The Barlows:
A Wounded General and his Wife
at the Spangler Farm

"Among our wounded, were three Colonels, Gen. Barlow, & Gen. Armistead."
— *Dr. Daniel G. Brinton*

On July 1, Brig. Gen. Francis Barlow arranged his XI Corps division on ground north of Gettysburg forever after known as Barlow Knoll. Unfortunately for the Union cause, it proved indefensible in the face of the aggressive enemy assault and was overrun. He was hit three times that afternoon. One of the bullets penetrated his left side halfway between his armpit and thigh and lodged in his pelvic cavity.

Confederates carried away the dangerously wounded general on a blanket to some shade next to Rock Creek. From there, Union prisoners carried him to the Josiah Benner house on Old Harrisburg Road. Three Confederate doctors examined the high-ranking officer and told him that day and the next that there was nothing they could do for him. An Army of the Potomac doctor working behind enemy lines agreed that Barlow's wound was mortal. The boyish-looking general was given morphine for the pain and told to keep cold water on his wounds. No

---

1 Brinton, "From Chancellorsville to Gettysburg, a Doctor's Diary," 313. Doctor Brinton was at the XI Corps hospital from July 1 to July 5, at which time he left with the Army of the Potomac to pursue Robert E. Lee.

Brig. Gen. Francis Barlow

Library of Congress

one believed Barlow would live long enough to reach the Spangler XI Corps hospital or survive the bumpy, fitful ride there.

Barlow spent a long and agonizing night at the Benner house before being moved to the John Crawford home on Harrisburg Street, where he remained for the last two days of the battle. Both locations were in Confederate hands. In fact, Lt. Gen. Richard Ewell, who commanded Stonewall Jackson's old corps, was served dinner with his staff at the Crawford house on July 1 and breakfast the following morning.

As it turned out, the 29-year-old New Yorker and son of a minister Barlow was very much alive on the morning of July 4, and to the surprise of many deemed fit enough to travel. He was placed in an ambulance and taken to the Spangler farm hospital with, or at about the same time as, Capt. Alfred E. Lee of the 82nd Ohio. Lee had been a patient on the first floor of the Crawford house, while Barlow was tended upstairs.

Lee was placed in the Spangler barn while Barlow was probably taken into the house where other officers were being treated with sufficient privacy befitting their ranks. (The Spangler family of six remained squeezed into one upstairs bedroom.) The other wounded general on the property when Barlow arrived on July 4 wore Confederate gray. Brigadier General Lewis Armistead was in the detached summer kitchen only a few yards from the house. He would die there the next day.

The 82nd Ohio's Captain Lee described what he saw when the wounded from the Crawford house arrived at the XI Corps hospital:

We were hurriedly carried to the ambulances and driven to a field-hospital established in a large barn a mile or more from Gettysburg. In and around that barn were gathered about fifteen hundred wounded soldiers, Union and Confederate. They were begrimed, swollen, and bloody, as brought in from the field, and, for the most part, had received as yet but little surgical treatment. Some were barely alive, others had just died, and many were in a state of indescribable misery.[2]

General Barlow was something of a VIP at Spangler. The young general graduated first in his class at Harvard before becoming a lawyer, which he put on hold in 1861 to join a New York unit as a private. In just two years he had shot up the ranks to brigadier general. His improbable rise was all the more amazing because he had no military training. Barlow was a dynamo, a young aggressive man who gained promotion after promotion by impressing his superiors with his intelligence, drive, discipline of troops, attention to detail, and strength and courage in battle. He bravely led from the front, and displayed the same fortitude after he fell wounded. He also had a tender side, as evidenced by his regular letters home indicating his love for his family.

Dr. Brinton had served in Barlow's division earlier that year before being transferred to von Steinwehr's division. Like so many others, Brinton had ample opportunity to witness another side of Barlow. The young general could be overly judgmental and condescending, and in his mind he was always right. Perhaps he was too tough and too proud of his own accomplishments. "Gen. Barlow . . . is a young man, about thirty, vastly puffed up at the idea of his elevation, and so puts on all manner of airs, which make him very generally disliked among his subordinates," explained Dr. Brinton in a letter to his father after Chancellorsville but before the army set out for Pennsylvania. "He commenced by overhauling me about a hospital over which he supposed I had jurisdiction. I objected to having much to due with it, as it was out of my province. So he constituted himself medical officer," he continued, "with the result that he was reported to Gen. Howard for interfering in an injurious manner in the medical affairs of the Division. The

2   Alfred E. Lee, "Reminiscences of the Gettysburg Battle," *Lippincott's Magazine*, July 1883, 60, GNMP Library, Box V8.

prospect of living amicably on his staff was not favorable. So I was not sorry to be sent here."[3] Now, on the Fourth of July, Brinton and Barlow were reunited.

The disastrous surprise and rout of Howard's XI Corps at Chancellorsville did not include Barlow's brigade, which was detached at the time. But his division was right in the middle of it when the XI Corps was swept from the field north of Gettysburg on the first day of the battle. The severely wounded Barlow, however, refused to accept blame for the affair. Instead, he placed it squarely on the Germans under his command. "These Dutch won't fight," Barlow fumed in a letter written three days after he arrived at the Spangler farm. "The enemy's skirmishers had hardly attacked us before my men began to run."[4]

It was an unfair slander, all the more so given the heavy casualties suffered by the men he placed in thin array on ground so far forward they could be attacked from multiple sides. Officers in both armies disagreed with his condemnation and claimed instead that the XI Corps soldiers put up an obstinate fight. Now resting at the Spangler hospital, Barlow was surrounded by many of those same Germans, some gravely wounded and dying, who had followed his orders and bravely moved too far out in front with him onto "Barlow Knoll."

"Among our wounded," wrote Dr. Brinton to his father, "were three Colonels, Gen. Barlow, & Gen. Armistead." The three colonels consisted of Eliakim Sherrill of the 126th New York, II Corps; Francis Mahler of the 75th Pennsylvania, XI Corps; and Hans Boebel of the 26th Wisconsin, XI Corps. Sherrill and Mahler would die in the Spangler house. Boebel had part of his right leg amputated, survived, and went home to Wisconsin.[5]

Evidence suggests that Barlow's wife, Arabella, was with him at the Spangler farm, and perhaps even earlier in Gettysburg. She was 39 that summer, making her 10 years older than her husband. Family and friends called them Belle and Frank. Barlow's thin build and boyish face made the age difference seem even more stark. Wealthy New York socialite and family friend Maria Lydig Daly called Frank the

---

3 Brinton to his father, May 29, 1863, Dr. Daniel Garrison Brinton Papers.

4 Barlow to his mother, July 7, 1863, and to Robert Treat Paine, August 12, 1863. Original letters in the Francis Channing Barlow Papers, 1861-1864, Massachusetts Historical Society, Boston. Copies in GNMP Library, Box B-70, File 85b, General Francis C. Barlow.

5 Brinton, "From Chancellorsville to Gettysburg, a Doctor's Diary," 313. All told, the Spanglers had four generals treated on their property. This number includes Gens. Samuel Zook and Winfield Hancock on July 2 and July 3, respectively, across the field from the Spangler barn at the First Division, II Corps hospital at the Granite Schoolhouse. Hancock was present there after his wound suffered during Pickett's Charge, and it is likely his medical condition was attended to during that time.

"boy-husband" of Belle, who mingled in literary circles in New York City and wowed those who knew her with her intelligence, energy, and loving personality. They married on April 20, 1861, and Frank left the next day for war.[6]

The former Arabella Wharton Griffith also went to war, volunteering as a nurse with the US Sanitary Commission, an organization that provided valuable nursing, sanitation, and provisions services to the Union army. Arabella was praised for her tireless efforts, which also allowed her to be close in proximity to Frank. She nurtured him for months after he was seriously wounded at Antietam on September 17, 1862, and she would do so again after he was nearly killed at Gettysburg.

Multiple accounts describe how she reached her husband in Gettysburg. Confederate Brig. Gen. John B. Gordon claimed to have spoken to the wounded Barlow on the battlefield and offered to contact Arabella and get her to him under a flag of truce. That night, Gordon later wrote, "She was carried to her husband's side . . . by my staff."[7]

General Howard recalled her presence during the battle, writing, "I can never forget how speedily, as if led by instinct, his good wife found her way from Frederick or Baltimore to our lines after they had been established on Cemetery Ridge. She said, as she found me not far from the Cemetery gates, "'Gen. Howard, my husband is wounded and left within the enemy's lines, I MUST GO TO HIM!'" Howard continued:

> Whether she tried Gen. Meade or not, to see if he would send her through by a flag of truce, I am not able to say. She said, 'They will not fire at me,' and so started rapidly down the Baltimore pike toward the court-house. But as the firing continued from church tower, housetops, house windows, and other places of shelter, the rifle-balls striking the earth and graveled street near her, she became alarmed for her safety and returned. 'I cannot go through there,' she said. She undertook this bold enterprise once again. I will go off there' pointing to the left,

---

6 Barlow did not mention Arabella in his letters, writing his mother, "I have our coloured man Horace & one convalescent left here as a guard." Barlow to his mother, July 7, 1863. Arabella Barlow's letters no longer exist. Francis Channing Barlow Papers, 1861-1864, Massachusetts Historical Society, and GNMP Library; Maria Lydig Daly, in Harold Earl Hammond, ed., *Diary of a Union Lady, 1861-1865* (New York, NY, 1962), 46.

7 John B. Gordon, "The Last Days of the Confederacy," a speech delivered October 24, 1896, in Kutztown, PA. The speech is on file at The Historical Society of Schuylkill County, Pottsville, PA. A copy is on file at the GNMP Library, Box 5, Participant Accounts, Gordon, John B.

The Francis Barlow statue
on Barlow Knoll.

Ron Kirkwood

'where both sides can see me.' She
did so, and this time succeeded in
passing through both skirmish-lines
and reaching her husband.[8]

"On the evening of the second
about dusk," recalled 18-year-old
Gettysburg resident Daniel Edward
Skelly, "Will McCreary and I were
sent on some errands down on
Chambersburg street and . . . we were
halted by two Confederate soldiers
who had a lady in their charge. She
was on horseback and proved to be
the wife of General Barlow who had
come into the Confederate lines under a flag of truce looking for her husband, who
had been severely wounded on July 1, and as she was informed, had been brought
into town."[9]

These accounts place Arabella with her husband on the night of July 1 at the
Benner house or on July 2 after Barlow had been moved to the Crawford home.
Another account indicates Arabella entered town in a carriage at the same time as
her husband. Did she find him at the Benner or Crawford homes? Did she arrive
with him at Spangler? Did they meet up later? Someday, perhaps, history will reveal
this secret.

Arabella probably stayed a little longer than one week, and probably on the
Spangler property. Barlow arrived there on Saturday, July 4, and wrote in a July 7

8   Howard, "A Wife's Devotion," clipping on file at the GNMP Library, File 85b, General
Francis C. Barlow.

9   Skelly, *A Boy's Experiences During the Battles of Gettysburg,* 17-18.

letter that he was in "a small house near Gettysburg, Penn. 3 miles out on the turnpike near Baltimore." The Spangler house isn't that far out, but a seriously wounded man unfamiliar with the area can be excused for misjudging the distance. There also is a report of him being taken to a house near Little Round Top. "I shall leave here on Friday & reach New York on Sat," he wrote in the same letter, which would have had him leaving town a little more than one week after receiving his life-threatening wound. XI Corps Assistant Medical Director Dr. Robert Hubbard was in charge of the Spangler farm hospital on July 10, and he spoke to the general that morning.[10]

Barlow left Gettysburg and continued his long recovery under Arabella's care. The general who was judged mortally wounded by multiple doctors returned to command, though in a weakened state, in April 1864 in the II Corps under an even more debilitated Hancock. Illnesses, perhaps the result of his severe wounds, resulted in several leaves of absence for Barlow.

Belle and Frank tried to get together whenever possible during breaks in the fighting, but she also was unwell. Her work and exposure to various diseases in medical facilities had exhausted and weakened her. She contracted typhus and struggled for weeks to regain her health. When she died on July 27, 1864, in Washington, D.C., her husband was fighting in the First Battle of Deep Bottom in Virginia. The news of his wife's death devastated Barlow, who took a leave of absence to bury her in her hometown of Somerville, New Jersey. She died at age 40 after three years of a marriage marked by civil war, illness, separation, and her husband's life-threatening battle wounds.

Spangler Farm Short Story

Francis Barlow ended the Civil War as a major general, a huge climb from his entry into service as a private. He continued his climb professionally after the war as secretary of state for New York and then as the state's attorney general, prosecuting New York City's politically corrupt Tammany Hall Boss Tweed ring. Afterward, Barlow returned to his law practice and was one of the founders of the American Bar Association. In 1867, he married Ellen Shaw, the sister of Col. Robert Gould

10 Barlow to his mother, July 7, 1863, Francis Channing Barlow Papers; Robert Hubbard Papers, Civil War Manuscripts Collection (MS 619), Manuscripts and Archives, Yale University Library (New Haven, CT). Copies on file at the GNMP Library. V5—Participant Accounts. Hubbard, Robert—Surgeon 17 CT INF.

Shaw, the commander killed while leading the famous charge against Battery Wagner at the head of his black 54th Massachusetts Infantry.

Barlow died at age 61 in 1896. One of his children, Charles, wrote to the National Park Service in Gettysburg in 1960 to offer the following story: "The spring before his death I went with my father to Thomasville, Ga. One night there was a knock on his door & a man came in who said 'Gen. Barlow I am the night watch man & was the Confederate soldier who picked you up in Gettysburg.'"

A statue of Barlow was dedicated in 1922 on modern-day Howard Avenue, where he led his troops on Barlow Knoll. The village of Barlow just south of Gettysburg is named after the Union general.

Barlow never specifically mentioned the XI Corps Spangler hospital in his writings.[11]

A Citizen's Account of the Search for Mrs. Barlow

"Towards the close of this memorable first day I was going up the street to attend to an errand when a Confederate rode up to me and said: 'Can you tell me where I can find Mrs. Barlow?'

"'Who is Mrs. Barlow?' I asked.

"'She's the wife of one of your Yankee generals. He's wounded and wants her.'

"Said I: 'Where does he say his wife is?'

"'He says he left her in a carriage in one of your streets.'

I told him I knew nothing of her, but if he would ask at the hotel near by he might find her.

"'Oh, d — n it,' he said. 'I believe if I'd ask the very man that had her in his house he'd be too scared to tell me anything.'

"I looked up to find about fifty Confederates standing around me. It was almost dark, and I found that I really was 'scared.' General Barlow was at a farmhouse Northeast of town, seriously wounded, and as Lee's army occupied the land I learned afterwards that it was with difficulty Mrs. B. succeeded in reaching her husband."[12]

11 Charles L. Barlow to Gettysburg National Military Park historian Harry Pfanz, March 21, 1960, GNMP Library, Box B-70, File 85b, General Francis C. Barlow.

12 "Days of Dread: A Woman's Story of Her Life on a Battlefield," *Gettysburg Compiler,* June 28, 1898.

Chapter 16

A Lingering Agony:
Nurse Rebecca Price's Spangler Experience

"So many times at night I lay on my stretcher weeping instead of sleeping."
— *Spangler nurse Rebecca Lane Pennypacker Price*

never got over what she witnessed at the Spangler farm. The suffering. The agony on their faces. The heart-rending forever farewells to those she had nursed, tenderly given water to, held hands with, and to whom she sang.

Rebecca Price cared deeply about these men. To nurse a 21-year-old soldier on his death bed was to know him and his family members because he told her so much about himself and his loved ones waiting back home. She listened to their life regrets and struggled with the calm courage of those dying so young. All of that made everything harder. "Why even now, after more than a quarter of a Century has passed, it makes me heart-sick to think of it," she confided to her children.[1]

Decades later, it still haunted her.

---

1 Nurse Price's 1894 letter to her children was provided by George Rapp, her second great-grandnephew. A copy of the letter is in the files of the Chester County Historical Society (West Chester, PA) MS 76602: "Rebecca Lane Pennypacker Price's Account of Her Experiences as a Nurse During the Civil War Written 1894 for Her Son," 26.

Rebecca Lane Pennypacker Price

M. B. Yarnall/Courtesy of George Rapp

* * *

Rebecca Lane Pennypacker Price didn't have to be at the XI Corps hospital after the battle of Gettysburg. She wasn't recruited, conscripted, or ordered to be there. Once she heard of the great bloody battle, though, she realized it was where she wanted to be. Indeed, it was where she needed to be. So she packed her bags, climbed aboard a small dark railroad cattle car in the middle of the night in Baltimore and got to Gettysburg within a couple days of the close of the fight.

Rebecca came from the prominent Pennypacker family of eastern Pennsylvania. First cousin Galusha Pennypacker would be a Union brigadier general by the end of the war at just 20, and he was awarded a Medal of Honor for his bravery at the Second Battle of Fort Fisher in North Carolina in January 1865. Samuel Whitaker Pennypacker, governor of Pennsylvania from 1903 to 1907, was her second cousin, and her fifth cousin was none other than George Armstrong Custer, the gallant cavalryman who fought at Gettysburg and throughout the Civil War only to die at the Little Bighorn in 1876. By the time she stepped off the cattle car in Gettysburg, her 22-year-old brother-in-law, Sgt. Elhanan Price of the 116th Pennsylvania, had been dead almost seven months, killed in the devastating December 1862 defeat at Fredericksburg. Nursing ran in the Pennypacker family: Rebecca's mother, Elizabeth, ran the Union Army hospital in Chambersburg, Pennsylvania, as its matron.

Rebecca was married to successful Phoenixville merchant Edwin Price. The union had yet to produce children when Fort Sumter was shelled by the Confederates on April 12, 1861. The news prompted her and other ladies of the town outside of Philadelphia to volunteer their help. The women made and purchased clothing for local soldiers and sent them off with Bibles and other goods.

When the number of ladies involved grew to more than 100, Edwin provided space in his store for the gatherings and Rebecca helped form the Ladies Union Relief Society. By 1863, more than a ton and a half of supplies and food had been donated by the community for the army's sick and wounded. Rebecca and Mattie Jones were selected to deliver the goods, and off they went on the long journey via train and ferry to the Union Windmill Point Hospital near Fredericksburg, Virginia, where up to 4,000 sick soldiers from the Army of the Potomac were obtaining care. Once there, the women shared a tent and worked in the snow, mud, and cold.

Rebecca was far from alone in her devotion to the sick and wounded. Some 20,000 women worked in Civil War hospitals in various capacities. Most were hired by the armies and served in the large general brick and mortar hospitals in cities. Those nurses, cooks, matrons, etc., were paid. Most at field hospitals like the one on the Spangler property weren't offered money, and if they were usually turned it down.

Rebecca was an idealistic 25-year-old and full of energy when she left Phoenixville first for Baltimore and then Gettysburg. She was on the tall side, judging by her photos. Her short dark hair, slight smile, and warm eyes suggested the compassion lingering inside while masking the toughness and strength that allowed her to take charge and handle horrific situations that most men and women could not stomach. She would need every ounce of that toughness and compassion at the Spangler farm.

History remembers Rebecca because she left a descriptive and detailed account of what she encountered at Gettysburg. Her writings of what transpired on the Spangler farm are unmatched in length and detail by any other individual, though many men from the 153rd Pennsylvania and 154th New York as well as Justus Silliman of the 17th Connecticut, Chaplain J. H. W. Stuckenberg of the 145th Pennsylvania, and the Rev. F. J. F. Schantz, among others, also deserve our gratitude. Rebecca wrote her account in a long letter to her children in 1894 in which she described her time at Windmill Point and Gettysburg.

Most of the Gettysburg portion of Rebecca's letter appears here. Author's notes are in brackets. Here is her Spangler story:

> How shall I begin to tell you of our labors at Gettysburg. To think of it fills my heart with sadness; to write about! How can I? You desire me to do so, and so dear children I will try.

Joseph MacAffee [McAfee], who was then, and had been for fourteen years, our Sabbath School Superintendent, was going as a delegate of the Christian Commission. We started with him, stopping at the rooms in Philadelphia, for his commission. I remarked that I wished Mrs. Spear [wife of Phoenixville stone mason Joshua Spear] and I could go as delegates. Mr. MacAffee spoke to Mr. Stuart [Philadelphia-based Christian Commission Chairman George H. Stuart] about it. He said they did not send any lady delegates, but when he heard my name he sent for me to come in his office. He remembered me as a nurse at Wind Mill Point, and was anxious to have me go as a delegate. He gave us a free pass, and a letter of introduction to the President of the Christian Commission at Baltimore, who received us kindly, and gave us our commission, with instructions to telegraph to him for any supplies we might need, fortunately there was no necessity for so doing.

We had about a ton weight with us, and then we were in Pennsylvania, where there was plenty. Farmers sent things to the Camp daily, and the Commission Rooms at Gettysburg, were kept well supplied so we did not have to go farther. We left Baltimore in cattle cars, seated on rough benches, no light except what little nature gave us, and thus after a long tiresome journey, we arrived in Gettysburg at 1 o'clock a.m. We had some difficulty in finding a place to rest, but finally a private family accommodated Mrs. Spear and I.

"The stench was sickening. The dead were not all off the field and then so many wounded!" she explained as she continued her story:

Can you possibly form an idea of what it would be in hot July weather? Every window in the house was fastened down tight, all doors kept shut; so it was stifling. Methought as I lay awake longing for a breath of fresh air, how little we, in our comfortable, cheerful homes knew of the suffering caused by the war. We could not realize its sad realities.

Next thing was to get to work, so after partaking of a cup of coffee with our kind host and hostess, we started out. An ambulance was passing which we hailed, and upon inquiring where we were needed, the driver said he was just going to the Eleventh Corps; 'Jump in, and I will take you there, no ladies there and you are needed.' We went with him; upon arriving at our destination the first person to greet us was Dr. Cantwell [Dr. Jacob Cantwell, 82nd Ohio], who had charge at Wind Mill Point Hospital. Two or three other Surgeons were there whom I knew;

Adjutant and 1st Lt. Joseph Heeney

Courtesy of George Rapp

you can well imagine how glad I was! It was so much pleasanter than being among strangers. The Surgeons expressed great delight to have me work with them again. Certainly the Lord directed us there! So much to do, and then by having previously worked with some in charge, I was free to do as I wished; no time wasted in hunting up a Surgeon to ask. Perfect liberty was given me over the entire Camp.

Soon as our boxes arrived, we opened them and went to work. Mrs. Spear was about twenty years older than me; she preferred doing the inside work, whilst I went from tent to tent. Three men were detailed to help us cook. Here we had every facility for work, and knowing from sad experience what was needed for our own comfort in such a life, we came prepared, bringing quilts, pillows, etc., with us.

Soon I stepped into the nearest tent to ours in which were four badly wounded men. Can I ever forget the glad smile, the look of surprise, comfort and joy, which spoke more eloquently than words? I felt that I was receiving a hearty welcome. I was a substitute for mother, wife and sister and in their eyes no stranger, but a friend. One occupant of that tent was Joseph Heeney [adjutant and first lieutenant, 157th New York, age 21.] Oh, how he suffered, and yet how patient! His pillow was an Army coat rolled up. I gave him my pillow, feeling so thankful I had brought it. When I placed it under his head, he looked at me with tearful eyes, beaming with gratitude, and said, 'Oh, what comfort.' One day he asked me to write a letter for him to the Hon. Gerrit Smith, of Peterboro New York. I did so, and frequently afterward. On the 22nd of July, his limb was amputated, on the 24th, he sank peacefully to rest. At his request, his body was embalmed and sent to his home. From the highest motives he volunteered as a private in the ranks, and in a year was promoted to Adjutant of his regiment. It was an excessively hot day when they carried him to the amputating table. As I held the umbrella over him to protect him from the sun, he said, 'How glad mother will be to know I am so tenderly cared for; tell her.' As we took him back, I felt that another of my brave boys would soon be gone. They were all my boys and I was 'Sister' to them. His last words were, 'Mother, Home, Heaven!'[2]

If he had been the only one! But to think of the hundreds whose lives were thus sacrificed! All missed Joseph, he was so cheerful and patient. In fact it was surprising how very patient the boys all were; no complaints, no murmurings, all bearing sufferings heroically!

Those who wore the gray, were cared for with our own boys in blue, and as they lay side by side in the same tents. . . . We never made any distinction, except it might be to give them the smallest oranges or apples. When able to be removed to places designated for prisoners, those of the gray left us. When seated in an ambulance ready to go, I would be sent for, as they wished to say 'Good-bye'; many of them wept as they thanked me for what I had done for them; how I pitied them! Some were driven in the Army at the point of the bayonet. One man said he was seated with his family at dinner, when officers came in, and ordered him to leave, without even finishing his meal; it was go, or die on the spot! Many of the confederates were thus forced into service. Seems to me they must have been poor soldiers, unwilling fighters. In the Northern Army no such extreme measures were used.

". . . About thirty yards from our tent, was the house and barn belonging to the owner of the farm. Then in possession of 'Uncle Sam,'" she explained. "On the barn floor side by side," she continued,

with only space enough to step between them, lay the worst cases. The Surgeon in charge asked me to take them under my special care. It was an unpleasant duty. One from which, for a moment I instinctively shrank! Just outside the barn, was the amputating table, and I thought, how can I pass it? Strength was given me, so

---

2 See Chapter 17 for more information on Joseph Heeney and his experience at the Spangler hospital. Heeney's name is spelled "Henry" on one of his regiment's index cards and his Civil War Muster Roll Abstract. Another index card spells it "Heeney," as does the National Park Service and Mrs. Price. The New York State Adjutant General's Office spells it "Henery" on the regiment's roster.

for many days and nights I passed and repassed it, often when operations were being performed. . . .

[One case] was one of those in the barn. He said he must see his father, he had something to tell him. The father was telegraphed for, and the young man kept alive by the nurses taking turns in pressing his wound. He knew the nurses were needed elsewhere, and he finally said, 'Let me die, father is not coming.' He could not be persuaded to communicate to anyone else, what he desired his father to know. As I witnessed his death, and closed his eyes, I felt that I could have made any sacrifice to have relieved his mind, so that he could pass away peacefully. His eyes were fixed upon the door with a strained, eager look, and his whole expression was one of dispair; thus he slowly bled to death. The grief of the father [who arrived hours after his son died] was heart-rending!

Oh! The sad scenes would fill a volume. My sympathy for suffering was too great to be removed by such scenes, so many times at night I lay on my stretcher weeping instead of sleeping. Frequently at night I would hear someone scratching on the tent, and when asked what was wanted, the response would be, 'Sister, Mr. —— is dying, and wants you,' so I would go to talk, read and sing to them, and perhaps . . . close their eyes in death! How thankful I was, that I could point them to a loving Saviour. When they felt a burden of sin, I could speak freely of His love, and I know that with God's help I was enabled to give peace and joy to many a burdened soul.

Dear Mrs. Spear was busy all the time, superintending the cooking and getting meals prepared on dishes, ready to be carried to the men; she worked early and late. After we had been there a few weeks, Mattie Jones [who had traveled with Rebecca from Phoenixville to Windmill Point earlier that year] came and remained until the Hospital was broken up. Mrs. Ashenfalter [Catharine Ashenfelter of Phoenixville], and Mrs. Levi B. Haler [Annie Haler of Phoenixville] brought on supplies, and staid with us a few days. We had ample provision, so could cater somewhat to their tastes. One man whose appetite I had been vainly trying to tempt, when asked if there was anything in the world he could eat, he said, 'Oh! Yes mum, I could eat cod-fish cakes.' I sent to the Commission rooms for fish, and he was soon enjoying the luxury of cod-fish cakes; his appetite was all right after that. Another craved, 'Rice pudding like mother makes.' He got the pudding and enjoyed it, whether it was like 'Mother's' or not; he said it tasted like home, and it certainly gave him an appetite for other things. It was a great satisfaction to be able to supply their needs. We used condensed milk for toast, puddings, etc. I often felt grateful to the one who discovered that method of putting up milk, for how could we have been supplied? Ladies from the surrounding country would occasionally bring us several quarts of fresh milk, but we had to use it at once. How gladly we welcomed the farmers and others who came with their wagons filled with supplies; sometimes the ladies brought food already prepared.

. . . I must tell you about our [French] Chaplain. . . . We found he was receiving considerable of the stores, as they came in, and I felt somewhat dubious about his distributing them as he ought, but had not time to watch carefully. A part of his duty was to go to the Commission rooms with the order for supplies for the day. One Sabbath it was near time for morning service, and nothing on hand to eat. I asked the Chaplain if he was not going for supplies; he said, 'It is time for service now, supplies can wait. I want you to come sing.' I told him I thought it was most important to have food for the mens' bodies so they could have strength to receive the Spiritual food. I saw he was angry, but was wholly unprepared for what followed; he insisted upon it that he would not go. Politeness vanished. I reported him, and suggested that his tent be searched. The Surgeon asked me to take the order. I jumped in the ambulance, was soon driven to the Commission rooms and returned with the needful, while the traitor was holding service. In the meantime, his tent was examined, and ample proof of his rascality found. He would hail the people as they came in with supplies, and take them. Of course, as he was Chaplain, they thought he would give them to us. He had fruits, wine, jelly, home-made cheese, and various things packed away, some opened and spoiled. Well, when service was over, and he found out what I had done, he poured forth a torrent of abuse. He was soon taken in charge, and I never saw or heard tell of him again; but the contents of that tent were something wonderful.

"Soon after this period, I noticed a Baltimore lady who came to the Camp to visit the wounded, halting longer at the bed of the confederates than with our men, and my suspicions were aroused," explained Nurse Price. "I watched her very closely, without seeming to do so. She had pencil and paper," continued her story,

and would write hurriedly as they talked, she all the while casting fugitive glances around. I felt assured she was a spy. I reported at Head Quarters, what I had seen, but told them not to rely upon what I said; to watch. She was watched and searched. After finding ample proof of her guilt, she was escorted out of camp under guard, and told never to return, or she would be our prisoner. Thus whilst caring for some of our enemies, I was having others dismissed. Notwithstanding every precaution was taken to prevent spies from entering our Camp; one would get in occasionally.

But I want to tell you more about my boys in the barn. Being some of the worst cases they were the last to be removed to the General Hospital, so I learned much of their home life, as I frequently wrote letters for them, and they loved to talk of home and dear ones. My heart often ached for those at home, whom I knew were anxious and worried about their wounded. Sometimes a letter would be given to me to read, containing expressions of thanks for our kindness; words like these, 'Oh! How relieved I am to know that a kind lady is caring for you.' 'Can I ever be grateful enough to the dear woman who is doing for you what I so long to do, but cannot? God bless her.' 'Give my love to the one who has taken her own life in her hand, to care for the Soldiers!' 'I feel relieved more than I can tell to know that a woman is nursing you. May the Virgin Mary bless her.' Why I could write nearly a page of similar expressions; they came before me so vividly, because at the time they did me so much good. When I would hear them read, or read them myself, I felt my work was not in vain. We were not only comforting the suffering in Camp, but the aching hearts at home. Wasn't I amply repaid? Friends sometimes say to me that I aught to have a pension, to be paid for my labor. Didn't I receive my pay in the heartfelt thanks of the sick and wounded, each hour of the day?

I was going from morning until night, all the time feeling that I could not do enough, often sitting up until nearly morning, writing letters from notes taken from the boys during the day. One night after writing until very late and being tired, I lay upon my stretcher hoping for a good sleep; soon I slept, but something disturbed me . . . I suddenly awakened to find myself in a puddle of water on the ground floor of our tent. A shower came up, and came in on my face; gathering myself up as quietly and quickly as possible, I soon had my valise which was doing duty as a pillow, opened and donned some dry clothing. Just then a call came for 'Sister, Lieut. Wheeler [1st Lt. Thomas Wheeler, 75th Ohio, age 25, wounded July 1, died July 28] is dying, and wants to see you.' No more sleep. As I went to the extreme end of the Camp, I wondered why he sent for me. A few days before, his parents came, and as they were with him, I had seen little of him, as there was so many to care for who had no one else. As I entered the tent, he looked at me and smiled, as I drew near he said, 'Oh! Sister I could not go without thanking you and saying farewell! Sing 'Rock of Ages.' As I sang, he passed away with a smile on his face, to be with God.

1st Lt. Thomas Wheeler

*Brady's National Photographic Portrait
Galleries/Courtesy of George Rapp*

My work with him was done, and it was time to begin my daily duty. How many, many times I was thankful to God for the gift of song! To the dying it brought comfort, and to the suffering, cheer, and sweet memories of home and friends. The dear sufferers needed all the comfort that could be given them; those were trying days to them. The intense heat, the stench from wounds, the annoyance from flies! Why even now, after more than a quarter of a Century has passed, it makes me heart-sick to think of it. What they suffered can never be told, and it was borne so uncomplainingly.

Those who were able to be sent home, went, some who had no special home or for some reason preferred it, were sent to a city Hospital. A General Hospital was established near Gettysburg, and many were sent there. Ere the cool weather set in, the Camp Hospitals were all broken up, and I turned my face homeward once more, glad for a rest.[3]

*   *   *

Rebecca served at the XI Corps hospital for about five weeks, almost the entire time it was open. She and Edwin went on to have daughter Cora in 1869 and son George in 1874. George became a professor and neurologist at Jefferson Medical

---

3 "Rebecca Lane Pennypacker Price's Account of Her Experiences as a Nurse During the Civil War Written 1894 for Her Son," 21-31.

Rebecca Lane Pennypacker Price and the National Association of Army Nurses of the Civil War at the Grand Army of the Republic encampment at Rochester, NY, in 1911. Mrs. Price is fourth from the right in the front row. *US National Library of Medicine Digital Collections*

College in Philadelphia. Rebecca spent the rest of her life doing charitable work. She prized a Red Cross pin given to her by Clara Barton, founder of the Red Cross, and was a member of and for a time president of the National Association of Army Nurses of the Civil War. That organization merged with the Grand Army of the Republic, which was made up of former Union Civil War soldiers, and she sometimes spoke at GAR encampments and meetings.

She spoke at the 1915 encampment in Washington, D.C. "I am glad to greet you this evening," she began. "It certainly is a great pleasure to once more stand before you,

> and I certainly enjoy the privilege, and I bring you the greetings of the National Association of Army Nurses of the Civil War, the women who tried to help you when you needed care when sick and wounded. We tried to—and we did, I think—nurse many of you back to life and health, so that you could go out again and fight for your country and your homes. After the war our ministrations did not cease for you. There were hospitals all over the country, and we labored in them for many, many months. But now our work seems to be practically ended. Well, not with all. Some of our nurses married some of you soldiers and we

are caring for you all through life. [Laughter and applause.] You see some of them are still very loyal.

Our labors for you are now over, but we still hold you in our hearts. As service for another generates love for that one, it is no wonder that then Army nurses have a particularly warm feeling for the Boys in Blue to whom they rendered such loving service. We have been bound even closer together since you gave expression of your kindness and feeling toward us, and your appreciation, in making us part of your organization at Boston in 1904, and we wear this bronze button or badge which you gave us; we wear it and honor it as much as you do your little bronze button. Our love for the flag under which we fought and labored, now waving over a united country, will never grow less. In the little time remaining to us, there is little we can do in the way of active service for our country, but we can do much to inspire the rising generation with the same love for our country that led the men and women of the war to give the best years of their young lives to preserve those blessings they now enjoy. We can do much to lead the rising generation to see the horrors of war rather than its glories that they may give their lives to preserve these blessings through peace. Peace is what we want, and not war.

"I am glad to have been able to say these few words. A few weeks ago I feared I should not be able to be with you. You see I am crippled, but I am not the only crippled soldier here," she said in conclusion. "I can sympathize with the men who lost their arms more than I ever did before in my life. Now, if we never meet again, I wish you all glory and honor and peace and happiness all through life, and a happy home Beyond."[4]

* * *

Rebecca's husband, Edwin, died in 1914 at age 82 after 55 years of marriage. She followed him in death five years later at age 81. At the time of her death, she was receiving a government nurse's pension of $12 a month. She and Edwin are buried in Morris Cemetery in Phoenixville, the same graveyard as her cousin, former Pennsylvania governor Samuel Whitaker Pennypacker.

---

4 Rebecca Lane Price, *Journal of the Forty-ninth National Encampment Grand Army of the Republic* (Washington, D.C., 1916), 216-217.

Civil War nurse Mary A. Gardner Holland remembered, "How the eyes of the old veteran fill with tears when, at our camp fires, some old lady is introduced, and the presiding officer says, 'Boys, she was an army nurse.' For a moment the distinguished officers present are forgotten, and they gather around the dear old lady, eager to grasp her hand and say some kind and loving word in appreciation of her services."[5]

Spangler Farm Short Story

Captain Augustus Vignos of the 107th Ohio (Adelbert Ames' brigade, Barlow's division), carried Rebecca Price's photo for 40 years. He didn't do it out of romantic love, but rather out of gratitude for how she helped save his life at the George Spangler farm.

Like so many others in the XI Corps, Vignos was severely wounded on July 1 on Barlow Knoll. Gangrene developed, and his right arm was amputated above the elbow on July 3 at the XI Corps hospital. His condition deteriorated, but Rebecca refused to give up on him. She made sure his blood-covered uniform was removed and he got into clean clothes, and day-after-day gave him tender attention. Eventually, he improved to the point that she was able to get him on a train home to Canton, Ohio. Even though he had only one arm and he could have stayed home, Vignos' health continued to improve and he returned to the army as a major and served through the end of the war.

He married in 1866, fathered nine children, and amassed substantial wealth as founder of the Novelty Cutlery Company and owner of the American Mine Door Company. He was a pall bearer at the funeral of his close friend President William McKinley. As far as Vignos was concerned, none of that family joy, countless friendships, or business successes would have transpired had it not been for the determined care of Rebecca Price at the XI Corps hospital. And he never forgot her for it. He showed her photo to fellow ex-soldiers at national gatherings in an attempt to find out where she might be and thank her, without luck.

Then, one day in 1906, a letter arrived. "Dear Sir: Do you remember the tall nurse at Gettysburg, who furnished you with clothing so that you could go home?" Mrs. Price had found him! "In looking over my photos taken in wartime I found one of yours," she continued, "which your sister Kate had sent to me. I was led to wonder if you were living, and if you were going to attend the G.A.R. encampment at Saratoga. I expect to be there, and would be glad to meet some of my 'soldier

5 Mary A. Gardner Holland, *Our Army Nurses: Interesting Sketches, Addresses and Photographs* (Boston, MA, 1895), 11.

Capt. Augustus Vignos

Courtesy of George Rapp

boys.' I would be glad to hear from you. . . . Now, in my declining years, my thoughts so often dwell upon those stormy times, and it gives me great pleasure to hear from or see those for whom I cared. Hoping you are enjoying health and prosperity."

Vignos replied that he looked forward to seeing her "with great pleasure." Their happy reunion took place at the 41st Grand Army of the Republic Encampment at Saratoga Springs, New York, on September 12, 1906, 43 years after they met at the Spangler farm. Vignos' wife, Phoebe, died later that same year. Vignos lived another two decades before dying in 1926 at the age of 87. After his death, a former comrade eulogized that Vignos had earned "the esteem of the entire regiment [and] was a generous hearted, noble souled man."[6]

6 Augustus Vignos Pension File No. 38556, National Archives and Records Administration, Washington, D.C.; *Reno* (NV) *Gazette-Journal*, September 12, 2007; M. J. Slutz, "Tribute to Major Augustus Vignos," delivered at a reunion of the 107th Ohio. Tribute shared by descendants of Major Vignos on Ancestry.com at www.ancestry.com/mediaui-viewer/ tree/31357887/person/12448279419/media/70d41c29-8e5b-4537-bd51-e04ed369035f?_ph src=iDS197&_phstart=successSource. Accessed September 29, 2017.

Chapter 17

Gerrit Smith, Lt. Joseph Heeney, and Nurse Price

"All missed Joseph, he was so cheerful and patient."

— *Nurse Rebecca Lane Pennypacker Price*

Smith was one of the richest men in the country and a powerful abolitionist when nurse Rebecca Price wrote letters to him for a dying Joseph Heeney at the XI Corps hospital.

The wealthy landowner's white-columned mansion in Peterboro, New York, was a regular stop on the Underground Railroad. There, Smith hid escaped slaves, provided them with money, and helped them on their way to freedom in Canada. He also gave away thousands of acres of land in upstate New York to black families. Smith spent millions of dollars to support his causes and the less fortunate. He helped finance John Brown's raid on Harpers Ferry in 1858, in which Brown tried to fuel a slave revolt, and he spent most of his adult life speaking out and writing about the injustices of slavery after attending an anti-slave meeting in 1835. Smith worked closely with fellow abolitionist Frederick Douglass and risked fines and imprisonment by violating the Fugitive Slave Act to the point of leading a mob to free a runaway slave who had been captured and jailed. Women's suffrage and the temperance campaign were two more causes close to his heart. Smith also served a term in Congress (1853-1854) and ran unsuccessfully for president of the United States three times on the Liberty Party ticket. By 1863, people across the United States had heard of Gerrit Smith, including Mrs. Price and others at the

Gerrit Smith

Library of Congress

Spangler farm. Those living in the Confederate states also knew who he was and what he stood for.[1]

Smith had taken in a young, poor go-getter named Joseph Heeney before the war and given him a job— an act of generosity that helped Joseph's widowed mother. Joseph left the Smith family in September of 1862 and went to war as a 21-year-old private in Company F, 157th New York. He was not yet 22 when he arrived in Gettysburg on July 1, 1863.

During that short stint in the service, however, his character and his spirit were so impressive that he advanced from private to first lieutenant. His first battle was the bloody fiasco at Chancellorsville, from which he emerged unscathed.[2]

As part of Brig. Gen. Alexander Schimmelfennig's brigade (Schurz's division, XI Corps), the 431 men of the 157th New York rushed north of Gettysburg and took up a position on the brigade's left. Heeney fell with a wound in his right leg when Brig. Gen. George Doles' Georgia Confederates assaulted the position from the north between the Mummasburg and Carlisle roads. Unable to walk, Heeney remained behind enemy lines until he could be rescued on July 4 or July 5. An

1 Mrs. Price's uncle, Elijah Pennypacker (1802-1888), was a leading abolitionist in Pennsylvania. Pennypacker opened his White Horse Farm near Phoenixville to the Underground Railroad and he personally helped hundreds of escaping slaves reach freedom. Pennypacker was president of the county and state anti-slavery organizations and he was active in the American Anti-Slavery Society, which was based in nearby Philadelphia. This information was taken from Miriam Clegg's "Secrets of Old Houses: Their Hidden Passageways," Historical Society of the Phoenixville Area newsletter, vol. 12, no. 1 (September 1988), 2-5.

2 http://dmna.ny.gov/historic/reghist/civil/rosters/Infantry/157th_Infantry_CW_Roster.pdf. Accessed January 30, 2019.

ambulance carried him to the XI Corps Spangler hospital and he was placed in a tent near the house and barn. It was there that Mrs. Price came into his life soon after both arrived at the farm.

Nurse Price provided him with her pillow for comfort and protected him from the sun with an umbrella when he was carried outside to have his leg amputated nearly three weeks after his knee had been shattered by a lead round. She was with him when he died on July 24. "Oh, how he suffered, and yet how patient!" she wrote of Heeney. "One day he asked me to write a letter for him to the Hon. Gerrit Smith, of Peterboro New York. I did so, and frequently afterward."[3]

On August 3, 1863, an unknown writer sent the following letter from Peterboro to John Crawford, the publisher of the *Oneida* (NY) *Dispatch*, regarding Gerrit Smith, Lt. Joseph Heeney, and Mrs. Price:

FRIEND CRAWFORD:

Another of the bravest and best of our young men has fallen a victim to the accursed 'Slaveholders' Rebellion.' Adjutant JOSEPH T. HENEY, of the 157th Regt. N.Y. Vol's, was badly wounded in the knee in the first day's battle at Gettysburg, Pa. He lay within the enemy's lines for several days without help or notice, and suffered greatly. He was finally reached by our men, and taken to the hospital at Gettysburg.

On the 22d of July the limb was amputated, and he died calmly on the 24th, the death of a christian and a soldier. His widowed mother and many friends have the great happiness to know, that during the confinement at the hospital, he was nursed, and cared for most tenderly. Mrs. Beckie L. Price of Phoenixville, Chester Co., Pa., one of the noble christian women of our land, who are ministering to the wants of our sick and dying soldiers, found our young friend in his distress, and with kindness, never to be forgotten, watched by his bedside, spoke words of comfort to his soul, and closed his eyes in death.

Adjutant Heney was born in Quebec. . . . His family moved from thence to Massachusetts, and afterwards to this State. He was for several years in the family of Hon. Gerrit Smith, and was by them most highly esteemed and beloved.

---

3 Nurse Price's 1894 letter to her children, 23.

Of uncommonly prepossessing manners, much personal beauty, possessing fine talents, he had a host of friends who deeply mourn his loss. His beautiful devotion to his widowed mother, whose main support he was, won for him the silent admiration of all. From the highest motives he volunteered as a private in the ranks about a year since, and rose rapidly to the honorable position of Adjutant of his regiment.

Gerrit Smith sent his son [Greene] to Gettysburg, but was too late to find our young friend alive. His remains arrived in Peterboro on Friday evening, July 31st. On Saturday our citizens assembled to pay their heartfelt respects to his memory. The services took place at the house of Gerrit Smith. The coffin was placed on the lawn in front of the mansion; and the banner of the country, for whose liberty he died, was the pall of the youthful soldier!

Appropriate hymns were sung. A touching prayer was offered by Hon. James Barnett, and some remarks, full of tender reminiscences of the deceased, were made by Gerrit Smith.

At the close a parting hymn was sung, and the honored remains of our dearly beloved young friend were borne away. The burial took place in the afternoon at the Catholic Cemetery at Oneida. G. W. P.[4]

Gerrit Smith believed the North shared some of the blame for slavery, and after the war provided part of the bond money to free former Confederate President Jefferson Davis from prison. Smith died in 1874 at age 77. His Peterboro mansion has since burned to the ground, but the Gerrit Smith Estate remains as a National Historic Landmark. The National Abolition Hall of Fame and Museum is in Peterboro.

Spangler Farm Short Story

It wasn't all grateful charity in Gettysburg, as there were many instances of civilians behaving badly toward the very soldiers who came to their rescue and sacrificed for them. There were reports of some Adams County farmers charging

4 https://dmna.ny.gov/historic/reghist/civil/infantry/157thInf/157thInfCWN.htm. Accessed October 2, 2017.

ridiculously high prices to soldiers for bread and other food and charging to take wounded soldiers to the railroad when military transport wasn't available. A few Adams County farmers refused to provide water to the wounded. Civilian grave robbers dug up corpses on the battlefield and stole from them. Many civilians were jailed for taking military equipment in an effort to sell it. Also, there were many Southern sympathizers in Adams County because it sits on the Mason-Dixon Line, and many of these sympathizers refused to help the Union wounded or charged exorbitant prices for their services.[5]

5 Gregory A. Coco, *On the Bloodstained Field* (Gettysburg, PA, 1987), 41, 45-46.

Chapter 18

Charity Pours In

"The members of the Christian Commission are here from Philadelphia & Baltimore & citizens from other places doing all they can to comfort the wounded & may God Bless them. You know nothing of the Horrors of War & cannot until you go & see it for yourself."

— *Pvt. James R. Middlebrook, hospital worker from the 17th Connecticut*

Reverend John B. Poerner knew horror and misery. The veteran of the US Christian Commission had served untold numbers of wounded after multiple battles and labored in many hospitals and camps, but he found a new level of agony when he arrived at the Spangler farm.

"I arrived at Gettysburg on the 6th of July, 1863, and was at once detailed on duty to the 11th Corps Hospital, then under the superintendence of Mr. James Grant, of Philadelphia who labored with one and other Delegates among about eighteen hundred patients," reported the Rev. Poerner. ". . . [F]rom five or six hundred were in a most pitiable and distressed condition." He continued:

On account of the heavy rains which poured down in streams upon our camp from the 4th to 9th of July, the whole field, but especially the level and lower parts of it, became in a certain sense a perfect lake in which the poor fellows laid, in their little shelter tents, two by two, literally covered in mud and rotten hay or straw, from three to five inches deep. I went to work at once, and with the consent of the Surgeon in charge, Dr. [James A.] Armstrong, proceeded with a squad of men through the surrounding country in search for lumber, but as I could not find any, I went on to Gettysburg and engaged all the empty boxes, barrels, and

A typical US Christian Commission field hospital setup. *New York Public Library*

hogsheads [a cask used for holding liquids or food], took them apart, and forwarded them to our 11th Corps camp. Another squad of men were sent to the woods to cut rails and forked pins, and after hauling them to our camp, commenced building up couches, and thus relieved that large number of suffering men from a muddy and watery grave, and just as fast as we built up and raised our wounded, we were furnished with comfortable hospital tents with which to cover them.[1]

Such was the life of a Christian Commission delegate in 1863.

The organization formed in Philadelphia in 1861 was much more than its name implied. The more modern 20th-century saying "find a need and fill it" would have been a perfect slogan for the 19th-century Christian Commission. The Rev. Poerner and James Grant did just that by finding physical and spiritual needs and filling them.

---

1 J. B. Poerner, *United States Christian Commission: Third Report of the Committee of Maryland* (Baltimore, MD, 1864), 265.

They weren't alone. Agents from individual states, nurses from ladies' relief societies, ministers, citizens, farmers from Gettysburg and beyond, and relatives of the wounded pitched in to help. Those generous organizations and individuals provided food, clothing, slings, bandages, bedticks, lint, crutches, cotton, mosquito nets, needles, sheets, and thread. All of these critically needed items, combined with the emotional support and dignity that these people displayed toward the wounded and dying, saved untold lives. Army tents, food, and medical goods had finally begun to arrive in Gettysburg on July 4, but make no mistake: This recovery was powered by the private sector.

The Christian Commission set up a tent at the XI Corps hospital and was supervised by Grant. Out of that tent poured food and other supplies as needed. A wagon arrived each morning at the Christian Commission headquarters in the John Schick store on the square in Gettysburg with a list of what was needed, which was promptly filled.

Bread was especially in need. If something wasn't available, it could be sent for and usually arrived within a day or two. Almost everything in the form of supplies and food was a donation from municipalities and organizations in the North. Ladies' relief societies were particularly reliable providing food, clothing, and medical supplies (such as lint, which was used to dress wounds), even though many of these groups suffered hardships getting to Gettysburg and additional discomforts after they arrived. A group of women from Lancaster County, Pennsylvania, for example, had to wait all night in Columbia for their turn on a ferry to Wrightsville and then on to Gettysburg because the bridge across the mile-wide Susquehanna River had been burned by Union militia during the campaign to prevent it from falling into Confederate hands.[2]

Christian Commission Founder and Chairman George Stuart of Philadelphia kept an eye on funding and issued calls for help in times of emergency such as Gettysburg. Responses to his pleas for assistance were often more than generous. "I drew up a long despatch, to be sent to leading cities, stating the facts and asking for the privilege of drawing for different amounts," he explained. "Boston I asked for ten thousand dollars; and the response came back the same day, 'Draw for sixty thousand!'"[3]

---

2 The burning of the Wrightsville bridge had a significant impact on the campaign and its aftermath. For more on this overlooked aspect of the Gettysburg Campaign, see Scott L. Mingus, Sr., *Flames Beyond Gettysburg: The Confederate Expedition to the Susquehanna River, June 1863* (Savas Beatie 2011).

3 George H. Stuart, *The Life of George H. Stuart* (Philadelphia, PA, 1890), 136.

The Reverend Poerner was different from most Christian Commission delegates in the field because he worked for most of the war. Most delegates were ministers who volunteered their time to the commission for a short period (six weeks or so) and then went home. Many Christian Commission nurses also worked far longer than six weeks, including Ellen Harris of Philadelphia at the II Corps hospitals in Gettysburg. She wore herself down through four long years of war.

The Reverend Poerner was born in Germany in 1816 and came to the United States in 1845 as a minister for the German Reformed Church. His main role as a Christian Commission delegate at Spangler was to conduct chapel and funeral services, write letters home for the soldiers, provide food and clothing, and minister to the wounded and dying, thus supplementing the work of regimental chaplains or substituting for them when none was present. His German background proved crucial at Spangler, where he could speak to the wounded in German or English as needed.

"During my fourth week's work at the 11th Corps hospital, we held daily Divine services, at different places, in the streets of our camp, so as to enable every man within the tents to listen to the singing of hymns, prayers, and preaching of God's Word," explained the Reverend Poerner. "The good which has been accomplished by the services Eternity alone will reveal. Many of the sufferers were made glad by the physical and spiritual aid they received from the Christian Commission through the hands, hearts, kind words, and earnest, as well as consoling entreaties of its Delegates." After laboring four weeks on the Spangler farm, the Reverand Poerner reported that he suffered from "perfect exhaustion" and contracted typhoid fever, which required two months of bed rest to recover.[4]

Spangler superintendent and Scotland native James Grant served on the YMCA committee in Philadelphia that called for a convention and created the Christian Commission in late 1861. Like the Reverend Poerner, but unlike most others, Grant's dedication to the Christian Commission lasted far longer than six weeks. He worked closely with the wounded at Second Bull Run and Antietam in an unpaid capacity. The Union surgeons were swamped with work at Antietam,

---

4 Poerner, *Third Report of the Committee of Maryland*, 265-266. The reverend and his wife, Esther, had five children, none of whom lived to adulthood. John died in 1862 at age 10; Augustus and Rosina died in 1864 at ages 17 and 15; and Sarah and Susanna died in August 1871 at 17 and 15. The entire family is buried at Kimmerlings Cemetery in Lebanon County, PA. An escort of former Civil War soldiers accompanied the Rev. Poerner's casket at his funeral in 1895. He visited Gettysburg one month before his death. *Lebanon* (PA) *Daily News*, August 2, 1895.

where Grant found a severely wounded soldier from the 72nd Pennsylvania and almost completely alone spent a week nursing him out of danger.

Although mostly an administrator of the Christian Commission post at the XI Corps hospital, in charge of bringing in and distributing supplies, the 34-year-old Grant recalled decades later a particular case that affected him deeply. "A soldier came to the tent and addressing me as 'Chaplain,' which was the general designation by which the delegates were called, said, 'There is a young man whose leg has been amputated that wants to see you down in the orchard,'" reminisced Grant, who continued:

> I at once accompanied him and was soon standing beside a table under the trees on which was lying a young man with pale face, black hair, and large dark eyes. His leg had just been cut off above the knee and he was weak and dying from the shock and loss of blood. Fixing his eyes upon me, he said, 'Chaplain, I have sent for you to take down my last message to my mother.' I took out my note book and he very calmly began with his name – 'John N. Edmonds, Battery H, 1st Ohio Light Artillery.' Then his mother's: 'Mrs. Emeline Van Fleet, Maunee [Maumee] City, Lucas Co., Ohio.'

Private Edmonds had been manning Cemetery Hill on July 2 when a shell nearly tore off his left foot. The first amputation was successful, but infection set in and a second amputation, this one "above the knee," was performed. It was then that Grant was called to his side. "To shew his perfect self-possession," continued the Christian Commission administrator,

> I understood him to say 'Catharine,' repeating the word after him, but he corrected me by saying 'not Catharine but Emeline.' . . . 'Tell her,' said he, 'that I died perfectly happy and without much suffering. That I am prepared to meet my God and die trusting in Jesus – to dispose of my things as she seems best – to live a christian and meet me in Heaven.' When this precious record was made we carried him tenderly from the table, laid him on the grass, and covered him with a fly tent remaining with him, ministering to his comfort, spiritually and physically till . . . his soul winged its flight to Heaven.[5]

---

5 James Grant, *The Flag and the Cross: A History of the United States Christian Commission*, Historical Society of Pennsylvania, Call No. Am. 7905 (Philadelphia, PA, 1894), 45-47.

Edmonds died July 15 and was buried on the Spangler property. Months later he was reburied in Soldiers' National Cemetery.

The Christian Commission's tender care included washing blood and dirt off the wounded, getting them into clean clothes, cooking for and feeding them, and burying some of the dead on the battlefield. In its 1864 annual report, the Christian Commission noted that it considered the XI Corps hospital "a field favorable to cultivation" for its mission of healing souls and bodies. "It was nearest the town of all the field hospitals,

> and was therefore easy to access. The number of wounded in it was large–nearly or quite two thousand. At first there was much destitution. Part of Monday night, after the battle, was spent . . . in giving to some hundreds of wounded soldiers the first soft bread they had tasted since the fight. Many of the men were Germans, and could be reached only by one who understood their language. For this post, therefore, Mr. Poerner was well fitted. In connection with other delegates, he conducted religious services in both the English and German language, and conversed privately with great numbers in regard to the interests of the soul. . . . Though it was our first duty to provide for our own soldiers, the rebels were not neglected.[6]

"A large amount of reading matter has been distributed in the different corps hospitals and in those in town," wrote commission delegate I. O. Sloan, "and a general effort has been made by all the delegates to commend the mercy and grace of Jesus, who calls the weary and heavy laden to come to him for rest, to all the suffering with whom they have mingled." Sloan was referring to the copies of the New Testaments and small pamphlets passed out as part of the commission's mission work. Each pamphlet usually consisted of four pages on an individual topic, such as "I'm Too Young," and "To the Sick, Who are Without Hope in Christ." Typical text included: "Perhaps you are beginning to fear that it is too late; that Jesus will not receive you; since no heart can conceive, no tongue can express, what a sinner you are. Blessed be God if it is thus with you! If indeed your soul

---

6 *United States Christian Commission for the Army and Navy for the Year 1863* (Philadelphia, PA, 1864), 77.

longs to be saved from sin and sanctified by grace. Jesus Christ is both able and willing to save the greatest sinners."[7]

In many cases, the men wanted not religious counseling but food, and so turned down the Christian offerings. The Christian Commission remained undeterred. "Surgeons estimated that more than one thousand lives were saved by the timely relief offered by the delegates and stores of the Christian Commission," noted the commission's report of Gettysburg. "Clergymen of age and experience, competent to judge, report that more than one thousand souls were there hopefully converted. We believe both of these estimates are short of the truth." Commission delegates likely teamed with regimental chaplains at the XI Corps hospital in their ministry if any of these chaplains remained in town. This merger happened with increasing frequency as the Civil War progressed.[8]

Aid efforts continued long after the armies left Gettysburg. A local committee of eight prominent Gettysburg-area citizens was formed on August 1, 1863, to aid the Christian Commission. One of its members was the Reverend Theodore Park Bucher of the German Reformed Church in Gettysburg. He owned nine acres on the southwest side of the 1863 intersection of Granite Schoolhouse Lane and the Baltimore Pike and handled donations and distributions for the commission. As a neighbor of the Spanglers, Bucher likely had the XI Corps hospital as part of his domain. His committee was still soliciting goods for the wounded more than a month after the battle, noting that the items most needed were butter, eggs, chickens, apple butter, dried fruit, dried beef, potatoes, onions, and pickles; also, sheets, pillows, cushions, ringpads, shirts, drawers, socks, and slippers.[9]

The Sanitary Commission, meanwhile, monitored the Army of the Potomac's movements and kept its supplies as close as possible. As a result, it was the first relief organization to get needed goods into town even as the battle was underway. Two Sanitary Commission wagonloads traveling with the XII Corps supply train arrived the evening of July 1 under the command of agent Sanford Hoag and Maj. J. C. Bush. Supply wagons were banned—even supplies from the government—so the troops could move faster and easier, but Hoag and Bush either ignored that order and slipped into town or it had not been received by the XII Corps. As a result, the XII Corps field hospital on the George Bushman farm was the only

7 I. O. Sloan to G. S. Griffith, *Baltimore Sun*, July 24, 1863; American Tract Society, "To the Sick, Who are Without Hope in Christ" (Boston, MA, n.d.), no. 110.

8 *United States Christian Commission Second Annual Report 1863* (Philadelphia, PA, 1864), 82.

9 *The Adams Sentinel*, August 4, 1863.

corps or division hospital that had enough food, medical, and patient supplies during the battle. Just down the road at the Spangler farm, however, they suffered without enough of anything. Once permission was given after the battle, the Sanitary Commission reported that it distributed more than 100 wagonloads of supplies in Gettysburg by July 7 with five railroad cars of additional supplies on the way.[10]

Hoag and Major Bush hustled between the hospitals they could find on July 2 distributing goods, including the XI Corps Spangler facility. The men emptied their wagons of such things as concentrated beef soup, crackers, condensed milk, coffee, shirts, pants, towels, blankets, quilts, bandages, and lint. "On telling the surgeons that I was on hand with sanitary stores," Hoag recalled, "I was almost invariably greeted with expressions like the following: 'You could never have come at a better time,' and once on mentioning sanitary stores, I received two hearty welcome slaps on the shoulder, one from the medical director of the corps, and the other the surgeon of the division."[11]

The Sanitary Commission was formed as a private agency by Congress in 1861 to aid the sick and wounded and monitor the army's sanitation in camps and field hospitals. Agents inspected hospitals and urged the military to make improvements for the good of the wounded and staff, pushing for cleanliness, improved sanitation, clean water, and better food. The commission worked more to prevent illness than treat it. Surgeons sometimes balked at these intrusions, but most of the doctors appreciated the efforts, knowing the commission also sought to help them.

The number of wounded at Spangler varied day by day, especially once the more stable wounded began to be shipped out shortly after the battle to larger general hospitals in other cities. A Sanitary Commission agent visited the XI Corps hospital each day to inspect conditions, find out what the medical staff needed, and record the names and types of wounds and send the information to Washington. According to commission reports, there were 1,800 Union and 100 Confederate wounded there at the peak of hospital traffic two days after the end of the battle.[12]

Like the Christian Commission, the Sanitary Commission solicited donations of goods and money to be used for the care of the wounded and met with similar

10 "Report on the Operations of the Sanitary Commission During and After the Battles at Gettysburg" in *Documents of the US Sanitary Commission*, 2 vols. (New York, NY, 1866), vol. 2, nos. 61-95, 10.

11 Ibid., 10.

12 Ibid., 24.

A wagon from the Spangler hospital collected supplies each day at the US Sanitary Commission's headquarters at the Fahnestocks' store in Gettysburg. *New York Public Library*

success—so much so that while the two organizations usually worked in harmony there occasionally was conflict and competition for credit. The Sanitary Commission also set up in Gettysburg, choosing the large Edward and Samuel Fahnestock store at Baltimore and Middle streets as its headquarters on July 7. The prescient Fahnestocks had mostly emptied the store of its valuable contents before the battle in anticipation of the arrival of the Confederate army. Once the move into town was underway, the commission closed its temporary headquarters at a school near White Run on the Baltimore Pike. The two commissions handled their logistics in similar fashion: Field hospitals sent a wagon to the Sanitary Commission store each day to pick up what was required. Unlike the Christian Commission, however, the Sanitary Commission was more interested in providing for the physical needs of the men than the spiritual. Also, except for volunteer nurses, the Sanitary Commission preferred to have a paid staff in the field, unlike the Christian Commission's mostly six-week volunteers.[13]

---

13 Skelly, *A Boy's Experiences During the Battles of Gettysburg,* 9, 24; *Documents of the US Sanitary Commission,* 12, 14.

The Confederates burned several railroad bridges in Adams County and neighboring York County prior to the battle, which prevented the arrival of supplies via railroad until about July 6. Once the bridges were rebuilt and the tracks reopened, the railroad hauled in tons of supplies and large numbers of workers from charitable organizations and the military who joined those already in the area or arriving via wagon, horseback, or foot.

Nurse Ellen Harris of the Ladies' Aid Society of Philadelphia left the II Corps hospitals and Gettysburg on July 10 because she believed there was enough help and supplies for the time being "except in the matter of bread and butter," and she might be needed in Maryland in case another battle transpired before Lee's army slipped across the Potomac River. "Since Saturday, the 4th, I have been on this 'field of blood,' seeing suffering of the most fearful character," she wrote on the day she left. "Every hour brought to my view my own boys, maimed and mutilated, whose joyful greetings almost break my heart."[14]

The Confederates had also burned a railroad bridge in Gettysburg, so the trains that arrived there bringing people and supplies and hauling away the wounded stopped about a mile out near the York Pike. There, the Sanitary Commission managed a temporary outdoor depot lodge with food, beds, and tents to feed and protect the crowds of wounded waiting for inconsistent train arrivals and departures to carry them to hospitals in Baltimore, Philadelphia, New York City, Annapolis, and elsewhere. Large numbers of wounded who were able to be moved left corps and division hospitals each day for the depot lodge. Most of the ambulances had left town with the Union army. Some of the men made it to the depot from the Spangler hospital in the two ambulances still there, others hitched rides with local farmers, and some who had been but lightly wounded walked or limped away from the farm. The Sanitary Commission moved its lodge from the York Pike into town at the railroad depot after the bridge was repaired a week after the close of the battle.[15]

Given the horrific conditions, the accomplishments of both commissions were extraordinary. The Sanitary Commission, for example, distributed the following food and supplies at Gettysburg: woolen shirts, 7,158; soap, 250 pounds; towels and napkins, 10,000; shoes and slippers, 4,000 pairs; candles, 350 pounds; fresh poultry and mutton, 11,000 pounds; butter, 6,430 pounds; eggs, 8,500 dozen;

---

14 Ellen Harris letter, July 10, 1863, in "Fifth Semi-annual Report of the Ladies' Aid Society of Philadelphia" (Historical Society of Pennsylvania, Philadelphia, PA, n.d.), 13-14.

15 *Documents of the US Sanitary Commission*, 13-14.

lemons, 116 boxes; oranges, 46 boxes; coffee, 850 pounds; chocolate, 831 pounds; brandy, 1,250 bottles; whiskey, 1,168 bottles; wine, 1,148 bottles; and codfish, 3,848 pounds. The perishables on the foregoing list were delivered in railroad cars packed with ice.[16]

"Car load after car load of supplies were brought to this place, till shelves and counter and floor up to the ceiling were filled, till there was barely a passage-way between the piles of boxes and barrels, till the sidewalk was monopolized and even the street encroached upon," Associate Secretary J. H. Douglas said of the conditions at the Sanitary Commission's Fahnestock warehouse. "These supplies were the outpourings of a grateful people."[17]

XI Corps Assistant Medical Director Dr. Robert Hubbard of the 17th Connecticut was but one of the many wounded and medical staff who praised the work of the commissions. He appreciated their efforts so much that he mentioned them in three letters from Gettysburg to his wife, Nellie:

July 7: I am in excellent health & with my acquaintance with the Sanitary & Christian Commission I get all I wish for my own comfort and I assure you they are doing a noble work for the wounded.

July 9: The Sanitary Commission & Christian Commission & kindred organizations are doing a noble work distributing clothing, food of all kinds with large supplies of fruit and vegetables.

July 13: I am very comfortable here, get plenty to eat and of excellent quality from the Sanitary Commission – eggs, chicken, crackers of every kind. It is wonderful, the amount of material that is sent us of every kind. They are doing a noble work as well as the Christian Commission and I risk nothing in saying that the wounded at no field hospitals of the world ever recd. such.[18]

US Army Medical Inspector John M. Cuyler also acknowledged "the immense aid afforded by the Sanitary and Christian Commissions. The promptness, energy, and great kindness uniformly exhibited by these benevolent associations doubtless helped to save the lives of many," he wrote, "and gladdened the hearts of thousands, who, with their friends scattered throughout our land, will hold their

16 Ibid., 21-22.

17 Ibid., 14.

18 Robert Hubbard Papers.

good and noble deeds in grateful remembrance." Cuyler also thanked the Adams Express delivery company, which voluntarily donated its drivers and wagons immediately after the battle to bring in wounded from the field "at a time when they were most in need."[19]

Many Northern states set up relief agencies to look after their own wounded, with New York taking its duty especially seriously. New York Agent Dr. Theodore Dimon reported to John F. Seymour when he arrived in Gettysburg on July 12. Seymour, the brother of New York Governor Horatio Seymour, was the state's agent for the relief of sick and wounded soldiers. He left town after instructing Dr. Dimon to provide whatever was required for New York's wounded. Dimon inspected every corps and division hospital, including the Spangler facility. "I found it located on a dry, airy knoll," he began,

> consisting mainly of well arranged hospital tents. A few of the wounded were deposited in a large barn. There was a sufficient detail here of surgeons, who appeared to be zealous in the performance of their duties. There was also a regular supply of hospital attendants. Agents of the Sanitary Commission and members of the Christian Commission were here also rendering aid. Several good women were encamped here, cooking for, and nursing the wounded, and the relatives of the soldiers, in considerable numbers, were each caring for his brother or son. The wounded lay upon stretchers, or upon ticks filled with hay or straw. Shirts and sheets were provided when needed. Food of good kind and variety and well prepared was furnished.
>
> Pads, compresses, and other appliances to relieve position or support painful parts, urinals, bed pans, basins, dishes, lanterns, etc. . . . had been freely distributed by the Sanitary Commission.[20]

Both Dr. Dimon and Agent Seymour assisted in the creation of Soldiers' National Cemetery later that year.

Individual contributions also poured in to the XI Corps hospital, as exemplified by the Reverend Franklin Jacob Fogel Schantz, 27, minister of three

---

19 John M. Cuyler, Official Report, July 27, 1863, in *The Miscellaneous Documents of the House of Representatives*, 25.

20 Theodore Dimon, "Report of the General Agent of the State of New York for the Relief of Sick, Wounded, Furloughed and Discharged Soldiers" (Albany, NY, 1864), Gregory Coco Box B-71, GNMP Library, File 136.

The Rev. Franklin Jacob Fogel Schantz

Archives and Special Collections,
Franklin and Marshall College

churches in the Catasauqua Charge near Allentown, Pennsylvania, and fellow German Aaron Seibert Leinbach, 38, soon to be minister of five churches in the Schwarzwald Charge in the area of Reading, Pennsylvania. The Reverend Schantz already had a tie to Gettysburg, for he had attended Lutheran Theological Seminary there for two years in the late 1850s. He returned to the battle-scarred town twice in July 1863, with each visit including a stop at the XI Corps hospital.

The Reverend Schantz discussed what he observed and included details of his work at the Spangler farm in an extraordinary 1890 address that is so invaluable it is worth quoting from at length:

> July 8: We visited the hospital of the 11th Corps. Houses and barns, outbuildings and tents were filled with the sick and wounded. We met a German Chaplain, Rev. Mr. Poerner, whom Pastor Leinbach and I had known for many years. He was delighted to see us. He wanted us to stay and help him in his work. He excused us after promising that on our return to our homes we would raise hospital stores and bring them or forward them to Gettysburg.

> July 22-27: The promise which I had given to the Chaplain of the 11th Corps Hospital was not forgotten. During the week following my return from Gettysburg, the good people of the Lutheran and Reformed Congregations at Catasauqua, White Hall and Altona were busy in preparing Hospital stores which they collected in promise from me that I would take them to Gettysburg and see to their proper distribution. On Tuesday, July 21st, I started for Gettysburg with four and a half large wooden boxes of stores from the church at Altona; four and a half similar boxes from Catasauqua and White Hall, and 2 boxes and 1 barrel from Coplay Station.

> On Friday afternoon I had a large wagon filled with Hospital stores and drove to the 11th Corps Hospital, some distance south of the town. I shall never forget

that ride. I wore a linen coat and a straw hat and smoked a clay pipe! Not many persons would have taken me for a parson. I reached the Hospital without any mishap. The German Chaplain, whom I had met when at Gettysburg on Wednesday after the battle, greeted me most cordially and rejoiced that I had kept my promise to bring stores for the sick and wounded. I distributed many articles myself from tent to tent, assisted by men in service at the Hospital. Many of the articles were distributed from the Tent of the Christian Commission. The men were delighted with what I brought. I had a large number of shirts, drawers and wrapper, and a large supply of lint. The home made bread, zwieback, butter, pickles, apple butter, canned fruit, large quantity of dried fruits, and other articles were very acceptable to the men. Many were the thanks I received to carry with me to the kind donors in the Lehigh Valley.

In the evening I preached first in German between rows of tents and subsequently in a large barn where I found many wounded soldiers lying in rows on the floor. I shall never forget the sad scenes in that barn. I heard many of the wounded soldiers speak of home, of their mothers, and other friends. I remember the sad plaintive utterances of many of the poor sufferers. A number of them gave me their names and the addresses of their friends and asked me to write to the latter what they dictated to me. Later I preached in English between tents. The poor sufferers seemed very grateful. I met at the Hospital, Chaplain Poerner, Dr. Ginkinger of Allentown [Assistant Surgeon William Henry Harrison Ginkinger, age 26, 27th Pennsylvania], Dr. Cram, Mrs. Price [Nurse Rebecca Lane Pennypacker Price, Phoenixville, PA], Mr. Smith of New Brunswick, NJ, and Mr. Ludlow of Rochester, NY. The German soldiers seemed very glad for the service in the German Language. I met a fine Swede. I was for some time with Louis [Lewis] Bishop. . . . He was the bold soldier who would not give up his flag when one of his legs was shot off. He stuck to his flag until he was wounded in the other leg. A sad case that of the dying infidel in the barn, who refused the services of clergymen.

On Sunday morning I left early to pay a second visit at the 11th Corps Hospital. . . . After I reached the 11th Corps Hospital, I visited the men in their tents. Some of them told me that since Friday they had received nothing but bread and coffee. I went at once to the tent of the Christian Commission and had the balance of what I had brought to the Hospital on Friday distributed among the men. After this distribution I went from tent to tent as far as I could and read scriptures, made what I regarded as suitable remarks, and prayed with the men, who appeared to be very grateful.[21]

The Reverend Schantz returned to Gettysburg that fall for the dedication of the Soldiers' National Cemetery and the Gettysburg Address by President Abraham Lincoln. He became a notable writer and lecturer after the war, continued his ministry, was a member of the Board of Trustees of Muhlenberg College, member and president of the Pennsylvania German Society, and one of the founders of the Lebanon County Historical Society.[22]

About a dozen sisters and Father James Francis Burlando from the Daughters of Charity in Emmitsburg waited out the July 4 torrential rains before arriving by wagon in Gettysburg on July 5 to begin their healing and spiritual work. More sisters arrived the next day determined to provide nursing duties, such as wrapping wounds, cooking, and ministering to the wounded. They also performed baptisms. The sisters dispersed throughout the Gettysburg area in teams of two or more. As far as we know, none of them mentioned the XI Corps hospital in their journals or letters. It is likely that none of them worked there, and no other writings mention seeing any of the sisters on the Spangler farm. We know some of the sisters worked at the Lutheran Theological Seminary, the Gettysburg courthouse, Pennsylvania College, St. Francis Xavier Roman Catholic Church, the Methodist Episcopal Church, a couple of field hospitals, and with the ambulances.[23]

The Seminary hospital took in some XI Corps men who fell wounded on July 1, so the sisters could have encountered them there, at one of the other hospitals, or on ambulances because XI Corps ambulance driver and Spangler worker Pvt. Jacob Smith of the 107th Ohio remembered them fondly after the war. "I have no doubt that scores of lives were saved through the care and attention given them by these sisters, that otherwise would have been lost," believed the private. "Many of

---

21 Schantz, "Recollections of Visitations at Gettysburg," Lebanon County Historical Society, 278-303.

22 Ibid.

23 Betty Ann McNeil, D.C., Vincentian Scholar-in-Residence, DePaul University, and author of *Balm of Hope: Charity Afire Impels Daughters of Charity to Civil War Nursing* (Chicago, IL, 2015), email interview, August 7, 2017.

the brave boys who were nursed through their afflictions by these good women, will remember them with affection and gratitude as long as life shall last."[24]

The XI Corps wounded and dying at the Spangler farm could be grateful for all of the charity relief that poured in after their sacrifice in battle. In some cases that charity turned agony into comfort or at least made things more bearable. In other cases it brought healing and made the difference between life and death or offered a tender hand and tender word to one whose life was fading. Sometimes it saved a soul.

"I had spent four days in the Hospitals of Gettysburg and learned the terrible consequences of war and how demoralizing it was for some men," recalled the Reverend Schantz. "I had also learned how much good can be done at such a place–a great field for spiritual ministrations–and for the exercise of the spirit of the Good Samaritan."[25]

Spangler Farm Short Story

Rowland B. Howard was the first Christian Commission delegate in Gettysburg, where he arrived with his brother, XI Corps Maj. Gen. Oliver O. Howard, on July 1. The second Christian Commission delegate to reach the field was John C. Chamberlain in the early morning of July 2. John was the brother of Col. Joshua Lawrence Chamberlain and Lt. Thomas Chamberlain of the 20th Maine. Howard and Chamberlain were short-term volunteer Christian Commission delegates, and Gettysburg was the only battle for each.

John Chamberlain spent the morning and afternoon of July 2 with his brothers bivouacked on Hanover Road and later on and around the Spangler farm. John rode to the top of Little Round Top side-by-side with his brothers in front of the 20th Maine and under fire late in the afternoon of the 2nd. There, Colonel Chamberlain told Thomas and John, "Boys, I don't like this. Another such shot might make it hard for mother." Thomas moved to the rear of the regiment and John to the rear of the Army of the Potomac line, where he began helping the wounded. He would do so for the rest of the battle mainly at the V Corps hospital. Rowland Howard treated the wounded all three days of the battle beginning July 1 on Cemetery Hill. "When the first broken line of limping, bleeding, 'wounded' halted along the Baltimore turnpike," he wrote after the war of the XI Corps

---

24 Smith, *Camps and Campaigns*, 125.

25 Schantz, "Recollections of Visitations at Gettysburg."

injured, "and I attempted, almost alone, the work of relief, I felt as never before war's cruel sacrifice of blood and life and limb."[26]

Ruch Report No. 5

At Spangler Farm
Private Reuben F. Ruch, Company F, 153rd Pennsylvania

"The natives brought in wagon-loads of bread, apple butter, and ham," began Ruch. "To get something from every wagon had to be worked by a sort of system,

and the way it was done was that two or three would escort the chaplain to the wagon, and the instruction to him was that he must tell the parties in charge of the wagon, that we in the barn had had nothing to eat for three days, which resulted in getting something out of every wagon. But the chaplain had to repeat this story every hour, and the consequence was we had plenty to eat and some left over when I left the barn. This was the only time in my life when I thought a preacher was any benefit to his fellow man. . . .

One word more about the chaplain. . . . I got into the barn on Saturday, and on Sunday morning the chaplain started to have services on the barn floor not over five feet from me. He got down on his knees and was offering a prayer to the Deity, and he was just getting nicely started when some hard Christian in the cow stable yelled, 'put the preacher out.' I felt sorry for my friend, the Chaplain, and praying seemed hard under the circumstances. The yelling was kept up during the service and consequently the prayer was cut short and the hymn shorter. I never was in a meeting where I felt so much like laughing, but as I was so near the preacher, out of respect for him, I controlled myself and kept in.[27]

* * *

26 Chamberlain, "Through Blood and Fire at Gettysburg"; Rowland B. Howard, "At Gettysburg," American Peace Society (Boston, MA, 1887).

27 Kiefer, *History of the One Hundred and Fifty-Third Regiment*, 223-224.

Nurse Marilla Hovey worked more than five weeks at the Spangler hospital, and she didn't stop delivering mercy when she left the wounded of Gettysburg and went home to Dansville, New York, for three weeks to recover her own health. There, the wife of Spangler doctor Bleecker Lansing Hovey (136th New York) was recruited to raise funds and materials for the state-sponsored New York Soldiers' Relief Association. The following excerpts are from a letter she wrote in August 1863:

Patriotic Ladies and Gentlemen of the State of New York:

Feeling a deep interest for our sick and wounded soldiers–that interest being increased by eight months experience visiting hospitals and on the battle field–I wish to say a few words in regard to relieving their sufferings. All know that we have a . . . Sanitary and Christian Commission which are doing a noble work. But few seem to know that each state has a relief association, the object being to appoint agents to look personally after their own sick and wounded. New York has probably done more than any other state in the Union. Yet she does not always get the credit for it, because she does it . . . not as much through our state association. I have heard our state soldiers say, with tears in their eyes, 'Where are our state agents? Why do not our people send such to look after us as other states do?' . . . But those of us who have been interested enough and had an opportunity, know that many states are looking after their own men so faithfully, that they have care almost as from their own families.

Now I wish to make an appeal to the patriotic ladies of our own state to send the articles of comfort which they are preparing, to our agent Mr. [Col. Samuel] North, at Washington. Rest assured they will be well appropriated, and when agents say these supplies were furnished by our state ladies, would not the same articles taste better, bandages set easier, lint be more soft? 'Perhaps a wife, a sister, or a dear mother has fixed this for me?'

I do not wish in the least to depreciate what our noble state has done. Go to the register of articles kept in Washington, and you will see that some portions of the state are responding nobly to the calls for supplies. The ladies of the Relief Society of Rochester in one year have forwarded (according to report) 16 bales, 14 boxes, 27 barrels and 32 kegs of articles. I have met agents from our state visiting and distributing in Washington, Virginia and Gettysburg. No pen describe the good they have done at Gettysburg. As I was taking notes to write to friends of one of our New York men who was dying [at Spangler], some gentlemen came along and stopped by the tent to witness the departing spirit, and make what enquiries they could. I told them I was going to write to the friends, that the body should be prepared so they could get it, but all the preparation that could be made was the articles prepared by the ladies. Do not be shocked when I tell you that their blankets were their winding sheets and coffins. One of the gentlemen kindly offered to furnish a coffin. Was he not an angel of mercy just at that time? I saw him going from hospital to hospital and from tent to tent, looking after our New York men. It was [attorney] John F. Seymour, whom his brother, the governor of our state, had sent to do what he could for the comfort of the suffering soldiers. It was very cheering to know that they were remembered at home. Some of our agents were there almost every day.

To furnish as far as possible, and by systematic visitation to cheer and console the suffering men of New York in these hospitals, is the object of the New York Soldier's Relief Society.

Mrs. B. L. H.[28]

28 Letter of August 1863, provided by Rex Hovey.

Chapter 19

The Spangler Surgeons

"For myself, I think I never was more exhausted."
— *XI Corps Surgeon Dr. Daniel G. Brinton*

 it got so bad the surgeons had no choice but to stop working and quietly stand next to their operating tables outside the Spangler barn to collect themselves and prevent a complete collapse. When occasion offered, they bent over and placed their blood-stained hands on their knees and rested for a few moments, or walked or stumbled into the shade of a tree to briefly get away from it all—as if that were possible on a farm packed with almost 2,000 wounded men.

The Union surgeons operated under the forebay extending out from the Spangler barn, which offered some protection from a glaring midday sun and bursts of rain. What they could not find protection from was the human suffering visible in every direction. Piles of bloody amputated limbs almost as high as their heads offered stark evidence of the untold misery in which they labored. The human arms, legs, fingers, and feet were already decaying or infected with gangrene, and the vomit-inducing smell only made matters that much worse. Buzzing flies and other biting insects feasted on the dead flesh and filled the air around the working medical men.

Many of the amputated limbs once belonged to young men they had doctored and helped raise back home. Others came from strangers they only met in passing once they were deposited, groaning or screaming or silent, on the blood-covered operating tables. Either way, it was a race against time to saw through this man's limb and save his shattered life.

Dr. Henry Van Aernam

New York State Military Museum

This assembly line of field surgery that began on the afternoon of July 1 continued day after day and night after night. "Would it ever end?" they surely wondered. Sleep, if it arrived at all, was taken in quick catnaps. Eating was an inconvenience when men needed their life-giving attention, a luxury more endured than enjoyed.

Surgeon Henry Van Aernam of the 154th New York was 44 years old that early July when he found himself covered in the blood of others. Like everyone, he was surrounded by the odor of human feces, body fluids, rotting flesh, and infection. His muscles ached after hours of standing for surgery, his eyes were losing focus, and his mind was shutting down from exhaustion. "My heart is sick contemplating the mutilations," he admitted in a letter home. On top of it all, he dearly missed his wife. Like most surgeons, his pain was both physical and mental.[1]

Most of these surgeons were just as tough as the toughest soldier, and they witnessed and survived scenes as bad or worse than experienced by any of the fighting men. As Dr. Van Aernam and his fellow Spangler surgeons would attest, it wasn't only the soldiers who had their spirits and health crushed by the Civil War. "For myself," confessed Second Division XI Corps Surgeon-in-Chief Daniel G. Brinton, "I think I never was more exhausted." Army of the Potomac Medical Director Dr. Jonathan Letterman understood Dr. Brinton's plight, and said as much in the report he penned that October. Some of the Gettysburg surgeons, he

---

1 Van Aernam to his wife, Amy Melissa, July 30, 1863, in Dunkelman *Brothers One and All*, 144.

Dr. Daniel G. Brinton

Chester County (PA) Historical Society

admitted, "fainted from exhaustion, induced by over-exertion, and others became ill from the same cause."[2]

As noted earlier, once the battle ended and the respective armies marched away, many of the surgeons were left behind, where they worked harder than ever. The first couple of days after a battle were always the worst, and the efforts continued, to a lesser degree, for months thereafter. Most of the initial primary operations and amputations were wrapped up within a week of the fighting. After that, the main focus was on treating wounds, keeping the men comfortable, and performing any further surgeries needed to repair anything else that was going wrong. According to his report, Dr. Letterman said 650 medical officers served under him at Gettysburg, and 106 were left behind when the army departed on July 5. They cared for 14,193 Union and 6,802 Confederate wounded, a total of 20,995.[3]

Probably about 14 surgeons, at one time or another, worked at the XI Corps field hospital from July 1-5, with at least twice as many assistant surgeons pitching in as well. The only surgeons known to still have been at Spangler after mid-July were Surgeon-in-Charge Dr. James A. Armstrong, Dr. Bleecker Lansing Hovey of the 136th New York, Dr. Jacob Y. Cantwell of the 82nd Ohio, and Dr. Henry K. Neff of the 153rd Pennsylvania, who transferred to Camp Letterman in late July. Many assistant surgeons remained, along with hospital stewards who served as pharmacists, and orderlies who helped wherever needed, such as holding down a patient who was having reflexive movements while under chloroform.

---

2 Brinton letter to his mother, July 9, 1863, Dr. Daniel Garrison Brinton Papers; Letterman, *OR* 27, pt. 1, 97.

3 Ibid., 198.

During the Civil War, more than 11,000 medical men assumed the job of Union doctor, and about half of them went home early on their own or were sent home. Civilian doctors volunteered after battles, but few impressed their military counterparts. Many of the civilian doctors were more in the way than helpful. Some only wanted to do amputations, while others didn't want to dress wounds or just didn't know how to cope with a situation this horrible. It took a special strength and special skill to handle this sort of work.

Each regiment had one surgeon and two assistant surgeons, and the assistants had it as bad as or worse than the surgeons. This was especially true during the battles because of the danger they faced managing aid stations immediately behind the line under fire. Many of these assistant surgeons were wounded, killed, or captured. Most doctors entered the war as regimental surgeons or assistant surgeons and were promoted from there.

At the Spangler hospital, Assistant Surgeon J. Mortimer Crawe of the 157th New York stuck around for more than a month and served as the recording officer, preparing the rolls of sick and wounded. Assistant Surgeon Dwight W. Day, 154th New York and assistant to Dr. Van Aernam, left Spangler in mid-July to escort hundreds of XI Corps wounded to Baltimore. Assistant Surgeon William H. H. Ginkinger of the 27th Pennsylvania is known to have stayed for most or all of July, as did Assistant Surgeon Amos Shaw, Jr., of the 41st New York. Assistant Surgeon John S. Whildin of the 145th Pennsylvania, II Corps, worked at the XI Corps hospital for a while during the battle because many 145th wounded were taken there. Assistant Surgeon William S. Moore, with the 61st Ohio, was mortally wounded on July 3 while serving behind the front line. He died at the Spangler facility on July 6, and thus holds the unfortunate record of being the only Army of the Potomac surgeon or assistant surgeon killed at Gettysburg.

In addition to exhaustion came the daily exposure to disease in unsanitary barns and tents. Most surgeons became ill themselves, and many left the army because of it and struggled with poor health for the rest of their lives. Some died early deaths as a result of their medical labors during the war.

William P. Bush of the 61st New York was one of the many II Corps First Division assistant surgeons working July 2-3 at Granite Schoolhouse. He was detailed to the main II Corps division hospitals after the battle and died that fall in Washington, D.C., at the age of 33 from typhoid fever, a disease he almost certainly contracted in a hospital or camp.

Surgeons suffered on the march like everyone. They usually rode behind the men or traveled in wagons, inhaling clouds of dust kicked up by those men and animals. Once in camp, they ate the same rations (often raw salt pork and hardtack) and drank the same unhealthful water. Sometimes only a couple of doctors comfortably shared a large tent with a stove and writing table, but just as often, especially early in the war, as many as five doctors were squeezed into tents so cramped they had to bend over and hobble to move around. Some nights were spent in the open in the rain, and they overheated and dehydrated in hot weather and humidity and suffered with the cold in winter. Lice, which were as abundant in hospitals as the flies, didn't discriminate between privates and doctors.

Homesickness, which coursed through every army, was just as strong amongst the Spangler doctors as it was in the ranks. Would they be forgotten by their loved ones? Were they missed? The strong desire to receive letters was a common plea when they stole a few moments to scratch out a letter home.

"I was sorely disappointed to night in not receiving a letter from you," Van Aernam wrote his wife, Amy Melissa, in May 1863. "I had looked for it so anxiously and so long that I could hardly believe our mail boy when he told me there was nothing for me to night. I thought he was mistaken & had him look the mail over again, and with, a little ill-concealed petulance he announced the result of his search 'I told you there was nothing!' I turned away disappointed and heartsick."[4] A month later, Van Aernam continued the same theme when he closed a letter home. "Write me often, for you cannot realize how glad I am to hear from you and home. Write often for a letter is the kiss of the absent–and were we together could we live a day without a kiss?"[5]

Robert Hubbard, who was surgeon of the 17th Connecticut before being promoted to assistant medical director of the XI Corps, also found himself hard at work on the Spangler farm. He, too, longed for letters from home. "This morning I recd. two letters from you one of the 25th and the other of the 26th of April," he wrote his wife Cornelia on May 8, "and this P.M. came an enormous mail requiring 4 horses to draw it & I thought certainly I should be favored with news from the dear ones at home of more recent date but I was greatly disappointed in only receiving yours of the 23rd of April."[6] One day later, he observed, "Your letters of late have become in army phrase great stragglers."[7]

---

4 Van Aernam to his wife, May 15, 1863, Henry Van Aernam Papers, US Army Heritage and Education Center, Box 1 of 1, Henry Van Aernam Correspondence (Originals).

5 Henry Van Aernam Papers, Henry Van Aernam Correspondence (Transcribed).

6 Robert Hubbard Papers, May 8, 1863.

7 Ibid., May 9, 1863.

Dr. Robert Hubbard

In addition to missing their loved ones, the doctors engaged in a little good-natured gloom over what the toil was doing to their appearance. "I have three large pictures," Van Aernam explained, "but I am sorry I had them taken now. . . . Care and anxiety and excitement and experience and sickness have chiseled away at that face of mine rapidly."[8]

Other grievances arose brought about by the stress of wartime work and the fact that they were human beings. A doctor at one of the two Spangler hospitals had complained before Gettysburg that some chaplains were inefficient, and told one with whom he was working that he wasn't as important as he thought. Without missing a beat, the chaplain shot back that the doctor would be better at his work if he drank less and was kinder to his patients. Another surgeon there grumbled that both of his assistant surgeons were trying to get out of the army, but that was fine with him because they were so lazy no less work would get done.

A surgeon at another field hospital in Gettysburg observed with some disgust that the hatred between two assistant surgeons was so strong that they refused to speak to each other or work together. The surgeon requested that for the good of the patients and the hospital staff that the two warring doctors be transferred and replaced.

The Reverend Franklin Jacob Fogel Schantz of Lehigh County, Pennsylvania, made two visits to the Spangler hospital in July, and during one of those he accused

---

8 Henry Van Aernam Papers, September 3, 1863.

a surgeon and/or assistant surgeon of theft, an interesting story worth relating at length:

> I was creditably informed on the Sunday morning that a Surgeon had appropriated for his own use one of the wrappers which I had brought for comfort of poor wounded soldiers. I dined at noon in a large tent with a number of Surgeons and Nurses in Chief. Six of us were seated at a table. I sat at one end and a Surgeon at the other. On each side sat a surgeon and a lady Nurse. In the course of conversation I remarked that before I had left home I had often heard that not all the goods sent for sick and wounded soldiers reached their proper destination, that I had always had contradicted the charge that had been made, but that I was sorry to say that on return to my home I could no longer contradict such charges for I had been informed that one of the wrappers which I had brought for the sick and wounded soldiers had been taken by some one who was well and receiving good pay.

> I said no more but in looking at the Surgeon at the other end of the table, I noticed that he had occasion to make a special examination of his knife and fork and no doubt found some relief in doing so, instead of looking at me, for he was the man who had been charged with the base act. After dinner I passed the Surgeon's quarters in a small wagon shed by the side of a barn and there I saw one of the wrappers I had brought. I asked the Surgeon's attendant where the wrapper was secured. His brief answer was, 'We got it.'[9]

Alcoholism also was a problem for a small fraction of the surgeons. More than enough medicinal whiskey, brandy, and sherry always seemed to be on hand, and the temptation proved to be too much for mortal men laboring under such grievous conditions. The predictable results were bad decision-making and uncomfortable confrontations.[10]

The doctors also had to be on alert for shirkers. One member of the 154th New York shot off two fingers from his right hand in 1862 in an attempt to get a

---

9 Schantz, "Recollections of Visitations at Gettysburg," 278-303.

10 Thomas Lowry and Terry Reimer, *Bad Doctors: Military Justice Proceedings Against 622 Civil War Surgeons* (Frederick, MD, 2010), 59.

disability discharge. Van Aernam, however, realized the wound for what it was and made him stay in the service.[11]

Being a surgeon had small perks if you could withstand the mental and physical toll of the labor. Doctor Brinton (and others) had a personal servant named Anthony to do laundry, cook non-army food, and take care of his horse. Servants were paid by the doctors who hired them. Doctors were allowed to shop for and purchase horses, and most did, though reimbursement wasn't guaranteed.

The pay was comparatively good. Union surgeons usually had a rank of major with a pay of $169 per month. Assistant surgeons were paid $115.50 with a rank of captain. In comparison, Army of the Potomac colonels were paid $212 per month and privates $13. Doctors paid for their own uniform, which identified them as medical men. The uniform included a green sash to be worn around their waist or over their shoulder and medical insignia and rank on their shoulder straps.

Many doctors who did not collapse from the gruesome work got used to it. One surgeon grew to enjoy performing amputations and experimental operations. "As soon as firing began he would roll up his sleeves and await the first man to be brought in with a positive appetite," recalled Capt. Louis Duncan of the US Army Medical Corps after the war.

As a whole, the Spangler doctors cared greatly for their patients and advanced the cause of medicine. They saved thousands of lives during the war under the most trying conditions. "The labor, anxiety and responsibility placed on them at this time," believed Captain Duncan, "was greater than of any other battle of the war."[12]

See Appendix 1 for more information, including biographies, on the Spangler farm surgeons.

Spangler Farm Short Story

Each Army of the Potomac regiment in the Civil War was supposed to have a chaplain, but many went months or years without one because the soldiers in the unit didn't consider it a priority. The quality of chaplains varied greatly, from the

---

11 Allen Williams to Northrup, July 1, 1895, Edwin Dwight Northrup Papers, Box 25, Carl A. Kroch Library, Cornell University.

12 Duncan, "The Greatest Battle of the War—Gettysburg," in *The Medical Department of the United States Army in the Civil War*, 22, 28.

Rev. John Henry Wilbrand Stuckenberg of the 145th Pennsylvania at the Granite Schoolhouse hospital who became one of the leading religious scholars of his time to men who had little or no religious training and considered reading military regulations once a week good enough for a chapel service.

The Lutheran Rev. Stuckenberg had a fellow outstanding II Corps chaplain comrade at Gettysburg in the Catholic Father William Corby, future president of the University of Notre Dame. Methodist ministers were the most common at Gettysburg. The XI Corps had a Jewish chaplain in Rabbi Ferdinand Leopold Sarner (54th New York). It's possible that Rabbi Sarner was treated at the Spangler hospital because he was wounded during the battle.

The best chaplains were often beloved by the men in their regiments. These chaplains risked their lives to get wounded men off the battlefield, wrote letters home before and after a soldier's death, offered basic first aid, visited the sick, stayed with dying men in their final moments, prayed with the men before combat, offered reminders of the love of God, handed out prayer books and Bibles, and preached. Despite all of this, wrote Pvt. John J. Ryder of the 33rd Massachusetts, XI Corps, "As a general rule army life is not conducive to religion; it rather tends the other way." According to US Christian Commission chaplain John B. Poerner, "A number of them as I have seen and heard are very profane. I will try with God's help, and by the power of His grace, to reform them." Spangler surgeon Dr. Daniel G. Brinton agreed: "The men are singularly immoral."[13]

Ruch Report No. 6

At Spangler Farm
Private Reuben F. Ruch, Company F, 153rd Pennsylvania

"There was a work bench in one end of the barn with a few tools," recalled the private, "and a comrade by the name of Jesse Soys

had the two middle fingers of his left hand cut off by a piece of a shell. He was busy making crutches, they were not very handsome, but they answered the purpose. I was the first doctor that had come to the barn . . . and I soon went

---

13 John J. Ryder, *Reminiscences of Three Years' Service in the Civil War* (New Bedford, MA, 1928), 47; Poerner, January 11, 1864, in *United States Christian Commission: Third Report of the Committee of Maryland* (Baltimore, MD, 1864), 156; Brinton to his mother, May 14, 1863, Dr. Daniel Garrison Brinton Papers.

to work dressing wounds. Sergeant Lantz was the first patient. We named him Dad. He had been shot through the thigh. Sergeant Lilly of Co. D was the next, he was also wounded in the thigh. Wm. Riehl was the third. He was shot in the shoulder, the ball was in his back. It was cut out the next day. Three of us sat on him while the surgeon cut out the ball. The ball was all battered, looking as much as if it had gone through a stone fence. I dressed wounds until I got out of bandages."

All four soldiers mentioned by Ruch were from the 153rd Pennsylvania and wounded on July 1 fighting north of town. Private Jesse Soys (35) lived to age 72; Sgt. Samuel L. Lantz (about 21) died in 1881; Cpl. Harrison W. Lilly (about 22) died in 1910; and Pvt. William H. Riehl (22), lived to age 78.[14]

---

14 Ruch wasn't a doctor, and was joking about being a so-called doctor. Kiefer, *History of the One Hundred and Fifty-Third Regiment,* 223.

Chapter 20

After the Fight

"The barn more resembled a butcher shop than any other institution. One citizen on going near it fainted away and had to be carried off."

— *Pvt. Justus Silliman, 17th Connecticut*

July 5, the Army of the Potomac left Gettysburg to begin its slow march south in chase of Robert E. Lee's retreating and defeated army. Many of the Union men were more than happy to leave Gettysburg, including Dr. Daniel G. Brinton. "I confess it was with a feeling of intense relief that I got my orders to leave this place where groans & cries had been resounding in my ears for days," he wrote to his mother on July 9. Brinton performed surgeries and amputations for five straight days at the XI Corps hospital.[1]

Private Jacob Smith of the 107th Ohio was also escaping the Spangler hospital. He and his fellow XI Corps ambulance workers had toiled day and night, often under fire, to haul wounded men to the farm hospital, and then helped wherever they could there. The ambulance corps spent all of July 4 and the morning of July 5 searching Gettysburg for additional wounded who had been left behind after the Confederates evacuated the town. Navigating the battlefield at night while exiting the town was something of a gamble. "There were no fences or landmarks of any kind left after the battle to serve as guiding points, and being very cloudy no stars could be seen to tell us the direction we wished to go," explained Smith. "The entire battlefield was without any trace of vegetation, and all signs of civilization and adornment by the inhabitants, were completely destroyed. There was nothing to be

---

1 Brinton to his mother, July 9, 1863, Dr. Daniel Garrison Brinton Papers.

found outside of the dread results of war; and here and there, half buried in the mud, would be found the dead body of some soldier that had been washed out of his shallow grave by the recent rains."[2]

Also departing on July 5 were most of the army's surgeons, assistant surgeons, and other medical staffers. The armies were on the move, and most of the men believed another large battle was in the offing within the next few days somewhere closer to the Potomac River. The loss of the doctors reduced the medical staff at Spangler and other hospitals to just 16 percent of what it was during the battle when the number of wounded and dying was at its peak. "What!" exclaimed Andrew Boyd Cross of the Christian Commission. "Take away surgeons here where a hundred are wanted, and where, if the men have not immediate help, hundreds must die for want of that attention. But so it is, and we can do no better."[3]

"There were some in churches, some in barns, some in tents among the fruit trees, some in tents in the fields, some under such shelter as a farmer would be ashamed to show for his cows," recalled Army of the Potomac Medical Inspector Dr. G. K. Johnston about the wounded on July 4-5. "Some were under blankets hung over cross-sticks, and some without even so much shelter as that. There were some scattered groups of men outside the hospitals. It sometimes appeared as if an experiment had been made to see how many wounded could be crowded into a given space in a house."[4]

The Army of the Potomac's departure emptied the Spanglers' 65 acres of wheat, grass, and woods north of Granite Schoolhouse Lane, though the wheat field below Powers Hill and much else were destroyed by the occupying Union army. The only things left on the Spangler land on the night of July 5 were the XI Corps hospital in and around their buildings, broken and unwanted Army of the Potomac debris, and nearly 2,000 wounded men.

With the armies filling the roads winding out of the area, family members of the victims of the fight, volunteers, and army medical and quartermaster staffers did their best to swim against the tide, with mixed success. Many relatives of the fallen traveled great distances via train to reach the battlefield, but had to wait days and even as long as a week to reach it because the Confederates had destroyed railroad bridges in the area.

2 Smith, *Camps and Campaigns*, 125.

3 Andrew B. Cross, "The Battle of Gettysburg" in *The War and the Christian Commission* (Baltimore, MD, 1865), 16.

4 *The Military Surgeon*, 220.

Hospital steward Cpl. William R. Kiefer of the 153rd Pennsylvania helped put up late-arriving hospital tents, but there were "not half enough." These shelters populated the grounds around the house and barn in a city of tents laid out in rows and spread to surrounding fields when more tents arrived. Another day of rain on July 5 maintained the high misery index. Shovels arrived to supplement those taken from the Spanglers and neighboring farmers, making the job of digging latrines and graves easier. Cooking equipment arrived about this time and made the job of putting warm food on the menu much easier. Lint and bandages and other medical items were also finally pouring in, or soon would be.[5]

Surgeries and amputations continued for several more days because of the steady flow of incoming wounded men and the short-staffed medical team. Many of those soldiers who fell on July 1 and didn't arrive at the Spangler farm until July 4-5 didn't survive because they did not receive proper care soon enough.

Forty-two-year-old hospital steward Pvt. Jacob T. Zehrung with the 73rd Ohio was shocked by the crowds of wounded and the suffering he witnessed on July 5. "Such a sight I never saw in all my life," he confessed.[6] "The barn more resembled a butcher shop than any other institution," recalled Pvt. Justus Silliman of the 17th Connecticut. "One citizen on going near it fainted away and had to be carried off."[7]

Private Henry D. Lock of the 157th New York was wounded in the foot north of town on July 1 and remained behind enemy lines until he was picked up by an ambulance four days later and hauled to the XI Corps hospital. He left a sparse but valuable daily account in his journal describing his post-battle experience:

"Sunday 5: We had to lay out doors on the wet ground it was rather tough on wounded men but thare is better day coming.

"Monday 6: Rained I hobbled around & found some of our company boys were wounded in every shape we have not much are thare . . . my foot is doing well as could be expected & that all for to day.

"Tuesday 7: Still keeps raining I feel just about the same I can hobble around & see the boys some of them looks hard but are in good spirits thare is three in our company we have not heard from.

5 Kiefer, *War Diary of William R. Kiefer.*

6 Lee A. Spangler, *Jacob Thomas Zehrung Civil War Diary* (Canal Winchester, OH, 2001), 11-13.

7 Silliman, *A New Canaan Private in the Civil War*, 45.

"Wednesday 8: Very warm & pleasant feel about the same still lie on the ground & pretty nasty the Ladys bring us provisions of all kinds they seem to be very kind to us & well they might."[8]

Confederate wounded from three divisions that participated in Pickett's Charge reached the XI Corps and other hospitals on July 3-4. Included among these arrivals was Pvt. Cameron L. Leonhardt from the 11th North Carolina, part of Brig. Gen. James Johnston Pettigrew's brigade, Henry Heth's division. The regiment had lost about one-third of its effective strength in the heavy fighting west of town on July 1 and participated in the charge on July 3. Leonhardt and his comrades had advanced directly against Cemetery Ridge and were wounded and captured near the Emmitsburg Road. Private Leonhardt was 20 or 21 years old when he was hit in the left shoulder on July 3. The Lincolnton native died at the XI Corps hospital on July 30 and was buried there with a marker.[9]

The Sanitary Commission estimated there were 100 Confederates at the Spangler farm at this time. They were in the wagon shed on the house side of the barn and in nearby tents. The medical staff usually but not always separated the wounded of the two armies. Most of the Spangler Confederates were handed over to the provost marshal by middle to late July for transfer to Camp Letterman outside of Gettysburg, to a general hospital, or to a prisoner-of-war camp. (Camp Letterman opened on July 22 and closed in November.)[10]

The few dozen men who survived the slaughter of the 2nd Mississippi in and around the Railroad Cut on July 1 also participated in Pickett's Charge. They fell in heaps as they approached the ridge just south of the Brian house on July 3. One of the wounded was Lt. William H. Moody, who had risen from private to third lieutenant. Moody was part of Company A (Tishomingo Riflemen) from Tishomingo County in northern Mississippi. Somewhere during the final yards of the attack the 21-year-old Moody fell with a neck wound. He survived long enough

---

8 H. D. Lock, diary, n.d., Division of Rare and Manuscript Collections, Carl A. Kroch Library, Cornell University.

9 J. W. C. O'Neal Collection, Adams County Historical Society, Gettysburg, PA, and Cameron Leonhardt's company muster roll cards on Fold3.

10 *Documents of the US Sanitary Commission,* 19.

to be hauled to the Spangler hospital but died soon after his arrival and was buried with a headboard.[11]

Wounded Confederates who survived the trip off the Spangler farm were often exchanged. Some took an oath of allegiance to the Union. Sergeant John F. Puckett, 7th Tennessee, was shot in the left arm during Pickett's Charge, captured, and taken to the XI Corps hospital. He suffered immense pain from a fracture and wound that would not heal. The nearly six-foot-tall, blue-eyed farmer was shipped to De Camp General Hospital on David's Island in New York City between July 17 and July 24. He was paroled there and transported to the Confederate States Hospital in Petersburg, Virginia, in November. Unfortunately, his exit wound was still discharging and his arm paralyzed. Puckett was admitted to a hospital in Richmond that December and spent most of 1864 in hospitals beginning in Petersburg, then Kittrell, North Carolina, Williamsburg, Virginia, and back to Petersburg. He was finally discharged on a surgeon's certificate of disability.[12]

* * *

It took many days to bury the dead. As a rule, Confederates were interred last. "On the Codori farm," 18-year-old Gettysburg resident Daniel Skelly recalled of July 6, "there were still some Confederate dead who had not been buried. They were lying on their backs, their faces toward the heavens, and burned as black as coal from exposure to the hot sun." Of July 7, Capt. Martin Stone of the 2nd Pennsylvania Cavalry noted, "The rebels were buried right where they had fallen for their bodies had become so putrid that it was imposible to move them but our men wer buried in good order." Army of the Potomac Capt. Henry B. Blood recorded that he buried 337 "dead rebels" on July 9 and 30 more the following day. He said he was still burying and burning horses on July 10-11. The stench from it all, including the burning carcasses, spread into Gettysburg.[13]

11 William H. Moody 2nd Mississippi July-August, September-October, and November-December 1863 Company Muster Rolls on Fold3.

12 John F. Puckett Roll of Prisoner of War Gettysburg July 1-2-3, List of Rebel Prisoners of War at DeCamp General Hospital July 17-24, 1863, November 1863 and May 1864 Reports of Surgical Cases at Confederate States Hospital in Petersburg, VA, December 22, 1863, Register of General Hospital No. 9 Richmond, VA, Feb. 22 Register of Episcopal Church Hospital in Williamsburg, VA, and 7th Tennessee, Jan.-Feb. 1865 Company Muster Roll, all on Fold3.

13 Skelly, *A Boy's Experiences,* 21; *Martin Stone,* diary, File V4-20. "Aftermath: Battlefield Descriptions & Accounts," GNMP Library; Henry Boyden Blood Papers, GNMP, Box B-4.

Gettysburg-area residents were slowly becoming used to the sight of dead bodies and carried on with getting their lives back to some semblance of normal. They cleaned their houses and threw out rugs spoiled by blood and other bodily fluids when the wounded were moved from their homes to area hospitals. Railroads returned to functioning order by July 7.

The medical pressures at Spangler began easing about a week after the battle with the primary operations done and the wounded being shipped away in larger numbers. Vermont Surgeon Henry Janes, 31, was put in charge of the military hospitals in town. He noted 7,500 wounded who were able to travel were sent away by July 9. Medical Director Jonathan Letterman raised that number to 11,300 by July 14, leaving fewer than half the wounded in Gettysburg. Hospitals in Baltimore and Philadelphia took in large numbers of wounded, but smaller towns closer to Gettysburg such as York, Carlisle, Chambersburg, and Harrisburg also received their share of injured. The fact that these wounded could travel didn't mean they were healed, and many from both sides died in other hospitals after their transfer.[14]

Assistant Surgeon Dwight W. Day of the 154th New York wrote to his parents on July 8 that he had taken 600 wounded from the XI Corps hospital to Baltimore and there were still 1,600 left on the Spangler farm. Doctor Day was actively involved in caring for the wounded of the 154th and many other regiments from the earliest hours until his departure. XI Corps Assistant Medical Director Robert Hubbard informed his wife, Cornelia, on July 14 that he was on the train to Baltimore overseeing the transfer of another 500 wounded.[15]

Within a week of the end of the battle, all of the volunteers, friends, and family members of the wounded and dead relying on the trains were finally able to join the mobs of visitors already in Gettysburg and at the corps and division hospitals. Some towns sent committees and individuals to check on their dead and wounded and report back. Members checking on the men of the 153rd Pennsylvania of Northampton County wrote home to local newspapers detailing who was dead, wounded, or missing and the nature of their wounds. This was often how a family member received definitive news about the fate of a loved one. For example, James W. Phelps of Great Valley, New York, visited the XI Corps hospital and wrote that five of the eight patients of the 154th New York who were in a tent together had

---

14 OR 27, pt. 3, 620, 699.

15 Dwight W. Day to his parents, July 8, 1863, in "From the Cattaraugus Regiment, 154th," *Cattaraugus Union,* July 24, 1863, *Brothers One and All,* 144; Hubbard to his wife, July 14, 1863, Robert Hubbard Papers.

died. He later provided a list of the regiment's dead and wounded to the newspaper *Cattaraugus Freeman*.[16]

Many family members, such as those of Assistant Surgeon William S. Moore of the 61st Ohio, traveled great distances to dig up their loved one from a Spangler grave and take him home for reburial in a family plot or local cemetery. The military put a stop to this practice later in July, and most of the rest of the Union dead were reburied that fall or winter in the new Soldiers' National Cemetery in Gettysburg.

Opinions varied about the quality of help provided by locals to the various hospitals. Spangler nurse Rebecca Price thought Adams County residents were generous. "Ladies from the surrounding country would occasionally bring us several quarts of fresh milk," she explained after the war. "How gladly we welcomed the farmers and others who came with their wagons filled with supplies; sometimes the ladies brought food already prepared." Hospital steward Kiefer of the 153rd Pennsylvania recorded the same thing, noting, "A number of citizens came with eatables," on July 7 and, "Many citizens to see us today," on July 9.[17]

Medical treatment, suffering, and dying continued through July, though not every wounded soldier accepted the care offered. "A color-bearer of the 107th Ohio was shot in the wrist and the ball passing up his arm, stopped near the elbow," remembered Alfred J. Rider of the same regiment. He might have been referring to Christian Taifel (age 22 or 23), who was wounded in the hand in the night-time fight on July 2 on East Cemetery Hill as he stood on a wall and waved the flag. "He walked around at the 11th Corps Hospital several days, and wouldn't let the Dr's cut out the ball," continued Rider. "I plead with him one evening when he was frying potatoes and onions to have the ball extracted. He swore he wouldn't and the next morning he was dead."[18]

Nineteen-year-old Pvt. Francis Eaton of the 157th New York was the strapping son of a deceased farmer who stood five feet 10 inches and was called Frank by his friends. He also was the sole provider for his widowed 56-year-old mother, Esther, who was at home in Groton, New York. When he enlisted, Frank set aside $10.00 of his monthly $13.00 paycheck for his mother. Bullets struck Frank in the right leg and near the left ear and exited his left eye when the 157th was

16 Letter of James W. Phelps, July 19, 1863, "The 154th New York," in *Cattaraugus Freeman*, July 23, 1863, in *Brothers One and All*, 148.

17 Price, "Rebecca Lane Pennypacker Price's Account of Her Experiences as a Nurse During the Civil War"; Kiefer, *War Diary of William R. Kiefer*.

18 Rider to Bachelder, October 3, 1885, *The Bachelder Papers*, vol. 2, 1,129.

overrun along the Carlisle Road north of town on July 1. The regiment lost about three-fourths of its men killed, wounded, and missing in its first day of combat and the fight on Culp's Hill the next day.

Eaton clung to life for a few days at the Spangler hospital and died sometime during July 8-10. A soldier's death in the Civil War was usually announced to his family via letter from a nurse or comrade. In this case, the letter to Eaton's mother was written by Sgt. J. Franklin Wright, who was being treated at Spangler for a chest wound. "Mrs. Eaton: It pains me to inform you of the death of your son Frank," began the sergeant, who continued:

> He died at 6 o'clock last night. We see that he had good care. One of the boys of the Reg't was his nurse. He was wounded on the first day of July through the head, entering near left ear & coming out left eye, rendering him delirious all of the time so he said nothing to us. Henry Douglass took his diary. He has gone to Baltimore. We saw him decently buried this morning & placed a board at the grave with his name, Regiment and Company marked on it. Lieutenant Waters will go to Cortland within two weeks & will give you full particulars. As he is wounded in right hand, he requested me to write. Serg't J. Frank Wright.[19]

Sometimes a grieving parent of a deceased soldier requested details from a comrade on his or her son's death. When Pvt. Henry A. Miller of the 153rd Pennsylvania died at the XI Corps hospital, Miller's father sought information on his son's wounding and demise. Corporal Rudolph Roessel of the same regiment collected the information and wrote back to the grieving father. "As you desired I went and got all the information I could concerning Henry," he began,

> I have inquired also of [Sgt.] David Moll, who says that Henry was wounded on the 2d of July in the evening. He was not with him at the moment he was wounded, but he saw him shortly afterwards. Henry spoke to David asking him to get a blanket for him if possible, and while he was gone in search of one an ambulance came along and removed him to the hospital. . . . He undoubtedly died on the Glorious 4th. How sad that we who were within a mile or two from

---

19 Letter from Sgt. J. Franklin Wright to Mrs. Esther Eaton, July 10, 1863, written at the Spangler farm, Fold3.

where he was wounded could not have been with him to at least pour cold water on his wounds. Henry was a good boy.[20]

John F. Seymour visited the XI Corps hospital as the New York agent for the relief of sick and wounded soldiers and was present for the deaths in mid-July of the 157th New York's Cpl. James E. Joyner, age 19, and Pvt. Daniel H. Purdy, 21, of the 17th Connecticut. Both died from wounds suffered on July 1. Seymour included Joyner and Purdy in his report of his visit to Gettysburg:

> A young soldier, James Joiner, from Cortland county, drew from his side, a bible stained with his own blood, and whispered to us, that it had never been absent from him in battle.
>
> Not far from his tent lay another soldier, Daniel H. Purdy, of Fairfield county, Conn. At nine o'clock at night he was reported to be dying. By the light of a candle held in a reversed bayonet, some of his fellow-soldiers, and a clergy-man and others gathered around his tent where he lay upon a bundle of hay. A prayer was offered up by the clergy-man that the way of death might not be dark to him.
>
> When the prayer ceased, young Purdy astonished the group around him by quoting text upon text, the most beautiful of all the promises of the christian religion; while repeating these, his ear caught the sound of a familiar hymn sung in a neighboring tent, and his face became radiant with devotion–death was not dark to him.[21]

Adding to the misery index at the farm, hospital steward Private Zehrung of the 73rd Ohio recorded each morning that it was either raining as he wrote in his diary or it looked like it was about to rain on 11 days between July 4 and July 26. On a couple of days he noted that it was "raining very hard" and another day described the downpour as "a big rain." On July 16 he wrote, "Some of our boys is doing well and some dieing."[22]

20 Kiefer, *History of the One Hundred and Fifty-Third Regiment*, 169.

21 John F. Seymour, "Report of the General Agent of the State of New York for the Relief of Sick, Wounded and Discharged Soldiers," 1864, File V5 – Dimon, Theodore, GNMP Library.

22 Zehrung diary.

Not all endings were unhappy. In fact, most of the injured treated at the Spangler hospital survived. Some wounded men healed well enough to return to their regiments directly from the XI Corps hospital or went home for a while or to another hospital before rejoining their commands. Some men survived because of their amputation or surgery and the advancements of the day in Civil War medicine. Patients had a 66 to 97 percent chance of survival after an amputation unless it was an amputation of the thigh (45% survival rate), knee joint (42%) or hip joint (16%).[23]

Some, such as Sgt. Louis Morell, age 19, of the 119th New York, went through years of hospitalization and survived almost out of sheer will. Morell was born overseas in Berlin. He was 17 years old, stood five feet seven inches, and was a student when he boarded a ship in Hamburg bound for New York City in January 1862. He enlisted one month after entering the United States. A year and a half later, on July 1, 1863, he suffered three wounds and spent four days mostly unconscious and without care. He eventually made it to the Spangler facility with a wound above his left knee, a bullet through his left eye, and another that entered his right side and exited through his back. That fact that he was still alive was something of a miracle. Morell was transferred from the Spangler farm to Camp Letterman on August 6, to a hospital in New York City that October, and to another hospital in May 1865. The German immigrant was finally discharged in August 1865 more than two years after being wounded. He became a US citizen in 1866 and re-enlisted as a hospital steward in 1867. Morell died in 1882 in Washington, D.C., and is buried in Congressional Cemetery.[24]

Private Chauncey G. Pinney of the 154th New York took a Minie ball in the left side of his chest that fractured a rib, passed partway through his body, and lodged in his right side. A Spangler surgeon—possibly Dr. Henry Van Aernam of the 154th—extracted the ball. It was reported after Pinney's transfer to Camp Letterman that he had developed a cough and difficulty breathing in early August, but by September 5 surgeons reported his health "much improved, cough disappeared." He transferred to a Philadelphia hospital in October and returned to duty on February 10, 1864, saved by Civil War medicine.[25]

23 Exhibit, National Museum of Civil War Medicine.

24 *The Medical and Surgical History of the War of the Rebellion*, vol. 2, pt. 2, 80.

25 Dr. Henry Janes, in the report "Presented by Henry Janes, M. D., to Prof. J. B. Wheeler, M. D.," Library of the University of Vermont and State Agricultural College (New York, NY, undated), GNMP Library, Henry Janes File 1-72.

Hospital steward Pvt. Emory Sweetland, age 27, 154th New York, liked hospital work and did it throughout the war, serving at the XI Corps hospital on the Spangler farm and at Camp Letterman in Gettysburg. He was placed in charge of a ward at the latter facility. "In the hospital we have enough to eat & of a better quality than we get in the Co.," he explained. "Another reason is the 2 shillings pr day extra wages we get. This is quite an object with me. . . . My lot has been easier than most of the regt. I am quite healthy and I think I am thoroughly acclimated. . . . I feel too that I have been of much use in alleviating the sufferings of the sick & wounded." Sweetland took the time to mention a specific incident in a letter home: "The nurse cried out that a man was bleeding like a stuck hog," he continued. "He had been wounded in the breast & was apparently doing well when some artery rotted off inside & the blood was spurting. Those around did not know what to do. I put my thumb on the artery & stopped it, & the doctors are going to cut into him and take it up. Such things as this are of daily occurrance (it is the second one today). Some days I hold the legs or arms of 4 or 5 men to have them taken off."[26]

The New York hospital steward shared another story in a letter home to his parents, perhaps in an effort to lessen their concern for their son. "Even amongst so much suffering and death, some things laughable will occur," he explained. "The other day we had some wounded Rebs in the cellar of the barn and, the door being open, a stray pig walked in. One of the Rebs entered a complaint to the Doctors' waiting boy that we allowed hogs to roam about among their wounded. The boy asked him if the hog recognized any acquaintances among the Rebs!"[27]

*   *   *

The death of Confederate Brig. Gen. Lewis Armistead on July 5 and the removal of Capt. Frederick Stowe of the Second Division XI Corps headquarters staff to another hospital in mid-July cleared out the Spangler summer kitchen. As the size of the hospital continued to shrink, the Spangler family began cleaning out the detached kitchen to use its beehive oven to bake bread for the wounded.

According to Army of the Potomac Medical Inspector John M. Cuyler, 16,125 wounded had been sent away from Gettysburg by July 27, leaving 3,000 to 4,000 from both armies, most of whom weren't well enough to leave town. Those left

---

26 Sweetland to wife Mary, January 26, 1863, and April 10, 1864, in Dunkelman, *Brothers One and All*, 83-84; ibid., 146.

27 Sweetland to his parents, July 26, 1863, Gregory A. Coco Collection.

behind were in the process of being moved from the field hospitals to Camp Letterman on the York Pike east of town near the railroad. Cuyler reported that he hoped the wounded at Camp Letterman "will have all the comfort and receive all the attention and kindness to which they are so justly entitled."[28]

On the same day Inspector Cuyler was reporting his tally, II Corps nurse Emily Bliss Souder was writing home of the hospitals, "The Twelfth Corps is entirely removed; the Eleventh Corps nearly so. The ambulances and litters are constantly passing through town. This morning," she continued, "the poor wearied horses attached to the ambulance refused to carry their burden up Cemetery Hill."[29]

On July 24, just a couple days after it opened, there were 97 Union and 37 Confederate wounded at Camp Letterman. That number swelled to 669 Union and 660 Confederate by August 11. More than 600 Federal and 138 Confederate attendants, together with 20 women attendants, helped them. Eleven men died there on August 11, while 25 Confederate wounded and 15 Union attendants were sent elsewhere from Letterman that day.[30]

Hospital steward Zehrung of the 73rd Ohio wrote that he was transferred from the Spangler farm to Camp Letterman on July 28. Private Franz Benda of the 26th Wisconsin was one of the last wounded men moved from the XI Corps hospital when he was transferred to Letterman on August 6. Benda, a native of what is now the Czech Republic and immigrant to Manitowoc, Wisconsin, was being treated for a gunshot wound to his left hip that fractured his femur. A surgeon reported on August 12 that in addition to his serious femur injury, Benda was also suffering "from diarrhea and hectic fever and is sinking rapidly." He lingered in agony until August 28, when he died "from exhaustion" at Camp Letterman just days after turning 19. He was buried at Letterman before being moved to the Soldiers' National Cemetery.[31]

And then it all ended. On the night of Thursday, August 6, 1863, the XI Corps hospital was gone. The Spanglers had their land and home back. Their 166 acres had been trampled and ravaged by thousands of men and hundreds of wagons, shelled by artillery fire, and jammed corner-to-corner with wounded and dying

---

28 John M. Cuyler letter to William A. Hammond, July 27, 1863, in *The Miscellaneous Documents of the House of Representatives*, 25.

29 Souder, *Leaves From the Battle-field of Gettysburg*, 62.

30 Janes, Camp Letterman General Hospital Orders and Correspondence Journal, July 26-September 9, 1863, University of Vermont, GNMP Library.

31 Janes, "Presented by Henry Janes, M. D., to Prof. J. B. Wheeler, M. D."

men, animals, and equipment. Most of the property was barely recognizable, but it was still theirs and it had survived, as had George, Elizabeth, and their four children.

At least 2,500 and perhaps as many as 3,000 men were treated in the II Corps and XI Corps hospitals on the Spangler property. Its fields, roads, and hills provided crucial staging areas, express travel lanes to the front, resting space, communication links, and protection for men and equipment. Their farm had played a huge role in the Army of the Potomac's victory at Gettysburg. After five weeks and two days of occupation, the six Spanglers stood alone on their bloodstained property.

On the morning of Friday, August 7, they began rebuilding that property and their lives.

Spangler Farm Short Story

Flies deposited eggs in open wounds or injuries covered by a moist dressing, and the resulting maggots posed a disgusting nuisance at Civil War field hospitals and for wounded soldiers left untreated on the battlefield. A wound could be covered with maggots within 24 hours of injury or amputation, a crawling annoyance to the patient and a disturbing sight for hospital staffers.

The 61st New York's Lt. Charles Fuller, age 21, was hospitalized for two days at Granite Schoolhouse. He discovered maggots on his amputated leg after being transferred to the II Corps First Division hospital farther back when he was bothered one night by "crawley feelings" on his wounded leg. The next day, he mentioned this to a visiting civilian doctor from Ohio. "He took the bandages off and found that there were a huge number of full grown maggots in the wound," recalled Fuller. "This discovery for the moment was horrifying to me. I concluded if all the other things did not take me off the skippers would, but the good doctor assured me that the wigglers didn't amount to much in that place, and he would soon fix them. He diluted some turpentine, took a quantity in his mouth and squirted it into the wound and over the stump. It did the business for the intruders," remembered the wounded officer, "and I had no more trouble of that sort."

Confederate doctors discovered shortly after Gettysburg that wounds infested with maggots healed faster because the maggots ate infected or dead tissue and left healthy tissue alone.[32]

---

32 Fuller, *Personal Recollections*, 102-103.

Ruch Report No. 7

At Spangler Farm
Private Reuben F. Ruch, Company F, 153rd Pennsylvania

"Among my patients in the ward was a case of typhoid fever. . . . I expected every hour to be his last . . . and all I had to give him was water. . . . [O]n the second day, another preacher came into the barn. He did not belong to the army . . . he had a big jug of whiskey . . . and a small glass, and coming up on my side of the floor gave each man a glass. . . . [M]y patient lay on the opposite side from me and when it came his turn he tried hard to get up, but he could not. The preacher told him that he felt sorry for him, but in his condition he dared not give him whiskey. The sick man begged for a drink, and when the gentleman shook his head the poor fellow looked disappointed. I could not stand this any longer, and as my mind was made up that the fellow was going to die anyhow, that if he wanted a little whiskey in this world before going to the next one he should have it. I interceded for him, telling the preacher that this man was one of my patients, that he had typhoid fever, and that the stimulant was just what he needed. The man replied that if I said so he should have it. He handed me a glass and I raised his head and gave it to the patient. He drank it and lay down to sleep. The thought with me was that will fix him, either kill or cure. In the last few days I had looked upon so many dead men, that one more made no difference. My patient took a long sleep, and I thought he would never again awake. But on that night he looked up and asked me for a drink of water. He said he felt better. The drink of whiskey had saved his life. On leaving the boys I went round to bid them good-bye and when I called on my patient he asked me to get his knapsack. He was sitting up, though very weak. . . . He presented me with a pair of canvass leggings. He was a zouave, and stated, 'I give you these leggings, to remember me by, for you have saved my life.'"[33]

---

[33] Kiefer, *History of the One Hundred and Fifty-Third Regiment*, 224. A few Civil War regiments modeled themselves after the North African troops that fought for the French beginning in the 1830s. These Zouaves were known as tough fighters and wore colorful uniforms with baggy pants and usually a fez or turban on their heads. Private Ruch's Zouave patient probably was a member of the 41st New York, the only Zouave regiment in the XI Corps at Gettysburg.

Chapter 21

The Other Spanglers

"We went over to the [Abraham] Spangler house and camped in the barn all night. You can bet when a bunch of boys like that get together there is going to be some fun."

— *Musician William Simpson, 28th Pennsylvania, XII Corps*

Of the immediate Spangler clan, the farms west of Gettysburg belonging to father Abraham and daughter Susannah were the first to experience the shock waves of war.

Susannah Herbst, George Spangler's half-sister, hid in the cellar of her home near the Fairfield Road on July 1 with her husband, John. Hiding with them were their five children, including two-year-old George. As their barn burned, Henry Heth's Confederates, part of A. P. Hill's Third Corps, moved through and around their property. The Herbst family hugged, ducked, cried, and prayed as the sounds of war exploded all around them.

To the northwest, Abraham Spangler's farm straddled the Chambersburg Pike. The southeast tip of his property was just across Willoughby Run from the northwest corner of his daughter's land. And like his daughter's property, Abraham's farm was front and center during the early hours of the battle when Heth's Confederate infantry and artillery pushed Union cavalrymen back toward Gettysburg. Abraham had another farm on the other side of town on the Baltimore Pike next to son George's place. The Baltimore Pike farm was so close to the action that on the second and third days of the battle, artillery shells flew over the house and barn from two directions, often at the same time.

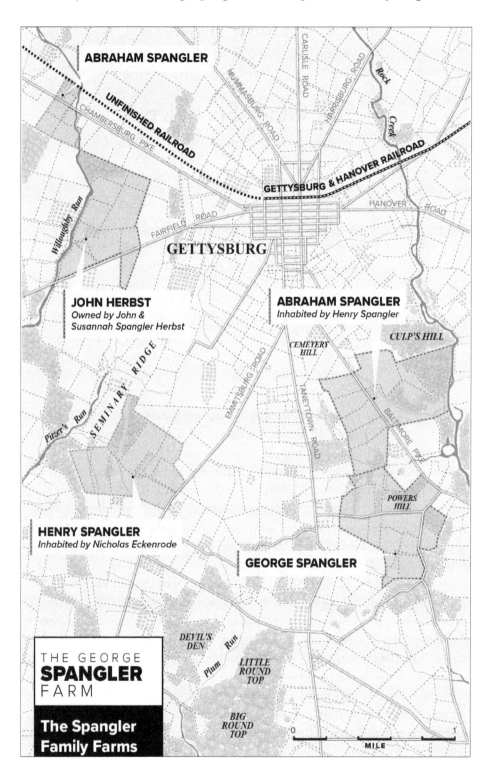

ABRAHAM SPANGLER

UNFINISHED RAILROAD

CHAMBERSBURG PIKE

CARLISLE ROAD

MUMMASBURG ROAD

HARRISBURG ROAD

Rock

Creek

GETTYSBURG & HANOVER RAILROAD

HANOVER ROAD

Willoughby Run

FAIRFIELD ROAD

GETTYSBURG

JOHN HERBST
*Owned by John &
Susannah Spangler Herbst*

ABRAHAM SPANGLER
Inhabited by Henry Spangler

CULP'S HILL

*CEMETERY
HILL*

EMMITSBURG ROAD

TANEYTOWN ROAD

SEMINARY RIDGE

Pitzer's Run

BALTIMORE PIKE

*POWERS
HILL*

HENRY SPANGLER
Inhabited by Nicholas Eckenrode

GEORGE SPANGLER

*DEVIL'S
DEN*

Plum Run

*LITTLE
ROUND
TOP*

THE GEORGE
SPANGLER
FARM

*BIG
ROUND
TOP*

0   1

MILE

**The Spangler
Family Farms**

Henry Spangler, George's half-brother, owned land near the Emmitsburg Road. Confederates used his property as a staging area, a jumping-off point from Seminary Ridge against Cemetery Ridge on July 2 and July 3. Like his sister's, Henry's barn burned to the ground.

Of the five Spangler farms, George's played the most important role in the battle because of its central location behind the Army of the Potomac line. As noted elsewhere, George's fields, roads, and Powers Hill provided indispensable logistical support. It was one of the keys to the Union victory. As much damage as George's farm endured from its use as a staging area and hospital and from Confederate artillery overshots, Susannah's, Abraham's, and Henry's farms suffered even more. George's 166-acre farm supported the battle and some of its aftermath, but the other four farms were right in the middle of the actual fighting and suffered accordingly.

Four Spanglers and five farms dragged into and changed forever by war. But they weren't the only Spangler farmers of the Abraham clan close to the action. George was the oldest Spangler child and the first of two from Mary Knopp. The second child, John, was born in 1817 less than two years before his mother died. In 1863, John owned a farm in Mount Joy Township. He could have watched part of the July 2 battle for Brinkerhoff's Ridge and the July 3 cavalry fight at Hanover and Low Dutch roads from his front porch.[1]

George and John's half-brother Daniel, age 39 at the time of the battle and the second child of Abraham's second wife, Elizabeth Lady, had his farm in Straban Township. Confederate Maj. Gen. Jeb Stuart's cavalry almost certainly trampled its way across his land on the way to the Hanover/Low Dutch roads fight, which unfolded on the farms next to Daniel's.[2]

According to Adams County tax records and an 1858 survey map, there were more than 20 Spangler farms spread throughout Adams County in 1858. Abraham, George, Susannah, and Henry had the only five Spangler farms in 1863 in Cumberland Township, which still surrounds the borough of Gettysburg today.

1 Map of Adams County Pennsylvania, from survey by G. M. Hopkins (Philadelphia, PA, 1858).

2 Ibid. There was another Spangler who owned land on the Day 3 cavalry battlefield. Brig. Gen. George Armstrong Custer and his Michigan brigade of cavalrymen used the Joseph Spangler farm as a staging area to launch charges against Confederate cavalry. After the battle, the house was used as a hospital and remains standing today. This Joseph Spangler was not of Abraham's immediate family. Abraham was the only one of his many siblings to settle in Adams County. The rest settled mainly farther west in Franklin County and farther south in Maryland. Abraham's children did not have any Spangler first cousins in Adams County.

This photo of three of Daniel Spangler's children was probably taken in the early 20th century. Left to right: John, George, and Laura. Daniel was George Spangler's half-brother.

William Tipton and the Adams County Historical Society

One of those other 20-plus farms belonged to a George Spangler in Freedom Township southwest of Gettysburg and was used as a bivouac on the morning of July 1 by part of the Army of the Potomac's I Corps.

* * *

The Abraham Spangler and Susannah Spangler Herbst farms west of town were aligned in such a way that Confederate troops hit Abraham's land first and John and Susannah's shortly thereafter during the initial thrust toward Gettysburg on the morning of July 1. Abraham purchased his farm in 1858 from his daughter's husband, John, and his brother, Samuel, after their father Jacob Herbst died in 1856.[3]

A roster of who fought across the 160-acre Herbst farm includes some of the most prominent officers and commands from both armies. Troopers from Brig. Gen. John Buford's cavalry occupied the Herbst farm on June 30 and the morning of July 1 and fought part of its delaying action there. Major General John Reynolds, commander of the Union I Corps, was killed at Herbst Woods on Susannah's property (known today as Reynolds Woods). His corps fought one of the most intense actions of the war that morning before a line of Confederate infantry so long that it surpassed the length of John and Susannah's property forced it east onto Seminary Ridge.

The Union Iron Brigade of the I Corps tore apart Brig. Gen. James Archer's brigade and captured its commander—the first Confederate general from Lee's

---

3 Tax Records, Cumberland Township, Box 1843-1859, Adams County Historical Society.

At the time of the battle, Herbst Woods (now known as Reynolds Woods) was on Susannah Spangler Herbst's farm. The monument in the background marks the spot where Maj. Gen. John Reynolds was killed on July 1, 1863. *Ron Kirkwood*

army taken prisoner during the war. The fighting in Herbst Woods was so close, so intense, and so unrelenting that the Iron Brigade (the 1st Brigade of the 1st Division of the I Corps) never fully recovered. After doing most of its fighting that day on the Herbst and McPherson properties, the 2nd, 6th, and 7th Wisconsin, 19th Indiana, and 24th Michigan suffered just under 1,200 casualties, the highest total of any Army of the Potomac brigade at Gettysburg. The 24th Michigan and 2nd Wisconsin lost more than 70 percent of their men. Though they lost the ground, they had helped buy the time necessary for the balance of the army to come up and occupy the land upon which the rest of the battle would be fought, inflicting horrendous Confederate losses in the process.[4]

Once the fighting rolled past his home, John Herbst ventured out of his cellar. It was about 4:00 p.m. His large Pennsylvania bank barn was on fire and a Confederate officer had orders to burn down the house because "the Yankees" had been firing from it. Herbst reported after the war that his house was spared only because a wounded Union soldier and two wounded Confederates—one of whom was too seriously hurt to be moved—were found inside and begged the Southern officer to spare the structure. The Herbst fields and woodlot were covered with dead and wounded from both sides. Many of these men would spend days without treatment or burial and many who died were never identified.[5]

Herbst filed a damage claim after the war for $2,689.36 for loss of property, equipment, crops, and animals, and was awarded $2,606.75 in 1871 by the commonwealth of Pennsylvania. Because of the losses, he sold the farm before he

4 Busey and Busey, *Union Casualties at Gettysburg*, 1,151-1,152.

5 Claims: John Herbst, File 14-CF-52, GNMP Library.

was compensated. He later served as county commissioner and director of the Adams County Almshouse.[6]

More heartache was just around the corner. Susannah Spangler Herbst died two months after the battle on September 2. She was just 37, and left behind five young children and her husband of 14 years. Susannah was the third of George's 10 siblings to die, following to the grave Anna (26) in 1848 and Lucy Ann (28) in 1857. John Herbst remarried and is buried in Evergreen Cemetery in Gettysburg with first wife Susannah and second wife Sarah Saltzgiver. Their graves are within a few feet of those of George and Elizabeth, Henry and Sarah, and Abraham and his wives Mary and Elizabeth.[7]

Father Abraham Spangler's 30 acres along Willoughby Run straddled the Chambersburg Pike west of Gettysburg. The eastern end of his farm met the western edge of the Edward McPherson farm, whose barn still stands today as a prominent battlefield landmark. The Railroad Cut was near Abraham's property. His farm no longer exists and has been divided into privately owned parcels.

Initially, Buford's Union cavalry occupied Abraham's land on the morning of July 1. When thousands of Confederate infantry and artillery under Heth pushed Buford back across Abraham's property, men and guns from Reynolds' I Corps joined in. More Confederate infantry poured across Abraham's fields in what would be several hours of fighting. And just like that, the fields belonging to 76-year-old Abraham Spangler and 63-year-old wife Elizabeth were wiped out, their farm firmly under the control of the Confederates for the next four days. It's not known where Abraham and Elizabeth Spangler spent the battle of Gettysburg.

As noted earlier, Abraham also owned 211 acres on the Baltimore Pike, the site of the famous Spangler's Spring. His son Henry and his family lived there during the battle while Henry's own 156-acre farm along the Emmitsburg Road, which he was renting to the Nicholas Eckenrode family, was also overrun.

Abraham's house on the Baltimore Pike near today's Hunt Avenue was in the hands of the Army of the Potomac, but the portion of Culp's Hill he owned and his fields to the east, including Spangler's Spring, were occasionally under the control of Confederate Lt. Gen. Richard Ewell's II Corps during July 2-3. This Spangler property was especially coveted because it straddled the Baltimore Pike, a key communications link for the Army of the Potomac. The Union also needed it in

---

6 Ibid.; *Gettysburg Compiler*, October 22, 1895.

7 Susannah Herbst gravestone at Evergreen Cemetery, Gettysburg.

The Abraham Spangler house on the Baltimore Pike as it looks today. Abraham's son Henry lived in the house in 1863.
Ron Kirkwood

order to protect the back side of its line and the ammunition train on the neighboring George Spangler farm.

The XII Corps artillery opened the fighting at about 4:00 a.m. on the morning of July 3 from George Spangler's and Nathaniel Lightner's Powers Hill and along the Baltimore Pike. Some of the Confederates they were aiming at were located on Abraham Spangler's property. In fact, there were Union cannons on Abraham's land firing at Confederate cannons that were also on his land.

Henry and his family evacuated the Baltimore Pike property before it was taken for a hospital during the battle on July 1 by the Second Division of the XII Corps. The Elliott's Map of the Battlefield of Gettysburg of 1864 shows 35 Army of the Potomac graves near this Spangler barn and house. This map shows another 44 Union graves in Abraham's fields for a total of 79, with burial records confirming 78 as identified. The Elliott map shows 55 Confederate graves on this farm. This is probably high, and is much higher than records made in the 1860s, but those records lumped many Abraham Spangler graves into the Culp's Hill dead. Neighbor Nathaniel Lightner described the scene on Abraham Spangler property, which was across the street from his own home: "Over on Culp's Hill I saw the Union soldiers burying Confederate soldiers in trenches thirty or forty feet long and only a few feet deep. They piled them in like cordwood."[8]

Musician William Simpson of the 28th Pennsylvania, XII Corps, worked as a hospital steward on Abraham's Baltimore Pike property when it was relatively quiet there on July 1 and again when it played a more central role on July 2-3. He wrote about his time there after the war:

8 "Horrors of Battle," an interview with Nathaniel Lightner.

Dr. William Altman [28th PA assistant surgeon] . . . gathered the drummer boys together to establish a field hospital. We went over to the Spangler house and camped in the barn all night. You can bet when a bunch of boys like that get together there is going to be some fun, especially when [musician] George McFetridge was around. He acquired his life-long nickname of 'fish' McFetridge that night. The Spangler house was unoccupied and McFetridge, nosing about, went down into the cellar. He found a kit of mackeral. He passed it to me through the cellar window and we opened it. We were in for a feast, but we soon found that hardtack and salt mackeral didn't go well together. So Mac took the kit over to Company K. If any of those Co. K boys are living today, they will remember it, for they were all hungry and enjoyed it.[9]

"While I was going over Baltimore pike I came across a strange sight," Simpson continued,

one that certainly looked odd in that war-torn country. An old couple were going along the road and from their dress I presumed that they were dunkards. He had on a stiff top hat and his dark blue coat had brass buttons; the old lady wore a blue furbelow and carried an umbrella. Two men who had been killed were brought along right in front of them. The old lady raised both hands and screamed, 'Isn't it awful?' The old man was just as horrified. They looked out of place on that road of death.[10]

Henry Spangler was George's half-brother. Confederate Maj. Gen. George Pickett massed his division of about 6,000 men on July 3 on Henry's farm west of the Emmitsburg Road. The men, Virginians all, waited in Henry's fields and in the shade of what is now known as Spangler Woods before stepping out and attacking Cemetery Ridge. The farm hosted Confederate commander Gen. Robert E. Lee and his chief of artillery, Brig. Gen. William Pendleton, throughout much of July 2. The Alabama brigade of Brig. Gen. Cadmus Wilcox and Floridians under Col. David Lang launched their early-evening assaults that day against Cemetery Ridge

9 *Philadelphia North American*, June 29, 1913; Gettysburg Field Hospital Research No. 2, Box B-70, File 68, Gregory A. Coco Collection, GNMP Library.

10 *The Philadelphia North American*. Abraham Spangler's house remains at 1118 Baltimore Pike. The former portion of his farm that was on the west side of the Baltimore Pike now consists of some of the National Park Service Museum and Visitor Center complex.

This circa 1888 photo shows Henry Spangler (center bottom) and members of his family. Henry's wife, Sarah, is on his right with her hand on his shoulder. Sons George (on the ladder) and Calvin are at top left, while daughter Ella is third from right and daughter Laura is at far right. The others are unknown. *Gettysburg National Military Park*

from Henry's farm. When the attack failed, Wilcox and Lang fell back and remained on Henry's property on July 3. They moved up to join the long line of artillery closer to the Emmitsburg Road that would take part in the pre-attack cannonade. It was from that point that they moved out, ostensibly to protect Pickett's exposed right flank. By the time they moved, however, the attack was already falling apart.[11]

Colonel Edward P. Alexander, 28, commanded much of the Confederate artillery for Pickett's Charge. He was ordered to select a spot for observation and chose "the advanced salient angle of the wood in which Pickett's line was now formed," which put him on and near the edge of Henry's farm. A portion of Maj. Gen. Isaac Trimble's division marched past Alexander on both sides, putting two of the three divisions in Pickett's Charge on Henry Spangler property at some point during the July 3 attack.[12]

11 John Bachelder, Map of the Battle Field of Gettysburg, July 2-3, 1863, Office of the Chief of Engineers US Army (Washington, D.C., 1876).

12 E. P. Alexander to J. William Jones, March 17, 1877, *Southern Historical Society Papers*, 52 vols. (Richmond, VA, 1877), vol. 4, 104.

Henry's barn burned to the ground July 2 after being hit by Union artillery fire. Henry, age 32, and his wife, Sarah, age 31, together with their family moved into this property after the battle and built a new barn of the same design on the same foundation. That barn also burned to the ground when it was hit by lightning in 1931. Today's barn was also built on the battle-era foundation and copies the original structure. The house that stands on the property today has gone through additions and remodeling and is larger than the 1863 building.[13]

Tenants Nicholas and Sarah Eckenrode escaped from the farm on July 1 before the Confederates took control of it. They returned after the battle to find the crops and fencing ruined, the barn and its contents destroyed by fire, the house stripped of its valuables, and the animals taken. Fresh graves dotted the property. By the time Sarah filed a claim after the war to the US Quartermaster General's Office for $2,272.14 in damages she was a widow. It was denied. The farm remained in Spangler family hands until it was sold to the National Park Service in 1955.[14]

The long reach of the Spangler name extended well past the battle of Gettysburg farms in the Civil War, with 124 Spanglers fighting for the Confederacy and 114 for Pennsylvania.[15]

Finally, it wasn't just farm land on George Spangler's side of the family involved in the battle of Gettysburg. The hours-long cavalry and infantry fight on July 2 on Brinkerhoff's Ridge along the Hanover Road took place on Henry Brinkerhoff's land. Henry was a cousin of George's wife, Elizabeth Brinkerhoff Spangler. The July 2 fighting at Hunterstown took place on land surrounded by Brinkerhoff farms.

Spangler Farm Short Story

Spangler's Spring on Abraham Spangler's property was a source of cool, fresh water for both armies and a spot for relaxation for Gettysburg-area residents long before and after the battle. As "proprietor of Paradise Grove," Abraham welcomed

---

13 *Gettysburg Compiler*, July 25, 1931.

14 Nicholas Eckenrode File, V14-CF-39, GNMP Library.

15 Janet B. Hewitt, ed., *The Roster of Confederate Soldiers, 1861-1865*, 16 vols. (Wilmington, NC, 1996), vol. 14, 346-347; Janet B. Hewitt, ed., *The Roster of Union Soldiers, 1861-1865*, 33 (Wilmington, NC, 1998), vol. 4, 16-17. George's half-brothers Elias, William, and Levi served during the war, but none were at Gettysburg. The 1870 federal census shows William Spangler living with his parents with an occupation of "hunter."

Fourth of July picnics to his property, Sunday school meetings, bands, and other gatherings. The spring was surrounded by a wall of flat stones near Rock Creek and offered plenty of shade. The July 12, 1850, *Gettysburg Star and Banner* reported a toast to Spangler at that year's Fourth of July celebration on his property that included, "May he live a thousand years and never come to want."

Contrary to popular myth, troops of both sides did not drink from the spring at the same time during a truce in the fighting. The spring changed hands during the battle, so whichever army controlled the water source got to drink from it. The spring can still be visited, but its source of water has been closed off.

Ruch Report No. 8

At Spangler Farm
Private Reuben F. Ruch, Company F, 153rd Pennsylvania

"I learned on the third morning of my stay in the barn, that a train left Littletown every afternoon, at five o'clock, for Baltimore, and all those who could get to Littletown could go on to Baltimore and Philadelphia. I did not like to leave three of my comrades and they could not walk, for it was eight miles to the station.

"Presently a native came along with a democrat or spring wagon, and one horse. I stopped him and asked him to take my three comrades to Littletown. Oh my! he did not have the time to spare and could not possibly do it. I called this fellow down in great shape. I told him he was not much of a man, that here were men who had driven the enemy from their homes, and protected their property, and that these men had gotten wounded in doing so, and were unable to get to a railroad station, and that he could not do them the small favor to haul them to the railroad station. He told me to let up; that I was right, and that he had not seen things in the true light. . . . He asked me how I was going to get there. I told him I would walk. He did not think I could make it, but I told him I had . . . over seven hours . . . to make eight miles and I would try it. I started with some others, but was soon left behind and did not get to the station until 5 p.m. . . . [M]y limb grew very bad from the effects of this walk. I got lunch in a charity place, for I had not one cent to my name. . . .

"By this time the train backed in, and I found it to be an army Pullman train, composed of box cars of a freight train, with a bundle of hay in each car. We entered and lay down on the hay. This was very comfortable. Our train stopped at Hanover, where the citizens handed in a big basket of eatables, with the request to return the basket, which we did with thanks. We arrived in Baltimore some time in the night.

Here we received the very kindest treatment; the people assuring us we deserved the best of the land. The invasion helped the citizens, making them very friendly."[16]

* * *

Private Reuben Ruch, age 19 at Gettysburg, made it home safely to the Allentown area. He married, had children, and died at age 76 in 1921 in Butler County, PA, where he worked in the oil fields. Ruch returned to Gettysburg for the 25th anniversary of the battle, where he met up with William H. Riehl, a wounded comrade in the Spanglers' barn and one of the three men who got a wagon ride to the train station in Littlestown thanks to Ruch's scolding of the wagon driver. "Rube," Riehl said when meeting up with Ruch, "I am poor but it does me more good to see you than it would to find a ten-dollar gold piece."[17]

16 Kiefer, *History of the One Hundred and Fifty-Third Regiment,* 225-226.

17 Ibid., 226.

Chapter 22

What Happened to the Spanglers?

"It is awful. Everything suffers in time of war; people all suffer; domestic animals suffer; plants suffer and droop and die; the little birds are killed or frightened away from their nests and their young; the trees are torn by shot and shell or are cut down ruthlessly for fires and breastworks; grains and grass are eaten up or trodden into the ground in an hour; springs and wells are the soldiers' boons and are quickly to the last drop. . . . War is all suffering."

— *Spangler neighbor Nathaniel Lightner*[1]

Nathaniel Lightner and his family were driven away by the blood, body fluids, and stench. Like the Spanglers, their house was used as a hospital for several weeks and they found a disaster area when they were allowed back. What hadn't been stolen or used was ruined or beyond disgusting.

"It made us all sick," Lightner admitted. "Towards spring I got a chance to take a stocked farm on shares, so I moved away and gave it to an old Dutchman, who did not seem to mind the smell and filth. Nine years afterward I took all the woodwork and plaster out, and made the house new from cellar to garret. Then we came back," he continued, "but my poor wife did not live long in our new home. She had never been well from the first time we tried to live in it."[1]

The Spanglers had stayed put in late June when many of Gettysburg's citizens evacuated as the two armies closed in around them. When the Union army arrived and confiscated their property on July 1, they had somehow persuaded the XI

1 Ibid.

The Lightners owned a farm (left) on the Baltimore Pike and shared ownership of Powers Hill (middle-background) with the Spanglers.

Center for Civil War Photography

Corps medical staff to allow them to remain on their farm. Now, on August 7, exposed to the same smell, filth, and ruin facing the Lightners and most of their neighbors, they again refused to vacate their land. The Spanglers were cut from a different cloth. They would rebuild their property and their lives.

But where to begin? Their house and large barn were heavily damaged and covered in human filth. Their crops had been destroyed, livestock killed or driven off, and walls and fences knocked down or consumed in campfires. A large swath of their land had been turned into a graveyard.

Perhaps George, Daniel, and Beniah began work on the barn that had hosted so many hundreds of wounded and dying men over the previous five weeks and two days that the hospital was there. Elizabeth, Harriet, and Sabina likely started their work in the house, teaming up to give it a thorough cleaning and airing out, though it likely took weeks or even months to fully rid the dwelling of its nasty smells. The bloodstains in the wood and elsewhere would have been nearly impossible to remove. What were the Spanglers to do with the hundreds of arms and legs and fingers that had been buried close by? Filling in the smelly latrines prepared by the hospital staff would have taken an enormous amount of time and effort.

For a while, food arrived from the United States Christian and Sanitary commissions, which continued working in Gettysburg for most of the rest of 1863. After that, the Spanglers likely relied on donations from friends and other family members or food sales from farmers outside of Gettysburg whose land wasn't impacted by the battle. They also probably purchased food shipped into town until they could get their farm producing again. Father Abraham and half-siblings Henry and Susannah were in much the same situation, for their farms had also been overrun by the hard hand of war, though Susannah died that September.

George and Elizabeth were probably more fortunate than many Gettysburg-area residents because they were a family of some means. They had purchased nearby land whenever it became available and increased the size of their farm from 80 to 166 acres between 1848 and 1863 and they used their resources to repair their buildings and property and buy new equipment and livestock. The railroad and a good road network provided access to modern-day goods. George later admitted they returned the land to good condition sooner than he had expected.

The Union dead in the Spangler orchards and field south of their house were exhumed later in 1863 or early 1864 and moved to the new Soldiers' National Cemetery on Cemetery Hill. Confederates remained on their farm until the early 1870s, when they were exhumed with private funds, transported south, and reburied.

By 1870, George was 55 and Elizabeth 52. Their 21-year-old son Beniah was the only child still living at home. Maria Mills, age 35, and Harriet Herbst, age 11, also lived there, listed in the 1870 census as "domestic servants." Harriet, however, was not a servant but a family member. She was the Spanglers' niece and the daughter of George's deceased half-sister Susannah Herbst.

The farm had a real estate value of $9,000 in 1870, up from $5,000 in 1860. The Spanglers increased the size of their house around that time by adding two bays on the south end and remodeling the main floor. The additions increased the house size from 28 by 26 feet (728 square feet) to 38 by 26 feet (988 square feet).[2]

Local painters Samuel Frey, William Frey, and Hiram C. Lady signed their names on the Spangler corn crib when they painted the barn in 1875; their autographs remain visible to this day. Beniah Spangler's name also still appears there.

The Spanglers filed three damage claims in the 1870s, one of which asked for $2,843.40. George's accompanying testimony was as follows:

> Had about 15 acres of corn growing in the field; most of it was about waist high and about half a mile from the line of battle. The troops marched through it and teams were driven through it, loose horses and cattle were in it, and teamsters staid there all night and fed their horses the corn. The crop was nearly destroyed. Succeeding in saving only about fifty bushels of ears. Had nineteen acres of wheat standing in the field in the different patches, not over half a mile from the Union line of battle. The teamsters parked their wagons in the wheat fields, principally, ambulance wagons.

2 Historic Structure Report.

One field of ten acres was nearly white with wagons, and the wheat was all tramped down and eaten by the animals. The other two fields were marched over by the troops, and wagons were parked in them, and the entire crop destroyed. Did not save any of the wheat. . . . Had twelve acres of oats . . . standing in the field uncut and one end of the field was not over a quarter of a mile from the Union line of battle. It was tramped down by the soldiers and by wagons being driven through the field. The entire crop was destroyed, did not save any of the oats. The meadow was close to the buildings, about half a mile from the Union breastworks. The grass was all standing uncut, and was trampled down by being marched over, and by driving wagons through it. Horses were also grazed on it to some extent, the entire crop of hay was destroyed. Supposes there were twenty five acres, cannot tell exactly. . . . Some acres injured by shells.[3]

George's neighbor, 70-year-old Franklin Swisher, testified for the Spanglers. Their land, he explained, "was wagoned over in every direction and the crops were completely destroyed. . . . Saw the soldiers sawing boards to make coffins. . . . Saw a great deal of claimant's timber cut down. . . . Some of the timber was destroyed by shells. Some was used in putting up hospital tents. . . . The farm was tramped up almost like the big road, the ground was wet and soft and was very much injured."[4]

Out of their three claims, the Spanglers were only awarded $90.00 for six tons of hay, for which they had received a receipt from Surgeon-in-Charge Dr. James A. Armstrong. There is no record that they actually received the money, and the likelihood is that it went to the attorney who helped them prosecute their claims.

"It is quite likely that some of the fencing was used for fuel, and it is also probable that a good many of the rails were used in the breastwork . . . the property appears to have been taken indiscriminately and without authority," reported US Quartermaster Agent Z. F. Nye. "With reference to this I would state that, during and after the battle of Gettysburg, self preservation and common humanity required the temporary occupation of buildings in the vicinity of the battle field for hospitals for wounded soldiers." The agent continued:

The emergency admitted of neither choice nor delay. The occupation, in this case, was only temporary and was occasioned by an overruling military

---

3 Spangler Damage Claim N-1892, 1875, Historic Structure Report.

4 Ibid.

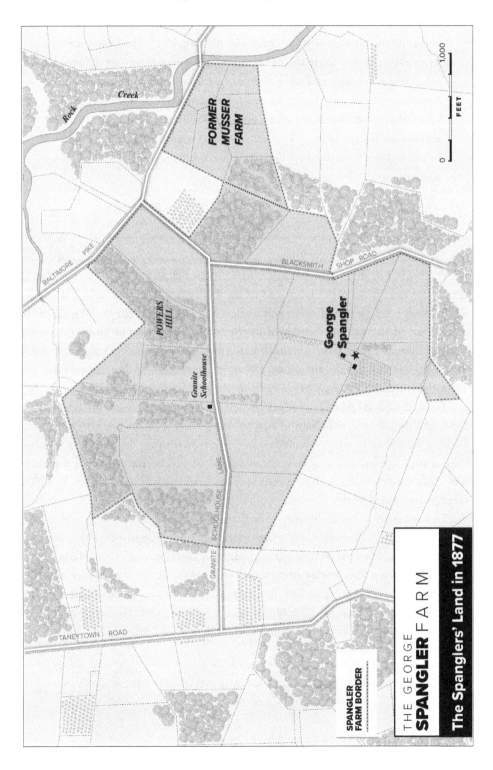

Rock Creek

FORMER MUSSER FARM

BALTIMORE PIKE

BLACKSMITH SHOP ROAD

POWERS HILL

George Spangler

Granite Schoolhouse

GRANITE SCHOOLHOUSE LANE

TANEYTOWN ROAD

1,000

FEET

0

SPANGLER FARM BORDER

THE GEORGE SPANGLER FARM

The Spanglers' Land in 1877

necessity, and there is no law covering uses of this kind. . . . The Union army, in its march on Gettysburg in July 1863, performed an imperative duty required by the public safety and that the Government of the United States is no more responsible for bringing on the battle fought there than it would have been had a tornado passed over that country causing as wide spread destruction as did that terrible engagement. . . . That situation was his misfortune, and he is not to be relieved therefrom by the United States as they were not responsible for the circumstances which created it.[5]

Cumberland Township tax records show an additional 16 acres for George and Elizabeth in 1878, so they probably purchased their second farm in 1877 and moved there. By this time the Spanglers were slowing down, with George at 62 and Elizabeth 59. No deed was recorded, and additional surveys list the farm as 18 acres. The land was on the west side of the Baltimore Pike just before it crosses Rock Creek heading out of town and owned by George Musser at the time of the battle. Part of the western border of the Spanglers' new farm abutted the eastern border of their original farm, making it a short walk from house to house and giving the Spanglers ownership of about 184 acres between the Baltimore Pike and Taneytown Road. (Today, this former Musser and Spangler property is a quarry.)

George and Elizabeth retained ownership of their Blacksmith Shop Road farm, and Beniah and wife Sarah Conover lived there and assumed the workload. Beniah, Sarah, and young daughter Mary lived there until the late 1880s, when Beniah gave up farming and they moved into town. The Blacksmith Shop Road farm was either vacant or had a tenant farmer or farmers until the early 1900s. George continued to pay the taxes on it after he moved next door.

George died at his Baltimore Pike farm on January 27, 1904, at age 88. "A remarkable fact," eulogized his obituary in the *Gettysburg Compiler* on February 3, "is that his married life covered sixty-three years. . . . The deceased only a week or two before his death was at work cutting wood and it is thought the exposure added to the infirmities of age, resulted in his death. . . . He was a staunch Democrat his whole life and was held in the highest esteem by every one that knew him." The *Adams Sentinel* on the same day called him "one of Cumberland township's most highly respected citizens."

Two weeks later on February 17, the *Gettysburg Compiler* ran a story called "A Memory of George Spangler" written by teacher William G. Black, whom Spangler

5 Ibid.

hired for Green Bush school in 1853 when he was president of the Cumberland Township School Board. "Mr. Spangler proved himself to be a very efficient school official," editorialized Black, "and made a lasting impression on my mind as a man of truthfulness and honesty in all things, and I lived to see my belief demonstrated time and again."

Elizabeth, who was also known as Eliza, moved in with Beniah and Sarah in town after her husband's death, and she died there in 1907. Like George, she was 88. "She enjoyed remarkable health during her life," observed the *Gettysburg Compiler* on May 29, 1907, "never having had any serious illness. Her health began to fail within the last few months."

George and Elizabeth's daughter Sabina and her husband, William Patterson, officially purchased the family farm in 1905, with the first known deed on the property recorded in April. Beniah handled the sale to his sister. The Pattersons sold the 65 acres north of Granite Schoolhouse Lane to the US government later in 1905 and sold the rest of the farm in 1910, ending 62 years of Spangler ownership of what is now sacred ground.[6]

Like many of their era and in the Gettysburg area, the Spanglers didn't write about their battle of Gettysburg woes except when they filed claims for damages to the government. Even then, it was just a matter-of-fact "here's what was damaged, destroyed, or taken, and here's what you owe us for it." They lived through a nightmare of sights, sounds, and smells that we can never understand today, but instead of complaining about it and telling future generations about their feelings and sufferings they moved on and set about fixing things and living their lives.

Humans were a hardy stock back then, taking satisfaction and pride in their labors. The Spanglers were among the hardiest. George worked in his fields until a week before he died at age 88. Beniah worked as a caretaker at the YWCA in his final years. Son Daniel went west to build houses on the frontier. Harriet and Sabina married farmers and survived through hard work by every family member.

Like so many others, religion was important to the Spanglers. George and Elizabeth had their children baptized within a year of their birth, and their faith undoubtedly helped get them through their 1863 ordeal. St. James Lutheran Church in Gettysburg and Christ Lutheran Church (Grace Lutheran today) in Two Taverns were the important churches in their lives. Beniah's daughter, Mary,

6 Historic Structure Report.

received a citation in 1960 for 52 consecutive years of service as a secretary of a Bible class at St. James Lutheran Church.[7]

The Spanglers took care of their community and one another.

George and Beniah were leaders at church as deacons and elders and both served on the Cumberland Township School Board, a service to the community they learned from George's father, Abraham. George was also on the committee that annually inspected the conditions at the county prison and poor house, served on multiple Adams County grand juries, and served as Cumberland Township justice of the peace. He also served on the board that managed Evergreen Cemetery and voted with the other members against allowing Confederates to be buried there. George did all of that work for the good of the community while running his 166-acre farm and then his second farm.[8]

One of many children, Elizabeth looked after her widower father in his later years and made sure his grave would be by hers. She moved in with Beniah's family after George died. Mary and husband William Stout lived with dad Beniah and mom Sarah for years, and Beniah moved in with Mary and William after Sarah died and lived with them at different addresses until he died. Harriet, Sabina, and Daniel each named a son George (Beniah did not have a son).

The Spanglers were also forgiving. Even though the government turned down their legitimate claims that totaled thousands of dollars in damages, they replied in the affirmative each time the government asked if it could buy a small portion of their land to erect a monument. Three sales took place in 1895. The Spanglers received $150 for the monuments to the 77th New York Infantry and Pennsylvania Light Artillery E on Powers Hill and the 4th New Jersey Infantry monument below Powers Hill at Blacksmith Shop Road and Granite Schoolhouse Lane. (As noted earlier in Chapter 7, the Spanglers sold for $75.00 a plot of land 25 feet square for a monument along Granite Schoolhouse Lane to Batteries B and L, 2nd US Artillery, 1st Brigade, Cavalry Corps in 1890. All of these monuments still stand.[9]

There is still much to learn even now from the Spanglers and others like them in Gettysburg. Theirs is a legacy that can and should live forever.

7 St. James Lutheran Church baptism records provided via email by church staff; *Gettysburg Times*, October 20, 1960.

8 *The Adams Sentinel,* July 3, 1863.

9 Cumberland Township tax records, Adams County Historical Society.

Family Notes

Abraham Spangler: George's father died in 1876 at age 88, the same age as George and Elizabeth when they died decades later. Abraham was a prominent landowner who served in a variety of leadership positions, including Cumberland Township School Board president, Cumberland Township treasurer, and director of the poor at the Adams County Almshouse. He was also voted vice president of a committee in 1866 tasked with formulating a plan to seek reparations for Adams County residents who suffered property losses during the battle. He is buried in Evergreen Cemetery in Gettysburg with first wife Mary Knopp and second wife Elizabeth Lady. Oldest son George served as his executor.[10]

Cornelius Brinkerhoff: Elizabeth Spangler's mother, Elizabeth Snyder Brinkerhoff, died in 1841 at age 48 and is buried somewhere in Gettysburg. Now a widower, Elizabeth Spangler's father, Cornelius Brinkerhoff, sold his 139-acre farm in 1844 and for reasons unknown became a resident of the Adams County Almshouse from 1861 until his death in 1871 at age 86. Supported by tax dollars, the almshouse served those who were poor, ill, or mentally or physically disabled. Cornelius was a resident of the almshouse when the area was caught in the middle of the July 1, 1863, combat north of town, and during the suffering of the hospital at the almshouse that followed. He is buried next to daughter Elizabeth and son-in-law George in Evergreen Cemetery.[11]

Harriet Jane Spangler: The Spanglers' oldest child, Harriet, married Samuel Schwartz in 1868 at age 26 and moved to a farm in Mount Joy Township, which borders where Harriet grew up in Cumberland Township. The passing of Elizabeth's husband, George, on January 27, 1904, set off a cascade of family deaths. Elizabeth's daughter, Harriet, followed her father to the grave at age 62 less than two months later on March 17. Harriet's daughter, Annie Catherine, died at age 33 four days after her mother. In less than two months, Elizabeth lost her husband, her daughter, and her granddaughter. Harriet and Annie died of "consumption" (tuberculosis). According to the 1900 census, Annie was still living with Harriet and Samuel at age 29. She worked as a school teacher in Two Taverns and it doesn't appear she married. Samuel never remarried and died in 1921 at age 77. Samuel, Harriet, and Annie Catherine are buried in Evergreen Cemetery.

---

10 *The Adams Sentinel*, February 20, 1866.

11 Almshouse Records box, "Almshouse Register" folder, Adams County Historical Society.

Sabina Catherine Spangler: The second Spangler daughter, Sabina, married William Patterson, the boy next door whose family land ran along the Taneytown Road and abutted Spangler land on the north side of Granite Schoolhouse Lane. This farm was used for a hospital during the battle and was hit consistently by Confederate artillery overshots, forcing the Pattersons to flee. William was 17 and Sabina 19 when their farms came under siege during the battle. William served as a private in Company G, 101st Pennsylvania, from March to June 1865, and returned home to marry Sabina in 1869 when she was 25. They continued to live and farm along the Taneytown Road and had eight children, one of whom, George, died as a toddler. Sabina lived to age 80 and William to 74. Her front-page obituary in the *Gettysburg Times* on September 25, 1924, recalled how the Spangler family baked bread for the wounded after the battle. Sabina and William are buried in Grace Lutheran Church Cemetery in Two Taverns.

Daniel E. Spangler: The Spanglers' first son was born in 1845 (though his gravestone and some other sources incorrectly list his birth year as 1843). Daniel left Gettysburg and moved west in the late 1860s and eventually settled down in Kansas, where he used his carpentry skills in the new state's growing housing market. The 1880 census lists him as a single 34-year-old carpenter living in a hotel in Abilene, where Wild Bill Hickok served as marshal in 1871. In 1892 he married Illinois native Effie Wilkie, who was 14 years younger, in Enterprise, Kansas. There, the new couple settled into a home and began raising a family while Daniel continued with his carpentry work. Their youngest son, Walter, drowned in the Smoky Hill River in Enterprise in 1912 when he was 15. Their other son, George Wilkie Spangler, died in Abilene in 1986. It's worth wondering if George or Elizabeth ever met their Kansas-born grandsons. Perhaps Daniel told his sons about what it was like to live on a farm overrun by war and turned into a hospital. We don't know, but it seems likely that grandson George visited Gettysburg at some point during his long life. Daniel died at age 91 in 1937, and Effie a few years later at age 83 in 1943. Both are buried with son Walter in Mount Hope Cemetery under two juniper trees among the rolling pastures and flat corn fields outside of Enterprise.[12]

Beniah John Spangler: Youngest child Beniah (also known as B. J.) was 14 in 1863 when the armies paid his farm a visit. He is the Spangler child who did the most to keep it running after the battle and was still living at home and working on

---

12 Dickinson County Cemetery Survey, Center Township, Mount Hope Cemetery (Abilene, KS, 1982), 358-359.

The Granite Schoolhouse, ca. 1886/87. Beniah Spangler is standing far left, and his only child, Mary Elizabeth, is third from the right in the second row with a large white collar standing next to a seated unidentified man. The daughters of Beniah's sister, Sabina Spangler Patterson, are also pictured: Alice Patterson (sixth from the left, second row) and Clara Patterson (third row behind the dog and in front of door). Teacher Maggie Schwartz stands on the right holding something in her left hand. Mary Elizabeth identified the people in this photo. *Mumper & Co. and the Adams County Historical Society*

the farm at 21 in 1870. He and his wife, Sarah Conover (born 1850), and their lone child, Mary (born 1879), became the sole residents of the property after George and Elizabeth moved to the Baltimore Pike property in about 1877. Mary attended Granite Schoolhouse on land donated by her grandparents, and a 1903 map of the battlefield by Schuyler A. Hammond shows a path from the house to the school. Mary and Beniah are the only two immediate members of the Spangler family who are in two photos from the 1800s that we know of today. One was taken in the mid-1880s at the school and the other probably in 1888 around the 25-year anniversary of the battle. Sarah is also in that photo, standing with the others in a field with the farm buildings behind them. Sabina's daughters Alice and Clara are also in the schoolhouse photo. In 1890, Beniah and his family were running a grocery store and living in town at 404 Baltimore Street. Today, the site is a popular ice cream shop just across the street from the Farnsworth House. They were all still living there in 1920, along with Mary's husband William K. Stout, a butcher whom she married in 1906 in neighboring York. Beniah's mother, Elizabeth, joined them after her husband George died. She lived there until her death in 1907.[13]

On April 6, 1910, the *Gettysburg Compiler* reported that Beniah and another man found the buried remains of a Confederate soldier thought to be from Louisiana while clearing brush on Gettysburg Water Company property on East Cemetery Hill. The soldier likely died or was mortally wounded there on the evening of July 2, 1863, when Louisiana and North Carolina troops charged up the slope of the hill. Beniah (81) was a widower in 1930 living with William (58) and Mary (50) at 159 Baltimore Street. He died of a stroke at 51 Hanover Street, age 84, in 1932. His obituary on the day he died in the December 29, 1932, *Gettysburg Times* recalled that he heard President Abraham Lincoln deliver the Gettysburg Address. Mary and William had one child (Fred), who died at just two weeks old in 1907. Beniah's mother died less than three months before his only grandchild died. Mary died as a widow in 1964 at age 85.

Beniah, Sarah, Mary, William, and Fred are buried in Evergreen Cemetery.

Spangler Farm Short Story

Spangler neighbors Catharine and Nathaniel Lightner's son Edward was a stonecutter who quarried most of the stone for the 77th New York and 4th New Jersey monuments on and at the base of Powers Hill. The land on Powers Hill for those two monuments as well as for Knap's Pennsylvania Light Artillery Battery E was sold by George and Elizabeth Spangler to the Gettysburg Battlefield Memorial Association for $150 in 1895.

The monuments stand today at or near the intersection of Blacksmith Shop Road and Granite Schoolhouse Lane. The Lightners owned a portion of the north side of Powers Hill, which they purchased from quarry owner Solomon Powers in 1858. The Spanglers owned the rest of the hill.

The third wall north of Granite Schoolhouse Lane (39°48'28"N 77°13'5"W) on the Baltimore Pike divides the former Spangler and Lightner properties. The battle of Gettysburg was just as difficult on the Lightners as it was the Spanglers, and like the Spanglers and most Gettysburg-area residents they were frustrated in their

---

13 Schuyler A. Hammond 1903 map, Gettysburg National Park Commission (Washington, D.C.).

attempt to find relief from the government, filing a $1,000 claim for damages and lost property and receiving but $33.00 in return.[14]

Owners of the George Spangler Farm, 488 Blacksmith Road, Cumberland Township, Adams County, Pennsylvania:

— John Dodds, 1798-1807;

— [gap in ownership, 1808-28];

— Henry Bishop, Sr., 1828-48;

— George Spangler, 1848-1904;

— Elizabeth Spangler and heirs, 1904-05;

— Sabina C. and William Patterson, 1905-10;

— Jacob Group, 1910;

— Frank and Minnie Mumper, 1910-28;

— Harris W. Cook, 1928-42;

— Grace E. and John M. Rider, 1942-53;

— Various Andrew family members, 1953-2008;

— Gettysburg Foundation, 2008-present. The Gettysburg Foundation purchased 80-plus acres for $1,887,500.[15]

14 Nathaniel Lightner Vertical File, V1-26, GNMP Library; *Gettysburg Times*, February 10, 1953; File 14-CF-64, Claims: Nathaniel Lightner, GNMP Library.

15 Historic Structure Report

Chapter 23

A Tour of the Modern Spangler Farm

"It was important to the Gettysburg Foundation to open the farm so visitors could see first-hand the barn, smokehouse, and summer kitchen and learn about family and farm life in 1863 and grasp the magnitude of the challenges this family faced when the soldiers invaded their lives."

— *Cindy Small, former vice president of the Gettysburg Foundation*

The Spanglers would be pleased. And very grateful. The Gettysburg Foundation should be pleased as well. And very proud.

This property was dead. The barn's foundation was crumbling, its siding falling off, and much of the wood rotten. The barn was in such bad shape there were concerns it would fall down in a strong wind. The equally fragile smokehouse wasn't safe to enter, and the house had a host of problems, including a basement with a foot of standing water. The summer kitchen, where a beloved Confederate general is thought to have died, was overgrown with weeds and rot.

But the members of the Gettysburg Foundation looked past all of that and believed the unique history of the Spangler farm was worth saving—that it could all be fixed, and that they could fix it. The fields and buildings were filled with stories that needed to be told.

In 2008, the Foundation made a daring $1,800,000 decision to purchase this dilapidated 80-acre property. If they rebuild it, will they come? It turns out they will, and people have done so by the thousands each year since the rejuvenated George Spangler Farm Civil War Field Hospital Site opened to the public for spring and summer weekends in 2013. The Gettysburg Foundation saved the farm by buying it, and in doing so preserved its history and stories for generations to come.

The George Spangler Farm Civil War Field Hospital Site in 2018. *Gettysburg Foundation*

"It was imperative to let visitors sense the power of place as they stood in the exact spots where those soldiers sought refuge and medical treatment and in some cases drew their final breath," explained Cindy Small, former vice president of the Foundation.

The Foundation has nursed the farm back to stunning health with a single-minded focus on historical detail. In almost every case, down to the animal hair in the mortar, all buildings except the house today look like they did in 1863 when the Spanglers lived there and the wounded and dying suffered there. If you want to see what 1863 looked like, take a walk around the Spangler farm.

Brian Shaffer, chief of facilities management for the Gettysburg Foundation, has been involved with the Spangler property since the 2008 purchase. He oversaw the construction, made the critical decisions regarding historical detail, and watched as the farm came to life. There is more to be done, of course, with work being completed as money is raised. But for now, Brian and other Foundation members past and present can enjoy the weekends when visitors and living historians fill the fields and buildings, knowing the crucial role they played in the resurrection of the Spangler farm.

Brian Shaffer

Ron Kirkwood

"It's been a real honor to be involved with something like this," Shaffer said, "especially when you saw what this place looked like . . . when we were thinking, 'What are we gonna do with it?' It sat for a year after we bought it. We didn't do anything with it," he continued. "Then we decided something had to be done or it was going to collapse. We just came out here at that point and made sure the electricity couldn't kill anybody. Put a sump pump in the basement [of the house] to get the water out. Posted no-trespassing signs. Just came out and checked up on it, and worked it from there."

One of the early believers in the property and the Foundation's dream was the Tourism Cares for America volunteer project, which is associated with the National Tour Association. Tourism Cares is a nonprofit public charity that mobilizes the travel and tourism industry to give back to society through grants to natural, cultural, and historic sites worldwide; through academic and service-learning scholarships for students of hospitality and tourism; and through the organization of volunteer efforts to clean up and restore tourism-related sites. More than 300 Tourism Cares volunteers traveled to Gettysburg in April 2009 to kick off rehabilitation efforts in earnest.[1]

An early major step came on January 25, 2010, when the Foundation sold an easement to the National Park Service for $750,000, handing the Park Service the right to use and help to oversee the land. Now there would be two top-notch organizations looking after the property.

With the help of a Historic Structure Report, the Gettysburg Foundation identified all the structures that were not on the property in 1863. All of them needed to be removed, including a detached shed, a shed attached to the north end of the barn, a chicken coop, a garage, a corn crib, and a concrete barnyard. Once that work was finished it was easier to visualize what the property looked like in 1863 (less a few outer buildings that were there then, but torn down prior to the Gettysburg Foundation's purchase).

Let's tour what's left from 1863 on the George and Elizabeth Spangler farm and what the Foundation has accomplished. One of our guides is Brian Shaffer. The other is David Maclay, barn preservation specialist for Historic Gettysburg Adams County. Maclay is an expert to the point of being able to look at a piece of wood or equipment and know how old it is.

---

1 George Spangler Farm Vertical File, V2-15c, GNMP Library. Gettysburg Foundation Press Release, 2008.

The Outer Limits

Today's lane entry into the property is exactly where it was in 1863, though back then it was dirt. According to period maps, the lane ended short of where it does now. The large rocks that today line part of the lane on each side are original and were put there by the Spanglers. The parking lot next to the summer kitchen is modern.

While facing the barn, turn right and look to the north while standing in the lane. It is thought that these and other fields were covered with hospital tents in July and early August of 1863.

According to the NPS, the walls on the property were at least three feet high and three feet wide. The stones along the lane are remnants of stone-and-rider fences, which had wooden rails above and along the sides of the stones to keep animals in and out. Stone-and-rider fences are visible today on the battlefield.

Large stones were a fact of life in Gettysburg-area fields in 1863. Farmers put the stones they dug up while plowing to good use as boundary walls and to divide up larger fields into smaller sections. They were skilled at building these straight

This stone-and-rider fence along the Taneytown Road runs next to the monument to the Army of the Potomac's chief of artillery, Brig. Gen. Henry J. Hunt. The Spanglers had similar fencing along part of their lane, west of the orchard, along Blacksmith Shop Road to Granite Schoolhouse Lane, and along portions of Granite Schoolhouse Lane. *Ron Kirkwood*

and level stone walls, an ability limited to only a select few individuals today. Back in 1863 in rocky Adams County, constructing perfectly balanced stone walls was just another part of running a farm. "Gettysburg's stone walls are the silent great testament to not only the battle but also a way of life that was here," explained Gettysburg National Military Park Division of Interpretation Historian John Heiser.

The walls were a help and a hindrance during the battle. Both armies used them for cover, but they also had to climb over them and in some places tear them down. The latter happened to some of the Spangler boundary and field walls, especially toward the west end of Granite Schoolhouse Lane and the west end of their property because of the sheer volume of men, horses, wagons, ambulances, and cannons on the land.

Soldiers on both sides built their own small stone walls for protection during fighting. You can find good examples on the west and south sides of Little Round Top (Union built), the summit of Big Round Top (Union), behind the 1st Vermont Cavalry monument on the southwest base of Big Round Top (Confederate), and a sharpshooter's wall at Devil's Den (Confederate).

The Spangler property, including the section on Powers Hill, was surrounded by a combination of stone, stone-and-rider, and Virginia worm fences. Most of these boundary stone walls and fences on Powers Hill, like those on the battlefield, were rebuilt in the 1930s by the Civilian Conservation Corps. A stone wall that spans the west end of the Spanglers' property is still in outstanding shape today in some places, which indicates it was rebuilt after the war and that little farming activity took place around it. All other remaining Spangler stone walls are worn down with large gaps, the stones having either been removed or buried. Four stone walls that were on the farm have vanished. The Spangler field walls were likely also used to contain animals such as hogs and horses. The former, in particular, were difficult to keep indoors because of their smell, and were a benefit when kept outdoors because they helped keep the undergrowth in check.

George Spangler was an impressive physical specimen if he was able to haul, lift, and place thousands of heavy stones, but it would have been nearly impossible to do alone, especially with all the other things that had to be done to keep the farm operational. His neighbors, siblings, hired hands, and sons Daniel and Beniah might have helped, depending upon how old the boys were when the walls were built. It is also possible George hired some or all of the work done.

The granite gatepost on the right of the driveway and in front of the barn today is original. (After decades of standing strong, part of it broke off in 2017.) Straps connected to a wooden gate would have been placed over the two pintles (or hooks) in the post. The gate connected to a post on the other side of the lane that is gone. Visitors should take note of the eleven quarry marks on the post, which were drilled or pounded in to help split the rock. It's possible this post came from a quarry on the Spangler property across Granite Schoolhouse Lane below Powers Hill, which at one time was owned by Solomon Powers. According to David Maclay, this is the only stone gate post he's seen in the area. "Someone was inspired one day," he said. "That is really neat."

Behind the gatepost is the barnyard, where piles of amputated limbs once reached several feet in height before being removed. The stone walkway leading from the barn to the summer kitchen, house, and smokehouse was there when the battle took place.

The Summer Kitchen

Summer kitchens were very popular on farms before the advent electricity because families could move their hot- weather cooking and baking out of the house. The Spanglers used a beehive oven to bake their bread, the opening of which can still be seen today in the interior fireplace area. The beehive oven was attached on the outside of the building. The exterior oven would have had a stone base a few feet high

The summer kitchen before the farm's purchase by the Gettysburg Foundation. *George Pyle Jr.*

and several feet wide. You can still see the shape of the doorway to the oven today on the exterior of the summer kitchen's east wall.

The Spangler beehive oven was attached to the exterior wall of the summer kitchen as depicted here. *Appalachia Building & Salvage Co.*

The Spangler fireplace area also probably had a wood cook stove, and they probably burned wood on grates to cook food in pots hanging over the fire. Canning and preserving took place in the summer kitchen. Happily, the black soot on the inner walls was not touched during renovations, giving today's visitors a feel for how often fire was used for cooking in the building. The actual cooking and its aromas, together with the ingredients, utensils, pots, pans, and cooked and preserved food that decorated the confined space made the summer kitchen homey and welcoming.

The Spanglers probably had a grape arbor in 1863 (such as the one shown in the accompanying photo; one is visible in an 1888 photo of the farm). In addition to grapes, this arbor provided shade next to the kitchen. The Foundation removed the grape arbor during cleanup. Summer kitchens were almost always located near the house for convenience, with the exterior often mimicking the house itself. The Spanglers' kitchen has a storage area upstairs.

Thanks to a donor, the summer kitchen was the first building renovated by the Gettysburg Foundation. It also required the least amount of effort. The work included replacing the floor and roof, patching the interior walls as needed, adding a fire-suppression system, tidying up the mortar, adding gutters and downspouts, patching the chimney, rebuilding the foundation, and replacing damaged window glass. The windows thought to still consist entirely of 1863 (or at least very old) glass can be found on the far right on the north side, and the roof window on the south side. The middle window on the north side has all original glass except the bottom right pane, as does the window by the door on the south side (except for the second pane from the bottom on the left).[2]

A bonus was the discovery of the Spanglers' main well under debris outside the kitchen on the west end. The well—stone-lined and about 18 feet deep—is a strong one that filled right back up after the Foundation pumped it out to see what was there.

The Foundation also moved the plaque honoring Confederate Brig. Gen. Lewis Armistead from the exterior wall by the door to a small post next to the building. (Most historians agree Armistead died in this building on July 5, 1863.)

The summer kitchen preservation work was completed in May 2013.

The Smokehouse

Before refrigeration and freezing, a smokehouse was used to preserve and store meats and fish. Meat, especially pork, was salted and hung on hooks from beams over a low smoky fire. The heat, smoke, and salt dried the meat so it would last much longer.

---

2 Historic Structure Report.

Before and after: The Spangler smokehouse.
Ron Kirkwood

The Friends of Gettysburg, the membership organization of the Gettysburg Foundation, together with hundreds of individual Friends, donated the $25,000 needed to demolish and rebuild the crumbling Spangler smokehouse—a victory by people who really care about this historic farm, Gettysburg, and their shared history.[3]

Only parts of the original foundation remain in today's smokehouse after the 2015-16 restoration. Horse hair from a nearby stable was used in the mortar to help with bonding, providing extra strength and preventing the mortar from snapping apart. This process was used in buildings of all kinds in the 1800s and in structures across the Spangler property. The smokehouse reconstruction took place at the same time as the barn's restoration.

The House

The Spangler dwelling served as the headquarters for the XI Corps' medical staff and, as we learned elsewhere in this book, many wounded men were cared for inside. The Gettysburg Foundation wanted to use the cellar as the electrical and

---

3 Friends volunteers have been involved in cleanup work on the farm for many years, and raised money to plant the apple orchard in 2017. Friends of Gettysburg volunteers, who today serve as expert docents at the farm, also helped with some of the research for this book. It is not a stretch to say that the Gettysburg Foundation would function far less efficiently without these dedicated volunteers.

The Spangler house still needed a massive amount of interior work in 2018. *Ron Kirkwood*

fire-suppression command center for the entire property, but to do so the crew had to engage in a massive clean-up and fix-up job.

One of the first things Foundation workers had to do was drain the water leaking through the walls that had flooded the basement so high it was possible to row a boat down there. Once that was done, the dirt floor was upgraded so water can be captured around the edges, and a sagging beam reinforced and supported. A ten-foot-square pit eight feet deep was dug in the middle of the floor to house the fire pump. Workers routinely came across large snakeskins during their work. Today, the cellar is so clean and dry it can be used for storage.

Once the water problem was resolved, the Foundation tore down an electrical pole on the property and installed a new underground line into the house. An electrical panel to run the farm was installed in the basement, as was the fire suppression system that controls the sprinkler system in the summer kitchen, barn, and house. An underground water tank was buried in the yard behind the house.

The Spangler house was renovated and expanded into offices and a conference center in 2019.

The Barn

The large Pennsylvania bank barn offered the Foundation several complex problems that had to be solved if its renovation was going to be called a success.

The first problem was the manure. The entire stable floor was covered with up to three feet of it. All of it had to be removed—the sooner the better. The manure created quite a stink, but that was only part of the problem. More practically, it was rotting support posts.

Once that mess was cleared out, volunteers with the Friends of Gettysburg stepped up again by painting plywood to temporarily cover and stabilize the hole-riddled siding. "I think the only reason it was preserved so well is because it was very, very holey when we got it," the Foundation's Shaffer said of the barn. "A lot of the doors were gone or just hanging on and there was constant air flow going through. If it would have been buttoned up tight this thing probably would have fallen, but [the holes] kept it dried up enough . . . from the air flow. We were afraid after Hurricane Sandy [in 2012]," Shaffer continued, "because we hadn't been able to act upon solidifying it at that point. We thought for sure it would be gone after Sandy, but it survived. Two weeks later, we had cables crossing inside supporting it." In a sense, he added, it was, "we want to say, shrink wrapped." T-11 plywood was put on "to tighten it up. We had rain spouting put on the entire way around and then drained the water away from the barn to preserve the foundation. Every time there was a windstorm," he added, "the metal would be peeled off the roof and

The barn was showing its age when the Gettysburg Foundation purchased the farm.
Gettysburg Foundation

David Maclay of Historic Gettysburg Adams County explains the exterior setup of a beehive oven. *Ron Kirkwood*

then we'd have to bring somebody out to refasten it. We patched the roof six, seven, eight, nine times."

Some work was still ongoing when the farm opened in 2013. "Everybody would say, 'The barn looks great,'" Shaffer recalled. "But that was just stabilization. When you walked in, there were cables that crossed from one side to the other."

The real renovation work began in the late summer of 2015 and ended in the following spring when the barn was taken apart piece by piece. The wood was spread out on the property. Anything that could be salvaged was used again. About 50 percent of the heavy timber was preserved, and most of the flooring upstairs was saved, including the original threshing floor upon which hundreds of wounded men had been placed. A lot of 1863 can still be seen and touched in the Spangler barn, and what isn't original to 1863 looks like it is because of the attention to detail by the contractors, the Gettysburg Foundation, and LSC Design, Inc. of York.[4]

The barn's foundation and stone work were also repaired. The siding was replaced, the metal roof swapped for red cedar shakes, vents replaced or rebuilt, floors repaired, and termite control and new lightning- and fire-suppression systems installed.

David Maclay of Historic Gettysburg Adams County appreciates everything the Foundation has done to preserve the Spangler barn. With his almost waist-length pony-tailed hair, friendly smile, and "Hey, man" greeting, you might at first think he is someone living in the 1960s, but if he is a '60s throwback, it would be more like the 1860s. He is knowledgeable and passionate about these old barns and he has made it his mission to preserve them.

Watching him investigate a barn is like watching a detective snoop for clues at a crime scene: This joint means this or that . . . this is hanging too high to be from the 1860s . . . look at how this wall is tilted . . . this bead is from a hand plane. Discoveries or examples of extraordinary craftsmanship elicit a happy response.

4 New wood is identified by a little metal tag.

Plenty of juicy clues remain for Maclay, even with the Gettysburg Foundation's 2015-16 restoration. Historians believe that when the Spanglers bought the property in 1848, they moved into a 26- by 24-foot log cabin with a 20 x 20 log stable. Maclay doesn't know about those log structures, but on a walk through the barn he spotted the evidence of a log crib barn right away and believes it dates to the late 1700s. His detective work always proves dead-on accurate.[5]

"There is a whole lot of recycling, particularly in the lower floor system," explained Maclay. "In 1798, 90 percent or more of the barns in the county were log crib barns. They were constructed just like log cabins with corner notches, and they built two log cabins essentially with the threshing floor between them and then put a roof over the whole thing. Most of them had forebays. As things became developed and people needed bigger barns," he continued, "there was better access to timber framing. Timber framing versus log crib gave you a lot more air space."

This recycling of wood more than 200 years old in today's Spangler barn is particularly evident in some of the overhead beams containing mortise joints, or cutouts. This "hole" in the wood indicates another beam was once attached. A joist above the door in the wagon shed leading into the stable offers a good example of recycled 1700s wood; its weathering and cut marks indicate it was hand-hewn with an axe or similar tool.

The large beams in the Spangler barn were hand-hewn on the property because they were too big to haul to a water-powered sawmill, which was likely used to cut the smaller original wood still in the barn. Vertical saw (or kerf) marks across the width of a board indicate a water-powered saw. There were many water-powered sawmills in the Gettysburg area in the 1850s when the Spanglers built this barn, including one just down the road on the Baltimore Pike. According to Maclay, most of the original wood in the barn is white oak, and some chestnut. The recycled timber from the original Spangler log crib barn had more chestnut than later wood they used.

Maclay was impressed with the rebuilt barn. "This was a big operation, and I think it's a great example of a barn of its type," he concluded. "Well crafted. Well engineered. Thankfully, well preserved. It's a gem. With its Civil War history that makes it even that much more valuable."

The Spangler barn, he explained, is an extended standard Pennsylvania barn with a basement drive-through. If you stand on the south side of the barn and look at it from the side, you'll see that the back-roof slope is longer than the front slope,

5 Historic Structure Report.

which was extended for storage purposes. The basement drive-through refers to the wagon shed on the south side of the building, and means it has back doors through which wagons could be driven. Some bank barns don't have these back doors. The main concentration of Pennsylvania bank barns are found in Franklin, Adams, Cumberland, Dauphin, York, and Lancaster counties. Immigrants from Switzerland and Germany did most of the bank barn building.

Maclay says it is highly unlikely George Spangler, his siblings, and other family members put up this barn themselves, though they probably helped. Instead, he explained, Spangler would have hired professional masons, carpenters, timber framers, and roofers to do a job that could have taken as long as three months. Some timber was likely taken from the trees on the Spangler property, and the work was probably done during the winter when there were fewer agricultural needs. According to Maclay, the stone work on the summer kitchen and the barn is so good and so similar that it is almost certain that the same "hot shot" mason worked on both buildings.

"I think it would have been a crew of masons getting the grade figured out and the ramp and foundation set up," he elaborated. "Most likely," he continued,

> they had a fairly small crew of timber framers that did the joinery and got the material on site. And then most likely the frame was raised in a couple of days, then sided and roofed over the course of a few weeks. In terms of calendar time, the foundation would take a while, but probably concurrently the timber framers would be out in the field, whittling away on the timbers; it would have taken weeks probably to do that. The siding probably would have taken, depending on the size of the crew, probably no longer than a week. And the roof they probably would have cranked out in a couple of weeks.

Ninety percent of the Pennsylvania barns in Adams County were built facing east to southeast, like the Spanglers' barn. This allows the sun to warm the animals in the stable and dry out the barnyard. It also helped with threshing their grain upstairs. The front and back doors on each side of the threshing floor were opened on breezy days when the Spanglers threshed their grain, which means separating the chaff from the good grain. The chaff would blow out of the barn in the west-to-east wind, leaving the edible grain behind.

The Spangler forebay extends seven feet from the front wall, which made it an ideal shelter for Civil War surgeons who needed fresh air, light, and cover for their operations and amputations. This forebay was built without support posts, but was sagging so badly that the Foundation needed to add them. Also on the front of the barn, the Foundation removed a large non-historic sliding door, rebuilt the wall, and replaced it with two smaller doors that match historic photos.

The corn crib next to the wagon shed has original and replacement wood. The gap between the wood panels indicates that Spangler put corn that was still on the cob or stalk into the crib so it could dry in the well-ventilated area. The corn crib has three doors so a wagon could be moved back and forth for easier unloading.

Maclay doesn't believe the hardware box on the right wall of the wagon shed is original to 1863 because the nails have round heads, and square heads were used until the 1880s. He does, however, believe it is indeed old. What looks like a ladder going nowhere next to this box is actually part of a winch system with a combination of original and newer equipment. The pulleys overhead were used to raise wagons for repairs. Horseshoeing could also have been done here. Many wounded Confederates were housed in the wagon shed during and after the battle.

The stable area inside is probably where wounded soldiers waited for their turn under the surgeon's saw. Later, the most seriously wounded were kept and treated here. Look to your right if you are standing in the middle of the stable on the main floor of the barn and facing the doors. That's where the Spanglers' horses were kept; along the south wall of the barn and nearest the house. There's a shelf in the wall to hold curry combs and hoof picks for grooming. Note that the front corners of the barn are rounded, which takes extra effort to build but allows for easier movement for animal and man. Note also the Dutch—or half—doors, which allowed the top half to be open for ventilation while the bottom half kept the horses in. Other livestock such as cows were kept in the rest of the stable. Maclay's keen eye picks out original nails in window jambs, doors, and other places as we walk through the stable.

Much of the wood around and above you in the stable is original. If it's tagged, it was installed in the 2015-16 rebuilding project. You can even see bark on some of the original pieces. Only the two doors in the center of the stable are recent additions. The others are all original, though they needed to be rebuilt, and the door hinges are either original or made to look original in 2015-16 by a blacksmith. The hanging hay feeders have a mixture of older and newer wood, but might have been installed after 1863 to replace the original.

The root cellar in the back of the stable was collapsing when Shaffer and his contractors tackled that job. It's unique in that most root cellars are not dug into the banks because of the extra expense of digging it and then lining it with stone. The work impressed Maclay, who notes the Spanglers' design, the original mason's skill, and the Foundation's work make it "an exceptional root cellar. Most of the ones we see are poorly executed. I'm blown away by their job of rebuilding this."

Jarred goods were placed on the shelf in the dark, cool root cellar with other foods on the floor, probably in baskets. According to Maclay, the sloping back wall next to the root cellar is designed to buttress that wall. Barns built into a bank have a lot of pressure from dirt and water, making the back wall one of the first things to blow out. "But they did a really nice job with this wall," he said.

Visitors who move outside to the back of the barn to check out the upper level will take note of the two posts behind the wagon shed and one behind the large doors on the bank. These posts are new and were installed by the Foundation for visitor safety to securely hold the doors open in the strong winds that can hit this side of the barn. Other non-1863 items added by the Foundation for safety or practicality include electricity, termite prevention boxes, vent screens to keep out birds, and the thresholds under doors to keep out animals.

The left bank wall (as you face the back of the barn) was falling down and rebuilt in 2015-16 with recycled stone from the property. The root cellar is beneath this bank. The top of the root cellar in the bank also had to be rebuilt. Wounded soldiers who were lying on the threshing floor just inside the big doors recalled Confederate artillery shells landing within 20 feet of the back of the barn here during the cannonade prior to Pickett's Charge.

Walk up the bank to the doors of the barn, step inside, and take a moment to absorb this top level, taking note of its size and beauty. You are standing on a double threshing floor, with a divider in the middle. Wounded men were placed on each side with their heads against the divider during the days the barn served as a hospital. Both threshing floors were covered in men, as were the hay mows on each end of the upper floor (and any other available space). According to a Union surgeon, this barn held 500 wounded men.

Based on the nails sticking out today, a wall about four feet tall once stood on the divider in the middle of the two threshing floors. Threshing machines were invented in the 1850s and greatly sped up and eased the process that up until then had been done by hand. It's not known if the Spanglers had one of the new machines, but it's easy to speculate that they did because of their attention to detail elsewhere on the property.

Most boards in the threshing floor are original to 1863, including the ones by the doors with holes. You can spot replacement boards in the upstairs floor by circular saw marks and round nail heads. Shaffer said it's easy to see the difference in original and replacement wood when the sun shines inside the barn.

A glance up allows you to take in the spaciousness and beauty of these Pennsylvania barns. It was a tough job to replace that roof and siding as the Foundation did, but it had to have been a great deal more difficult and dangerous when the barn was built with 1850s technology.

Hay was stored as high as possible in the hay mows, with the ladder on each one for access. Someone climbed the ladder with a pitchfork, climbed into the mow, and dropped the hay into a wagon below. One of the threshing floors could be used for overflow hay. That trolley at the peak of the barn was part of a hay carrier system developed after the Civil War that used ropes and was pulled by a horse.

Just to the right and up the steps after you walk in through the bank doors is the five-bin granary. There, the Spanglers stored grains such as wheat, rye, oats, and barley after threshing for use later as animal feed. A trap door in the granary floor made it easier to load bags into the wagon shed below.

The threshing floor and other parts of the upper level also could have been used for storage of wagons and other items.

Finally, upstairs are five vertical frames of heavy timber—called bents—that hold the structure together. These bents were assembled on the ground and installed by hand. They divide the upper Spangler barn into four bays.

Every contractor who worked during the 2015-16 restoration of the barn and smokehouse was from Maryland or Pennsylvania. Workers included one general contractor in addition to masons, timber guys, roofers, a lightning-rod system installer, electricians, a blacksmith, and a sprinkler company. "We took this barn apart piece by piece," the Foundation's Shaffer said. "We kept finding more and more of the interior structure that needed to be replaced; almost all of the roof rafters had to be replaced after you peeled the roof off. You could see one side of it was rotten, but you couldn't see that until you actually got up there and took all the roof off. And then," he continued, "when we called in for extra wood we needed to make sure it was reclaimed wood. A lot of work and decisions were made as we went through the job to try to keep it true to form. It was really, really inspiring to see the transformation of this place."

As noted on the marker on the front of the corn crib, the barn is No. 159 in the Historic Gettysburg Adams County Farm Preservation Project. To place a barn on the registry, HGAC measures and surveys it, notes special features, and comes up with an idea for its age. The barn's owner then qualifies for product discounts and grants for restoration.

The Gettysburg Foundation and the Spangler farm received HGAC's 2017 Barn Preservation Award. "They dedicated themselves to the preservation of this farm and have done so much to bring it back to life," Maclay praised. "It was in pretty rough shape when they took ownership of it. A lot of money. A lot of commitment."

And a lot of history saved, for generations to come.

Spangler Farm Short Story

The size of the Spangler orchard in 1863 is not known, but in 1880 the federal and agricultural census recorded that the property had 20 apple trees on three acres that produced 20 bushels of apples, and a peach orchard with 75 trees that bore 100 bushels of fruit. Those trees were long gone when the Foundation purchased the property, so 50 apple trees were planted in 2017 in the former apple orchard's location just south of the house. The varieties planted by the Foundation include Stayman, GoldRush, Arkansas Black, and Northern Spy. The Foundation uses these apples to make cider.[6]

6 Historic Structure Report.

Appendix 1

Army of the Potomac Surgeons
Known to Have Worked at the XI Corps Hospital

The II Corps and XI Corps surgeons who labored on the Spangler property in July 1863 were among the best of the best by this point of the war. Most unqualified doctors had been weeded out by this time. Those who had the talent to wield a knife and the fortitude to withstand the horrendous conditions advanced up the ranks. As a result, the vast majority of the Spangler surgeons were men of skill, passion, compassion, and leadership. They showed those same characteristics after the war when they returned to their communities and slid into leadership roles at the local, state, and national levels, including in the US Congress. The following is a biographical list of the surgeons known to have worked at the Spangler farm:

James A. Armstrong, 75th Pennsylvania. Surgeon-in-charge, age 28. XI Corps Medical Director Dr. George Suckley left Spangler on July 5. His assistant, Dr. Robert Hubbard, who was often busy working in town, left on July 14. That gave Surgeon-in-Charge Armstrong full control of the Spangler hospital.

It was Dr. Armstrong who gave the Christian Commission permission to scrounge Gettysburg for lumber or boxes that could be used to get the Spangler patients out of the mud. It was Armstrong who detailed musician Alfred J. Rider of the 107th Ohio to bury the Spangler dead, record their names, and turn their effects over to him. And it was Armstrong who signed off on the determination that a wounded soldier was well enough to return to some form of duty.

Armstrong remained at the Spangler farm through July and probably until the hospital closed on August 6. In an article that appeared on July 14 in the *Philadelphia Inquirer*, the Reverend Jacob Hanson (or Hinson) described Dr. Armstrong as "a most able and efficient medical officer, who is working nobly for the welfare and comfort of the wounded. The doctor has charge of the Eleventh Corps Hospital, and I find the wounded more comfortable here than at any other place." Armstrong had risen from assistant surgeon to surgeon-in-charge. He likely took personal interest, as time allowed, with 75th Pennsylvania comrade Col. Francis Mahler, who was mortally wounded July 1 and died on the Spangler farm.

Armstrong graduated from the Philadelphia College of Pharmacy and the University of Pennsylvania Medical School before the war, and practiced both pharmacy and medicine after it ended. He served 15 years as coroner, and died suddenly of what was then called "apoplexy" (stroke) in 1885 at the age of 50 in Camden, New Jersey. His funeral, noted the *Philadelphia Times*, "will be attended by the entire County Medical Society."[1]

Daniel G. Brinton, surgeon-in-chief, Second Division, XI Corps, age 26. "My horse, like myself is pretty well worn out," he scribbled in a letter home to his mother on July 5, 1863. The Yale and Jefferson Medical College graduate finally had a chance to catch his breath that day after the frenzied July 1-4 workload that had driven him into a state of exhaustion. The doctor took a well-deserved break and toured a portion of the sprawling battlefield before shipping out with the Second Division on July 5. "The dead had just been buried," he wrote, "but the ground still bore abundant evidence of the desperation with which the fight had been carried on." He was promoted to medical director in charge of all XI Corps doctors and hospitals in the fall of 1863.

Brinton was an especially learned man with an active mind. After the war, he became a professor at the University of Pennsylvania and a noted anthropologist with an emphasis on the study of American Indians. He was also a prolific postwar author of more than 20 books, including Ancient Phonetic Alphabet of Yucatan and Lenape and Their Legends.[2]

Jacob Y. Cantwell, 82nd Ohio, age 38. Doctor Cantwell was wounded in the left thigh at the Battle of Cross Keys in Virginia 13 months before Gettysburg and needed a leave of absence to recover. His brother, Col. James Cantwell (also of the 82nd Ohio), was killed two months later at Second Bull Run in August 1862. Doctor Cantwell had already lived through more than two years of war, personal sacrifice, and hospital horrors, but there he was at the XI Corps hospital working as surgeon-in-chief, Second Brigade, Third Division.

Cantwell was known for his friendly presence and dedication to his work, both of which had a calming effect on nurse Rebecca Price, who had worked with Cantwell earlier in 1863 and arrived at Spangler a couple of days after the battle. "Upon arriving at our destination the first person to greet us was Dr. Cantwell, who had charge at Wind Mill Point Hospital," she wrote years later. "Two or three other Surgeons were there whom I knew; you can well imagine how glad I was! . . . Certainly the Lord directed us there!"

Cantwell also made an impression on XI Corps Medical Director George Suckley, who told him so in a July 4 letter before Suckley left Gettysburg with the army the next day:

> My dear Doctor. While about taking leave . . . I cannot refrain . . . from writing you a few lines expressing my honest appreciation of the faithful, industrious, and energetic manner in which you have conducted yourself as a Medical Officer. . . . I have been obliged to

---

1 "Twenty-second Annual Report of the Alumni Association," Philadelphia College of Pharmacy, 1886, 141; *Philadelphia Times*, November 3, 1885.

2 Brinton, "From Chancellorsville to Gettysburg, a Doctor's Diary," 314; Brinton to his mother, July 7, 1863, Dr. Daniel Garrison Brinton Papers.

respect you, and honor you for your earnest, practical, and high toned professional conduct. . . . Your operations are performed with judgement, skill, dexterity and humanity. I now leave knowing well that our poor wounded cannot be left in better hands.

The rigors of his sojourn at the XI Corps hospital weakened the industrious Cantwell, who required another leave of absence to recover his health. He stuck it out through the balance of the war and was promoted to brevet lieutenant colonel. Once the firing ended, Cantwell settled in Alabama, where he died in 1883 at the age of 58. He is buried in his hometown of Mansfield, Ohio.[3]

Henry C. Hendrick, 157th New York, age 35. Civil War surgeons left wounds open after an amputation so fluids could drain when the inevitable infection set in. As chief of the dressing department at Spangler during the peak surgery period of July 3-4, Dr. Hendrick "dressed" these wounds by applying a moist covering and then closely monitoring the healing. Hendrick was one of the surgeons who examined Confederate Brig. Gen. Lewis Armistead at the XI Corps hospital and was surprised by his death.

Hendrick received his medical degree from the University of Michigan and practiced medicine prior to the war. He served throughout and returned to his practice in New York. When he mustered out, the medical director of the South, Lt. Col. Meredith Clymer, told him, "It gives me great pleasure to testify to your uniform excellent conduct as an officer and gentlemen since you have been on duty in this department."

Hendrick returned to Gettysburg in 1886 with other former members of the 157th New York and gave a speech at the unveiling of the regiment's monument. He died in 1911 at the age of 83.[4]

Isaac Newton Himes, 73rd Ohio, age 28. Doctor Himes was born in Shippensburg, Pennsylvania, just 29 miles west of Gettysburg, and still had family there during the battle. He left the Spangler farm on July 5, and on July 6 wrote a letter from Emmitsburg to his sister in Shippensburg. "You have probably been in Gettysburg Cemetery," he began. "We have had the severest battle that I have yet been in, at Gettysburg, Pa. Our corps suffered severely. . . . Although our hospital was only about a mile or two from Gettysburg, I did not get into Gettysburg after we had driven the enemy, and did not get to see any of our friends

---

3 Price, "Rebecca Lane Pennypacker Price's Account of Her Experiences as a Nurse During the Civil War," 22; "Letters Received by Commissioner Branch, 1863-1870," C715—C1109 C769—Cantwell, J. Y., and "Heitman's Register and Dictionary of the US Army," 280, Fold3; Compiled Military Service Records No. 453, National Archives.

4 "The Cortland County Medical Society," in Henry Perry Smith, ed., *1885 History of Cortland County*, 172; Meredith Clymer to Henry C. Hendrick, July 12, 1865, www.usgenweb.info/nycortland/books/1885-16.htm. Accessed October 20, 2017.

or acquaintances," he continued, because "I was operating surgeon of our division and had no time at all."

Himes received his medical degree before the war from the University of Pennsylvania. After the war, he traveled and studied in France, Germany, and the western United States before settling down and starting a practice in Cleveland, where he also taught at the Cleveland Medical College. He was president of the Cuyahoga County Medical Society, the American Medical Association, and the Society of Medical Sciences, and dean of faculty at what is now Case Western Reserve University. "He always had something of value to present, and yet with the most unobtrusive modesty," editorialized the Cleveland Medical Gazette. "Many a man with half the worth would have made twice the noise about it." Doctor Himes died in 1895 at the age of 60.[5]

Bleecker Lansing Hovey, 136th New York, age 45. Doctor Hovey, wife Marilla, and son Frank worked at Spangler for five-plus grueling weeks, from the day it opened until the day it closed. They served together through the end of the war. He mustered out in August 1865 as a brevet lieutenant colonel. The Hoveys relocated from Dansville, New York, to Rochester after the war, where he operated his practice. He was a respected and prominent citizen and studied deeply the subject of insanity. "He stands today as a most distinguished representative of the medical fraternity," noted a 1902 biography, "a man who through the long years of an active practice has kept in constant touch with the advancement and progress being made in the profession and has therefore made his service of the greatest possible value to his fellow men."

Hovey, the oldest doctor to work at the XI Corps hospital, died at the age of 89, outliving his wife and son. The surgical kit he used at the Spangler farm has been passed down through his family for generations and as of the time of this writing is in the hands of his great-nephew, Rex Hovey.[6]

Robert Hubbard, XI Corps assistant medical director/medical inspector, age 37. Doctor Hubbard was surgeon of the 17th Connecticut just prior to Gettysburg when XI Corps commander Maj. Gen. Oliver O. Howard promoted him to headquarters staff. Together with Dr. Armstrong, Hubbard took control of administrative and surgical functions at the Spangler hospital while continuing to perform surgeries when XI Corps Medical Director Dr. George Suckley and most of the Army of the Potomac left Gettysburg on July 5. The Yale graduate also personally attended Capt. James J. Griffiths, Howard's aide-de-camp, who was mortally wounded during a reconnaissance west of town on July 5. Hubbard

5 "A War Letter From Dr. Himes," *The Western Reserve Medical Journal,* vol. 3, no. 8 (Cleveland, OH, May 1895), 317; Albert R. Baker and Samuel W. Kelley, eds., *The Cleveland Medical Gazette,* 15 vols. (Cleveland, OH, 1895), vol. 10, 287-288.

6 *The Biographical Record of the City of Rochester and Monroe County, New York,* 36.

remained in downtown Gettysburg at the shared home/office of Drs. William Taylor and James Cress. It is believed Captain Griffiths was also in this house until he died on July 10.

Hubbard commuted to Spangler as time allowed and described his Spangler and Gettysburg experiences in regular letters home to his wife, Cornelia, whom he called "Nellie," in Bridgeport. "It would be superfluous to say that I have been busy after stating that the wounded from our Corps alone were far over 1400 & that I have the supervision of them. As for operating, I have every opportunity & have performed a large number of all kinds," he penned in one letter. "Our wounded are fast being sent to Baltimore & other places. I visit the Genl Hospital daily but the Capt. is unwilling that I should stay long so that I cannot do as much there as I wish." Dr. Hubbard left Gettysburg in the middle of July.

His beloved Nellie died in 1871 at about age 37. Hubbard spent his postwar life with his Bridgeport medical practice, surgical work, a term in the Connecticut General Assembly, as president of the Connecticut Medical Society, studying botany, and with his children. He died at age of 71 in 1897. "[T]he professional preeminence of Dr. Hubbard dominated our medical field," wrote one of his medical partners. Dr. Hubbard was "of commanding and dignified presence . . . his muscular strength was that of a trained athlete [and] his generosity to the poor and unfortunate emulated that of the good Samaritan."[7]

Jay Kling, 55th Ohio, age 34. Doctor Kling wrote a letter to the *Atlanta Journal Constitution* that was published October 13, 1896. The letter described the arrival, treatment, and death of Confederate Brig. Gen. Lewis Armistead at the XI Corps hospital, and included, "His body was buried in the rear of the garden connected with the cottage." Kling probably left the Spangler farm with the 55th Ohio on July 5.

He received promotions to brigade and division surgeon in 1863 and was mustered out in Atlanta on October 12, 1864. He was captured by Confederate cavalry not far from Atlanta on his way home to Ohio and sent to notorious Libby Prison in Richmond, where his health declined before his release in January 1865. He filed a claim to the US government "for losses sustained and expenses incurred" during his time as a prisoner, but the claim was denied because his capture happened on his way home after he had mustered out. "The service of the claimant having expired previous to his capture," was how the denial read. Dr. Kling returned to his medical practice but battled ill health for the rest of his life. He eventually moved south and settled in Atlanta, just miles from where he was captured.[8]

7 Robert Hubbard Papers; *Proceedings of the Connecticut Medical Society, 1898* (Bridgeport, CT), 357-359.

8 Hartwell Osborn et al., *Trials and Triumphs: The Record of the 55th Ohio Volunteer Infantry* (Chicago, IL, 1904), 241-242; *Reports of Committees of the House of Representatives for the Second Session of the Forty-second Congress, 1871-72* (Washington, D.C., 1872).

Louis G. Meyer, 25th Ohio. Surgeon-in-chief, First Division, XI Corps, age about 40. His bravery at the debacle at Chancellorsville two months earlier earned him the love and respect of the men of his 25th Ohio. "The self-denial he exhibited at Chancellorsville," wrote Bvt. Col. Edward C. Culp of the 25th regiment after the war, "when he allowed himself to be captured in order to take care of our wounded who were left upon the field, will never be forgotten by those whose lives he saved." That admiration was still there when Meyer mustered out of the service in July 1864. "The loss of [Dr. Meyer] was universally lamented by the entire Regiment," admitted Culp. "He came out as its first surgeon, and remained faithfully at his post until the expiration of his term of service, never having accepted a leave of absence."

Meyer was born and educated in Germany, emigrated to America, and obtained his medical degree at Case Western Reserve University School of Medicine in Cleveland. The lifelong bachelor practiced medicine in Cleveland until his death at the age of 73. The Cleveland Medical Gazette noted, "In the death of Dr. Louis G. Meyer . . . Cleveland lost one of her oldest physicians and one of the most esteemed, especially among the German population."[9]

Henry K. Neff, 153rd Pennsylvania, age 41. Like many of the wounded he treated, Dr. Neff also suffered the effects of Army life even before setting foot on Spangler property. Government pension applications and letters set forth his story. Neff became ill with bilious pneumonia about the time of Chancellorsville in early May 1863. He was seriously ill when he was captured during the battle and shipped to Libby Prison, where his health further deteriorated during his four weeks of captivity.

After his time as a POW, he worked to exhaustion at Spangler and thereafter was weak and ill. "After much suffering, there was an abatement of the general symptoms, but cough, pain with sense of stricture through the lungs, difficulty of breathing, emaciation, loss of appetite, and general debility continued," reported another physician. Even in his weakened state, Dr. Neff treated the wounded. He was transferred from Spangler to Camp Letterman in late July, where he was placed in charge of a section of the hospital until relieved of that duty on August 17, when he went home to Huntingdon, Pennsylvania. A doctor who examined him in October 1864 noted that Neff had ". . . almost constant cough and expectoration, accompanied with difficult respiration, and disturbed action of the heart." The physician also reported continuation of extreme physical debility and

9   Edward C. Culp, *The 25th Ohio Infantry in the War for the Union* (Topeka, KS, 1885), 99; Samuel W. Kelley, ed., *The Cleveland Medical Gazette*, vol. 13 (Cleveland, OH, 1898), 58; CMSR No. 1987, National Archives.

emaciation, jaundiced eye, and sallow appearance of the skin. Neff never fully recovered from his illnesses, and died in 1868 in Huntingdon at the age of 45.[10]

Enoch Pearce, 61st Ohio, age 30. Doctor Pearce rushed from the Spangler hospital through sporadic firing on the morning of July 3 to get to the side of friend and comrade Assistant Surgeon William S. Moore of the 61st Ohio. Moore had been moving wounded men away from the front line when he was mortally wounded and carried on a stretcher to Catherine Guinn's log cabin along the Taneytown Road. Pearce found him there weak and in shock. Pearce had Moore moved to the Spangler facility when it became safe to do so at the conclusion of Pickett's Charge, and he died there on July 6 with Pearce at his side. Moore's care was one of Pearce's final duties for the 61st Ohio and at the XI Corps hospital, for he left Gettysburg and was promoted to assistant surgeon and then surgeon, United States Volunteers. He was a brevet lieutenant colonel by the end of the war. Pearce was born in Maryland and raised in Steubenville, Ohio. He graduated from Jefferson Medical College in Philadelphia in 1854 and returned to Steubenville to practice medicine. He was present for and passed through unscathed about 20 battles and campaigns. He returned home to Steubenville after the war and married, raised a family, and became a successful dentist in addition to remaining a surgeon. The *Cincinnati Enquirer* took note of his death in 1916 at the age of 83. "He was a prominent member of the Ohio State Medical Society, medical writer of prominence and widely known throughout the state," eulogized the paper. According to an earlier biography, "He is an . . . upright, worthy man and his record, whether viewed from a civil, military or professional standpoint, is thoroughly honorable and eminently creditable."[11]

George Suckley, XI Corps medical director, US Volunteers, age 32. Of all the doctors who served at the Spangler facility, George Suckley had among the most interesting prewar careers. George and Elizabeth Spangler's farm changed from a division to a corps hospital early in the battle, and Dr. Suckley was either personally involved in the selection of the Spangler property or he approved it. He was the chief administrator in charge of everything going on at the hospital and reported directly to Jonathan Letterman, the Army of the Potomac's medical director.

Suckley's duties were myriad. In addition to selecting or approving the site of the Spangler farm, he made sure the hospital received adequate supplies and oversaw the ambulance corps, the duties of each surgeon, and the recordkeeping of the wounded as well

10 Letter in Henry K. Neff's Invalid Pension File No. 84659 from examining surgeon Jas. H. Oliver, October 30, 1864; "Camp Letterman General Hospital Orders and Correspondence: Journal of Dr. Henry Janes [3rd Vermont] July 26, 1863-Sept. 9, 1863," University of Vermont, Burlington. File in GNMP Library.

11 *History of the Upper Ohio Valley* (Madison, WI, 1891), vol. 2, 305-307; *The Cincinnati Enquirer*, January 15, 1916.

as their diet. Suckley also monitored sanitation, compiled casualty reports and passed them along to Letterman, promoted the improvement of medical care by providing specimens and case studies for review, decided which surgeons to leave behind once the army moved away, managed the removal of wounded, and monitored each doctor's behavior and work. Suckley left the XI Corps hospital with the Army of the Potomac on July 5 after turning his duties over to Assistant XI Corps Medical Director Robert Hubbard.

The New York City native born in 1830 had lived a full life by the time he arrived at the Spangler farm. After graduating from the College of Physicians and Surgeons (now part of Columbia University) in 1851, he worked in a New York City hospital before traveling west in 1853 to participate in surveying the route of the Northern Pacific Railroad, an expedition led by Isaac I. Stevens (who would later rise to the rank of Union general and be killed during the Civil War at Chantilly on September 1, 1862). Suckley collaborated with others to publish a book on the natural history of Washington territory in 1859. As a naturalist, he collected, identified, and wrote about various specimens in the 1850s in the West and Panama. The shark Squalus suckleyi (Girard, 1855) and fish Catostomus sucklii (Girard, 1856) are named after Suckley.

A bullet pierced Suckley's clothing but left him unharmed at Chancellorsville, where he was taken prisoner and held for about two weeks. He died of kidney disease in 1869 at age 38.[12]

William H. Thome. Surgeon-in-chief, Third Division, XI Corps, age about 27. Doctor Thome graduated from Pennsylvania College in Gettysburg and grew up 53 miles away in Palmyra, so he was on familiar ground when he arrived with the Army of the Potomac. He received his medical degree from the University of Pennsylvania in 1858 and went on to accomplish what few other surgeons did during his four years of wartime service: He advanced from regimental surgeon of the 41st Pennsylvania to medical director of the XVI Corps. Dr. Thome was wounded in the arm by a shell at Chancellorsville, but he kept working. Malarial fever laid him low for a time and he was treated in Washington, D.C., soon after leaving the Spangler farm.

He returned to Palmyra to practice medicine after the war and never married. His health deteriorated, exacerbated by his field hospital service during the war and a hard fall in 1876 during which he was trampled by his horse. Thome's invalid pension filing in 1897 listed a host of problems, including leg weakness, an arm fracture, contraction of the gullet (esophagus), rheumatism, an injured right ankle, and the note that he was "broken down

---

12 George Suckley, William Cooper, et. al., *The Natural History of Washington Territory and Oregon; With Much Relating to Minnesota, Nebraska, Kansas, Utah, and California . . . Being Those Parts . . . Northern Pacific Railroad Route . . .* (New York, 1859); For a brief bio., see www.famousamericans. net/georgesuckley/SmithsonianNationalMuseumof NaturalHistory.

physically." He checked himself into the US National Homes for Disabled Volunteer Soldiers in Hampton, Virginia, in 1904 and died of tuberculosis at age 69 one year later.[13]

Henry Van Aernam, 154th New York, age 44. The surgeon-in-chief of the First Brigade, Second Division was a passionate opponent of slavery and after the war argued for full civil rights for blacks. "[T]he curse of God visits on all that come in contact with this atrocious institution," exclaimed Dr. Van Aernam in a letter 16 days before arriving at the Spangler farm. He had made abolitionism the centerpiece of his agenda during his single term in the New York State Assembly prior to the war, and he continued to push civil rights for blacks during his four terms as a US Congressman after the conflict ended. Also, President Ulysses S. Grant appointed him to a term as commissioner of pensions.

After retiring from government work, Van Aernam returned to his medical practice in Franklinville, New York. "A part of the time I was where the minnie balls were plenty–and all the while shells were frequent, and familiar visitors," he wrote recalling his time at the XI Corps hospital. "There were five horses killed by shells right about the hospital . . . and several horses wounded. . . . Shells . . . fell very thickly about our hospital, especially on the 3rd day. For a while, from 1 to 3 or 4 o'clock it was a perfect shower."[14]

Charles L. Wilson, 75th Ohio, age 31. "Bill! I've been shot! Take me to Dr. Wilson," cried Pvt. Norman Brooks of the 75th Ohio to his friend and fellow private William A. Southerton during the July 2 evening fight on East Cemetery Hill. Years after the war, Southerton described how he assisted his friend with the serious facial wound down the Baltimore Pike past Evergreen Cemetery and Culp's Hill to the Spangler barn, where they found Dr. Wilson frantically working on other wounded men.

Wilson enlisted as an assistant surgeon in 1861 and was promoted to surgeon after Chancellorsville, so Gettysburg was his first battle as surgeon. Wilson likely left the Spangler hospital with the 75th Ohio on July 5, then he resigned from that regiment in October and joined the 141st Ohio as surgeon, mustering out in 1864. He practiced medicine for most of the rest of his life in Atlanta and Indianapolis. He died in 1918 at the age of 86 and is buried in his hometown of Athens, Ohio.[15]

13 *The Journal of the American Medical Association* (Chicago, IL, 1905) vol. 44, 1,696; OR 27, pt. 1, 232; *Lebanon, PA, Daily News,* June 14, 1876; Pension Application 1.197.809, September 4, 1897; Register for the US National Homes for Disabled Volunteer Soldiers, 1866-1938; CMSR, Can No. 20539, National Archives.

14 Van Aernam letter to his wife, June 15, 1863, Henry Van Aernam Papers, Box 1, Henry Van Aernam Correspondence (Transcribed), 1862-1864; Van Aernam letter to his wife, July 30, 1863, Box 1, Henry Van Aernam Correspondence (Transcribed), 1862-1864.

15 "Reminiscences of William B. Southerton"; www.civilwarindex.com/armyoh/rosters/75th_oh_infantry_roster.pdf. Accessed February 13, 2019.

Dr. Alexander N. Dougherty

US Army Heritage and Education Center

Doctors at the Granite Schoolhouse

Alexander N. Dougherty, medical director, II Corps, age 41. Under constant fire on the afternoon of July 3, the man in charge of the II Corps' medical care rushed between his three division hospitals on Granite Schoolhouse Lane and the Taneytown Road to oversee the evacuation of men and materials to a safer spot along Rock Creek. The selection of the new site that put the three division hospitals in proximity farther behind the line had been ordered by Dougherty. As this was transpiring, Dougherty received word that II Corps commander Winfield Scott Hancock had been seriously wounded on Cemetery Ridge. Dougherty rushed to Hancock's side, used his finger to probe the wound on the general's upper thigh, and pulled out a nail. Dougherty stayed in the ambulance with Hancock after the defeat of Pickett's Charge as the general was transported to the new hospital setting, though they stopped briefly at Granite Schoolhouse.

Dougherty was a graduate of Oberlin College in Ohio and received his medical degree from the College of Physicians and Surgeons in New York. He served four years during and after the Civil War, rising from surgeon of the 4th New Jersey to command of the II Corps medical staff. He left the army as a brevet colonel in late 1865. After the war, he settled in his hometown of Newark, New Jersey, to practice medicine. He was an expert on kidney disease, studied in Paris, and was in charge of the New Jersey Home for Disabled Soldiers. He died in 1882 at the age of 60.[16]

William W. Potter, 57th New York. Surgeon-in-charge, First Division, II Corps, age 24. Doctor Potter—who was captured and confined for a short time in Libby Prison in Richmond in 1862—performed operation after operation outside the Granite Schoolhouse in between personally attending the mortally wounded Brig. Gen. Samuel K. Zook (on and off the schoolhouse site) and preparing the hospital to move out of the range of enemy gunfire. "The first Division caught the heaviest of the blow, many killed and wounded were the result, and the latter were now being brought to the hospital in great numbers," he wrote regarding the fighting on July 2. "After working till the small hours of the morning of the 3d, I laid down and obtained a little sleep, but was up and at it again by daylight."

Potter was awarded a degree from Buffalo University Medical College. He returned to Buffalo after the war and was one of the founders of the American Association of Obstetricians and Gynecologists. He was also the president of the Medical Society State of New York, Medical Society County of Erie, Buffalo Medical and Surgical Association, New York State Board of Medical Examiners, and the National Confederation of Medical Examining and Licensing Boards. Potter also owned and edited the Buffalo Medical Journal. He died in 1911 at the age of 72, following his wife, Emily, (who died in 1906) and his only son, Frank, also a doctor (1891).

Dr. Potter made headlines in Buffalo newspapers by leaving his entire estate to a single female friend and nothing to his two daughters and two grandsons.[17]

R. C. Stiles, medical director, First Division, II Corps, age 32. Confederate artillery rounds fired at Union positions on Powers Hill had been falling all morning on July 3 on the First Division II Corps hospital at the Granite Schoolhouse. Dr. Stiles knew his hospital had to be moved even before it came under attack again a few hours later, this time during the pre-Pickett's Charge cannonade. It was time to leave the George Spangler property for a safer locale farther behind the lines. Most of the hospital and most of the wounded were packed up and moved by that afternoon.

This hospital ran full throttle and handled masses of wounded and dying for two days on Granite Schoolhouse Lane next to the little school and the little stream and directly beneath the Spangler-owned Powers Hill. Only remnants of the hospital remained on July 4.

Dr. Richard Cresson Stiles was cut out for this type of leadership and work. The native of West Chester, Pennsylvania, graduated from Yale in 1851 and the University of Pennsylvania Medical School in 1854. He studied for three years in Europe and returned to chair the Physiology departments at the University of Vermont and Berkshire Medical College.

He joined the army in 1862 and screened the health of drafted men in Pittsburgh before joining the Army of the Potomac's II Corps in 1863. Stiles relocated to Brooklyn after the war and continued to lead. Dr. Stiles authored a landmark study regarding the health risks associated with poor ventilation in crowded public buildings and rooms and made the first progress in figuring out the cure for the deadly and costly Texas cattle fever.

17 *Buffalo Medical Journal*, vol. 67, August, 1911 to July, 1912 (Buffalo, NY, 1912); Potter, "Three Years With the Army of the Potomac," 438-439; *Buffalo Medical Journal*, vol. 66, 1911, 509-510; *The Buffalo Enquirer*, November 16, 1911; *The Buffalo Commercial*, November 16, 1911.

Sadly, in the midst of all of his leadership roles, hard work, and scientific progress, he died in 1873 at the age of 42.[18]

Charles S. Wood, 66th New York. Chief operator, First Division, II Corps, age 38. Dr. Charles Squire Wood looked down at a large hole in his patient's chest. Without even bending over or cutting, he could see deep inside the injured man and see his heart beating. The wound, he announced matter-of-factly, is mortal. There would be no operation. Priority had to be given to those who stood a chance at living. Brigadier General Samuel K. Zook, who is memorialized with a monument in the Wheatfield, was carried on a stretcher from Granite Schoolhouse by two broken-hearted staff members to die somewhere else. Dr. Wood quickly and quietly amid a chorus of moans and screams moved on to the next man at the Granite Schoolhouse Lane hospital.

The II Corps' First Division chief operator performed untold numbers of operations and amputations over the next 24 hours before his hospital was moved off Spangler property. Wood was a strong, sturdy man who grew up working hard on his family's farm, but his endurance was tested at Gettysburg. The only breaks he took, all of them short, were when his mind and body were close to or past the breaking point.

He graduated from Jefferson Medical College in Philadelphia and wrote his thesis in French. He began as an assistant surgeon with the 66th New York and advanced to surgeon, US Volunteers, working through the war. Afterward, he practiced in New York City and was president of the Northwestern Medical and Surgical Society and New York County Medical Association. Dr. Wood died in 1890 at the age of 64 and is buried in his childhood hometown of Litchfield, Connecticut. His son Walter had died at the age of two and his daughter Sarah at just nine months.[19]

Those XI Corps regimental surgeons who worked as prisoners of war behind Confederate lines probably stayed where they were after the Confederates retreated on July 4 or stopped in at the Spangler facility and left town with their regiments on July 5 after their wounded men were moved to the Spangler hospital.

18 Frank B. Green, "History of the Medical Profession of the City of Brooklyn, 1822-1884" in *History of Kings County, Including Brooklyn, N.Y.* (New York, 1884); "Poison in the Air," *New York Herald,* February 14, 1870.

19 Charles A. Leale, "Memoir of Dr. Charles S. Wood, M.D.," in E. D. Ferguson, ed., *Transactions of the New York State Medical Association for the Year 1884-1899,* 16 vols. (New York, NY, 1891), vol. 7, 507, 509.

Appendix 2

The XI Corps at Gettysburg*

Corps Commanders
Maj. Gen. Oliver O. Howard
Maj. Gen. Carl Schurz

Headquarters Escort and Guards
1st Indiana Cavalry (Companies I and K)
8th New York Independent Company
17th Pennsylvania Cavalry (Company K)

First Division
Brig. Gen. Francis C. Barlow
Brig. Gen. Adelbert Ames

First Brigade
Col. Leopold von Gilsa
41st New York / 54th New York
68th New York / 153rd Pennsylvania

Second Brigade
Brig. Gen. Adelbert Ames
Col. Andrew Harris
17th Connecticut / 25th Ohio
75th Ohio / 107th Ohio

Second Division
Brig. Gen. Adolph von Steinwehr

First Brigade
Col. Charles R. Coster
134th New York / 154th New York
27th Pennsylvania / 73rd Pennsylvania

Second Brigade
Col. Orland Smith
33rd Massachusetts / 136th New York
55th Ohio / 73rd Ohio

Third Division
Maj. Gen. Carl Schurz
Brig. Gen. Alexander Schimmelfennig

First Brigade
Brig. Gen. Alexander Schimmelfennig
Col. George von Amsberg
82nd Illinois / 45th New York
157th New York / 61st Ohio
74th Pennsylvania

Second Brigade
Col. Wladimir Krzyzanowski
58th New York / 119th New York
82nd Ohio / 75th Pennsylvania
26th Wisconsin

Artillery Brigade
Maj. Thomas W. Osborn
1st New York Light, Battery I
13th New York Light
1st Ohio Light, Battery I
1st Ohio Light, Battery K
4th United States, Battery G

Strength: 9,245 men; 26 guns
Casualties: 480 killed; 2,016 wounded; 1,473
missing or captured. Total = 3,969 (42.9%).

* OR 27, pt. 1, 182-183; Busey and Martin, *Regimental Strengths and Losses at Gettysburg*, 83-92; Busey and Busey, *Union Casualties at Gettysburg*, vol. 3, 1,234-1,235.

Appendix 3

The Army of the Potomac
Artillery Reserve at Gettysburg

Commander
Brig. Gen. Robert O Tyler[1]
Capt. James M. Robertson

Headquarters Guard
32nd Massachusetts Infantry, Company C

First Regular Brigade
Capt. Dunbar R. Ransom
1st US Light, Battery H
3rd US Light, Batteries F and K
4th US Light, Battery C
5th US Light, Battery C

First Volunteer Brigade
Lt. Col. Freeman McGilvery
5th Massachusetts Battery E (10th Independent
New York attached)
9th Massachusetts Battery
15th New York Independent Battery
Pennsylvania Independent Batteries C and F

Second Volunteer Brigade
Capt. Elijah D. Taft
2nd Connecticut Light Battery
5th New York Independent Battery

Third Volunteer Brigade
Capt. James F. Huntington
1st New Hampshire Light Battery
1st Ohio Light, Battery H
1st Pennsylvania Light, Batteries F and G
1st West Virginia Light, Battery C

Fourth Volunteer Brigade
Capt. Robert H. Fitzhugh
6th Maine Battery
1st Maryland Light, Battery A
1st New Jersey Light, Battery A
1st New York Light, Battery G
1st New York Light, Battery K

Train Guard
4th New Jersey Infantry

---

1 OR 27, pt. 1, 878, and Busey and Busey, *Union Casualties at Gettysburg*, vol. 3, 697, 1,256-1,260;
Gettysburg Battlefield Monument Association.

Appendix 4

Where was the 2nd Connecticut Light Battery?

The whereabouts of the 2nd Connecticut Light Battery on July 2, 1863, varies by report. According to Brig. Gen. Robert O. Tyler, commander of the Artillery Reserve at the Spangler farm, he sent the 2nd Connecticut from the farm to the left of the Army of the Potomac line on July 2:

> At 3:30 p.m., pursuant to instructions received, I ordered Major [Lt. Col. Freeman] McGilvery with two batteries (Fifteenth New York Battery and C and F, Pennsylvania artillery) of his brigade to report to Major-General [Daniel] Sickles [Third Corps]. Afterward, as the action went on, I sent forward, as they were called for, the remaining batteries of that brigade, and, in addition, those commanded by Captains [John. W.] Sterling (Second Connecticut Battery) and [Capt. Nelson] Ames (G, First New York Artillery), making in all six batteries of thirty-four guns.[1]

Tyler's report appears definitive, but the Connecticut Adjutant General's Office offered an 1869 report on the unit's wartime activities based on records in its office. According to that office, the 2nd Connecticut was only involved July 3 at Gettysburg. That, too, is pretty definitive.[2]

An Artillery Reserve Second Volunteer Brigade sign on the Baltimore Pike outside Evergreen Cemetery supports General Tyler's report. It claims that on July 2, the 2nd Connecticut Light Battery: "Reinforced Third Corps line and late in the day retired and formed line under Lieut. Col. F. McGilvery on left of the Second Corps."

Respected Connecticut judge David B. Lockwood, who served as a corporal with the 2nd Connecticut at Gettysburg, wrote years after the war: "On arriving at Gettysburg on the afternoon of Friday [Thursday], the second day of the battle, the Battery was ordered into position to the left of the center, where the enemy made a bold but ineffectual attempt to break through our lines, and just as the gallant Sickles was being borne to the rear."[3]

---

1 OR 27, pt. 1, 872.

2 C. M. Ingersoll, *Catalogue of Connecticut Volunteer Organizations (Infantry, Cavalry and Artillery)* (Hartford, CT., 1869), 120.

3 www.civilwardata.com/active/hdsquery.dll?RegimentHistory?111&U. Accessed April 18, 2017.

Lieutenant Edwin B. Dow of the 6th Maine recalled that his battery restlessly waited at Spangler "until late in the afternoon, and until every other Battery was called away." That would seem to indicate that the 2nd Connecticut had come and gone from Spangler property.[4]

However, in addition to the Connecticut adjutant general's report, three 2nd Connecticut artillerymen (whose quotes follow below) wrote home within a week after the battle reporting they remained at Artillery Reserve headquarters and were not engaged on July 2. All three also discussed the Confederate shelling that hit the Spangler farm early Friday morning.

Private William Wilcoxon: "We started Thursday Morning for Gettysburg and got there at noon we did not go in to the fighting that day. . . . Friday morning the Rebs Sheld us out . . ."[5]

Private Eldridge B. Platt of the 2nd Connecticut was wounded by one of those Confederate shells that fell on Spangler property that Friday morning. His descriptions indicate that he likely was treated at the Granite Schoolhouse First Division II Corps hospital, which was across Granite Schoolhouse Lane from the cultivated Spangler fields. Platt wrote that his battery did not go into action on July 2. He described his battery's time at and around the Spangler farm and the shelling that the farm received in a letter to his parents on July 6, one day after the 2nd Connecticut left Gettysburg:

> We got thair thursday July 3rd [July 2] a bout 12 oclock and the fight comenced a bout 3 oclock and lasted till night but we did not go in that afternoon but the next morning they comenced a bout five oclock and we was in the rear in the range of thear guns and ours and I tell you the way the rebel shells came over in to our camp [from Culp's Hill] was not slow they had not fired more than 5 minutes before we got or [orders] to join to batle and jest as we got limbered up and started before a shell came over and struck right squar down by my feet and drove the dirt clear threw the skin ... my face all sweld up and my eyes so that I could not see hardly anything for 2 days Captin came up and told me to go in to the hospital and so i did and the doctor gave me some stuf to wash my eyes and face in and made it feel some beter I stayd there over night and they moved their hospital back a bout a mile back in to a peace of woods.[6]

Finally, Pvt. William B. Sniffen, in a letter to his mother on July 5, penned the following:

4 Edwin B. Dow manuscript, Records of the Adjutant General of Maine, Box 110 (2202-0402), Maine State Archives. Copy in Box B-1, GNMP Library.

5 William Wilcoxon letter to his sister, July 10, 1863, William L. Clements Library, University of Michigan. Copy in GNMP Library. File 6-CT2-ART.

6 Eldridge B. Platt letter to his parents, July 6, 1863, Eldridge B. Platt Papers, 1862-1866, no. 4767, Southern Historical Collection, Wilson Library, Univ. of North Carolina at Chapel Hill.

We came in about noon [Thursday the 2nd] and took position in the rear with the rest of the reserve Artillery. . . . Between 4 & 5 p.m. . . . the batteries began to leave so . . . we were about the last in that one place and . . . finely the orders came for us, we started out but it was most dark and the battle for the night stopped before we could get in line with the rest. About dark the fight stoped. We staid just in the rear with shells flying past. . . . Our horses of course standing in harnesses all night as they have now for several days, we lay by them on the ground that night next. [Friday the 3rd] They bid us good morning about 4 o'clock with a shell which we did not think much of untill several more followed in quick succession raining . . . shells among our guns and over our heads in a manner not at all agreeable. . . . We got out pretty quick. We were ordered to the front.[7]

So which is it? Did the 2nd Connecticut Light Battery rest on Spangler property on July 2, or did it go into action? Unfortunately, no official report from Capt. John W. Sterling, commander of the 2nd Connecticut, has been found. Captain Elijah D. Taft, who was in charge of the Second Volunteer Brigade—to which the 2nd Connecticut belonged—understandably wrote only about his own New York Light 5th Battery, which was positioned far away on Cemetery Hill.

Both stories are plausible and both have holes, but here's why it is far more likely that the 2nd Connecticut remained at the Spangler farm on July 2:

— Three 2nd Connecticut artillerymen definitively wrote in letters that they stayed there.

— There are no flank markers for the 2nd Connecticut around the Peach Orchard and Wheatfield Road or anywhere along General Sickles' line.

— A III Corps Artillery Brigade marker at the Peach Orchard tells what Artillery Reserve batteries came to its aid, but does not mention the 2nd Connecticut.

— We know when and to where the other Artillery Reserve batteries in the area retreated on July 2, but we know nothing of the 2nd Connecticut.

John B. Bachelder's battlefield maps for each day of the fight were years in the making. He contacted officer after officer to make sure each unit's placement and movement for each army was accurate and precise. His maps are of impressive detail. But the 2nd Connecticut doesn't appear on Bachelder's Day 2 map. That would be a huge oversight by

---

7 William B. Sniffen letter to his mother, July 5, 1863, William B. Sniffen Papers, "Letters written to his family dated November 2, 1862 through Dec. 31, 1863," Box 1 of 1, 2nd Connecticut Light Battery, 1862-1863. US Army Education and Heritage Center.

someone so careful. He does, though, have the 2nd correctly placed along the "Plum Run Line" not far south of the Pennsylvania monument on Day 3.

In his book *The Peach Orchard–Gettysburg*, John Bigelow of the 9th Massachusetts Battery does not mention the 2nd Connecticut as being involved in his account of the battle.

Casualties for the 2nd Connecticut at Gettysburg are listed as three wounded and two missing. It is highly unlikely that the battery could have fought on the southern end of the July 2 battlefield in what was a brutal firestorm, and then through the pre-Pickett's Charge bombardment, and suffered such light losses.

General Tyler was in charge of 19 Artillery Reserve batteries at Gettysburg and received much-deserved credit for his work. But he and those batteries were in harm's way both on the Spangler farm and on the battlefield and units were rushing in and out at a frenetic pace in a scene of uncommon frenzy. Tyler did not issue his report for almost two months. Despite his brilliant and steady work in Gettysburg, he might not have remembered accurately this one point. (Was the sign at Evergreen Cemetery noting the 2nd Connecticut's work on Day 2 based on General Tyler's report?)

Also, the 2nd Connecticut had difficulty getting ammunition because it was the only battery in the Army of the Potomac that used 14-pounder James rifles and 12-pounder howitzers. In addition, all other batteries used just one type of cannon per battery. The type and variety of cannons used by the 2nd Connecticut limited its use in battle.

Finally, Captain Dow's comment that the 6th Maine was the last to be called from the Artillery Reserve at Spangler on July 2 can be explained. Because of the large undulating Spangler fields and stands of timber, a man can stand in some places and not see a wagon or a gun just 100 yards away. As a result, it is more than conceivable that one battery might not be aware of another. Or, perhaps Lieutenant Dow was referring to after the 2nd Connecticut departed, not knowing that it would later pull back without having been engaged. Keep in mind also that the Artillery Reserve was large and various batteries likely spilled into neighboring fields.

Based on all of the above, it is more likely than not that both General Tyler and the marker in front of Evergreen Cemetery are wrong.

Appendix 5

The XI Corps Hospital Wounded

The number of wounded soldiers who received medical care at the XI Corps hospital on the George and Elizabeth Spangler farm varies widely depending upon the source. For example, Assistant Surgeon Dwight W. Day, 154th NY, recorded the number as "More than 2,200," while the US Christian Commission report put it at "Nearly or quite 2,000." Other sources and tabulations include the following:

US Sanitary Commission report: 1,900
The Rev. John B. Poerner, US Christian Commission: 1,800
The Rev. Jacob M. Hinson of Philadelphia: 1,700
Captain Alfred E. Lee, 82nd Ohio: 1,500
Gettysburg National Military Park Commission in 1914: 1,400.[1]

Conditions at the farm were not conducive to accurate recordkeeping. There were too many wounded and dying men in various stages of duress filling the fields and buildings and too few hospital staff available to treat them. This was especially true July 1-5 when the Spangler hospital saw the greatest influx of cases. Surgeons and staffers were working almost around the clock to save lives, and they had more pressing issues than counting the wounded, not to mention recording everyone's name, rank, company, regiment, manner of wound, and treatment, together with any additional remarks. Once treated, some of the ambulatory wounded simply walked away and were never recorded as having been treated there.

The Christian and Sanitary commissions took pride in their recordkeeping, but members were not allowed into town until July 4. It probably was July 5 when they made their estimates of 1,900 to 2,000 wounded at Spangler (with the Sanitary Commission recording that about 100 of that number were Confederates). The number of wounded men at Spangler fell slowly at first, with some men leaving on their own over the coming days, and then faster starting July 7 as groups of wounded were collected and shipped elsewhere for treatment. Like many other things relating to the Civil War, we'll

---

1 *Cattaraugus Union*, in Dunkelman's *Brothers One and All*, 144; *United States Christian Commission for the Army and Navy for the Year 1863*, 77; *Report on the Operations of the Sanitary Commission During and After the Battles at Gettysburg* (New York, NY, 1863), 24; Poerner, "Third Report of the Committee of Maryland," 265; *Philadelphia Inquirer*, July 14, 1863; *Lippincott's Magazine of Popular Literature and Science*, 60.

never know the exact number of patients treated at the XI Corps hospital, but we have enough information to produce a number that is reasonably accurate.

Four lists follow. The first is from Pennsylvania Register 554 ("Register of the Sick and Wounded") from the US Surgeon General's Office at the National Archives and Records Administration in Washington, D.C. This list, handwritten in pencil in 1884, is a copy of the XI Corps hospital register for Gettysburg that has since been lost. The lost register listed only the names of the men treated at the Spangler farm, while PA Register 554 includes men from many hospitals. As a result, it can be difficult to decipher who was treated at what Army of the Potomac hospital, and many men were at more than one hospital. Thankfully, though, this copy exists or many Spangler names would be lost to history.

PA Register 554 includes about 1,300 Spangler names. Unfortunately, many are misspelled, the list is obviously incomplete (many men known to have been at the Spangler farm are not on the list, including such prominent names as Armistead, Barlow, and Stowe) and factual errors abound. These errors have been corrected for publication, but it is possible as many as 200 to 500 men were omitted from this list either through oversight or because over-stressed doctors did not have time to keep track of everyone during the early July days.

The second list is a shortened version of one that contained 236 names believed to have been submitted by Chaplain Hinson at the Spangler farm and printed in the July 14, 1863, *Philadelphia Inquirer.* The Rev. Hinson said he compiled the list with the help of Spangler Surgeon-in-Charge Dr. James A. Armstrong. He said he would submit more names when he found the time, but he never did. The names in the *Inquirer* that did not make the surgeon general's "Register of the Sick and Wounded" were added here.

The chaplain probably was a Methodist minister from Philadelphia, writing to the *Inquirer:* "This week eight hundred were sent off to Baltimore, nine hundred still remaining," Referring to July 7-13.

The third list is from my own research from other sources and includes names that did not make the first two lists. Taken together, that accounts for more than 1,430 names. If you combine that with however many men remained uncounted, the Rev. Hinson's 1,700 seems a reasonable figure, especially since he came up with that number in consultation with XI Corps hospital administrator Dr. Armstrong. But when one takes into account the ambulatory wounded and still others who passed through, the 1,900 range estimated by the Christian and Sanitary commissions is well within easy reach.

Forty-six confirmed Confederates are on the lists presented here, which could be an indication that the Sanitary Commission's estimate of 100 is high. The Confederates were shipped out in groups throughout July to prison hospitals in Baltimore and on David's Island in New York Harbor. Many were shipped to regular prisons or paroled and a few took the Oath of Allegiance to the United States.

Capt. Ozni R. Brumley of the 20th North Carolina was shipped from the Spangler hospital to David's Island on July 20, 1863, and then to Johnson's Island prison on Lake Erie near Sandusky, Ohio, on September 18. He was sent to Point Lookout, Maryland, on February 1, 1864, on to Fort Delaware in Delaware a few months later on June 25, and then to a Union-held prison in South Carolina on August 20. By October 20 he was at yet another Union prison, this one at Fort Pulaski,

Georgia. The initial wound coupled with the rigors of POW life were too much for Captain Brumley, and he died of double pneumonia in March 1865, mere weeks before the end of the war.[2]

Brumley and fellow former Spangler patient 2nd Lt. John B. Bentley of the 22nd Georgia were literally caught in the middle of the war at a time when both sides had difficulties caring for large numbers of prisoners. Bentley and Brumley were part of the "Immortal Six Hundred," a group of Confederate officers intentionally starved in retaliation for the treatment of Union POW officers, and they were used as human shields during an artillery bombardment of Charleston, South Carolina. Unlike Brumley, Bentley survived the war.

Many amputations were not recorded by the surgeons for reasons unknown, so more such surgeries took place than noted here. A "compound fracture" is a strong indicator that an amputation took place even if it is not noted as such. This type of break almost always resulted in an infection followed by gangrene or blood poisoning and then death if the limb wasn't amputated within 48 hours of receiving the wound.

A "flesh wound" in 1863 meant that no bones were broken. Flesh wounds often caused life-threatening damage with large gouges of skin and tissue destroyed.

A "water dressing" was the application of an ointment to a wound covered with a wet cloth. It was the most popular treatment at the Spangler hospital and an example of why Civil War-era hospitals needed to be near a supply of cold, fresh water in order to keep wounds clean. The Spanglers had one well next to their summer kitchen and another somewhere near Granite Schoolhouse. In addition, a pair of small streams flowed through their property (as they do now) and their farm was a short walk or ride to Rock Creek. The XI Corps hospital was the only Gettysburg corps or division hospital in PA Register 554 that listed water dressing as a treatment, though it was undoubtedly used in all Gettysburg army hospitals because it was the treatment of choice at that time. The task of changing water dressings regularly fell to soldiers pulled from the ranks to work in hospitals. The wet cloths were cleaned between each use but not sterilized.

Many soldiers from corps other than the XI were treated at the Spangler facility. A. C. Registers 96 and 97 at the National Archives are not complete but list 846 names of wounded First Division II Corps men, many of whom undoubtedly were treated at Granite Schoolhouse. First Division Chief Operator Charles S. Wood of the 66th New York said in Register 97, "We were obliged to move the hospital four times in order to get out of line of fire creating ... confusion and rendering it impossible to present a correct record."

Not all who died at the XI Corps Spangler hospital were listed among the dead in this report by the surgeons. Some listed as having died there might have died elsewhere after they were moved because many patients spent time at multiple hospitals. The surgeons recorded the name, rank, regiment, company, wound, treatment, and made a remark for most patients, but not all of them.

Many Spangler surgeons only spoke English, which resulted in spelling and other factual errors because so many of the XI Corps wounded were German immigrants. Some of their names were recorded in German, some in English, and some in a combination of both German and English.

2 Company muster rolls, Fold3.

Out of the 26 XI Corps infantry regiments that fought at Gettysburg, the 26th Wisconsin had the most wounded men (135) treated on the Spangler property, according to this list. This was true even though the majority of the wounded from this regiment spent July 1-3 trapped behind the Confederate line in hospitals in and around Gettysburg. The other four regiments with the most wounded at the Spangler farm were the 157th New York (117), 134th New York (109), 153rd Pennsylvania (109), and 107th Ohio (98).

Unless otherwise noted, this list of wounded is compiled from PA Register 554.[3] Corrections to the original records have been made for the list that appears below. All of the wounded served in the XI Corps unless otherwise indicated. (CSA = Confederate States of America; author's notes appear in parentheses.)

Patients at the Spangler Farm XI Corps Hospital

Aber, David, Sgt., 82nd OH, K, right side, water dressing;

Adams, William F., Pvt., 73rd OH, C, mid 3rd both legs, water dressing;

Aeigle, John, Pvt., 107th OH, K, right side, died July 19, water dressing;

Agan, Peter, Pvt., 157th NY, G, fracture lower 3rd left thigh, splints;

Ahrens, John H., Pvt., 75th OH, A, right thigh, water dressing;

Albert, Philip J., Pvt., 153rd PA, K, left hip & left leg, ball extracted from hip;

Albreck, Frederick, Pvt., 45th NY, A, left shoulder, water dressing;

Albro, John, Sgt., 119th NY, H, left arm flesh wound, water dressing;

Allen, Charles B., Cpl., 134th NY, C, upper third left thigh, water dressing;

Allen, John B., Pvt., 107th OH, E, left thigh, water dressing;

Allison, John S., Cpl., 75th OH, K, right knee & arm, compound fracture, water dressing;

Alters, Joseph B., 1st Lt., 75th OH, A, flesh wound upper 3rd left thigh, water dressing;

Anderson, John, Sgt., 54th NY, I, lower 3rd left leg, compound fracture, water dressing;

Anguish, Horace, Cpl., 157th NY, I, right shoulder, died July 31, fracture resection head of humerus;

Annis, Roe H., Pvt., 136th NY, C, left hand, 2 first fingers amputated;

Anson, Ernest, Pvt., 55th OH, C, right knee, ball extracted;

Armlin, William W., Cpl., 134th NY, D, flesh wound mid 3rd left thigh, water dressing;

Arndt, Carl, Pvt., 26th WI, E, upper 3rd left forearm & side, water dressing;

Ash, David, Pvt, 154th NY, E, left arm, compound fracture, splints;

Ashley, A., Pvt., 157th NY, B, lower & right thigh, water dressing;

Atwater, Clayton J., 2nd Lt., 157th NY, D, left shoulder, water dressing, contusion;

Atwood, John R., Pvt., 19th ME, 2nd Corps, E, upper 3rd of right thigh, water dressing;

Auer, Fred, Pvt., 134th NY, A, mid 3rd leg, water dressing;

Auger, Charles, Cpl., 26th WI, E, wounded in right foot, water dressing;

Austin, Jacob, Pvt., 17th CT, G, index finger, water dressing;

3 PA Register 554 "Register of the Sick and Wounded," Office of the United States Surgeon General, and Carded Medical Records Volunteers, Mexican and Civil Wars, 1846-1865, Records of the Adjutant General's Office, National Archives.

Axtell, John, Pvt, 82nd OH, C, flesh wound calf of both legs, water dressing;

Babcock, George M., Pvt., 157th NY, D, mid 3rd right leg, water dressing;

Backer, John, Cpl., 107th OH, F, right leg, water dressing;

Backoff, Joseph, Pvt., 41st NY, G, rheumatism;

Bader, Jacob, Pvt., 74th PA, G, left leg, water dressing;

Bagley, George F., Pvt., 119th NY, A, right side of head, water dressing;

Baje, Charles, Pvt., 26th WI, C, upper 3rd left hip & mid 3rd left arm, water dressing;

Baker, Henry, Pvt., 75th OH, D, back contusion, water dressing;

Baker, John, Pvt., 25th OH, K, gunshot left shoulder, sent to general hospital July 8;

Balde, Frederick, Cpl., 75th PA, D, left arm, compound fracture & amputated upper 3rd;

Ball, Charles L. S., Sgt., 134th NY, K, right ankle & lower 3rd left arm, water dressing;

Ballard, Richard, Pvt., 157th NY, E, left breast, simple cerate;

Ballentine, William, 2nd Lt., 82nd OH, E, left thigh, water dressing;

Ballew, Auguste, Pvt., 68th NY, C, fever;

Balluff, Charles, Pvt., 26th WI, I, left breast, water dressing;

Balmes, Joseph, Pvt., 26th WI, C, right hip, died July 14, water dressing, compound fracture;

Baltus, Charles, Cpl., 134th NY, K, upper 3rd right arm & head, water dressing;

Banzhof, John G. Pvt., 17th CT, H, diarrhea;

Barber, Zack, Pvt., 136th NY, K, 2 fingers of right hand & right shoulder, 2 fingers amputated;

Barnum, Henry C., Pvt., 143rd PA, 1st Corps, H, right knee, water dressing;

Barrett, Joseph, Pvt., 73rd OH, G, right knee, died July 18, water dressing, compound fracture;

Barrette, Edward, Pvt., 25th OH, F, upward portion of nose, water dressing, compound fracture;

Barry, Jeremiah, Pvt., 134th NY, E, gunshot, died July 31;

Barth, Francis, Pvt., 41st NY, E, right heel, water dressing;

Barth, Joseph, Cpl., 75th PA, D, lower 3rd right leg, water dressing;

Barthauer, William, Cpl., 45th NY, D, right side of head, water dressing;

Bartlett, Erastus, Pvt., 33rd MA, A, hand, water dressing;

Bartley, James, Pvt., 75th OH, H, upper 3rd right leg, water dressing;

Bartsch, August, 1st Lt., 26th WI, D, upper 3rd left arm & side, water dressing;

Bates, Adam, Pvt., 73rd OH, G, right hip, water dressing;

Batteson, John H., Pvt., 17th CT, F, contusion hip & back, water dressing;

Battles, Edward D., Pvt., 33rd MA, E, head, water dressing;

Bauer, Joseph, Cpl., 119th NY, C, upper 3rd left leg, water dressing;

Beal, Joseph, Pvt., 33rd MA, I, right eye, died July 30, water dressing;

Beaver, Peter, Cpl., 134th NY, K, small of back, died July 10, water dressing;

Beck, August, Pvt., 54th NY, D, flesh wound throat, water dressing;

Beck, John, Pvt., 45th NY, D, right breast, died July 20, water dressing;

Beck, Ludwig, Pvt., 26th WI, H, flesh wound left foot, water dressing;

Beck, Stephen, Pvt., 107th OH, C, flesh wound mid 3rd thigh, water dressing;

Becker, William, Pvt., 134th NY, K, left shoulder, simple cerate;

Beckmann, Henry, Pvt., 41st NY, E, upper 3rd left leg, water dressing;

Beers, J. L., Sgt., 150th PA, 1st Corps, G, right shoulder, water dressing;

Behler, Heinrich, Pvt., 26th WI, H, upper 3rd left arm, water dressing;

Behling, Carl, Pvt., 26th WI, E, left shoulder, water dressing;

Beiswanger, Jacob, Sgt., 75th PA, B, right shoulder, water dressing;

Beltz, John A., Pvt., 107th OH, E, mid 3rd right leg, water dressing;

Benda, Franz, Pvt., 26th WI, F, left hip, ball extracted;

Benedict, John H., Cpl., 17th CT, C, left arm & lower 3rd right thigh, arm splinted;

Benjamin, Fred A., Sgt., 157th NY, A, flesh wound neck, water dressing;

Benjamin, John W., 2nd Lt., 157th NY, E, left knee, water dressing;

Benson, Frank, Pvt., 17th CT, C, lower 3rd right thigh, compound fracture, splints;

Bentley, John B., 2nd Lt., 22nd GA, Hill's Corps, CSA, F, right groin & hip, water dressing;

Berghofer, Adam, Pvt., 107th OH, F, flesh wound right side neck & right ear, simple cerate;

Berlage, Joseph, Cpl., 26th WI, A, left thigh, water dressing;

Bernard, Wilhelm, Pvt., 75th PA, B, flesh wound back, water dressing;

Bertsche, Bernhart, Pvt., 74th PA, G, flesh wound head, water dressing;

Bevens, William, Pvt., 134th NY, D, left arm, fracture, resection shoulder;

Beverly, Balts, Pvt., 107th OH, C, back below shoulder blades, died July 14, water dressing;

Bice, Benjamin B., Pvt., 134th NY, A, flesh wound left shoulder, died July 31, water dressing;

Bickford, James C., Pvt., 25th OH, I, flesh wound upper 3rd left thigh & right wrist, water dressing;

Biddle, Daniel, Cpl., 107th OH, A, lower 3rd left thigh, water dressing;

Billings, S., Sgt. 19th ME, 2nd Corps, C, left leg, dead, compound fracture, amputation mid 3rd thigh;

Billings, William, Pvt., 73rd OH, C, front of head, water dressing;

Birchard, J. D., Pvt., 134th NY, E, right hip, compound fracture, dressed with splints;

Bird, Francis A., Pvt., 119th NY, A, right hand, water dressing;

Bisbe, Stephen, Pvt., 157th NY, F, flesh wound upper 3rd & lower 3rd arm, water dressing;

Bishop, George W., 2nd Lt., 134th NY, A, left hip, water dressing;

Bishop, Lewis, Sgt., 154th NY, C, left knee fracture, died July 31, amputation lower 3rd left leg;

Bitzer, Socrates, Cpl., 73rd OH, A, through penis, privates & left hip, died July 7, water dressing;

Black, William, Pvt., 27th PA, K, lower 3rd right thigh, water dressing;

Blaisdell, Richard, Pvt., 19th ME, 2nd Corps, K, contusion, water dressing;

Blakeman, James Henry, Pvt., 17th CT, D, left side, water dressing;

Blanchard, Sylvanus, Pvt., 33rd MA, D, upper 3rd left arm, water dressing;

Blasche, Franz, Pvt., 75th PA, A, right hip, water dressing;

Blee, Charles A., Sgt., 73rd PA, I, upper 3rd left leg, water dressing;

Bodenschatz, Christopher, Cpl., 107th OH, K, left hip, water dressing;

Boebel, Hans, Lt. Col., 26th WI, right foot, compound fracture, 2nd & 3rd toes amputated;

Bohrer, Casper, Pvt., 107th OH, G, lower 3rd right leg & side, died July 16, compound fracture, amputed mid 3rd right leg;

Boileau, Joseph, Cpl., 75th OH, E, right shoulder, water dressing;

Boman, William, Pvt., 25th OH, B, right thumb, fractured, amputated near hand;

Bond, Alexander, Pvt., 27th PA, K, mid 3rd leg, water dressing, compound fracture;

Bookman, Charles, Pvt., 154th NY, D, right side of head, water dressing;

Borger, Gideon, Pvt., 153rd PA, H, gunshot, died July 7;

Bornemann, Conrad, Cpl., 26th WI, F, through right foot, water dressing;

Boroway, Jacob M., Pvt., 107th OH, A, neck, water dressing;

Boroway, William, Pvt., 107th OH, A, left side neck, simple cerate;

Boslough, Melville, Cpl., 150th PA, 1st Corps, H, right hip, water dressing;

Botkin, Wallace W., Pvt., 73rd OH, F, flesh wound right thigh, water dressing;

Bouton, John W., Pvt., 17th CT, C, upper 3rd left forearm, ball extracted;

Boyd, John, 1st Sgt., 136th NY, H, head & lower 3rd thigh, water dressing, fractured thigh;

Braasch, William, Pvt., 26th WI, B, upper 3rd left thigh, water dressing;

Braatz, August, Pvt., 26th WI, B, through the head, compound fracture, water dressing;

Bradley, Lucius, Cpl., 136th NY, B, right lung, water dressing, penetrating wound;

Bradley, Woodward, Pvt., 157th NY, C, mid 3rd right thigh, water dressing;

Bradt, Joseph C., Pvt., 134th NY, C, flesh wound right hand, water dressing;

Brady, Levi S., Pvt., 153rd PA, E, head, water dressing;

Brand, Andrew L., Cpl., 134th NY, I, upper 3rd both thighs, water dressing;

Brandenburg, Jesse W., 1st Sgt., 55th OH, K, left hip, water dressing;

Brandes, Julius, Pvt., 68th NY, I, left thigh, water dressing;

Brandt, Conrad, Pvt., 75th PA, E, left arm, water dressing;

Brannigan, Thomas, Pvt., 73rd PA, K, mid 3rd left leg, water dressing;

Braun, Joseph, Sgt., 107th OH, C, breast, water dressing;

Braun, Samuel, Pvt., 107th OH, I, lower 3rd right leg, compound fracture & amputated lower 3rd;

Braun, Xavier, Pvt., 26th WI, E, right hand & left leg, water dressing;

Bray, David R., Sgt., 75th OH, I, contusion right shoulder, water dressing;

Brayton, Thomas, Pvt., 157th NY, D, upper 3rd right leg, water dressing;

Breckenridge, George A., Pvt., 82nd OH, C, right knee, water dressing;

Brent, Edmund V., 1st Lt., 61st OH, D, left wrist & arm, water dressing;

Bresee, William H., Cpl., 134th NY, D, flesh wound left forearm, water dressing;

Briegel, Otto H., Cpl., 82nd IL, D, flesh wound left hand 3rd & 4th fingers, simple cerate;

Briggs, Leonard F., Capt., 157th NY, I, upper 3rd left leg, water dressing, compound fracture;

Britt, Edward, Pvt., 27th PA, D, flesh wound left forearm, water dressing;

Brixs, Jenaes, Pvt., 119th NY, D, left thigh & left wrist, water dressing;

Brodmerkel, George, Pvt., 74th PA, B, right breast, water dressing;

Brooks, Norman, Pvt., 75th OH, B, chin & right side of face, water dressing;

Brooks, Samuel J., 1st Sgt., 25th OH, I, both thighs, water dressing;

Brooks, Socrates, Pvt., 55th OH, B, lower 3rd left leg, water dressing;

Bross, Frederick, Pvt., 107th OH, C, right side, water dressing;

Brown, Charles, Pvt., 74th PA, B, left leg, water dressing;

Brown, Charles S., Sgt., 157th NY, D, right forearm, water dressing;

Brown, John, Pvt., 25th OH, B, diarrhea;

Brownlee, James, Cpl., 134th NY, G, right lung & upper 3rd right thigh, water dressing;

Brubaker, Benj., Pvt., 75th OH, C, left hip, water dressing;

Brubaker, Jacob, Pvt., 55th OH, B, upper 3rd left thigh, water dressing;

Bruckert, Charles, 2nd Lt., 26th WI, I, lower 3rd right leg, died July 16, compound fracture & amputated mid 3rd;

Brumley, Ozni R., Capt., 20th NC, Ewell's Corps, CSA, B, left thigh & back, water dressing;

Brunner, Albert, Pvt., 1st NY Light Artillery, I, right foot, died Aug. 2, water dressing, compound fracture;

Bryer, James, Cpl., 157th NY, B, neck & jaw fracture, water dressing;

Buck, Alden, Pvt., 73rd OH, K, right hip, water dressing;

Buckley, Patrick, Pvt., 17th CT, A, right shoulder, water dressing;

Buechner, Casper, 1st Sgt., 26th WI, E, right breast, water dressing;

Bunt, Jacob H., Pvt., 134th NY, I, shoulder, water dressing;

Burkhardt, Anton, Pvt., 107th OH, I, paroled prisoner;

Burneman, Conrad, Pvt., 26th WI, F, through right foot, water dressing;

Burnheimer, Aaron, Pvt., 107th OH, D, right thigh, ball extracted;

Burns, George E., Pvt., 15th MA, 2nd Corps, G, flesh wound mid 3rd right thigh, died July 14, water dressing;

Burtis, Warren J., Pvt., 17th CT, H, flesh wound left foot, water dressing;

Bush, John A., Sgt., 154th NY, D, right shoulder, bone extracted, fracture;

Bushey, Taylor, Pvt., 82nd OH, F, hip flesh wound, water dressing;

Butcher, John, Pvt., 5th NH, 2nd Corps, F, right breast, water dressing;

Butler, John, Pvt., 157th NY, I, fracture right foot, water dressing;

Butt, John, Pvt., 73rd OH, D, shoulder, water dressing;

Cahill, John, Pvt., 157th NY, B, lower 3rd left leg & right foot, water dressing, fracture;

Cain, Reuben, Pvt., 134th NY, D, flesh wound mid 3rd left leg, water dressing;

Call, William R., Pvt., 73rd OH, B, died July 16, ball extracted;

Callahan, Jacob W. B., Pvt., 82nd OH, C, lower 3rd left thigh, water dressing;

Camp, Alonzo, Pvt., 136th NY, D, back contusion, water dressing;

Campbell, Jesse M., Pvt., 25th OH, C, upper 3rd left leg compound fracture, amputation lower 3rd left thigh;

Campbell, John A., Sgt. Maj., 157th NY, upper 3rd left thigh, water dressing;

Canfield, Amos, Pvt., 82nd OH, E, right knee, water dressing, fracture;

Carl, James M., Pvt., 107th OH, A, lower 3rd left leg, water dressing;

Carl, Peter, Cpl., 107th OH, I, upper 3rd right leg, water dressing;

Carlisle, Henry H., Pvt., 16th VT, 1st Corps, C, upper 3rd right thigh, water dressing;

Carman, Cassius M., Sgt., 157th NY, I, flesh wound right hip, water dressing;

Carpenter, Frederick H., Cpl., 17th CT, D, mid 3rd left forearm, water dressing, fracture;

Carpenter, W. W., Pvt., 157th NY, D, left hip, splints, fracture lower 3rd;

Carr, Orson S., Sgt., 13th VT, 1st Corps, E, gunshot, died July 3;

Carr, Solomon, Pvt., 157th NY, C, flesh wound privates, water dressing;

Carroll, Benjamin, Cpl., 134th NY, F, mid 3rd right thigh, water dressing;

Carroll, Vincent, Sgt., 25th OH, E, upper 3rd forearm, water dressing, compound fracture;

Cause, John, Pvt., 107th OH, E, middle finger & mid 3rd left thigh, ball extracted;

Cave, Franklin, Pvt., 9th NY Cavalry, Cavalry Corps, I, right breast, water dressing;

Chaffee, J. M., Pvt., 55th OH, C, mid 3rd left leg & hip, water dressing, fracture;

Chalett, Charles, Pvt., 25th OH, K, both hips & left knee, water dressing;

Chalker, Charles H., Cpl., 73rd OH, K, upper 3rd left thigh, water dressing;

Champlin, Stanton, Pvt., 134th NY, E, left thigh, water dressing;

Chapman, George, Pvt., 134th NY, A, lower 3rd left arm, water dressing;

Chase, D. D., Pvt., 157th NY, F, upper 3rd right thigh, water dressing;

Chase, James F., Pvt., 154th NY, D, right hip & privates, died July 31, water dressing;

Christ, John, Cpl. 136th NY, E, right foot, water dressing, contusion;

Clark, Horace S., 1st Lt., 73rd OH, E, left thigh, water dressing;

Clark, Michael, Pvt., 17th CT, I, back & hip, liniment, run over by horse;

Clenings, Francis M., Pvt., 73rd OH, C, upper 3rd left leg, water dressing, compound fracture;

Clewell, William, Pvt., 153rd PA, I, lower 3rd left thigh, water dressing;

Clifford, Robert, Pvt., 106th PA, 2nd Corps, C, flesh wound lower 3rd left leg, water dressing;

Clohosey, Thomas, Pvt., 72nd PA, 2nd Corps, B, penetrating wound in privates, water dressing;

Cloninger, Jonas S., Cpl., 28th NC, Hill's Corps, CSA, B, right elbow, water dressing;

Cloom, James, Pvt., 75th PA, D, right shoulder, water dressing;

Clute, Christian H., Pvt., 134th NY, A, both feet & right hand, water dressing;

Coan, Andrew, Cpl., 82nd IL, A, gunshot left foot, sent to general hospital July 8;

Coe, Edward D., Pvt., 154th NY, F, mid 3rd left arm, water dressing;

Coe, William W., Sgt., 21st NC, Ewell's Corps, CSA, M, lower 3rd both thighs, water dressing, compound fracture & flesh wound;

Colgrove, Alva, Pvt., 33rd MA, H, chronic diarrhea;

Collins, John, Pvt., 17th CT, B, lower 3rd right leg & knee, water dressing;

Colvin, Otis, Cpl., 157th NY, K, left thumb & throat, water dressing;

Comstock, Samuel, Sgt., 17th CT, H, compound fracture upper 3rd left thigh, water dressing & splints;

Conger, Charles H., Cpl., 25th OH, K, right side & lung, water dressing;

Conklin, Andrew L., Cpl., 119th NY, K, penetrating wound right lung, water dressing;

Conner, George W., Pvt., 157th NY, D, left hip, died July 20, water dressing;

Conner, Samuel L., Pvt., 82nd OH, E, mid 3rd right thigh, died July 16, water dressing, resection;

Connor, Nicholas, Pvt., 136th NY, E, lower 3rd right thigh, water dressing, compound fracture;

Connor, Peter, Pvt., 136th NY, K, upper 3rd right thigh, water dressing;

Cooper, Samuel, Pvt., 82nd OH, G, mid 3rd left arm fracture amputation upper 3rd;

Cooper, William, Pvt., 82nd OH, A, left elbow, water dressing, fracture;

Coover, William, Pvt., 82nd OH, E, left arm & lung, water dressing;

Corcoran, Daniel, Cpl., 119th NY, I, upper 3rd left thigh, water dressing;

Cordier, Charles, Pvt., 107th OH, H, back contusion, water dressing;

Corl, Robert, Pvt., 134th NY, H, right ankle & left shoulder, died July 19, water dressing;

Corman, John, Pvt., 107th OH, I, right breast, water dressing;

Costin, John, Capt., 82nd OH, F, left hip, water dressing;

Cotton, William, Pvt., 134th NY, H, flesh wound right leg, water dressing;

Coverny, William, Pvt., 33rd MA, D, lower 3rd left arm, compound fracture, amputation;

Crabtree, Francis M., Pvt., 73rd OH, D, left side of face, water dressing;

Cramer, Daniel, Pvt., 107th OH, A, left hip, water dressing;

Cramer, Henry C., Sgt. 134th NY, F, left leg, water dressing;

Creighton, Robert, Pvt., 25th OH, A, mid 3rd right thigh & lower 3rd left thigh, water dressing;

Crisher, Peter, Pvt., 26th WI, C, gunshot, died July 12;

Criswell, Joshua E., 2nd Lt., 82nd OH, A, head, water dressing;

Crosby, Abijah, Sgt., 19th ME, 2nd Corps, C, left leg, died July 12, amputation mid 3rd left thigh;

Crum, Michael, Pvt., 82nd OH, F, mid 3rd both legs, water dressing;

Cullen, James, Pvt., 73rd OH, E, left middle finger, water dressing;

Cullinan, Jeremiah, Pvt., 136th NY, F, left side, water dressing;

Culver, Miles A., Pvt., 157th NY, E, left lung, died July 16, water dressing;

Culver, Otis, Pvt., 157th NY, H, flesh wound right knee, water dressing;

Cunningham, Joseph W., Cpl., 25th OH, I, left knee, died July 31, ball extracted;

Cupps, Samuel, Pvt., 82nd OH, F, lower 3rd right thigh, water dressing;

Curtis, Lafayette, Pvt., 157th NY, A, flesh wound upper 3rd left forearm, water dressing;

Cuthbertson, Thomas, Cpl., 25th OH, G, right foot, water dressing, toe broken;

Cutter, Frederick, Pvt., 33rd MA, E, back of head, water dressing;

Dag, John, Pvt., 74th PA, H, right shoulder, water dressing;

Dailey, Zachariah, Cpl., 25th OH, I, back of neck, water dressing;

Dale, John, Sgt., 119th NY, I, flesh wound privates, water dressing;

Damboch, Mathias, Pvt., 26th WI, B, mid 3rd right thigh, water dressing;

Dana, Philip, Pvt., 134th NY, E, right hip, died July 12, water dressing;

Danford, M. F., Pvt., 25th OH, H, face, water dressing;

Danner, Samuel, Pvt., 82nd OH, F, leg, water dressing;

Darling, Ira, Pvt., 157th NY, I, left foot, water dressing, fracture;

Darr, Franklyn, Pvt., 107th OH, A, left hip, died July 29, water dressing;

Daul, Bernhard, Pvt., 26th WI, G, back between shoulder blades, water dressing;

Davenport, Orville O., Pvt., 157th NY, E, mid 3rd right leg & right forearm, water dressing;

Davidson, Daniel, Pvt., 153rd PA, K, left hip, water dressing;

Davis, Austin, Pvt., 157th NY, A, upper 3rd right thigh, water dressing;

Davis, J. L., Pvt., 8th VA, Longstreet's Corps, CSA, D, left ankle, water dressing;

Davis, John, Pvt., 75th OH, K, mid 3rd right thigh & lower 3rd left thigh, died July 10, water dressing;

Davis, John C., Sgt., 119th NY, I, through the neck, water dressing;

Davis, L. M., Pvt., 82nd OH, C, left side, water dressing;

Davis, William B., 1st Sgt., 73rd OH, E, right shoulder, water dressing, contusion;

Deady, Jeremiah, Cpl., 82nd OH, G, lower 3rd right thigh, water dressing;

DeForrest, Henry W., Pvt., 17th CT, G, hip & privates, water dressing;

Deibold, Jacob, Pvt., 74th PA, G, upper 3rd right thigh, water dressing;

Deitrich, Jesse, Pvt., 153rd PA, G, left side, water dressing;

Delacroy, John, 2nd Lt., 20th NY State Militia (80th NY), 1st Corps, F, mid 3rd both thighs, water dressing;

Delancy, James F., Pvt., 82nd OH, F, right forearm, water dressing;

Dellanbach, George, Pvt., 26th WI, G, left side, water dressing;

Dennis, Morris, Pvt., 153rd PA, I, left arm, compound fracture, amputation;

Denton, Joseph, Pvt., 119th NY, H, right leg, water dressing;

Deshler, Charles H., Sgt., 75th OH, B, flesh wound mid 3rd right thigh, water dressing;

Detty, E. M., Pvt., 73rd OH, G, scrofula abscess in neck;

Deutschmann, Max, Sgt., 54th NY, I, both legs & right hand, water dressing;

Devany, Patrick, Pvt., 61st OH, B, middle finger left hand, water dressing;

Dewhirst, William S., Pvt., 17th CT, D, left side of head, water dressing;

Deyo, John G., Pvt., 157th NY, F, left ankle, water dressing;

Dickerson, Baruch, Sgt., 82nd OH, G, upper 3rd left leg, water dressing;

Dickerson, William, Pvt., 75th OH, K, great toe right foot, water dressing;

Diehl, Carl, Pvt., 119th NY, D, right hip, water dressing;

Diemer, John, Pvt., 74th PA, K, contusion left leg, water dressing;

Dietrich, Franz Louis, 1st Lt. & Adj., 58th NY, D, died July 3;

Dietrich, Nicholas, 107th OH, K, flesh wound right breast, water dressing;

Dietzel, John, Pvt., 45th NY, G, left groin, water dressing, contusion;

Dilbert, Gottlieb, Pvt., 119th NY, C, compound fracture, lower 3rd right hip, dressed with splints;

Dine, William, Pvt., 107th OH, D, flesh wound forearm, water dressing;

Dingman, Reuben, Cpl., 134th NY, E, flesh wound face & left foot, water dressing;

Dixon, Joseph, Pvt., 25th OH, C, right knee, water dressing;

Dixon, Levi, Pvt., 17th CT, H, knee, compound fracture, amputation lower 3rd thigh;

Doherty, George M., Capt., 73rd Ohio, F, left hip, died July 10, ball extracted;

Dorman, John S., Pvt., 157th NY, D, left shoulder, water dressing;

Dotterer, John N., Pvt., 153rd PA, C, flesh wound left side, water dressing;

Dougall, John E., Pvt., 134th NY, H, lower 3rd left hip, water dressing;

Douglas, Henry W., Cpl., 157th NY, E, flesh wound left forearm, water dressing;

Dove, Dennis, Pvt., 82nd OH, K, mid 3rd right leg, water dressing;

Dowd, James, Cpl., 157th NY, H, right leg, water dressing, compound fracture;

Dowell, A. J., Cpl., 73rd OH, G, left hip, water dressing, fracture;

Draper, William, Pvt., 157th NY, I, flesh wound right shoulder & right hip, water dressing;

Dreher, Anton, Pvt., 82nd IL, E, back contusion, water dressing;

Drehmer, George, Pvt., 136th NY, B, upper 3rd right thigh, water dressing;

Drippard, Reuben, Cpl., 25th OH, K, shoulder, water dressing;

Driscal, James, Cpl., 134th NY, E, right leg, water dressing;

Droeber, Henry, Pvt., 119th NY, B, left 3rd right thigh, water dressing;

Duboise, John, Pvt., 24th MI, 1st Corps, I, right lung, died July 22, water dressing;

Duehring, William, Pvt., 26th WI, B, upper 3rd right thigh, water dressing;

Dunbar, William J., Pvt., 153rd PA, G, bayonet wound in back, water dressing;

Duncan Albert A., Cpl., 27th PA, I, through right hand, water dressing, bones fractured;

Duncan, Stephen A., Cpl., 57th VA, Longstreet's Corps, CSA, A, thigh, water dressing;

Dye, Joseph, Sgt., 82nd OH, C, right foot, water dressing;

Dye, Samuel H., Pvt., 136th NY, I, upper 3rd arm & right hand, compound fracture & flesh wound, splints;

Dyke, William, Pvt., 157th NY, D, upper 3rd right arm, water dressing;

Eagan, Dennis, Sgt. 17th CT, I, right forearm, water dressing;

Eaton, Francis, Pvt., 157th NY, E, left ear & right leg, died July 8, water dressing;

Ebert, Nicolaus, Pvt., 119th NY, C, below crest ilium, piece of shell extracted;

Eckert, Edward, Pvt., 119th NY, D, left foot, water dressing;

Eckert, Max, 1st Lt., 68th NY, H, upper 3rd forearm, water dressing;

Eckstein, David, Sgt., 41st NY, B, mid 3rd forearm, water dressing;

Eddleblute, Jacob, Pvt., 82nd OH, I, flesh wound left wrist, water dressing;

Eddleblute, Lewis, Pvt., 82nd OH, I, fractured left cheek, bones extracted;

Edgecomb, Gordon, Pvt., 119th NY, I, flesh wound right leg, simple cerate;

Edmonds, John, Pvt., 1st Ohio Light Artillery, Artillery Reserve, H, left ankle, died July 16, compound fracture, amputation left leg mid 3rd;

Edwards, Thaddeus S., Pvt., 17th CT, C, upper 3rd right thigh, water dressing;

Eggleston, Julius, Pvt., 134th NY, E, flesh wound left leg, simple cerate;

Ehrig, Samuel, Pvt., 153rd PA, B, upper 3rd left thigh, water dressing;

Ehrmann, William, Pvt., 26th WI, H, mid 3rd left leg, water dressing;

Eichhorn, George, Pvt., 74th PA, K, right foot, water dressing;

Eickler, Adam, Pvt., 74th PA, A, flesh wound right hip, water dressing;

Eisler, John, Pvt., 107th OH, K, flesh wound mid 3rd left leg, water dressing;

Ellarson, Charles, Pvt., 134th NY, E, right knee, water dressing;

Ellenberger, Reuben, Sgt., 153rd PA, G, pleurisy, cupping & anodynes;

Ellenberger, Robert J., Pvt., 153rd PA, G, cholic, paroled prisoner;

Emmons, William H., Sgt., 75th OH, G, left breast & mid 3rd left arm (fractures of clavicle), water dressing;

Endres, Friedrich, Pvt., 41st NY, B, flesh wound head, water dressing;

Ensley, Philip, Pvt., 153rd PA, F, right foot, water dressing;

Ernst, Ruppert, Sgt., 68th NY, C, right foot, amputation 1st & 2nd toes;

Ervin, James, Pvt., 73rd PA, G, gunshot, died July 3;

Eskew, James, Pvt., 42nd MS, Hill's Corps, CSA, H, right hand & arm, water dressing;

Evans, Reuben, Pvt., 153rd PA, G, paroled prisoner;

Evans, Sampson B., Pvt., 73rd OH, C, left side & left thigh, water dressing;

Evans, Simeon, Pvt., 75th OH, H, left cheek & neck, water dressing;

Eyssenhardt, Adelbert, Pvt., 26th WI, A, knee joint, water dressing;

Faiss, Andreas, Pvt., 54th NY, C, left breast, water dressing;

Farr, Haskell, Pvt., 55th OH, G, both hips (fractures of femur), water dressing;

Farrell, James, Pvt., 119th NY, I, mid 3rd right leg, compound fracture, splints, amputation lower 3rd right thigh;

Fathaeur, Ernest H., Pvt., 107th OH, B, flesh wound left hand, resin cerate;

Faulkner, Dorr, Cpl., 136th NY, B, upper 3rd left arm, compound fracture, resection 4 inches of humerus;

Feeley, Daniel, Pvt., 33rd MA, I, head, water dressing;

Feist, Louis, Cpl., 74th PA, I, head, water dressing;

Feldkamp, Henry, Sgt., 107 OH, E, upper 3rd left thigh, water dressing;

Fenstermacher, Josiah, Cpl., 75th PA, C, great toe, water dressing, compound fracture;

Ferris, William H., Sgt., 75th OH, D, lower 3rd right thigh, water dressing;

Ferry, Francis H., Pvt., 17th CT, C, fracture right forearm, ball extracted;

Fiero, John M., Cpl., 136th NY, E, flesh wound right side, ball extracted;

Filsburg, Carl, Cpl., 119th NY, D, left thigh fracture, amputation mid 3rd;

Finkenbiner, Henry, Pvt., 107th OH, D, flesh wound both hips, simple cerate;

Fischer, Daniel, Pvt., 27th PA, C, through left side, ball extracted from left side;

Fischer, Edward, Sgt. Maj., 119th NY, right foot, water dressing;

Fisher, Harry, Pvt., 23rd PA, 6th Corps, G, left hand, water dressing;

Fisher, William, 1st Lt., 107th OH, F, left shoulder, water dressing;

Fitting, John, Pvt., 26th WI, G, upper 3rd forearm, water dressing;

Fitzke, August, Cpl., 45th NY, C, upper 3rd thigh, water dressing;

Flanagan, John, Pvt., 73rd OH, F, upper 3rd right thigh, water dressing;

Fleig (or Fleck), Adolph, Pvt., 68th NY, E, mid 3rd right leg, water dressing;

Fletcher, Thomas, Pvt., 2nd NY State Militia (82nd NY), 2nd Corps, I, right leg, compound fracture, amputation;

Flora, Harrison, Acting 2nd Lt., 107th OH, D, right breast, water dressing;

Flory, Milton, Pvt., 136th NY, I, right side, water dressing, contusion;

Flynn, James, Pvt., 17th CT, E, elbow, compound fracture, amputation lower 3rd left arm;

Foley, John W., Pvt., 157th NY, B, left side face, water dressing, contusion;

Folger, George F., Pvt., 33rd MA, I, upper 3rd right leg, water dressing;

Folmsbee, John, Pvt., 136th NY, G, left side & shoulder, water dressing;

Foote, Baldess, Pvt., 136th NY, B, flesh wound upper 3rd left leg, water dressing;

Foote, Joseph, Pvt., 17th CT, C, dysentery, anodynes;

Ford, Alonzo, 1st Lt., 75th OH, D, lower 3rd left leg, water dressing;

Ford, Henry, Pvt., 157th NY, A, lower 3rd right arm, water dressing;

Foskett, Milton, Pvt., 136th NY, E, flesh wound left shoulder, water dressing;

Fox, John D., Pvt., 157th NY, I, left forearm, water dressing;

Franksen, William, Sgt., 26th WI, D, back of neck, water dressing;

Frantz, Charles, Pvt., 153rd PA, I, right side, water dressing;

French, Wilson, Capt., 17th CT, G, right elbow joint, water dressing, fracture;

Frensz, Charles, Pvt., 26th WI, G, flesh wound left elbow & upper right thigh, water dressing;

Frensz, Christian, Cpl., 26th WI, G, left hip, water dressing;

Fresche, Charles, Pvt., 1st Ohio Light Artillery, I, left heel, water dressing;

Freund, Heinrich, Pvt., 119th NY, D, flesh wound above cheek ilium, water dressing;

Frey, Charles, Pvt., 73rd PA, A, flesh wound lower 3rd right leg & left ankle, water dressing;

Frey, Matthias, Sgt., 107th OH, B, left knee, died July 19, water dressing, fracture;

Friederici, Julius, Sgt., 119th NY, D, back, penetrating, died July 15, water dressing;

Friend, Peter, Pvt., 134th NY, I, flesh wound left forearm, water dressing;

Frosch, Theodore, Pvt., 119th NY, B, right side, water dressing, contusion;

Fuerstenberg, Hermann, 1st Lt., 26th WI, G, mid 3rd right leg, water dressing;

Fuller, Daniel H., Pvt., 157th NY, E, flesh wound upper 3rd left leg, water dressing;

Fulse, David, Pvt., 153rd PA, K, right side, water dressing;

Furlong, William, Pvt., 153rd PA, G, left eye, compound fracture;

Furman, Granville S., Pvt., 143rd PA, 1st Corps, K, left foot, water dressing;

Gabeler, Herman, Pvt., 41st NY, H, mid 3rd left leg, water dressing;

Gable, Jacob, Sgt., 27th PA, D, mid 3rd right thigh, water dressing;

Gabriel, Monroe, Sgt. 23rd NC, Ewell's Corps, CSA, K, head & left shoulder, water dressing;

Gaines, Richard T., Sgt., 28th VA, Longstreet's Corps, CSA, G, flesh wound right ankle, water dressing;

Gale, Morton, Pvt., 33rd MA, A, lower 3rd left arm, water dressing;

Gallagher, Daniel, Pvt., 119th NY, F, through the cheek, water dressing;

Gant, William, Pvt., 25th OH, I, mid 3rd right thigh, water dressing;

Gates, Frank E., 2nd Lt., 157th NY, G, flesh wound left groin, water dressing;

Gaus, Emil, Cpl., 68th NY, B, flesh wound lower 3rd right thigh, water dressing;

Gebauer, Carl, Cpl., 107th OH, K, back, died July 17, water dressing, compound fracture;

Geimer, Michael, Pvt., 136th NY, C, right thumb, amputation;

Geiser, Jacob, Sgt., 68th NY, C, flesh wound right side, water dressing;

Gephart, George W., Sgt., 73rd OH, E, flesh wound left thigh, water dressing;

Gerber, William, Pvt., 26th WI, C, both thighs, water dressing;

Gerhaeuser, John, Pvt., 26th WI, D, fracture right arm, amputation;

Gerlach, Philip, Pvt., 54th NY, H, face, water dressing;

Gesell, Henry, Pvt., 54th NY, D, head, died July 19, water dressing;

Getman, Jefferson T., Pvt., 157th NY, D, right side face, water dressing;

Getter, Charles, Pvt., 153rd PA, D, right knee, died July 18, water dressing;

Getter, Jacob, Pvt., 153rd PA, F, lower 3rd left thigh, water dressing;

Giese, Emil, Pvt., 82nd IL, D, compound fracture left leg, amputated;

Gifford, Emery, Pvt., 157th NY, D, right knee contusion;

Gilbert, Isaac W., Pvt., 17th CT, A, flesh wound back, water dressing;

Gilbert, S. P., Pvt., 57th VA, Longstreet's Corps, CSA, E, mid 3rd forearm, fracture of ulna, straight splint applied;

Gnau, Peter, Pvt., 107th OH, A, flesh wound right arm, sent to general hospital on July 10 (One Volunteer Carded Medical Record says he was at the XI Corps hospital and another says the VI Corps hospital.);

Goble, Jacob, Pvt., 153rd PA, G, flesh wound knee, ball extracted;

Goble, Oscar, Pvt., 153rd PA, G, upper 3rd left thigh & right knee, ball extracted from thigh;

Godskelk, Walson, Pvt., 82nd IL, I, fracture mid third right thigh, water dressing;

Goelz, Adam, Pvt., 26th WI, H, flesh wound left side neck & right cheek, water dressing;

Goess, John, Pvt., 26th WI, K, left hip & shoulder, water dressing;

Gohlke, Ludwig, Pvt., 5th WI, 6th Corps, C, left hand, water dressing;

Gomb, Barney, Pvt., 119th NY, D, flesh wound upper 3rd right thigh, water dressing;

Goodspeed, James H., Cpl., 75th OH, D, right hip, died July 19, ball extracted;

Goss, John, Pvt., 6th US Cavalry, Cavalry Corps, C, flesh wound lower breast, water dressing;

Gough, David, Pvt., 73rd OH, H, flesh wound upper 3rd right arm, water dressing;

Grace, William, Pvt., 17th CT, K, lower 3rd left thigh, water dressing;

Graham, Martin, Pvt., 136th NY, D, abdomen & right hand, water dressing;

Graves, George A., Capt., 22nd NC, Hill's Corps, CSA, G, upper 3rd right arm, water dressing;

Gray, John L., Cpl., 73rd OH, I, right breast, water dressing;

Green, Aaron, Pvt., 134th NY, A, left forearm, water dressing;

Green, Charles M., Sgt. 157th NY, B, mid 3rd right thigh, water dressing, compound fracture;

Gregg, James M., Pvt., 75th OH, E, contusion of hip, water dressing;

Greiner, George B., Cpl., 73rd OH, G, compound fracture mid 3rd left leg, died July 15, water dressing;

Greiner, John, Pvt., 27th PA, D, right cheek, water dressing;

Griffin, Cyrus, Pvt., 134th NY, C, flesh wound mid 3rd left thigh, water dressing;

Griffin, John L, Pvt., 75th OH, B, upper 3rd left leg, water dressing;

Griffin, Thomas A., Cpl., 107th OH, B, flesh wound mid 3rd right thigh, water dressing;

Grimes, William, Pvt., 73rd PA, D, mid 3rd right thigh, water dressing;

Grochowsky, Charles, Cpl., 26th WI, K, flesh wound through neck, water dressing;

Grode, Conrad, 2nd Lt., 26th WI, A, right shoulder, water dressing;

Groetter, Wilhelm, Pvt., 1st NY Light Artillery, I, flesh wound left thigh, water dressing;

Gropp, John, Cpl. 54th NY, D, both hips, water dressing;

Gross, Charles, Pvt., 153rd PA, H, left hip by bayonet, water dressing;

Gross, John Ludwig, Pvt., 26th WI, E, flesh wound right shoulder, water dressing;

Grube, Charles W., Pvt., 153rd PA, F, left foot, water dressing, fracture;

Gruntish, Jacob, Pvt., 55th OH, K, right knee, water dressing;

Guengerich, Daniel, Pvt., 74th PA, H, flesh wound lower 3rd both legs, water dressing;

Guffin, James, Pvt., 134th NY, G, flesh wound right side chest, water dressing;

Guhl, Jacob, Pvt., 54th NY, D, lower 3rd right arm, water dressing;

Gunther, Charles, Pvt., 134th NY, C, right thigh & mid 3rd left arm, water dressing;

Guttman, Peter, Sgt. 26th WI, D, flesh wound head & left foot, simple cerate;

Haas, Rudolph, Sgt., 68th NY, B, rifle bullet wound right leg, water dressing;

Haberstich, Bernhardt, Pvt., 74th PA, H, contusion right arm, water dressing;

Hacker, Henry, Pvt., 26th WI, F, bayonet wound calf of right leg, water dressing;

Haertley, Mathias, Pvt., 26th WI, E, flesh wound wrist & right hip, water dressing;

Haffermann, Charles, Pvt, 26th WI, G, flesh wound upper right leg, water dressing;

Hagar, Abijah, Pvt., 17th CT, A, flesh wound right hand, water dressing;

Hagen, Paul, Pvt., 119th NY, E, flesh wound left elbow, water dressing;

Hague, Samuel, Pvt., 119th NY, A, shell wound ankle, died July 16, piece of shell extracted;

Haines, David P., Sgt., 12th NH, 3rd Corps, K, contused abdomen, water dressing;

Hale, George, Cpl., 17th CT, E, left hip, water dressing;

Haley, Thomas, Pvt., 157th NY, E, compound fracture lower thigh, died July 15, amputation mid 3rd;

Hall, Samuel P., Sgt., 26th NC, Hill's Corps, CSA, C, flesh wound right thigh, ball extracted;

Halstead, Vernum, Pvt., 20th NY State Militia (80th NY), 1st Corps, G, compound fracture left hand, 4 fingers amputated;

Ham, John J., Pvt., 134th NY, I, flesh wound upper 3rd both thighs, water dressing;

Hamman, Gottfried, Pvt., 74th PA, K, shot through the head, died July 3;

Hammon, Jacob, Pvt., 75th OH, I, flesh wound mid 3rd thigh, water dressing;

Hammond, Calvin L., Pvt., 157th NY, K, flesh wound upper 3rd left thigh, water dressing;

Hand, Henry, Pvt., 27th PA, K, compound fracture hand, one finger amputated;

Handrahand, Martin, Pvt., 157th NY, A, flesh wound right hand, water dressing;

Hannan, John, Pvt., 74th PA, G, flesh wound left hip, water dressing;

Harbaugh, James, Pvt., 75th OH, C, shell wound right leg below knee, water dressing;

Harbison, Robert, Pvt., 134th NY, B, flesh wound right wrist, water dressing;

Hardesty, Israel, Cpl., 73rd OH, C, fracture through right foot, water dressing;

Hardy, Adolphus, Cpl., 4th US Artillery, G, contusion left foot, water dressing;

Hardy, Warren B., Pvt., 33rd MA, A, flesh wound mid 3rd left leg, water dressing;

Harper, John, Pvt., 73rd OH, I, left side privates & right side, water dressing;

Harriman, Charles, Pvt., 19th ME, 2nd Corps, E, flesh wound left leg, compound fracture both legs, died July 10, amputation left leg;

Harrington, John H. Pvt., 17th CT, G, ankle, water dressing;

Harrington, William, 1st Sgt., 157th NY, B, right hip & left foot, ball extracted from hip;

Hart, Joseph, Pvt., 157th NY, G, mid 3rd right thigh, water dressing;

Hartley, Benjamin F., Pvt., 75th OH, E, compound fracture lower 3rd right leg, died July 17, water dressing;

Hartmann, Adolph, Sgt., 41st NY, I, flesh wound upper right leg, water dressing;

Hartmann, William, Pvt., 26th WI, B, fracture right knee, water dressing;

Hartnagle, Joseph, Pvt., 54th NY, F, flesh wound left thigh, water dressing;

Hartshorn, Henry H., Pvt., 19th ME, 2nd Corps, D, contusion, left thigh, water dressing;

Hartz, Louis, Pvt., 41st NY, B, flesh wound right foot, water dressing;

Harvey, George, Pvt., 157th NY, B, flesh wound mid 3rd right leg, water dressing;

Harvey, Ralph Dayton, Pvt., 157th NY, K, face & right eye, water dressing;

Hasenboeler, David, Pvt., 107th OH, K, contusion from being run over, water dressing;

Haskell, Chauncey, Pvt, 82nd OH, F, compound fracture upper 3rd right leg, amputated above knee;

Hassman, Theobald, Cpl., 107th OH, I, flesh wound top left shoulder, water dressing;

Hatch, Albert, Pvt., 157th NY, I, fracture through head, died July 10;

Hawley, Hiram, Pvt., 157th NY, K, flesh wound lower 3rd both thighs, water dressing;

Hay, Andrew J., Sgt., 153rd PA, E, contusion, water dressing;

Hay, Thomas H., 1st Lt., 54th NY, B, compound fracture left ankle & left thigh, water dressing;

Hayes, George R., Pvt., 17th CT, D, fracture left leg & arm, water dressing;

Hayes, John L., Pvt., 17th CT, F, flesh wound right thigh, water dressing;

Hayes, M. J., Pvt., 26th WI, C, flesh wound right shoulder, water dressing;

Hays, Franklin L., Sgt., 157th NY, F, flesh wound upper 3rd left leg, water dressing;

Hazelton, Albert M., Sgt., 157th NY, C, compound fracture & flesh wound great toe & left thigh, water dressing;

Heald, Nathan, Pvt., 73rd OH, F, gunshot, died July 3;

Hearn, George, Pvt., 9th GA, Longstreet's Corps, CSA, G, compound fracture left side face, water dressing;

Heath, Ebenezer, Sgt., 154th NY, F, flesh wound back, water dressing;

Heath, Elijah, Sgt., 134th NY, F, flesh wound back, water dressing;

Heberling, William, Pvt., 153rd PA, D, flesh wound little toe left foot, back & left arm, water dressing;

Heeney, Joseph, Adj., 157th NY, lower 3rd knee, splints, bone splintered;

Heilig, Anton, Capt., 74th PA, H, compound fracture through head, died July 15, ball extracted;

Heimerdinger, Fred, Pvt., 68th NY, D, through face, water dressing;

Heims, Carl, Pvt., 68th NY, D, flesh wound left knee, water dressing;

Heinle, Fritz, Sgt., 74th PA, K, right leg & left lung, water dressing, straight splints, compound fracture;

Heinz, Jacob, Pvt., 26th WI, G, flesh wound left ankle, water dressing;

Heiss, William H., Pvt., 107th OH, B, flesh wound right ankle, water dressing;

Heldebrandt, Charles, Pvt., 134th NY, F, flesh wound head, simple cerate;

Heldeman, Joseph, Pvt., 153rd PA, K, flesh wound left shoulder, water dressing;

Heller, Carl, 1st Sgt., 54th NY, I, flesh wound right leg, water dressing;

Helwig, Adam, Pvt., 157th NY, I, flesh wound right foot, water dressing;

Hemmerling, John, Sgt., 107th OH, B, mid 3rd left leg, water dressing;

Henry, William, Pvt., 75th OH, E, flesh wound lower 3rd right thigh, water dressing;

Henson, John, Pvt., 73rd OH, E, flesh wound right thigh, water dressing;

Herbstritt, Charles, Sgt., 74th PA, D, flesh wound back of head, water dressing;

Herman, Stephen, Pvt., 153rd PA, H, flesh wound left hip, water dressing;

Hermonson, L. B., Pvt., 82nd IL, I, flesh wound abdomen, water dressing;

Herring, Carl, Pvt., 68th NY, G, flesh wound right foot, water dressing;

Herschfeld, Edward, Pvt., 73rd PA, G, flesh wound left foot, water dressing;

Hess, Abraham, Pvt., 153rd PA, G, flesh wound upper 3rd left hip, water dressing;

Hess, Lewis, Pvt., 26th WI, D, flesh wound left shoulder, water dressing;

Hess, Reuben, Pvt., 153rd PA, G, left knee, amputation lower 3rd thigh;

Hess, William H., Pvt., 153rd PA, G, flesh wound upper 3rd right leg, water dressing;

Hetzel, Heinrich, Pvt., 75th PA, A, compound fracture left leg & head, water dressing;

Hic, Walter M., Pvt., 157th NY, K, compound fracture right wrist, water dressing;

Hick, Frank, Sgt., 74th PA, G, flesh wound left knee, water dressing;

Hickey, John, Pvt., 28th MA, 2nd Corps, C, flesh wound upper 3rd right leg, water dressing;

Higgins, Norman, Pvt., 157th NY, E, flesh wound left forearm, water dressing;

Highman, Duncan, Pvt., 25th OH, B, flesh wound both legs & left ankle, water dressing;

Hilger, Joseph, Pvt., 26th WI, D, flesh wound mid 3rd right leg, water dressing;

Hilgers, Peter, Sgt., 73rd PA, D, gunshot, died July 5;

Hineline, Joel F., Pvt., 153rd PA, F, left knee, water dressing;

Hines, Samuel, Pvt., 61st OH, H, flesh wound right thumb & left knee, water dressing;

Hitzel, Julius, Pvt., 68th NY, E, right foot, compound fracture, amputation;

Hix, Dennis B., Pvt., 157th NY, K, flesh wound left hip, water dressing;

Hoagland, Peter, Pvt., 1st PA Light Artillery, 1st Corps, B, gunshot, died July 4;

Hoagland, Thomas, Pvt., 107th OH, D, compound fracture right hand, water dressing;

Hoessli, Daniel, Pvt., 82nd IL, E, left behind on account of general disability;

Hoffman, DeWitt, Pvt., 153rd PA, B, flesh wound upper 3rd left thigh, water dressing;

Hoffman, John, Cpl., 119th NY, G, flesh wound mid 3rd right arm, ball extracted;

Hoffman, John, Pvt., 74th PA, I, flesh wound in head, water dressing;

Hoffman, Peter, Cpl., 107th OH, B, fracture left knee, amputation lower 3rd left leg;

Hoffmann, Augustus, Pvt., 74th PA, E, compound fracture left shoulder, water dressing;

Hogan, Michael, Pvt., 134th NY, F, compound fracture mid 3rd right leg, water dressing;

Hoisington, Samuel, Pvt., 75th OH, D, flesh wound right forearm, water dressing;

Holden, Henry F., Pvt., 55th NC, Hill's Corps, CSA, I, flesh wound left thigh & contusion back, water dressing;

Holland, T. C. (Thomas), 1st Lt., 28th VA, Longstreet's Corps, CSA, G, flesh wound left cheek & neck, water dressing;

Hollinger, William, Pvt., 82nd OH, B, flesh wound upper 3rd left thigh, water dressing;

Hollinger, Xavier, Pvt., 74th PA, E, flesh wound upper 3rd right forearm, water dressing;

Holloway, Jerome C., Sgt., 73rd OH, C, compound fracture upper 3rd left thigh, large piece of shell extracted;

Holm, Jeremiah J., 1st Sgt., 107th OH, G, compound fracture right knee & lower 3rd left thigh, shell extracted from left leg;

Holzbrink, Rudolph, 1st Sgt., 119th NY, E, flesh wound left foot, water dressing;

Hooper, James B., Sgt., 157th NY, G, flesh wound right shoulder, water dressing;

Hopkins, James, Pvt., 33rd MA, C, compound fracture lower 3rd right leg, water dressing;

Horn, Herman, Pvt., 82nd IL, C, rheumatism;

Hornaday, William, Pvt., 75th OH, G, shell wound above right eye, water dressing;

Horsey, John, Sgt., 73rd OH, D, flesh wound in head, water dressing;

Hosley, James A., Pvt., 33rd MA, E, compound fracture mid right forearm, water dressing;

Hough, Broughton, Pvt., 157th NY, K, left hip, died July 13, water dressing, ball not extracted;

Hubbard, Michael, Pvt., 134th NY, E, flesh wound face & shell contusion back, water dressing;

Huber, Adolphus, Pvt., 41st NY, D, flesh wound mid 3rd left forearm, water dressing;

Huffman, Wesley, Pvt., 157th NY, D, shell contusion mid left leg, water dressing;

Hughes, George, Pvt., 73rd OH, D, flesh wound left hip, water dressing;

Hughes, William, Pvt., 26th WI, G, flesh wound right foot, water dressing;

Hull, Daniel V., Pvt., 136th NY, G, flesh wound mid 3rd right thigh, died July 12, water dressing;

Hull, George, Pvt., 17th CT, G, diarrhea;

Hull, John, Pvt., 23rd NC, Ewell's Corps, CSA, B, flesh wound lower 3rd left thigh, water dressing;

Hummel, Jacob, Pvt., 27th PA, I, compound fracture left elbow, amputated above elbow;

Hummel, Jacob, Pvt., 153rd PA, F, contusion, water dressing;

Hunfeld, Augustus, Pvt., 41st NY, C, flesh wound right side, water dressing;

Hunk, Fritz, Pvt., 74th NY, C, gunshot, died July 8;

Hunkel, Philip, Pvt., 26th WI, B, mid 3rd right leg, water dressing;

Hunt, Benjamin, Pvt., 57th VA, Longstreet's Corps, CSA, G, compound fracture mid 3rd left arm, water dressing, resection;

Hunzicker, Rudolph, Pvt., 26th WI, C, mid 3rd right thigh, water dressing;

Hutzelman, Michael, Pvt., 107th OH, C, compound fracture upper 3rd right arm & hand, amputation arm & finger;

Hyler, James R., Sgt., 25th OH, H, mid right leg, water dressing;

Ingmire, Thomas, Pvt., 73rd OH, A, flesh wound mid 3rd right arm, ball extracted;

Ingram, James, 2nd Lt., 20th NC, Ewell's Corps, CSA, H, flesh wound small of back, water dressing;

Ira, John, 2nd Lt., 73rd OH, H, flesh wound mid 3rd left leg, water dressing;

Isenhour, Jerome B., Cpl., 136th NY, K, flesh wound wrist & forehead, water dressing;

Jackson, Jeremiah, Pvt., 134th NY, E, compound fracture upper 3rd right forearm, water dressing;

Jagemann, Henry, Cpl., 74th PA, G, head & mid 3rd thigh, water dressing;

Jahns, Albert, Pvt., 26th WI, B, flesh wound left shoulder, water dressing;

Jansen, Ludwig, Musician, 54th NY, H, flesh wound lower & mid 3rd left thigh, simple cerate;

Jenner, Nicholas, Cpl., 26th WI, E, flesh wound mid 3rd left arm, water dressing;

Johnson, Benjamin, Pvt., 134th NY, B, flesh wound right hip & upper 3rd left thigh, water dressing;

Johnson, David, Pvt., 1st MN, 2nd Corps, B, flesh wound lower 3rd right thigh, water dressing;

Johnson, George, Pvt., 153rd PA, A, rheumatism;

Johnson, James H., Pvt., 23rd NC, Ewell's Corps, CSA, K, flesh wound left side, water dressing;

Johnson, Jerry, Cpl., 157th NY, C, gunshot, died July 6;

Johnson, John, Pvt., 153rd PA, A, flesh wound lower 3rd left leg, water dressing; (amputation);

Johnson, John, Pvt., 153rd PA, K, compound fracture mid 3rd left arm, died July 22, amputation arm;

Johnson, Simeon, Pvt., 73rd OH, I, flesh wound left foot, water dressing;

Jones, Deloss T., Sgt., 157th NY, E, flesh wound mid 3rd left forearm, water dressing;

Jones, Martin, 1st Sgt., 134th NY, G, flesh wound mid 3rd thigh, water dressing;

Jones, Stephen, Pvt., 42nd MS, Hill's Corps, CSA, C, right groin, water dressing;

Jones, William, Pvt., 82nd OH, F, flesh wound left knee, water dressing;

Jones, William R., Pvt., 157th NY, C, compound fracture left hand forefinger, amputation;

Jordan, Frank, Pvt., 4th US Artillery, G, concussion head & abdomen;

Joslin, George W., Cpl., 119th NY, E, flesh wound mid 3rd left leg, water dressing;

Joyner, James, Cpl., 157th NY, E, flesh wound right lung, water dressing;

Juenger, Sigmund, 2nd Lt., 26th WI, A, compound fracture thumb left hand, water dressing;

Juengling, Frederick, Pvt., 107th OH, C, flesh wound left shoulder, water dressing;

Julian, John F., Pvt., 14th CT, 2nd Corps, D, compound fracture head, died July 6;

Jura, Wenzel, Pvt., 26th WI, F, fracture right thumb & forefinger, water dressing;

Justice, Purnell, Pvt., 73rd OH, C, fracture toe of right foot, water dressing;

Kahl, Claus, Sgt. Maj., 75th PA, shoulder & mid 3rd left leg fractured, amputation;

Kappel, John, Pvt., 1st NY Light Artillery, I, flesh wound left shoulder, water dressing;

Kastner, Charles, Pvt., 107th OH, H, flesh wound left hand & left foot, water dressing;

Kaufmann, Christian, Pvt., 68th NY, E, elbow right arm, compound fracture, amputation;

Keeler, Eli J., Pvt., 17th CT, G, contusion shoulder & hip, water dressing;

Kehrein, Eduard, Pvt., 26th WI, D, flesh wound upper 3rd left thigh, water dressing;

Keller, Julius, Cpl., 45th NY, A, shell privates, water dressing;

Kelley, Charles, Sgt., 12th NH, 3rd Corps, F, rheumatism;

Kelley, John, Pvt., 157th NY, I, flesh wound head & shoulder, water dressing;

Kelly, John M., Pvt., 1st Ohio Light Artillery, K, penetrating wound in back, water dressing;

Kelly, William, Pvt., 73rd OH, H, flesh wound right thigh, water dressing;

Kempf, John, Pvt., 26th WI, F, flesh wound both hips, water dressing;

Kent, James, Cpl., 11th VA, Longstreet's Corps, CSA, G, flesh wound upper 3rd left leg, water dressing;

Kent, Oscar D., Pvt., 157th NY, H, flesh wound left knee, water dressing;

Kern, Charles, Sgt., 75th PA, I, flesh wound mid 3rd left thigh, water dressing;

Kerns, Henry, Pvt., 73rd OH, A, right shoulder, water dressing;

Kerns, Samuel, Pvt., 153rd PA, C, flesh wound left wrist, water dressing;

Kerr, Richard, Cpl., 154th NY, D, flesh wound right side of head, water dressing;

Ketelmann, John, Pvt., 68th NY, G, compound fracture left leg, water dressing;

Kieffer, Joseph, Musician, 107th OH, D, flesh wound through left side of face, water dressing;

Killian, William, Pvt., 23rd NC, Ewell's Corps, CSA, F, compound fracture right ankle, water dressing;

Kincade, Charles, Pvt., 157th NY, E, flesh wound left side of right leg & midarm, water dressing;

King, Lawrence, Pvt., 134th NY, G, flesh wound upper 3rd right arm, water dressing;

King, Samuel L., Musician, 136th NY, K, flesh wound left foot, water dressing;

Kinney, William H., Pvt., 157th NY, H, flesh wound back of neck, water dressing;

Kirby, John, Pvt., 82nd OH, C, flesh wound mid 3rd left thigh, water dressing;

Kircher, Charles, Pvt., 82nd IL, D, rheumatism;

Kirkland, William, Pvt., 82nd OH, K, flesh wound mid 3rd left arm, water dressing;

Kirksey, John, Pvt., 11th MS, Hill's Corps, CSA, E, flesh wound right shoulder & left cheek, water dressing;

Kissinger, George, Pvt., 26th WI, A, flesh wound left hand, water dressing;

Kissinger, Philip, Cpl., 26th WI, A, flesh wound right hip, water dressing;

Kittle, James E., Cpl., 134th NY, A, left knee, water dressing;

Kleckner, Jacob H., Pvt., 53rd PA, 2nd Corps, I, upper 3rd right arm, compound fracture, amputation;

Klein, Henry, Cpl., 107th OH, C, flesh wound mid 3rd of thigh, water dressing;

Klein, Michael, Pvt., 107th OH, C, flesh wound mid 3rd right arm, water dressing;

Klein, Nicolaus, Sgt., 54th NY, B, left shoulder, water dressing;

Kleppinger, Joseph, Pvt., 153rd PA, D, gunshot, died July 7;

Kletzin, Abraham, Pvt., 26th WI, F, flesh wound upper right forearm, water dressing;

Kline, Barna, Pvt., 55th OH, C, shell left shoulder, water dressing;

Klingaman, Henry, Cpl., 107th OH, H, upper 3rd right leg, water dressing;

Klinker, Henry, Cpl., 26th WI, C, mid 3rd left leg, compound fracture, dressed with splints;

Knapp, Epaphroditus W., Pvt., 157th NY, F, minnie ball privates, water dressing;

Knapp, William S., 1st Lt., 17th CT, F, enlargement of liver;

Knecht, Edwin F., Pvt., 153rd PA, F, compound fracture upper 3rd right leg, splints;

Knecht, Stephen, Pvt., 153rd PA, F, contusion left knee, water dressing;

Knighton, James, Pvt., 73rd OH, G, (penetrating) flesh wound right side, water dressing;

Knowlden, Mark A., 1st Sgt., 75th OH, K, flesh wound left foot, water dressing;

Knust, Frederick, Pvt., 136th NY, K, flesh wound mid 3rd of arm, water dressing;

Koddermann, Julius, Pvt., 54th NY, C, ribs broken & flesh wound, water dressing;

Koenig, John, Pvt., 153rd PA, A, flesh wound face, arm & both legs, water dressing;

Kohn, Christopher, Pvt., 134th NY, F, flesh wound left side chest, left hip & wrist, water dressing;

Koken, John, Pvt., 153rd PA, F, flesh wound right breast & lung, water dressing;

Kopp, George, Pvt., 74th PA, E, left side, water dressing;

Korte, Heinrich, Pvt., 26th WI, D, flesh wound right side & right breast, water dressing;

Kraus, John, Pvt., 68th NY, K, flesh wound right foot, water dressing;

Kreisher, Fred W., 1st Sgt., 107th OH, A, fracture left shin bone & left thigh, water dressing;

Krenscher, Peter, Pvt., 26th WI, C, flesh wound left side, died July 12, water dressing;

Kridler, Wesley, Pvt., 82nd OH, A, fracture mid 3rd right thigh, water dressing;

Kroehl, John, Pvt., 68th NY, H, flesh wound upper 3rd right thigh, water dressing;

Krueger, Henry, Pvt., 74th PA, D, flesh wound right forearm, & right foot, water dressing;

Krueger, Gottlieb, Pvt., 26th WI, F, flesh wound calf left leg, water dressing;

Krueger, William, Sgt., 74th PA, B, flesh wound mid 3rd right thigh, water dressing;

Kuckhan, Bernhard, Pvt., 26th WI, B, flesh wound both forearms, water dressing;

Kuhlmann, Charles, Pvt., 26th WI, B, flesh wound left hand, amputation little finger;

Kuhn, Andreas, Cpl., 82nd IL, A, flesh wound great toe left foot, simple cerate;

Kuhn, George, Pvt., 136th NY, I, flesh wound right breast and left shoulder, ball not extracted;

Kuhn, Peter, Pvt., 26th WI, G, compound fracture lower 3rd right leg, died July 9, splints;

Kummer, Arnold, Capt., 68th NY, G, flesh wound lower 3rd right thigh, water dressing;

Kuneck, Anton, Cpl., 74th PA, G, flesh wound in cheek, water dressing;

Kunz, Albert, Pvt., 26th WI, F, flesh wound mid 3rd both thighs, water dressing;

Landon, Emlin, Pvt., 107th OH, H, flesh wound head, water dressing;

Langenberg, Henry, Sgt, 68th NY, I, flesh wound upper 3rd right thigh & shoulder, water dressing;

Lantz, William, Pvt., 153rd PA, F, flesh wound hip, water dressing;

Laraba, Jonathan, Pvt., 75th OH, E, compound fracture lower 3rd left leg, amputation mid 3rd;

Larkin, George, Sgt., 61st OH, B, flesh wound right forearm & abdomen, water dressing;

Laubli, Jacob, Asst. Surg., 68th NY, compound fracture foot, water dressing;

Lavery, James, Pvt., 136th NY, E, penetrating wound left side of head, water dressing;

Layton, William C., Sgt., 82nd OH, E, flesh wound lower 3rd right thigh, water dressing;

Leake, Elisha L., Pvt., 73rd OH, G, fracture jaw right side mouth & right eye, died July 8;

Leapold, Hirish, Pvt., 82nd IL, C, contusion left leg, water dressing;

Lebal, John, Pvt., 26th WI, F, flesh wound right knee, water dressing;

Lebold, John, Pvt., 25th OH, A, flesh wound right hip, ball not extracted, water dressing;

Leeper, Franklin W., Pvt., 28th NC, Hill's Corps, CSA, B, contusion mid 3rd forearm, water dressing;

Lees, Edward, 2nd Lt., 17th CT, E, compound fracture lower 3rd left leg, amputation mid 3rd;

Leffler, John A., Pvt., 107th OH, F, flesh wound upper 3rd right thigh, simple cerate;

Leger, John, Pvt., 68th NY, H, compound fracture lower 3rd left thigh, water dressing;

Legrand, Jones, 1st Sgt., 134th NY, I, severe flesh wound genitals, left testicle removed;

Leifer, Frederick, Cpl., 107th OH, A, flesh wound left leg, simple cerate;

Lesher, William, Pvt., 153rd PA, K, neuralgia, not wounded;

Lester, Alanson, Pvt., 134th NY, H, flesh wound right shoulder, water dressing;

Light, David, Pvt., 17th CT, I, flesh wound left breast, left hand & thigh, water dressing;

Light, William, Pvt., 27th PA, K, compound fracture little finger, water dressing;

Lightle, James, Pvt., 73rd OH, I, compound fracture left hand, 3 fingers amputated;

Lilly, Solomon, Pvt., 153rd PA, H, flesh wound right shoulder & side, water dressing;

Lines, Samuel D., Cpl., 134th NY, C, flesh wound upper 3rd left arm, water dressing;

Link, Charles, Sgt., 45th NY, C, upper 3rd both legs;

Link, Peter, Pvt., 134th NY, K, flesh wound mid 3rd left hip, died July 10, water dressing;

Litle, William, Pvt., 107th OH, D, consumption;

Litz, Frederick, Pvt., 136th NY, E, fracture lower 3rd left forearm, splints;

Lober, George, Sgt., 74th PA, H, flesh wound left foot, water dressing;

Lock, David B., Pvt., 146th NY, 5th Corps, H, chronic diarrhea;

Lockwood, Joseph, Pvt., 17th CT, B, paroled prisoner;

Logeman, Henry, Pvt., 82nd IL, C, flesh wound head, water dressing;

Lohner, Theodore, Pvt., 134th NY, K, flesh wound mid 3rd left thigh & right knee, water dressing;

Long, William N., Pvt., 25th OH, B, flesh wound left hand, water dressing;

Lopendall, Nicholas, Pvt., 107th OH, G, flesh wound right arm, water dressing;

Lorenz, John, Pvt., 73rd PA, D, flesh wound ankle, water dressing;

Lovall, Stephen, Pvt., 25th OH, I, compound fracture lower 3rd right thigh, pieces of bone extracted;

Love, George, Pvt., 157th NY, D, flesh wound mid 3rd left arm, water dressing;

Lovejoy, Ira, Pvt., 33rd MA, A, fever, not wounded;

Luce, Edwin, Pvt., 136th NY, B, flesh wound right side foot, water dressing;

Ludwig, William, Pvt., 68th NY, H, flesh wound upper 3rd left arm, water dressing;

Ludwig, William, Pvt., 75th PA, I, flesh wound right side, water dressing;

Luenberger, Samuel, Pvt., 107th OH, I, flesh wound upper 3rd leg, water dressing;

Lynch, Edward, Sgt. Maj., 3rd US, 5th Corps, flesh wound upper 3rd both thighs, water dressing;

Lyon, Joseph H., Cpl., 157th NY, C, flesh wound left hip, simple cerate;

Madden, Francis, Pvt., 40th NY, H, sent to general hospital on July 8;

Madden, John, Pvt., 2nd US Light Artillery, Cavalry Corps, B, burned in face, left side & hands, water dressing;

Maddox, Matthew W., Pvt., 73rd OH, G, flesh wound calf left leg, water dressing;

Mahan, Abner A., Pvt., 57th VA, Longstreet's Corps, CSA, E, compound fracture cheek & nose, water dressing;

Mahler, Francis, Col., 75th PA, abdomen, died July 5;

Maier, Jacob, Pvt., 75th PA, D, flesh wound sole of right foot, water dressing;

Maley, Pat, Pvt., 73rd OH, F, flesh wound right thigh, water dressing;

Malone, Joseph E., Cpl., 136th NY, F, flesh wound right wrist, water dressing;

Manly, Charles H., Pvt., 1st MI, 5th Corps, A, fracture left arm, water dressing; (Records aren't clear. Information likely is correct.)

Mann, William H., Pvt., 153rd PA, K, exhaustion;

Manning, Nathaniel J., Capt., 25th OH, K, flesh wound right thigh, ball extracted;

Maple, Reason. B., Pvt., 73rd OH, G, flesh wound privates, water dressing;

Marbeck, Anton, Pvt., 75th PA, G, flesh wound left side, water dressing;

Marble, Martin, Cpl., 157th NY, D, flesh wound left side face, water dressing;

March, William, Pvt., 13th VT, 1st Corps, D, (cannon ball through both legs), died July 3;

Marsh, Milton, 1st Lt., 82nd OH, G, flesh wound mid 3rd right leg, water dressing;

Marsh, Thomas, Pvt., 17th CT, D, flesh wound upper 3rd left shoulder, water dressing;

Marshall, Barney, Pvt., 17th CT, D, flesh wound back of neck, ball extracted;

Marshall, James, Pvt., 73rd OH, G, compound fracture mid 3rd left arm, amputation upper 3rd;

Marsteller, William, Pvt., 153rd PA, F, flesh wound mid 3rd right arm, water dressing;

Martin, George, W., 1st Lt., 25th OH, B, compound fracture right arm, amputation;

Martin, John, Pvt., 54th NY, G, flesh wound left 2nd finger;

Martin, Rudolph, Pvt., 119th NY, C, flesh wound breast, water dressing;

Martling, Ralph, 2nd Sgt., 119th NY, F, compound fracture upper 3rd left arm, amputation upper 3rd;

Marx, Christopher, Pvt., 41st NY, D, flesh wound upper 3rd left forearm, water dressing;

Maschauer, Joseph, 2nd Lt., 26th WI, H, left groin & right thigh flesh wound, water dressing;

Masterson, Thomas J., Pvt., 61st OH, G, flesh wound, water dressing;

Mathes, Philip, Pvt., 26th WI, H, fracture left heel, water dressing;

May, Philip, Pvt., 107th OH, I, flesh wound left groin, water dressing;

Mayberry, Andrew, Cpl., 20th ME, 5th Corps, D, gunshot iliac region, died July 3;

Mayers, Simon, Pvt., 73rd OH, D, flesh wound upper 3rd forearm, water dressing;

McCarter, Charles, Pvt., 157th NY, B, flesh wound right leg, water dressing;

McCarty, Nathan, Pvt., 73rd OH, D, flesh wound right hand, water dressing;

McClaflin, Edwin M., 1st Ohio Light Artillery, I, flesh wound left hip, water dressing;

McCoy, Theodore, Sgt., 119th NY, F, flesh wound mid 3rd left arm, water dressing;

McCracken, Uriah, Cpl., 153rd PA, G, gunshot, died July 8;

McCurley, Edward, Pvt., 157th NY, F, flesh wound right forearm, water dressing;

McDargh, Joseph, Pvt., 157th NY, E, flesh wound upper 3rd right leg, water dressing;

McDermot, John, Sgt., 140th NY, 5th Corps, K, flesh wound left leg, simple cerate;

McDermot, Matthew, Pvt., 73rd PA, E, mid left leg, water dressing;

McDevitt, Fenton P., Cpl., 99th PA, 3rd Corps, H, mid 3rd left leg, water dressing, bone slightly injured;

McDonough, Henry, Sgt., 17th CT, E, flesh wound upper 3rd thigh, water dressing;

McElroy, Charles, Pvt., 17th CT, K, flesh wound mid left leg & right side, water dressing;

McElroy, William, Cpl., 82nd OH, H, right leg broken, splints;

McGee, William, Pvt., 73rd OH, D, flesh wound right side of neck, water dressing;

McHenry, Michael, Pvt., 1st US Light Artillery, 2nd Corps, I, flesh wound left side head, water dressing;

McHugh, John, Pvt., 17th CT, E, flesh wound left knee & upper 3rd right leg, water dressing;

McIntee, Arthur, Pvt., 33rd MA, H, compound fracture left hand, water dressing;

McIntyre, John, Cpl., 61st OH, D, flesh wound left hip, water dressing;

McKay, Fred, Cpl., 17th CT, K, flesh wound back of head, ball extracted;

McKinney, James, Pvt., 73rd OH, H, flesh wound upper 3rd right thigh, water dressing;

McKinney, Lanson, Pvt., 107th OH, D, shell flesh wound right cheek, water dressing;

McKinny, Jacob, Pvt., 107th OH, D, aque (aqueous humour);

McKirahan, John, Cpl., 25th OH, A, flesh wound left hip, simple cerate;

McLaughlin, Levi, Pvt., 25th OH, H, flesh wound right thigh, water dressing;

McMillen, Alexander G., Sgt., 134th NY, F, flesh wound left arm, water dressing;

McMurrin, William J., Pvt., 134th NY, A, compound fracture left thigh, water dressing;

McNutt, Henry J., Pvt., 75th OH, B, fracture left shoulder blade, water dressing;

McPeck, George M., Sgt., 82nd OH, H, flesh wound mid 3rd forearm, water dressing;

Meiners, Heinrich, Cpl., 26th WI, H, flesh wound right hip, water dressing;

Melchior, Leopold, 2nd Lt., 26th WI, D, flesh wound upper 3rd right leg & right hip, water dressing;

Mellor, Thomas, Cpl., 134th NY, F, fracture fibula upper 3rd leg, water dressing;

Mencer, William, Pvt., 1st PA Light Artillery, Artillery Reserve, G, gunshot;

Mendin, George A., 1st Sgt., 25th OH, B, right arm amputated above elbow;

Mericle, Albert, Cpl., 154th NY, H, flesh wound & fracture right leg & abdomen, died July 10;

Messing, Gottlieb, Pvt., 119th NY, E, right shoulder, water dressing;

Metzel, Alexander, Sgt. Maj., 26th WI, flesh wound, water dressing;

Metzner, Gottlieb, Pvt., 26th WI, G, right shoulder, water dressing, fracture;

Meyer, Jacob, Pvt., 74th PA, H, flesh wound head, water dressing;

Meyer, Joseph, Capt., 74th PA, G, compound fracture 3 fingers left hand, water dressing;

Meyer, Peter, Pvt., 107th OH, G, flesh wound wrist & forehead, water dressing;

Meyers, Peter, Sgt., 82nd IL, B, flesh wound mid 3rd right thigh, water dressing;

Michael, Simon, Pvt., 153rd PA, I, flesh wound upper 3rd right leg, water dressing;

Michel, Charles, Pvt., 54th NY, E, flesh wound left forearm & hand, water dressing;

Mick, Simeon, Pvt., 73rd OH, I, flesh wound left shoulder, water dressing;

Mickle, George, Pvt., 134th NY, G, flesh wound left thigh, simple cerate;

Mignell, A. H., Bugler, 82nd IL, D, fracture lower 3rd forearm, amputation mid 3rd;

Miller, Albert, Pvt., 13th NY Light Artillery, dysentery;

Miller, Charles, Pvt., 73rd PA, D, contusion left foot, water dressing;

Miller, Charles, Pvt., 153rd PA, D, flesh wound left side of neck, water dressing;

Miller, Charles H., Pvt., 157th NY, F, flesh wound hip & back, water dressing;

Miller, Christian, Pvt., (possibly 7th US, 5th Corps), E, penetrating wound left lung, water dressing;

Miller, David A., 2nd Lt., 75th OH, H, flesh wound left hip, water dressing;

Miller, Emerick, Pvt., 73rd PA, D, flesh wound mid 3rd thighs, water dressing;

Miller, Henry, Cpl., 26th WI, G, flesh wound face & neck, water dressing;

Miller, Henry, Cpl., 119th NY, C;

Miller, Henry A., Pvt., 153rd PA, B, gunshot, died July 5;

Miller, John, Pvt., 153rd PA, H, flesh wound right thigh, water dressing;

Miller, John H., Pvt., 134th NY, I, flesh wound head, simple cerate;

Miller, Matthew, Cpl., 82nd OH, G, flesh wound abdomen, water dressing;

Miller, Reuben, Pvt., 153rd PA, K, flesh wound left shoulder, water dressing;

Miller, Warren, Pvt., 73rd OH, B, compound fracture right shoulder, left arm & side (penetrating), water dressing;

Miller, William, Pvt., 136th NY, I, flesh wound back of neck, water dressing;

Miller, William, Pvt., 25th OH, G, left knee joint, died July 22, water dressing;

Miller, William, Pvt., 153rd PA, E, compound fracture mid 3rd left leg, died July 9, amputation;

Miller, William, Pvt., 157th NY, G, flesh wound hand, water dressing;

Millhollan, Charles, Pvt., 25th OH, K, flesh wound left thigh & upper left arm, water dressing;

Milton, John, Sgt., 25th OH, H, bone fracture mid right forearm, ball extracted;

Miner, Clinton H., Pvt., 136th NY, A, flesh wound mid 3rd right forearm, water dressing;

Miner, George W., Pvt., 157th NY, C, flesh wound right shoulder, simple cerate;

Minster, John, Cpl., 153rd PA, H, flesh wound left shoulder, water dressing;

Mitchell, Jacob, Pvt., 55th OH, C, flesh wound lower 3rd left leg & upper 3rd right arm, died July 30, water dressing;

Mitchell, William, Capt., 82nd OH, H, fracture right ankle & right arm, ball extracted;

Monteith, James, Pvt., 17th CT, E, contused right breast, water dressing;

Montgomery, Henry, Sgt., 157th NY, F, compound fracture mid 3rd left leg, water dressing;

Montgomery, John, Sgt., 61st OH, K, flesh wound left hand, water dressing;

Moody, William, 3rd Lt., 2nd MS, Hill's Corps, CSA, A, flesh wound neck, water dressing;

Moon, William W., Pvt., 134th NY, A, flesh wound right hand 3rd finger, simple cerate;

Moore, John, 4th Sgt., 5th AL, Ewell's Corps, CSA, E, flesh wound upper 3rd left thigh, water dressing;

Moore, William S., Asst. Surg., 61st OH, flesh wound upper 3rd left thigh, died July 5, water dressing;

Moose, John J., Pvt., 25th OH, B, mid 3rd right arm broken, splints;

Morell, Louis, Sgt., 119th NY, D, flesh wound left knee & back, water dressing;

Morgan, Moses, Cpl., 4th MI, 5th Corps, G, gunshot right leg, sent to general hospital on July 8;

Morrow, Samuel, Pvt., 75th OH, K, upper 3rd left thigh, water dressing;

Moser, James W., Cpl., 153rd PA, D, not wounded, recaptured prisoner;

Moser, Joseph, Pvt., 153rd PA, D, tarsal bones injured right foot, water dressing;

Mosher, George, Pvt., 136th NY, H, compound fracture mid left arm, water dressing;

Mott, Thomas B., Cpl., 119th NY, H, flesh wound both thighs, water dressing;

Moyer, William, Pvt., 153rd PA, I, flesh wound right hip, water dressing;

Muckley, Michael, Pvt., 107th OH, D, ankle sprain, water dressing;

Mueller, Jacob, Pvt., 75th PA, H, gunshot right hand, sent to general hospital on July 8, amputation 1st finger;

Mueller, Julius, Pvt., 26th WI, B, flesh wound right shoulder, water dressing;

Mueller, Martin, Pvt., 107th OH, C, flesh wound upper 3rd left thigh, water dressing;

Muir, Lyndock B., Sgt., 16th MI, 5th Corps, E, gunshot left side slightly, sent to general hospital on July 8;

Muller, Christian, Pvt., 45th NY, F, flesh wound back, water dressing;

Muller, Edward, Pvt., 68th NY, C, flesh wound lower 3rd right hip, water dressing;

Muller, Henry, Pvt., 41st NY, B, right hip & mid 3rd right arm, died Aug. 4, water dressing;

Muller, John, Pvt., 74th PA, E, flesh wound left side, water dressing;

Multer, Joseph, Pvt., 134th NY, C, flesh wound left leg, water dressing;

Munch, Gustavus, Sgt., 68th NY, C, flesh wound upper 3rd right leg, water dressing;

Mundloch, Hubert, Pvt., 26th WI, K, flesh wound lower 3rd left leg & upper 3rd right hip, water dressing;

Munger, Bennett, Capt., 44th NY, 5th Corps, C, gunshot left thigh & groin, sent to general hospital on July 8;

Munroe, John, Sgt., 4th US Light Artillery, G, penetrating wound right lung, water dressing;

Murphy, Daniel, Pvt., 61st OH, C, severe cough;

Murphy, Jerry, Pvt., 157th NY, G, flesh wound mid 3rd thigh, water dressing;

Murphy, John, 1st Sgt., 75th OH, E, flesh wound lower 3rd right leg, water dressing;

Mus, Peter, Pvt., 136th NY, H, compound fracture right shoulder, water dressing;

Musgrove, Stephen L., Pvt., 75th OH, H, rib broken right side, water dressing;

Myer, Jacob, Pvt., 1st Ohio Light Artillery, K, flesh wound head, water dressing;

Myers, Aaron J., Cpl., 153rd PA, I, gunshot, died July 7;

Myers, Adolpheus, Pvt., 25th OH, G, compound fracture left foot, water dressing;

Myers, Homer, Pvt., 157th NY, B, elbow, water dressing;

Myers, Jeremiah, Cpl., 153rd PA, I, compound fracture right leg, water dressing;

Nash, Wells G., Pvt., 136th NY, C, flesh wound lower 3rd right thigh & lower 3rd right leg, water dressing;

Neal, Elijah, Pvt., 75th OH, K, flesh wound upper left forearm, simple cerate;

Nebelsick, Otto, Pvt., 119th NY, D, flesh wound left breast, water dressing;

Nelson, Joseph, Pvt., 73rd OH, B, compound fracture upper 3rd left forearm, water dressing;

Nest, Max, 1st Sgt., 68th NY, C, flesh wound left hand, water dressing;

Neumeister, Julius, Pvt., 26th WI, I, flesh wound left leg, water dressing;

Neumeyer, Joseph, 2nd Lt., 74th PA, G, compound fracture right side, water dressing;

Neville, Patrick, Pvt., 157th NY, B, compound fracture left great toe, amputation;

Newland, Andrew, Cpl., 82nd OH, E, flesh wound back & left side, water dressing;

Newmyer, Henry C., Pvt., 153rd PA, A, flesh wound left hip pelvis, water dressing;

Nicholas, George, Pvt., 134th NY, A, flesh wound right foot, water dressing;

Nichols, Lansing, Pvt., 157th NY, F, flesh wound right leg, water dressing;

Nichols, Thomas, Pvt., 73rd OH, G, flesh wound left knee, water dressing;

Niephaus, Gerhard, Pvt., 26th WI, F, flesh wound left hip, water dressing;

Nisel, George, Sgt., 74th PA, D, flesh wound left side, water dressing;

Nist, Joseph, Cpl., 74th PA, H, flesh wound head, water dressing;

Nixon, George, Pvt., 73rd OH, B, flesh wound right hip & side, died July 10, water dressing;

Nolan, Daniel, Pvt., 33rd MA, F, flesh wound left thigh, water dressing;

Noland, Sylvester, Pvt., 73rd OH, F, slight fracture mid 3rd left leg, water dressing;

Noonen, William, Cpl., 136th NY, H, compound fracture upper 3rd right thigh, ball extracted;

Northrop, Ira, Pvt., 157th NY, B, flesh wound calf of left leg, water dressing;

Norton, Charles H., Pvt., 157th NY, D, flesh wound right side head, water dressing;

Norton, Michael, Cpl., 73rd OH, F, flesh wound left arm & left thumb shot off, amputation;

Nowlan, John, Pvt., 2nd NY State Militia (82nd NY), 2nd Corps, E, flesh wound left knee, water dressing;

Nuckols, Edward G., Pvt., 1st VA, Longstreet's Corps, CSA, H, flesh wound lower 3rd left forearm, water dressing;

O'Doharty, Philip, Pvt., 17th CT, I, right shoulder, water dressing;

O'Garra, Thomas, Pvt., 75th OH, F, penetrating wound left lung, water dressing;

O'Gorman, William, Pvt., 134th NY, G, flesh wound lower 3rd right thigh, water dressing;

Olson, Gotskalk, Pvt., 82nd IL, I, mid 3rd right thigh, water dressing;

O'Neal, Ezra, Sgt., 73rd OH, F, fracture right knee joint, water dressing;

Orr, Henry C., Pvt., 136th NY, H, compound fracture mid 3rd right forearm, water dressing;

Ott, John, Cpl., 75th PA, D, fracture mid 3rd left thigh (fractures of femur), water dressing;

Outon, John, Pvt., 106th PA, 2nd Corps, I, flesh wound ankle, water dressing;

Owen, Darius, Pvt., 157th NY, C, flesh wound mid 3rd right leg, water dressing;

Paheeher, John, Pvt., 134th NY, K, compound fracture right eye, water dressing;

Paine, David, Pvt., 73rd OH, C, compound fracture left hand, water dressing;

Palmer, George H., Sgt., 25th OH, K, flesh wound upper 3rd left leg, water dressing;

Paris, Charles, Pvt., 134th NY, G, flesh wound left foot & right hip, water dressing;

Parish, Stephen, Pvt., 21st NC, Ewell's Corps, CSA, C, penetrating wound abdomen;

Park, Andrew, Pvt., 154th NY, B (One Carded Medical Record says he was at the 11th Corps hospital and another one says the 6th Corps hospital.);

Parker, Daniel, Pvt., 33rd MA, E, flesh wound left foot, water dressing;

Pattberg, Peter, Sgt., 68th NY, I, flesh wound lower 3rd left thigh, water dressing;

Patterson, Frank, Cpl., 19th ME, 2nd Corps, E, flesh wound lower 3rd right leg, water dressing;

Paugh, John, Pvt., 154th NY, I, flesh wound mid 3rd right thigh, died July 12, water dressing;

Paulus, Nicolaus, Pvt., 26th WI, C, flesh wound right elbow, water dressing;

Payne, George R., Sgt., 134th NY, E, poisoned both legs;

Pease, William, Pvt., 157th NY, G, right shoulder, splints;

Peaslee, George H., Pvt., 134th NY, A, flesh wound left thigh & leg, water dressing;

Peck, Aaron, Pvt., 17th CT, G, flesh wound right hand, water dressing;

Pense, Jesse, Pvt., 73rd OH, C, flesh wound lower 3rd left leg, water dressing;

Perry, Augustus, Pvt., 157th NY, A, flesh wound upper 3rd left leg & left foot, water dressing;

Perry, Henry, Cpl., 157th NY, F, contused left breast, water dressing;

Perry, Roland E., Pvt., 75th OH, B, compound fracture finger, amputation;

Person, James, Cpl., 153rd PA, D, flesh wound mid 3rd right arm, simple cerate;

Petrie, Willard, Pvt., 157th NY, F, flesh wound upper 3rd left leg, water dressing;

Pfeifer, Philip, Pvt., 153rd PA, C, flesh wound mid 3rd right arm, water dressing;

Pfeifer, William, Pvt., 27th PA, I, flesh wound right ankle, water dressing;

Phelps, Richard D., Pvt., 25th OH, E, penetrating wound right breast, water dressing;

Pierce, Charles H., Pvt., 33rd MA, E, flesh wound upper 3rd left forearm, died July 7, water dressing;

Pinney, Chauncey G., Pvt., 154th NY, D, flesh wound left side (penetrating, rib fractures), water dressing;

Plom, Andrew, Pvt., 58th NY, I, sick not wounded;

Plunkett, Amos E., Sgt., 82nd OH, I, arm fractured, ball extracted at wrist, above elbow amputation;

Poetzsch, Herrmann, Pvt., 54th NY, G, flesh wound left hip, water dressing;

Pommerich, John, Pvt., 26th WI, E, flesh wound mid 3rd right thigh, water dressing;

Porr, Jacob, Pvt., 41st NY, I, compound fracture elbow, amputation mid 3rd;

Post, Jacob, Pvt., 136th NY, F, flesh wound lower 3rd left leg, water dressing;

Potts, Joseph L., Cpl., 75th OH, H, flesh wound upper 3rd right hip (fractures of femur), water dressing;

Powers, Daniel S., Pvt., 157th NY, K, flesh wound upper 3rd left leg & mid 3rd right leg, water dressing;

Prengel, Theodore, Cpl., 26th WI, B, flesh wound left side neck, water dressing;

Preston, Henry, Cpl., 134th NY, H, flesh wound lower 3rd right leg & mid finger, water dressing;

Price, David B., Pvt., 136th NY, I, flesh wound neck, water dressing;

Priefer, Gustav, Pvt., 107th OH, B, flesh wound upper 3rd right thigh & finger, water dressing;

Purdy, Daniel H., Pvt., 17th CT, C, flesh wound left shoulder & lungs, dead, water dressing;

Purdy, Vincent, Cpl., 17th CT, I, fracture right side, water dressing;

Quillien, John W., Pvt., 27th PA, I, left arm pit, water dressing;

Raabe, Gottlieb, Pvt., 26th WI, B, flesh wound face, water dressing;

Raasch, August, Pvt., 26th WI, B, flesh wound left side, water dressing;

Raber, August, Pvt., 107th OH, F, flesh wound left forearm, died Aug. 4, water dressing;

Racely, Serenus, Pvt., 153rd PA, G, flesh wound right side of head, water dressing;

Rader, John F., Pvt., 153rd PA, K, flesh wound left shoulder, water dressing;

Raeish, John, Pvt., 54th NY, C, flesh wound mid right leg, water dressing;

Randolph, Arbagh, Sgt., 68th NY, B, flesh wound upper 3rd left arm, water dressing;

Ratd, Joseph, Pvt., 82nd IL, G, flesh wound left great toe, simple cerate;

Rausche, Frederick, Sgt., 26th WI, H, flesh wound mid 3rd left thigh, water dressing;

Rauth, Michael, 2nd Sgt., 27th PA, A, flesh wound right hand, water dressing;

Raven, Rudolph, 1st Lt., 54th NY, A, flesh wound chest, water dressing;

Rawlings, Henderson, Pvt., 75th OH, K, flesh wound knee & head, water dressing;

Ray, John B., Pvt., 136th NY, C, flesh wound right shoulder, water dressing;

Rechtenbach, Gustavus, Pvt., 27th PA, A, fracture right leg, splints;

Rector, William, Pvt., 134th NY, B, flesh wound right shoulder, water dressing;

Reed, David, Pvt., 134th NY, C, flesh wound mid 3rd left leg, water dressing;

Reed, Joseph, Cpl., 73rd OH, B, flesh wound right arm & left hip, ball extracted from hip;

Reed, William L., Pvt., 134th NY, E, compound fracture right knee, water dressing;

Reedy, Thomas A., Pvt., 73rd OH, A, flesh wound mid 3rd right leg, water dressing;

Regele, George M., 134th NY, H, flesh wound back & hips, died July 19, water dressing;

Regensburger, John, Cpl., 119th NY, G, left side of head, ball extracted;

Reichenbach, Frederick, Pvt., 107th OH, C, flesh wound upper 3rd left leg, water dressing;

Reimel, John, Cpl., 153rd PA, K, compound fracture right breast, water dressing;

Reinhardt, Charles, Sgt., 45th NY, C, flesh wound head, water dressing;

Reinhardt, Charles, Pvt., 1st Ohio Light Artillery, I, flesh wound mid 3rd both thighs, died July 12, water dressing;

Reininger, Samuel, Pvt., 61st OH, K, compound fracture lower 3rd arm, splints;

Reis, Peter, Pvt., 107th OH, F, flesh wound right knee, died July 8, water dressing;

Reiser, Conrad, Pvt., 68th NY, E, flesh wound lower 3rd left thigh, water dressing;

Remert, George, Pvt., 68th NY, B, left side jaw broken, water dressing;

Resh, Benjamin, Pvt., 107th OH, A, compound fracture lower 3rd left arm, amputation mid 3rd;

Retter, Martin M., Cpl., 68th NY, C, flesh wound right leg & forehead, water dressing;

Reynolds, Thaddeus, Drummer, 154th NY, I, flesh wound left hand & hip, died July 12, 2 fingers amputated;

Rezac, Fran, Pvt., 26th WI, I, flesh wound shoulder, water dressing;

Rheinisch, John, Pvt., 134th NY, K, compound fracture lower 3rd left thigh, water dressing;

Rhimes, August, Pvt., 1st Sgt., 73rd PA, I, flesh wound upper 3rd left leg, water dressing;

Rhoad, John A., Pvt., 153rd PA, B, flesh wound back, water dressing;

Rhoades, Henry, Pvt., 108th NY, 2nd Corps, B, flesh wound left side, water dressing;

Rice, Stephen, Pvt., 153rd PA, H, fracture right shoulder blade, water dressing;

Rice, Thomas W., Sgt., 73rd OH, B, right side of head skull fracture, died July 17, water dressing;

Richards, George, Cpl., 33rd MA, B, flesh wound lower 3rd left forearm, water dressing;

Richards, Isaac, Pvt., 82nd OH, A, compound fracture head & arm, died July 9, amputation upper 3rd arm;

Riebe, Hermann, Pvt., 68th NY, F, compound fracture, left foot, water dressing;

Riegger, Benedict, Pvt., 26th WI, C, contusion back, water dressing;

Riese, Carl, 1st Lt., 68th NY, mid 3rd right thigh, water dressing;

Riest, Louis, Pvt., 74th PA, K, flesh wound right side, water dressing;

Rissmiller, George, Pvt., 153rd PA, I, compound fracture mid 3rd left leg, water dressing;

Ritter, Eugene, Pvt., 153rd PA, A, flesh wound right breast, water dressing;

Ritter, John, Cpl., 45th NY, G, flesh wound lower 3rd right arm, water dressing;

Ritter, Joseph, Pvt., 153rd PA, A, flesh wound mid 3rd thigh, water dressing;

Rix, Christian, Cpl., 54th NY, G, contused right arm, water dressing;

Roantree, James, Cpl., 157th NY, B, flesh wound left foot, water dressing;

Roberts, Jacob, Sgt., 61st OH, K, contusion right foot, water dressing;

Robinson, Franklin W., Pvt., 134th NY, E, flesh wound both hips, ball extracted;

Rode, John, Cpl., 134th NY, K, flesh wound right shoulder, water dressing;

Roe, John H., Pvt., 157th NY, G, flesh wound right side face, water dressing;

Roeder, Peter, Pvt., 107th OH, F, flesh wound left side, water dressing;

Romig, Stephen C., Pvt., 153rd PA, F, flesh wound left knee, water dressing;

Romus, Christian, Pvt., 68th NY, B, flesh wound left side, water dressing;

Rosebille, Charles, Pvt., 119th NY, H, flesh wound through neck, died July 12, water dressing;

Rosenthal, Henry, Pvt., 26th WI, D, flesh wound upper 3rd right leg, water dressing;

Ross, Amos, Pvt., 73rd OH, I, flesh wound right leg, water dressing;

Ross, John, Sgt., 61st OH, K, compound fracture upper maxillary, water dressing;

Ross, William, Pvt., 73rd OH, E, contusion right heel, water dressing;

Ross, William J., Pvt., 154th NY, B, compound fracture left shoulder, water dressing;

Roth, John, Pvt., 75th OH, F, flesh wound left shoulder, water dressing;

Rothermel, Frank, Pvt., 107th OH, B, compound fracture both temples, water dressing;

Rothlauf, George, Cpl., 119th NY, E, flesh wound mid 3rd right leg, died July 10, water dressing;

Rounds, Sylvester, Pvt., 17th CT, D, flesh wound left shoulder, water dressing;

Rudel, George W., Pvt., 73rd OH, A, contused mid 3rd left leg, water dressing;

Ruebsaamen, Carl, Pvt., 26th WI, E, flesh wound mid 3rd forearm, water dressing;

Ruesch, William, Pvt., 68th NY, H, flesh wound left hand, mid finger amputated;

Ruhl, Henry, Cpl., 45th NY, E, flesh wound upper 3rd right leg, water dressing;

Ruland, Walter, Pvt., 119th NY, I, flesh wound right hip, water dressing;

Ruley, Thornton, Cpl., 73rd OH, I, right hand fracture & abdomen, water dressing;

Rull, Leman, Pvt., 134th NY, E, flesh wound head, water dressing;

Ruppel, George, Sgt., 54th NY, flesh wound neck, water dressing;

Russell, George W., Cpl., 33rd MA, G, flesh wound mid 3rd right thigh, water dressing;

Rustow, John, Pvt., 68th NY, F, flesh wound head, water dressing;

Ruth, Franz, Pvt., 54th NY, E, flesh wound mid 3rd right thigh, water dressing;

Rutlidge, Joshua, Pvt., 5th AL, Ewell's Corps, CSA, E, flesh wound hip & right heel, water dressing;

Sagendorf, Andrew, Pvt., 134th NY, E, flesh wound left thigh, ball extracted;

Sanders, James, Pvt., 25th OH, F, right hip, water dressing;

Sanford, Lewis, Bugler, 73rd OH, C, fracture left leg, died July 12, amputation lower 3rd;

Sarabaugh, David, Pvt., 107th OH, A, compound fracture left shoulder, water dressing;

Sasse, Friedrich, Pvt., 26th WI, K, flesh wound upper 3rd right hip, water dressing;

Sawdey, John H., Pvt., 157th NY, C, flesh wound right shoulder & first finger left hand, water dressing;

Schaefer, Christian, Cpl., 75th PA, B, flesh wound left foot, water dressing;

Schaefer, Thurlius, Cpl., 26th WI, C, flesh wound mid 3rd left leg, water dressing;

Schafer, John, Pvt., 82nd IL, D, struck in breast by shell at Chancellorsville fight May 2, 1863, unfit for duty;

Schaffer, Emanuel, Pvt., 153rd PA, C, flesh wound lower 3rd left thigh, water dressing;

Schaffer, William, Pvt., 107th OH, B, flesh wound lower 3rd left leg, water dressing;

Schall, Absalom, Pvt., 153rd PA, H, flesh wound chin, right breast & arm, water dressing;

Schallett, James, Pvt., 25th OH, F, compound fracture jaw & front of ear, paste board splint;

Schartzman, Andrew, Pvt., 134th NY, K, mid 3rd hip & right arm broken, splints;

Scheib, Peter, Sgt. 107th OH, I, upper 3rd left arm, water dressing;

Schild, Casper, Pvt., 107th OH, I, flesh wound head, water dressing;

Schlabach, Benjamin, Pvt., 153rd PA, D, flesh wound right hand & left hip, water dressing;

Schmahl, Joseph, Pvt., 153rd PA, H, flesh wound left side, water dressing;

Schmidt, Andrew, Sgt., 75th PA, I, flesh wound upper 3rd left hip, water dressing;

Schmidt, Anton, 1st Sgt., 27th PA, G, flesh wound upper 3rd left arm & left foot, water dressing;

Schmidt, Conrad, Pvt., 54th NY, B, flesh wound both hips, water dressing;

Schmidt, Lucas, Pvt., 73rd PA, D, flesh wound right shoulder, water dressing;

Schmidt, William, Pvt., 68th NY, F, compound fracture mid 3rd right arm, water dressing;

Schmitt, George, Cpl., 41st NY, K, contusion back, water dressing;

Schneider, Carl, Pvt., 82nd IL, H, compound fracture right wrist, water dressing (amputation);

Schneider, Michael, Pvt., 26th WI, F, flesh wound lower 3rd both thighs (amputation), water dressing;

Schneller, John, Pvt., 26th WI, E, penetrating wound left breast, water dressing;

Schneller, Peter, Cpl., 26th WI, K, flesh wound upper 3rd left thigh, water dressing;

Schonhart, Francis, Pvt., 25th OH, C, flesh wound right leg, water dressing;

Schroeder, Albert, Pvt., 45th NY, F, flesh wound left foot, water dressing;

Schuler, Conrad, Sgt., 75th PA, E, flesh wound left shoulder & left side (penetrating), water dressing;

Schultz, John, Sgt., 26th WI, G, compound fracture left cheek, water dressing;

Schultz, Theodor, Cpl., 68th NY, A, fracture left hand & flesh wound leg, water dressing;

Schulz, Hermann, Pvt., 26th W, B, flesh wound upper 3rd left leg, water dressing;

Schwab, Samuel, Pvt., 107th OH, I, flesh wound mid 3rd left leg, ball extracted;

Schwister, Mathias, Pvt., 26th WI, F, gunshot, died July 7;

Seaman, Robert, Cpl., 134th NY, H, flesh wound right leg, water dressing;

Seas, Henry, 1st Sgt., 82nd OH, D, compound fracture knee & upper 3rd left leg, water dressing;

Seeliger, Eduard, Cpl., 26th WI, A, flesh wound left breast, water dressing;

Seerey, John, Pvt., 17th CT, K, fracture lower 3rd left leg, amputation mid 3rd;

Seiberich, John, Pvt., 136th NY, F, gunshot, died July 6;

Seifarth, Herbert, Pvt., 75th PA, F, flesh wound mid 3rd right leg, water dressing;

Seiple, John, 1st Sgt., 153rd PA, F, flesh wound left hip, water dressing;

Seiple, Henry, Pvt., 153rd PA, K, flesh wound upper 3rd both thighs, water dressing;

Seiter, Jacob, Pvt., 82nd IL, F, rheumatism;

Selden, William K., Pvt., 136th NY, C, contusion right shoulder, water dressing;

Seng, Tobias, Pvt., 41st NY, A, compound fracture left foot, amputation leg;

Sentz, Hermann, Pvt., 26th WI, A, flesh wound upper 3rd left thigh, water dressing;

Setzler, Philip, 1st Lt., 107th OH, H, contusion back, water dressing;

Shaffer, William, Pvt., 20th NY State Militia (80th NY), 1st Corps, G, flesh wound left thigh, water dressing;

Shapley, Daniel, Pvt., 157th NY, E, compound fracture right hand, water dressing;

Shaum, Benjamin, 1st Lt., 153rd PA, A, flesh wound lower 3rd left thigh, water dressing;

Shaw, Harrison, Pvt., 25th OH, I, flesh wound calf of right leg, water dressing;

Shelhamer, John, Pvt., 33rd MA, C, flesh wound left foot, water dressing;

Sherrill, Eliakim, Col., 126th NY, 2nd Corps, gunshot, died July 3;

Sherwood, Lovett, Cpl., 136th NY, C, flesh wound mid 3rd right thigh, water dressing;

Shimerick, John (possibly John Simonek), Pvt., 26th WI, F, flesh wound upper 3rd left forearm, water dressing;

Shiplin, Philip, Sgt., 75th OH, F, penetrating wound right breast, right side & right knee, died July 12, water dressing;

Shoder, Reuben (possibly Hubert Schroeder), Cpl., 26th WI, K, flesh wound left hip, water dressing;

Shrock, William A., Pvt., 73rd OH, H, flesh wound right breast, water dressing;

Shufelt, Lorenzo, Pvt., 157th NY, C, fracture left shoulder, ball & pieces of bone extracted;

Siegendall, William H., Pvt., 153rd PA, D, flesh wound left eye, water dressing;

Sigler, William, Pvt., 73rd OH, G, flesh wound left ankle & upper 3rd left thigh, water dressing;

Sill, William J., 1st Lt., 75th PA, C, compound fracture mid 3rd left leg, amputation upper 3rd;

Silliman, Justus, Pvt., 17th CT, H, flesh wound head, water dressing;

Silsby, Alonzo, Pvt., 1st Ohio Light Artillery, I, compound fracture mid 3rd left forearm, amputation;

Simons, John, Pvt., 153rd PA, H, flesh wound left hip, water dressing;

Simpkins, Charles H., Pvt., 12th NJ, 2nd Corps, K, flesh wound upper 3rd thigh, water dressing;

Simpson, Richard, Sgt., 26th PA, 3rd Corps, E, flesh wound right hip, water dressing;

Sloyer, Edward, Pvt., 153rd PA, F, flesh wound upper 3rd right thigh, water dressing;

Slutts, Mahlon, Pvt., 107th OH, D, flesh wound upper right leg, water dressing;

Smith, Charles, Pvt., 27th PA, K, flesh wound side of elbow joint, water dressing;

Smith, Frederick, Pvt., 134th NY, A, flesh wound left breast, died July 25, water dressing;

Smith, George P., Pvt., 157th NY, D, flesh wound left forearm, water dressing;

Smith, Isaac, Pvt., 153rd PA, K, flesh wound right shoulder, piece of ramrod extracted;

Smith, J., Pvt., 136th NY, B, gunshot, died July 20;

Smith, Jacob, Pvt., 1st Ohio Light Artillery, K, leg broken, ball entered at knee, ball extracted from upper 3rd thigh;

Smith, John H. Cpl., 119th NY, H, flesh wound left wrist, water dressing;

Smith, Lucien J., Cpl., 136th NY, G, flesh wound right heel 5/6 rib out, died July 17, water dressing;

Smith, Nelson, 2nd Lt., 157th NY, F, fracture left foot, amputation;

Smith, Reuben, Pvt., 153rd PA, G, flesh wound right thigh, water dressing;

Smith, Samuel, Pvt., 33rd MA, F, flesh wound mid 3rd left forearm, water dressing;

Smith, Samuel B., Pvt., 153rd PA, E, flesh wound mid 3rd left forearm, water dressing;

Smith, William Henry, Pvt., 17th CT, C, flesh wound right shoulder, water dressing;

Smuck, Henry, Pvt., 25th OH, E, flesh wound left hand & lower 3rd left thigh, water dressing;

Snow, Miller, Pvt., 18th NC, Hill's Corps, CSA, I, flesh wound left shoulder & contusion arm, water dressing;

Snyder, James, Pvt., 25th OH, B, both legs;

Snyder, John W., Pvt., 73rd OH, F, slight fracture upper 3rd right leg, water dressing;

Southard, Edwin, Pvt., 119th NY, H, flesh wound right hip, water dressing;

Sowers, Paul, Pvt., 73rd OH, C, flesh wound right foot, water dressing;

Spears, William B., Pvt., 75th OH, B, flesh wound mid 3rd right thigh (fractures of femur), water dressing;

Speier, William, Capt., 107th OH, I, severe flesh wound right shoulder, water dressing;

Spence, Thomas, Sgt., 119th NY, A, flesh wound both thighs, water dressing;

Sperbeck, Orlando, Pvt., 134th NY, G, fracture both arms, ball extracted from left arm;

Sperry, Isaac, Pvt., 73rd OH, G, gunshot, died July 5;

Spore, John C., Pvt., 134th NY, I, flesh wound left shoulder, water dressing;

Spurrier, Dennis, Cpl., 55th OH, H, flesh wound upper 3rd left leg, water dressing;

Stahl, Daniel, Pvt., 107th OH, A, flesh wound lower 3rd thigh, water dressing;

Stalter, Bartholomew, Pvt., 157th NY, H, flesh wound mid 3rd left leg, ball extracted;

Stanton, Thomas, Pvt., 75th OH, G, flesh wound mid 3rd left leg, water dressing;

Stark, Albert, Sgt., 68th NY, D, compound fracture right elbow, splints; resection upper 3rd ulna;

Stawitzky, Thomas, Pvt., 82nd IL, E, flesh wound left leg, water dressing;

Steadman, Henry C., Pvt., 12th IL Cavalry, Cavalry Corps, I, gunshot, died July 3;

Stebbins, William S., Pvt., 136th NY, B, flesh wound left foot, water dressing;

Steckle, Jacob, Pvt., 153rd PA, H, flesh wound left arm, water dressing;

Steiner, Barnet T., Capt., 107th OH, D, flesh wound left shoulder & breast, ball probably in or against pleura;

Steinhaus, Friedrich, Pvt., 26th WI, H, flesh wound lower 3rd right leg & mid 3rd right arm, water dressing;

Steinmeyer, William, 2nd Lt., 26th WI, B, flesh wound left foot, water dressing;

Stephan, Philip, Pvt., 45th NY, D, contusion upper 3rd left leg, water dressing;

Stepping, Jacob, Pvt., 26th WI, H, flesh wound left side, water dressing;

Stevens, Abednego, Pvt., 25th OH, E, flesh wound mid 3rd left leg, water dressing;

Stevens, George, Pvt., 33rd MA, E, flesh wound right eye, water dressing;

Steward, George W., Pvt., 55th OH, H, flesh wound left shoulder, died July 15, water dressing;

Stewart, Andrew G., Sgt., 25th OH, G, left shoulder compound fracture, water dressing;

Stier, Charles, Sgt., 26th WI, E, flesh wound mid 3rd left leg, water dressing;

Stier, Christian, Pvt., 26th WI, F, penetrating wound small of back, died July 16, water dressing;

Stofflet, Francis, Pvt., 153rd PA, D, compound fracture left elbow, water dressing;

Stoldt, Gustavus, Capt., 58th NY, compound fracture left knee, died July 21, water dressing;

Stommel, Julius, 2nd Lt., 41st NY, I, flesh wound right breast & upper right arm, water dressing;

Stouffager, Datney, Pvt., 75th OH, I, flesh wound mid 3rd right thigh, water dressing;

Strasser, Elias, Pvt., 75th PA, I, flesh wound mid 3rd right leg, water dressing;

Strickland, Francis, 1st Sgt., 154th NY, I, right elbow, amputation;

Strobel, Lucas, Pvt., 107th OH, A, compound fracture mid 3rd right thigh, died July 25, splints;

Stubanus, Andreas, Pvt., 26th WI, G, flesh wound left thigh, water dressing;

Stutzel, George, Pvt., 68th NY, G, compound fracture upper 3rd right hip & knee, splints; & water dressing;

Style, John, Pvt., 26th WI, I, flesh wound right heel, water dressing;

Sullivan, David, Pvt., 33rd MA, D, flesh wound left knee, water dressing;

Sutlief, James, Pvt., 1st Ohio Light Artillery, I, contusion left foot, water dressing;

Swackhamer, Jacob, Pvt., 73rd OH, G, compound fracture upper 3rd right thigh, died July 20, pieces of shell extracted;

Swales, Samuel, Cpl., 134th NY, F, flesh wound back, died July 9, water dressing;

Swarthout, James H., Cpl., 134th NY, C, flesh wound right shoulder & right leg, water dressing;

Swarts, Solomon, Sgt., 136th NY, I, flesh wound left shoulder, water dressing;

Sweet, George, Pvt., 73rd OH, A, compound fracture upper 3rd left leg, water dressing;

Sweetland, Andrew, Pvt., 55th OH, I, flesh wound right foot, water dressing;

Swindler, John J., Cpl., 7th WV, 2nd Corps, E, flesh wound mid 3rd right thigh, water dressing;

Taffender, Abraham, Pvt., 4th US Light Artillery, G, flesh wound left hip, water dressing;

Tallarday, William H., Cpl., 134th NY, I, flesh wound back, water dressing;

Taylor, John, Pvt., 33rd MA, H, flesh wound mid 3rd left leg, water dressing;

Taylor, Perry, Pvt., 75th OH, G, flesh wound mid 3rd left leg, water dressing;

Tebbetts, Joseph F., Sgt., 33rd MA, H, flesh wound lower 3rd right arm, water dressing;

Temple, Jesse, Pvt., 1st PA Light Artillery, B, 1st Corps, flesh wound lower leg & mid 3rd forearm, water dressing;

Templin, William C., Cpl., 73rd OH, A, compound fracture through left ankle, water dressing;

Ten Eyke, Henry, Cpl., 157th NY, B, flesh wound left breast, water dressing;

Terry, John, Pvt., 73rd OH, B, fracture upper 3rd left thigh, amputation;

Tescher, John F., 1st Lt., 107th OH, G, right thigh, water dressing;

Teter, Daniel, Pvt., 134th NY, D, flesh wound right breast, water dressing;

Textor, Anton, Pvt., 26th WI, H, flesh wound left shoulder, water dressing;

Thiele, Friedrich, Pvt., 26th WI, H, flesh wound lower 3rd right arm, water dressing;

Thieme, Charles, Pvt., 26th WI, A, flesh wound left side of neck, water dressing;

Thomas, John B., Cpl., 134th NY, E, flesh wound right hip, died July 19, water dressing;

Thomas, Thurston, Pvt., 134th NY, D, flesh wound mid 3rd left leg, died July 20, water dressing;

Thomson, Alexander (possibly Elias Thompson), Pvt., 134th NY, E, flesh wound head, water dressing;

Thomson, William H., Pvt., 82nd OH, H, flesh wound left hip, water dressing;

Timmons, Joseph, Pvt., 73rd OH, C, flesh wound upper 3rd both legs, water dressing;

Tinkler, Christian, Pvt., 107th OH, D, flesh wound left side of head, water dressing;

Todl, Adolph, 3rd Sgt., 26th WI, F, flesh wound lower 3rd left thigh, water dressing;

Toensing, Fredrick, Pvt., 107th OH, B, compound fracture lower 3rd (leg), amputation;

Toggenberger, John, Pvt., 82nd IL, G, flesh wound left leg, water dressing;

Townsend, James, Sgt., 75th OH, E, flesh wound upper 3rd right thigh, water dressing;

Trachsel, Frederick, Pvt., 107th OH, I, flesh wound mid 3rd left thigh, water dressing;

Trautman, Peter, Pvt., 107th OH, H, flesh wound 3 fingers left hand, water dressing;

Treisch, Leonard, Pvt., 68th NY, G, flesh wound left leg, simple cerate;

Troemel, Otto, 1st Lt., 26th WI, F, mid 3rd left thigh, water dressing;

True, Henson W., Pvt., 25th OH, I, flesh wound upper 3rd right arm, water dressing;

Trumpelman, Otto, 1st Lt., 119th NY, C, compound fracture right foot, water dressing;

Tucksbury, David, Pvt., 73rd OH, H, flesh wound mid 3rd leg, water dressing;

Turner, Daniel, Pvt., 157th NY, K, penetrating wound left side, water dressing;

Twele, David, Pvt., 74th PA, K, flesh wound right side of head, water dressing;

Unangst, Edward, Pvt., 153rd PA, C, flesh wound mid 3rd right leg, water dressing;

Unangst, Henry, Pvt., 153rd PA, C, right shoulder, water dressing;

Underer, Charles, Pvt., 54th NY, A, flesh wound left shoulder, water dressing;

Van Bencoten, Jerome, Pvt., 134th NY, A, flesh wound left hip, water dressing;

Van Denburg, Corydon, Pvt., 157th NY, D, flesh wound right breast & shoulder, water dressing;

Van Epps, George O., Pvt., 134th NY, B, flesh wound upper 3rd right arm, simple cerate & ball extracted on the 3rd July;

Van Hoesen, Gerret S., 1st Sgt., 157th NY, D, flesh wound left foot 2nd toe, simple cerate;

Van Patten, Harmon, Pvt., 134th NY, B, compound fracture left foot, water dressing;

Van Vost, William, Cpl., 157th NY, K, flesh wound lower 3rd right thigh (fractures of femur), water dressing;

Van Wagoner, Peter, Pvt., 20th NY State Militia (80th NY), 1st Corps, G, flesh wound mid 3rd left leg, water dressing;

Vanater, William, Cpl., 64th NY, 2nd Corps, C, contusion right ankle, water dressing;

Vandermerlin, Henry, Pvt., 111th NY, 2nd Corps, D, right shoulder blade, water dressing & ball extracted;

Vanderslice, Aaron, Cpl., 27th PA, E, flesh wound upper 3rd left leg, water dressing;

Vangorder, Francis, Cpl., 55th OH, C, compound fracture left hand, water dressing;

VanWald, Leonhard, Pvt., 26th WI, K, flesh wound upper 3rd left thigh, water dressing;

Vasolt, Sebastian, Pvt., 58th NY, H, flesh wound right leg, water dressing;

Vaughn, Robert, Cpl., 134th NY, G, flesh wound popliteal space, water dressing;

Veer, George H., Cpl., 134th NY, A, flesh wound lower 3rd thigh, water dressing;

Vogel, Charles, Pvt., 136th NY, G, flesh wound lower 3rd left thigh, water dressing;

Vogel, Frank, Pvt., 74th PA, G, flesh wound mid 3rd right leg, water dressing;

Vollmer, Matthaus, Pvt., 136th NY, D, flesh wound lower 3rd left leg, water dressing;

Von Wienskowski, Hans, Cpl., 119th NY, D, flesh wound right foot, water dressing;

Voorhees, John, Pvt., 153rd PA, K, flesh wound mid 3rd right thigh, simple cerate;

Vorhies, Simon L., Pvt., 25th OH, A, flesh wound lower 3rd left leg, water dressing;

Vroman, Albert L., Pvt., 134th NY, E, flesh wound lower 3rd left arm, simple cerate;

Wagenfuhr, August, Sgt., 82nd IL, E, flesh wound mid 3rd left arm, water dressing;

Wagner, August, Pvt., 45th NY, E, compound fracture shoulder joint, amputation at shoulder;

Wagner, Conrad, Sgt., 73rd PA, H, contusion mid 3rd right thigh, water dressing;

Wagner, John, Pvt., 134th NY, K, compound fracture leg, water dressing;

Wahler, Charles, Pvt., 107th OH, F, flesh wound right side face, simple cerate;

Wainwright, William, Pvt., 61st PA, 6th Corps, H, rheumatism;

Waizenegger, Charles, Sgt., 75th PA, D, flesh wound left hip, water dressing;

Wald, Christian, Pvt., 68th NY, C, compound fracture right leg, amputation mid 3rd;

Walker, Anderson, Pvt., 75th OH, K, flesh wound left shoulder blade, water dressing;

Walker, Samuel, 2nd Lt., 4th MI, 5th Corps, H, gunshot left forearm, slight;

Wallace, Thomas, Cpl., 73rd OH, H, flesh wound right thigh, water dressing;

Wallace, William, Pvt., 17th CT, K, flesh wound right knee, water dressing;

Walter, John, Cpl., 26th WI, G, flesh wound by shell right hip, water dressing;

Walter, Levi F., Pvt., 153rd PA, E, knee, water dressing;

Walter, Peter, Pvt., 26th WI, G, flesh wound left side, water dressing;

Walther, Joseph, 1st Lt., 41st NY, C, flesh wound right shoulder & upper right arm, water dressing;

Walton, George, 1st Lt., 153rd PA, H, flesh wound right knee, water dressing;

Walton, Matthew, Cpl., 61st OH, K, fracture 2nd & 3rd toes left foot, 1 toe amputated;

Walzer, Louis, Cpl., 107th OH, C, fracture left hand front finger, water dressing;

Ward, George, Pvt., 4th MI, 5th Corps, E, gunshot left thigh, severe;

Ward, Samuel, Cpl., 73rd OH, B, flesh wound upper 3rd right arm, water dressing;

Warner, Orrin, Sgt., 134th NY, C, flesh wound head, water dressing;

Warren, David, Sgt., 55th OH, C, flesh wound lower 3rd right leg, water dressing;

Warren, Edmund, Pvt., 75th OH, D, flesh wound mid 3rd right arm, water dressing;

Warren, George, Cpl., 134th NY, C, gunshot right leg, sent to general hospital July 8;

Warren, Henry B., 1st Sgt., 55th OH, C, flesh wound left wrist, water dressing;

Warren, Rufus, Pvt., 17th CT, C, compound fracture mid 3rd left leg, died July 17, amputated upper 3rd;

Wasson, Andrew J., Pvt., 134th NY, H, fracture upper 3rd arm & flesh wound, water dressing;

Waters, Alexander S., Pvt., 157th NY, E, right leg broken, amputated above knee;

Waters, Henry D., 1st Lt., 157th NY, E, compound fracture 2 fingers right hand, amputation;

Weaver, Levi E., Sgt., 153rd PA, C, flesh wound upper 3rd right leg, water dressing;

Weaver, Lorenzo, Pvt., 153rd PA, K, mid 3rd leg, amputation upper 3rd;

Weaver, Theodore, Pvt., 153rd PA, K, fracture mid 3rd right thigh, water dressing;

Weaver, Theodore A., Pvt., 153rd PA, C, spine, water dressing;

Webb, Henry I., Pvt., 17th CT, F, exhaustion & fatigue;

Wechsel, Louis, Pvt., 54th NY, E, flesh wound right arm, water dressing;

Weed, James M., Pvt., 134th NY, E, flesh wound right shoulder, water dressing;

Weiffenbach, John, Pvt., 26th WI, B, flesh wound upper 3rd left leg, water dressing;

Weigner, Nathaniel, Pvt., 153rd PA, F, concussion from shell, rest & quiet;

Weikert, Carl, Pvt., 68th NY, H, flesh wound right hip, water dressing;

Weinberg, Francis, Pvt., 17th CT, H, flesh wound mid 3rd left thigh, water dressing;

Weinmann, Leopold, Sgt., 107th OH, F, water dressing;

Weis, Joseph, Pvt., 107th OH, H, flesh wound upper 3rd right leg, water dressing;

Weisensa, George, Sgt., 73rd OH, B, flesh wound elbow left arm, water dressing;

Weiss, Christian, Pvt., 26th WI, E, flesh wound mid 3rd left hip, water dressing;

Weller, Jacob, Pvt., 1st NY Light Artillery, I, right arm & right hip & both legs, arm amputated upper 3rd;

Wells, Charles S., Pvt., 17th CT, D, flesh wound lower 3rd right thigh, water dressing;

Wells, John, Pvt., 2nd US, 5th Corps, K, mid 3rd right leg, water dressing;

Welsh, James, Pvt., 73rd OH, E, slight flesh wound middle finger & left leg shin bone, water dressing;

Wendorff, Friedrich, Pvt., 26th WI, B, flesh wound neck, water dressing;

Wenke, Heinrich, Cpl., 68th NY, E, compound fracture lower 3rd right thigh, straight splints;

Wentz, Friedrich, Pvt., 41st NY, I, compound fracture upper 3rd right arm, amputation & water dressing;

Wentzel, Conrad, Pvt., 75th PA, B, head and arm, water dressing;

Wergin, Bernhard, Pvt., 26th WI, D, flesh wound upper 3rd left leg, water dressing;

Werkler, Wilhelm, Drummer, 82nd IL, E, flesh wound right breast & left leg, water dressing;

Werner, August, 1st Sgt., 68th NY, A, flesh wound left hip & left hand, water dressing;

Wessles, Harmon, Pvt., 134th NY, A, flesh wound mid 3rd left thigh, water dressing;

West, William, Pvt., 55th NC, Hill's Corps, CSA, K, flesh wound right ankle, water dressing;

Westhoff, August, Pvt., 26th WI, D, flesh wound left arm, water dressing;

Westlake, William W., Cpl., 17th CT, A, fracture lower 3rd right leg & upper 3rd left leg, amputated mid 3rd right thigh;

Wheeler, Anthony, Pvt., 25th OH, B, flesh wound right side, water dressing;

Wheeler, George E., Pvt., 19th ME, 2nd Corps, H, flesh wound lower 3rd left thigh, water dressing;

Wheeler, Thomas, 1st Lt., 75th OH, A, flesh wound right side & right leg & left groin & lower 3rd left arm, water dressing;

White, William, Pvt., 25th OH, A, fracture right knee, water dressing;

Whitesell, Daniel A., Sgt., 5th US Light Artillery, Artillery Reserve, C, lower left leg shot off & right side wounded, amputation leg lower 3rd;

Whitlock, Joseph S., Pvt., 17th CT, C, bone fracture lower right arm, died July 16, bones extracted & hand amputated;

Whitlock, Nephi, Pvt., 17th CT, C, flesh wound upper 3rd left leg, water dressing;

Whitman, Charles, Pvt., 157th NY, I, compound fracture lower 3rd left thigh, straight splints;

Whitmer, Daniel, Cpl., 107th OH, A, compound fracture left foot, water dressing;

Whittlesey, Samuel F., Pvt., 17th CT, D, flesh wound left side of neck, water dressing;

Whyte, William H., Pvt., 134th NY, F, flesh wound head, simple cerate;

Wiebel, John, Pvt., 68th NY, G, flesh wound left eye, water dressing;

Wiedemann, Joachim, Pvt., 26th WI, G, flesh wound right shoulder, water dressing;

Wiegand, Johann, Sgt., 41st NY, A, flesh wound left foot, water dressing;

Wightman, Cyrus B., Pvt., 134th NY, G, flesh wound mid 3rd right leg, water dressing;

Wilbur, Frank, Pvt., 2nd RI, 6th Corps, A, contusion back from shell, water dressing;

Wilcox, Alvia E., Cpl., 17th CT, D, died July 7;

Wild, Julius, Pvt., 45th NY, A, flesh wound back, water dressing;

Wiles, Benjamin, Pvt., 7th MI Cavalry, Cavalry Corps, G, contusion by fall of horse, liniments;

Wiley, William, Pvt., 25th OH, I, mid 3rd right leg & mid 3rd right forearm, leg fractured, leg, arm amputated upper 3rd;

Wilkie, William G., Cpl., 134th NY, B, flesh wound right forearm, water dressing;

Willey, George H., Cpl., 19th ME, 2nd Corps, H, penetrating wound abdomen, died July 24, water dressing;

Williams, Albert, Pvt., 74th PA, ball extracted;

Williams, David, Pvt., 25th OH, F, flesh wound right shoulder, water dressing;

Willmann, Henry, 1st Sgt., 54th NY, F, compound fracture lower 3rd left thigh, died July 10, amputated mid 3rd;

Wilson, Charles, Pvt., 119th NY, H, flesh wound left shoulder, water dressing;

Wilson, David, Pvt., 119th NY, H, flesh wound right thigh, water dressing;

Wilson, Henry C., Pvt., 73rd OH, D, flesh wound left side, water dressing;

Wilson, William H., Sgt., 134th NY, C, gunshot left thigh, sent to general hosp. on July 8;

Wiltse, Emerson, Cpl., 154th NY, D, flesh wound right shoulder, water dressing;

Winewright, George H., Pvt., 134th NY, D, left foot & left hip & right hand, water dressing;

Winkler, John B., 1st Sgt., 74th PA, B, flesh wound right groin, water dressing;

Winkler, Morris, Pvt., 26th WI, C, flesh wound right side head over eye, water dressing;

Wires, Warren, Pvt., 75th OH, D, flesh wound back between shoulder blades, water dressing;

Witbeck, George H., Pvt., 134th NY, E, compound fracture mid 3rd right leg, amputation upper 3rd;

Witbeck, Pelet, Pvt., 134th NY, C, flesh wound left side abdomen, simple cerate;

Withey, Leman W., Pvt., 136th NY, C, left cheek & eye, water dressing, eye destroyed;

Wolff, Emil, Pvt., 54th NY, K, mid 3rd right hand broken, splints;

Wolfley, Thomas, Sgt., 61st OH, C, flesh wound left breast, water dressing;

Wolfgram, Friedrich, Pvt., 26th WI, I, flesh wound upper 3rd right leg & lower 3rd left thigh, water dressing;

Woller, Ferdinand, Pvt., 26th WI, E, flesh wound of scalp, water dressing;

Wood, George H., Pvt., 12th NJ, 2nd Corps, C, flesh wound head, simple cerate;

Wortman, Henry D., 1st Sgt., 75th OH, I, fracture left index finger, amputation 2nd joint;

Wright, Charles M., Pvt., 75th OH, H, flesh wound right hip, water dressing;

Wright, Franklin J., Sgt., 157th NY, E, flesh wound right breast & shoulder, striking the bone not breaking it;

Wright, George, Pvt., 136th NY, A, compound fracture upper maxillary, bone extracted;

Wright, James R., Pvt., 157th NY, B, flesh wound left foot, water dressing;

Wright, John, Sgt., 61st OH, H, flesh wound left breast, water dressing;

Wright, John, Cpl., 136th NY, B, flesh wound left foot, water dressing;

Wunch, Joseph, Bugler, 27th PA, I, flesh wound left leg, water dressing;

Yan, Andrew, Pvt., 157th NY, B, contusion of head;

Yantiss, Joseph J., Cpl., 82nd OH, H, flesh wound left wrist, water dressing;

Yeager, Peter, Pvt., 153rd PA, E, flesh wound mid 3rd left thigh, water dressing;

Yost, Jacob, Pvt., 75th PA, D, flesh wound neck, water dressing;

Young, F. (possibly Ferdinand Lund), Pvt., 33rd MA, K, flesh wound right foot, water dressing;

Young, Henry, Sgt., 107th OH, B, flesh wound upper 3rd left hip, water dressing;

Young, John, Pvt., 27th PA, B, compound fracture left maxillary, water dressing;

Young, Nicholaus, Pvt., 26th WI, G, flesh wound mid 3rd right hip, water dressing;

Youngs, Benjamin F., Pvt., 157th NY, D, flesh wound left shoulder, water dressing;

Zann, Peter, Pvt., 1st NY Light Artillery, I, contusion mid 3rd right leg, water dressing;

Zapfe, August, Cpl., 26th WI, E, penetrating wound chest, water dressing;

Zbitowsky, Joseph, Pvt., 26th WI, D, flesh wound upper 3rd thigh, water dressing;

Zeiger, Franz, Pvt., 26th WI, H, flesh wound both hips, water dressing;

Zeiner, Levi, Pvt., 153rd PA, F, cap off elbow, water dressing;

Zimmerman, Anton, 2nd Sgt., 27th PA, H, flesh wound left upper 3rd Hem, water dressing;

Zink, Amandus, Cpl., 74th PA, G, flesh wound left leg, water dressing;

Zink, John, Pvt., 54th NY, K, flesh wound mid 3rd right elbow & left thigh, water dressing;

Zubler, Rudolph, Cpl., 134th NY, A, compound fracture left arm, amputation at shoulder.

Others at Spangler Farm

from the *Philadelphia Inquirer,* July 14, 1863

Antonieski, Edward, Capt., 58th NY, A, leg;

Armistead, Lewis A., Brig. Gen., Longstreet's Corps, CSA, arm & leg;

Cochran, John Scott, Capt., 5th FL, Hill's Corps, CSA, D, lungs, shoulder;

Cole, Leroy, Cpl., 157th NY, C, sick;

Ellmer, Charles, 3rd Lt., 57th NC, Ewell's Corps, CSA, G, left eye out;

Green, Henry F., Sgt., 22nd GA, Hill's Corps, CSA, K, shoulder;

Judd, Theophilus, Cpl., 2nd GA, Longstreet's Corps, CSA, C, scrotum;

Labar, John C., Cpl., 153rd PA, G, thigh;

Lackner, Francis, Capt., 26th WI, B, right leg;

Laubach, George A., Sgt., 153rd PA, D, wrist;

Lazaro, Charles, Pvt., 74th PA, E, ankle;

Lee, Aaron W., Cpl., 17th CT, G, left thigh;

Lee, Alfred E., Capt., 82nd OH, E, right hip;

Lerielle, Charles, Cpl., 27th PA, C, left hip;

Longenbach, James, Pvt., 153rd PA, D, wrist;
Love, Earl, Cpl., 151st PA, 1st Corps, A, thigh;
Martin, George W., Sgt., 75th OH, C, left arm;
McConnell, James B., Capt., 82nd OH, G, breast and shoulder;
McGimsey, William C., 1st Lt., 8th LA, Ewell's Corps, CSA, A, lung;
Murrell, J. P., Sgt., 8th LA, Ewell's Corps, CSA, G, lung;
Preiser, Emil, Cpl., 27th PA, E;
Puckett, John F., 1st Sgt., 7th TN, Hill's Corps, CSA, E, arm;
Reynolds, James M., Capt., 61st OH, B, arm, dead;
Sullivan, Daniel O., 2nd Lt., 61st OH, K, left breast;
Vignos, Augustus, Capt., 107th OH, H, arm amputated;
Watson, James H., 1st Lt., 47th NC, Hill's Corps, CSA, K, cheek;
Williams, Robert, Pvt., 153rd PA, I, hip.

Additional Names from Other Sources

Barlow, Francis C., Brig. Gen., 1st Division, left side;
Black, John D., Adj., 145th PA, 2nd Corps, E, breast;
Bowie, James, Pvt., 102nd NY, 12th Corps, I;
Brockway, Green B., Pvt., 1st OH Light Artillery, I;
Cheney, Matthew B., Capt., 154th NY, G;
Clehener, Charles, Pvt., 26th WI, B;
Crandall, Alonzo, Pvt., 136th NY, A;
Crubaugh, Jeremiah, Pvt., 75th OH, C;
Feldmann, Philipp, Pvt., 26th WI, I;
Finch, Martin, Pvt., 136th NY, A;
Gasler, Joseph, Pvt., 107th OH, K;
Germann, Bernhard, Pvt., 119th NY, D;
Gilleran, Thomas, Pvt., 61st OH, F;
Halbing, George, Pvt., 119th NY, G;
Hof, Jacob, Pvt., 107th OH, E;
Hubert, Mark A., Pvt., 5th TX, Longstreet's Corps, CSA, K, leg;
Jones, Nelson W., Sgt., 3rd ME, 3rd Corps, I;
Ladd, Charles, Sgt., 25th OH, E;
Lahmiller, Andrew, Pvt., 107th OH, A;
Lantz, Samuel L., Sgt., 153rd PA, F, thigh;

Leonhardt, Cameron L., Pvt., 11th NC, Hill's Corps, CSA, I, left shoulder;
Lilly, Harrison W., Cpl., 153rd PA, D, thigh;
Lock, Henry D., Pvt., 157th NY, E, foot;
McCarty, Thomas, Pvt., 8th LA, Ewell's Corps, CSA, I;
McVey, William, Pvt., 73rd OH, H;
Mead, James A., Pvt., 136th NY, A;
Mesnard, Luther B., Sgt., 55th OH, D, arm;
Moll, David, Sgt., 153rd PA, B;
Moore, Willard H., Pvt., 97th NY, 1st Corps, B, left thigh;
Pollock, William E., Pvt., 55th OH, C;
Reynolds, John W., Capt., 145th PA, 2nd Corps, A, head;
Riehl, William H., Pvt., 153rd PA, F, shoulder, ball extracted;
Ruch, Reuben, Pvt., 153rd PA, F, each leg;
Russel, James W., Pvt., 6th NC, Ewell's Corps, CSA, G, right knee & upper forearm;
Ruth, William, Pvt., 153rd PA, A, back of left shoulder;
Rykert, Gilbert M., Cpl., 154th NY, C, arm amputated;
Schmid, Bernhard, Cpl., 74th PA, E;
Snyder, Adam, Pvt., 107th OH, H;
Soys, Jesse, Pvt., 153rd PA, F, left hand;
Spencer, Israel, Pvt., 136th NY, A, left shoulder;
Stowe, Frederick, Capt. & Assist. Adj. Gen., 2nd Division, shell fragment to right side of head;
Taifel, Christian, Sgt., 107th OH, E, arm;
Weisensel, John C., Cpl., 45th NY, E;
Wilbur, Philip C., Pvt., 134th NY, E.

Names Recorded by XI Corps Surgeons that Could Not be Verified with Confidence

Arman, Charles, Pvt., 54th OH (not at Gettysburg), C, mid 3rd left leg & right arm, water dressing;
Bollard, Stephen E., Pvt., 157th NY, E, face & left forearm, water dressing, contusion;
Conbaugh, Perry;
Durwin, John E., Cpl., 1st PA Cavalry, E, right foot, water dressing, compound fracture;
Heidrich, Pvt., 41st New York, H;

Kelley, James B., Pvt., 9th VA, Longstreet's Corps, CSA, I, penetrating wound lower 3rd right leg, water dressing;

Marander, W., flesh wound back, water dressing;

Ney, W. M., 73rd OH, died July 7;

Oliver, John S., Pvt., 75th OH, died July 19;

Resppersberg, U. R., Pvt., 68th NY, G, rheumatism;

Silas, Pvt., flesh wound calf left leg, water dressing; (Possibly Silas Schulur, 107th OH, A);

Stephens, James F., Pvt. 158th PA, I, flesh wound wrist, water dressing; (Possibly James F. Stevens, 150th PA, 1st Corps, I, gunshot, arm amputated. Admitted to Jarvis US General Hospital in Baltimore on July 9);

Tanner, Samuel, Pvt., 82nd OH, F, flesh wound lower 3rd left leg, water dressing;

Weiss, Charles, servant, fracture left forearm & wrist, amputation left arm.

Appendix 6

The XI Corps Hospital Dead

Those who died at the XI Corps hospital likely were taken to a tent called a "dead house" close to the makeshift cemetery in a peach and apple orchard south of the Spangler house. There, the bodies were prepared for burial or gathered to wait until workers had time to bury them. Once wounded began to be shipped away and space was cleared, it's also possible that an isolated part of the Spanglers' barn was procured for a dead house, such as one of the hay mows upstairs.

Soldiers' personal and military information was recorded and sent to Washington, D.C. Effects were collected for return to family members, often via comrades. Some men were embalmed, but most were not. It depended on whether comrades or family members arranged to have the body transported home for burial, or the embalmers who followed the armies thought they could make money off a particular body.

Bodies were usually wrapped in blankets and placed inside hastily made caskets made from wood found on the farm. Each grave was supposed to be marked with an identifying board with the decedent's name written in pencil, carved, or painted.

The Elliott's Map of the Battlefield of Gettysburg shows 20 Confederate burials at Spangler, but only five have been identified. Two of those Confederate casualties arrived on the night of July 2 from East Cemetery Hill, one from the 6th North Carolina and the other from the 8th Louisiana. The other three known Confederate dead had been mortally wounded during Pickett's Charge on July 3, including Brig. Gen. Lewis Armistead. I have confirmed the names of 46 Confederates treated at Spangler, all of whom lived except the five just mentioned. The Elliott's map is a valuable resource, but it has not always proven precisely reliable. As a result, we will never know precisely how many Confederates were buried on the Spangler farm, but it was probably closer to five than 20.

The identity of the four Confederates other than General Armistead who died at the XI Corps hospital come courtesy of Dr. John W. C. O'Neal of Gettysburg, who collected their names while at Spangler. Doctor O'Neal, a Pennsylvania College graduate who became a beloved member of his Gettysburg community through his decades of doctoring and leadership prior to his death at age 93 in 1913, took a special interest in recording Confederate burials. His notes are on file at the Adams County Historical Society in Gettysburg.

The Elliott's map shows 185 Union graves. The records show only 118 confirmed Spangler deaths and 19 probable deaths, so the number is almost certainly high.

The crews began moving the Union dead to the new Soldiers' National Cemetery on Cemetery Hill in late October 1863. The dead in and around Gettysburg had to be disinterred from all sorts of terrain. It was a well-organized if complicated, gruesome, delicate, and painstaking endeavor. An attempt was made to identify each man and gather effects buried with him to return to his family, but many personal items had been stolen by grave robbers, a big problem in and around Gettysburg in the weeks and months following the battle. Many soldiers were buried in the new cemetery as unknowns.

Although Soldiers' National Cemetery was dedicated November 19, 1863, when President Abraham Lincoln delivered his Gettysburg Address, the reburial of the Army of the Potomac's Gettysburg dead remained unfinished and would not be complete until March 1864. The Union dead were disinterred from George Spangler's land and moved to Cemetery Hill between late October

1863 and late March 1864. Most of the 25 men buried in the fourth row of the Ohio plot of the cemetery are found on the Spangler burial list in this appendix.

General Armistead's body was removed from the Spangler plot in October 1863 and reburied by his family at Old St. Paul's Cemetery in Baltimore. Most of the Gettysburg Confederate dead remained in the area until they were reburied in the early 1870s, mainly in Raleigh, North Carolina, Savannah, Georgia, Charleston, South Carolina, and Richmond, Virginia.[1]

Each death was mourned by friends and family members back home, and in many cases the tragic news also meant the loss of income—doubling the sorrow. Corporal John S. Allison of the 75th Ohio was wounded in the knee north of Gettysburg on July 1 and eventually made it to the Spangler hospital. Allison worked a double shift on the railroad back home in Cincinnati to support mother Nancy and ailing stepfather Wesley, who had "chronic rheumatism and general disability" and could not support himself. Allison gave his mother money every month before enlisting and continued to do so during the war, though one month $20 was lost in the mail. Allison died July 17, ending his support for his mother and stepfather. "I also know that John looked after the comfort of his mother at all times and he seemed to be impressed with the idea that he was her mainstay, and that he bought coal & provisions for his mother's family continually," claimed a letter in his pension file in support of his mother's claim for government help. Allison's mother was awarded a pension of $8.00 a month, but only after his stepfather swore to the pension office that he is "strictly temperate in his habits and uses no intoxicating drinks."[2]

Examples of economic hardship abound. Private Casper Bohrer of the 107th Ohio was a chair maker in Berea outside Cleveland whose father was unable to work because of a hernia. Before the war, Bohrer gave $200.00 a year for four years to his mother, Apollonia. He gave her another $200.00 during the war. Bohrer was wounded and suffered a compound fracture below his right knee on July 1, and underwent an amputation. He died at the XI Corps hospital on July 16. His mother was eventually provided with $8.00 a month.[3]

The higher the rank, the more the dependent received per month. When Colonel Francis Mahler of the 75th Pennsylvania died at the Spangler hospital, his widow then received $30.00 per month. Children under the age of 16 increased pensions $2.00 a month. Pensions were terminated if the widow remarried, and they were often denied if the surviving family member could not prove an inability to earn an income. Pensions were raised during the ensuing decades.

Sometimes a death was made even more painful by its timing. James Chase arrived at the Spangler farm on August 1 after a long journey to see his wounded son, Pvt. James F. Chase of the 154th New York. When he inquired of his son's whereabouts, the father was told he had died just one day earlier. XI Corps staff showed the grieving father his 25-year-old son's grave and headboard with his name, company, and regiment painted on the rough wood, and gave him his clothing and effects. Private Chase was later reburied in Soldiers' National Cemetery.[4]

---

1 Mary H. Mitchell, *Hollywood Cemetery: The History of a Southern Shrine* (Richmond, VA, 1999), GNMP Library, Box 14A, Folder #4, "Burials at Camp Letterman," 146-159. A listing of the dead in Hollywood Cemetery in Richmond does not contain any known Spangler dead.

2 Pension Claim No. 98.223, Fold3.

3 Pension Claim No. 133.187, Fold3.

4 Pension Claim No. 120.701, Fold3; CMSR 228, National Archives.

Benjamin F. Hartley, a private in the 75th Ohio, and wife Margaret had a three-year-old son (William) and one-year-old daughter (Sedalia) at home in Chauncey in southern Ohio. On the afternoon of July 1, he was wounded in the right leg north of town and taken to the Spangler farm. Assistant Surgeon Amos Shaw Jr. of the 41st New York picks up the story in a letter written at Private Hartley's request to Margaret on July 16:

> He was struck in the thigh just above the knee with a double canister shot which buried itself partly in the bone. I assisted in the taking out of the bullet and found that the bone was but little shattered and supposed that he would get along very well. Since that time he has not been under my care and I have not seen him until today when some of his friends called me in and I found him in a very low condition. His leg below the knee has become Gangrenous and the only chance that remains for him is amputation. At present he is not able to bear the operation; but should he get strength sufficient to bear it the chance will be given him.
>
> Everything that could be done for him has been done by the Surgeon who attends him, but it seems that all efforts to save his limb have proved unsuccessful. Perhaps I have told you too much already, but I deem it my duty to tell you the worst. Pardon me if by so doing I should awake such feelings of dispair that I know will be aroused in the reception of such news. The Angel of Death may be near and ready to sever the cords which yet bind him to Earth and to Life. Should death come it will be merely for him a change from this evil world to a world of Happiness and Bliss. Your Husband sends his love to you to his Mother & Father and all his Friends.

Hartley died the next day. Margaret rushed to Gettysburg upon receipt of the letter, but discovered soon thereafter that she was a widow. Someone guided her to her husband's grave in the Spangler field not far from the house.

Gettysburg showed no mercy, even to those behind the lines. Private Thomas Gilleran enlisted in the 61st Ohio in 1861 at 42. He and wife Honora were married 21 years earlier in their homeland of County Roscommon, Ireland, and now lived in Cincinnati. Gilleran was working as a cook on Cemetery Hill when he was mortally wounded, as Capt. William H. McGroarty reported in a letter dated August 17, 1863, to the pension office in Cincinnati. Gilleran "was killed [mortally wounded] on the 2nd of July in the eavening being detailed to help the cooks bring coffee to the men," explained the captain, "killed whilsc carrying the kettles back to where they were cooking after the men had finished their supper the reason of his helping the cook at the time was on account of one of them being sick." He died a couple of days later at the Spangler hospital and was buried there before eventually being reburied in the Ohio section of Soldiers' National Cemetery. Captain McGroarty was also not long for this world, and would be killed at Lookout Valley, Tennessee, just two months later. Mrs. Gilleran was awarded a pension of $8.00 a month.[5]

As noted in this book, speedy treatment was often the difference between life and death. Many of the Army of the Potomac men listed here were wounded on July 1 but had to wait three and sometimes four days or more for treatment. One was Spangler casualty Cpl. Aaron J. Myers of the 153rd Pennsylvania, who carried water to suffering comrades even though he had been wounded in

---

5 Pension Claim Nos. 103.659 and 319.41, Fold3; Ibid., No. 16.221, National Archives.

the leg. "I cautioned him to be careful," recalled Lt. Benjamin F. Shaum after the war, "but I understood he died in four or five days."[6]

The following list of men who perished at the XI Corps hospital was taken from a report compiled by Gettysburg resident J. G. Frey in 1863, together with other firsthand sources. Many XI Corps soldiers were initially buried upon their death at the Adams County Almshouse, private residences, in orchards, Kuhn's Brickyard, church graveyards, the XII Corps hospital, a schoolyard, and other locations where they fell across the sprawling battlefield.

The second-largest Gettysburg burial site for the XI Corps after the Spangler farm was Josiah Benner's cornfield north of town, where 13 men were buried, including eight from the 73rd Ohio. Many men died after being transferred from Spangler to Camp Letterman and larger out-of-town general hospitals.[7]

Identified Burials
at the XI Corps Hospital

* Now buried in Soldiers' National Cemetery in Gettysburg

** Now buried in Evergreen Cemetery in Gettysburg

\# On Gettysburg resident J. G. Frey's list of burials at Spangler,
but name or other info could not be resolved

Confederate Dead
from the Army of Northern Virginia

Armistead, Lewis A., Brig. Gen., brigade commander,
Pickett's division, Longstreet's Corps
Leonhardt, Cameron L., Pvt., 11th NC
McCarty, Thomas, Pvt., 8th LA
Moody, William H., Lt., 2nd MS
Russel, James W., Pvt., 6th NC

6 Kiefer, *History of the One Hundred and Fifty-Third Regiment*, 137-138.

7 Kathleen Georg Harrison, Transcription of J. G. Frey's Book of Union Interment Sites, by Farm Area. File 7-14a, GNMP Library. Original book owned by A. Larson. Other sources include: letters, diaries, regimental rosters, Gettysburg Foundation research, books, state adjutants general reports, US Registers of Deaths of Volunteers, 1861-1865, Gettysburg National Military Park files, Busey and Busey's *Union Casualties at Gettysburg*, and in Washington, D.C., from the National Archives and Records Administration's Compiled Military Service Records, Volunteer Carded Medical Records, Register 554, and pension files.

Union Dead
from the Army of the Potomac

** Allison, John S., Cpl., 75th OH
* Barrett, Joseph, Pvt., 73rd OH
* Benson, Frank J., Pvt., 17th CT
* Bishop, Lewis, Sgt., 154th NY
Bitzer, Socrates S., Cpl., 73rd OH
* Bohrer, Casper, Pvt., 107th OH
* Borger, Gideon, Pvt., 153rd PA
* Bowie, James, Pvt., 102nd NY
Brockway, Green B., Pvt., 1st OH Lt Art
* Call, William R., Pvt., 73rd OH
* Chase, James F., Pvt., 154th NY
* Conner, George W., Pvt., 157th NY
* Conner, Samuel L., Pvt., 82nd OH
* Crubaugh, Jeremiah, Pvt., 75th OH
* Culver, Miles A., Pvt., 157th NY
* Dana, Philip, Pvt., 134th NY
* Davis, John, Pvt., 75th OH
* Dietrich, Franz Louis, 1st Lt. and Adj., 58th NY
Duboise, John, Pvt., 24th MI
Duding, James, C, 28th PA
Eaton, Francis, Pvt., 157th NY
* Edmonds, John, Pvt., 1st OH Lt Art Bty H
* Ervin, James, Pvt., 73rd PA
Feldmann, Philipp, Pvt., 26th WI
* Flynn, James, Pvt., 17th CT
* Friederici, Julius, Sgt., 119th NY
* Gasler, Joseph, Pvt., 107th OH
* Germann, Bernhard, Pvt., 119th NY
Getter, Charles, Pvt., 153rd PA
* Gilleran, Thomas, Pvt., 61st OH
Goble, Jacob A., Pvt., 153rd PA
Gyngusch, Daniel, D, 134th PA
* Hague, Samuel, Pvt., 119th NY
* Halbing, George, Pvt., 119th NY
* Haley, Thomas, Pvt., 157th NY
* Hamman, Gottfried, Pvt., 74th PA
* Hanson, Austin, Cpl., 17th ME
* Harriman, Charles, Pvt., 19th ME
* Hartley, Benjamin F., Pvt., 75th OH
* Haskell, Chauncey, Pvt., 82nd OH
* Hatch, Albert, Pvt., 157th NY
* Heald, Nathan, Pvt., 73rd OH
Heeney, Joseph, 1st Lt., 157th NY
* Heinle, Fritz, Sgt., 74th PA
Heldeman, Joseph, Pvt., 153rd PA
Hess, K., PA
* Hilgers, Peter Sgt., 73rd PA
* Hoagland, Peter G., Pvt., 1st PA Lt Art Bty B
* Hof, Jacob, Pvt., 107th OH

* Hough, Broughton, Pvt., 157th NY
* Hull, Daniel V., Pvt., 136th NY
* Johnson, Jerry, Cpl., 157th NY
Johnson, John, Pvt., 153rd PA, Co. A
Johnson, John, Pvt., 153rd PA, Co. K
* Jones, Nelson W., Sgt., 3rd ME
* Joyner, James E., Cpl., 157th NY
* Ladd, Charles, Sgt., 25th OH
* Lahmiller, Andrew, Pvt., 107th OH
* Leake, Elisha L., Pvt., 73rd OH
* Link, Peter, Pvt., 134th NY
Mahler, Francis, Col., 75th PA
* March, William J., Pvt., 13th VT
* McCracken, Uriah, Cpl., 153rd PA
* McVey, William, Pvt., 73rd OH
* Mericle, Albert, Cpl., 154th NY
# Meyer, Adolph, D, 25th PA
Miller, Henry A., Pvt., 153rd PA
* Miller, William, Pvt., 25th OH
* Miller, William, Pvt., 153rd PA
* Mitchell, Jacob, Pvt., 55th OH
Moore, William S., Asst. Surg., 61st OH
* Muller, Henry, Pvt., 41st NY
* Nixon, George, Pvt., 73rd OH
# Ott, John, Cpl., D, 75th PA
* Paugh, John, Pvt., 154th NY
* Pierce, Charles H. Pvt., 33rd MA
* Pollock, William E., Pvt., 55th OH
* Preiser, Emil, Cpl., 27th PA
* Purdy, Daniel H., Pvt., 17th CT
* Raber, August, Pvt., 107th OH
* Regele, George M., Pvt., 134th NY
* Reimel, John, Cpl., 153rd PA
* Reinhardt, Charles, Pvt., 1st OH Lt Art Bty I
Reynolds, James M., Capt., 61st OH
* Reynolds, Thaddeus L., Musician, 154th NY
* Rice, Thomas H., Sgt., 73rd OH
# Richards, Charles, Battery I, OH
* Richards, Isaac, Pvt., 82nd OH
* Rosebille, Charles, Pvt., 119th NY
* Rothlauf, George, Cpl., 119th NY
Schmid, Bernhard, Cpl., 74th PA
Schmidt, Conrad, Pvt., 54th NY
Seas, Henry, Sgt., 82nd OH
Seiple, John, Sgt., 153rd PA
Sherrill, Eliakim, Col., 126th NY
* Shiplin, Philip, Sgt., 75th OH
Smith, Lucien J., Cpl., 136th NY

* Snyder, Adam, Pvt., 107th OH
* Sperry, Isaac, Pvt., 73rd OH
* Strobel, Lucas, Pvt., 107th OH
* Swackhamer, Jacob, Pvt., 73rd OH
* Thomas, Thurston, Pvt., 134th NY
# Unknown, I, 41st NY
Warren, Rufus, Pvt., 17th CT
* # Weight, William, K, 34th NY
* Weisensel, John C., Cpl., 45th NY
* Wentz, Friedrich, Pvt., 41st NY
Westlake, William W., Cpl., 17th CT
Wheeler, Thomas, 1st Lt., 75th OH
* Whitlock, Joseph S., Pvt., 17th CT
* Wilbur, Philip C., Pvt., 134th NY
* Willey, George H., Cpl., 19th ME
* Willmann, Henry, Sgt., 54th NY

Spangler Patients Who Likely Died at the XI Corps Hospital

* Anguish, Horace, Cpl., 157th NY: Buried with 12 other Spangler patients in Soldiers' National Cemetery.
* Balmes, Joseph, Pvt., 26th WI: Buried next to three fellow Spangler patients from the 26th Wisconsin.
* Barry, Jeremiah, Pvt., 134th NY: Buried with 12 other Spangler patients.
* Beal, Joseph, Pvt., 33rd MA: Buried next to a confirmed Spangler death and 33rd Massachusetts comrade Charles H. Pierce.
* Beaver, Peter, Cpl., 134th NY: Buried with 13 other Spangler patients.
* Bice, Benjamin B., Pvt., 134th NY: Buried with 13 other Spangler patients.
* Bruckert, Charles, 2nd Lt., 26th WI: Buried next to fellow Spangler patient Christian Stier of the 26th Wisconsin.
* Carr, Orson S., Sgt., 13th VT: Died before patients were moved to a general hospital or other corps or division hospitals. He is buried in Gettysburg next to 13th Vermont comrade Pvt. William J. March, who records show died at the Spangler hospital.

* Cunningham, Joseph W., Cpl., 25th OH: Buried with other Spangler patients.
* Kleppinger, Joseph, Pvt., 153rd PA: Died before patients were moved to general hospitals.
* Krenscher, Peter, Pvt., 26th WI: Buried next to three fellow Spangler patients from the 26th Wisconsin.
* Kuhn, Peter, Pvt., 26th WI: Buried next to three fellow Spangler patients from the 26th Wisconsin.
Mayberry, Andrew, Cpl., 20th ME: Died before patients were moved to general hospitals or other corps/division hospitals. Left behind wife Hannah and five kids six months to 11 years in Windham, Maine.
Myers, Aaron J., Cpl., 153rd PA: Died before patients were moved to general hospitals.
* Schwister, Mathias, Pvt., 26th WI: Died before patients were moved to general hospitals. He is buried next to three fellow Spangler patients from the 26th Wisconsin.
* Stier, Christian, Pvt., 26th WI: Buried next to fellow Spangler patient Charles Bruckert of the 26th Wisconsin.
Swales, Samuel, Cpl., 134th NY: Reported to have died in the "camp hospital."
* Thomas, John B., Cpl., 134th NY: Buried among 13 other Spangler patients.
** Wilcox, Alvia E., Cpl., 17th CT: Died before patients were moved to general hospitals.

Spangler Patients Who Likely were Moved and Died at the XII Corps Hospital[8]

* Aeigle, John, Pvt., 107th OH: Buried in Soldiers' National Cemetery in Gettysburg with other deceased Spangler patients. Gettysburg resident J. G. Frey recorded that Aeigle was initially buried down the road from the Spanglers at the XII Corps hospital on the George Bushman farm, so he could have been moved there before he died.
* Beverly, Balts, Pvt., 107th OH: Buried in Soldiers' National Cemetery with other deceased Spangler patients. J. G. Frey recorded, however, that Beverly was

---

8 Aeigle, Beverly, Goodspeed, and Greiner are buried in the midst of more than 30 Ohioans at Soldiers' National Cemetery known to have died at the Spangler hospital—a strong indicator they also died there. That makes it at least possible that J. G. Frey's record is wrong about these four men, and that they were treated and also died on George Spangler's farm. It also remains possible they were transferred from the Spangler facility to the Bushman farm before or after their deaths and were buried there and then reburied with their XI Corps Ohio comrades on Cemetery Hill. Frey's painstaking recording of Army of the Potomac burial sites in the Gettysburg area in 1863 remains the most accurate and appreciated work of its kind.

initially buried down the road from the Spanglers at the XII Corps hospital on the George Bushman farm, so he could have been moved there before he died.

** Frey, Matthias, Sgt., 107th OH: J. G. Frey recorded that Sgt. Frey was initially buried down the road from the Spanglers at the XII Corps hospital on the George Bushman farm, so he could have been moved there before he died.

* Goodspeed, James H., Cpl., 75th OH: Buried with other deceased Spangler patients. J. G. Frey recorded, however, that Goodspeed was initially buried down the road from the Spanglers at the XII Corps hospital on the George Bushman farm, so he could have been moved there before he died.

* Greiner, George B., Cpl., 73rd OH: Buried with other deceased Spangler patients. J. G. Frey recorded, however, that Greiner was initially buried down the road from the Spanglers at the XII Corps hospital on the George Bushman farm, so he could have been moved there before he died.

Former Spangler Patients Known to Have Died at Camp Letterman

* Benda, Franz, Pvt., 26th WI: Died Aug. 28. Age 19;

* Bond, Alexander, Pvt., 27th PA: Died Sept. 30 of exhaustion. Age 37;

Coe, William W., Sgt., 21st NC: Admitted to Spangler on July 2. Transferred from Spangler after right leg amputation to Camp Letterman on Aug. 2. Died Sept. 17;

Comstock, Samuel, Sgt., 17th CT, H, died Sept. 17. Resided in New Canaan;

* Droeber, Henry, Pvt., 119th NY, B: Died Aug. 27. Age 25;

Grube, Charles W., Pvt., 153rd PA: Admitted to Camp Letterman with an amputated left leg. Died Sept. 4. Age 31;

* Laraba, Jonathan, Pvt., 75th OH: Died Aug. 20 of pneumonia. Remains removed to Soldiers' National Cemetery as Lavenden. Age 19;

* Taylor, Perry, Pvt., 75th OH: Died Oct. 15. Age 34;

* Young, Nicholaus, Pvt., 26th WI: Died Aug. 8.[9]

"[P]robably at no other place on this continent was there ever congregated such a vast amount of human suffering."

— *Surgeon Justin Dwinelle,*
II Corps, Army of the Potomac, after the Battle of Gettysburg

9 GNMP Library, Box 14A, Folder #4, "Burials at Camp Letterman."

Bibliography

Newspapers

Adams (PA) *Sentinel* (Gettysburg)
Atlanta Journal-Constitution
Baltimore Sun
Brooklyn Daily Eagle
Buffalo Commercial
Buffalo Enquirer
Cattaraugus (NY) *Freeman*
Cincinnati Enquirer
Dansville (NY) *Advertiser*
Democrat and Chronicle (Rochester, NY)
Duluth (MN) *Herald*
Geneva (NY) *Courier*
Gettysburg Compiler
Gettysburg Star and Banner
Gettysburg Star and Sentinel
Gettysburg Times
Independent (MT) *Record*
Lebanon (PA) *Daily News*
Marietta (OH) *Sunday Observer*
New York Herald
Oneida (NY) *Dispatch*
Philadelphia Inquirer
Philadelphia North American
Philadelphia Times
Reno (NV) *Gazette-Journal*

The Blade (Toledo, OH)

Washington (D.C.) *Evening Star*

Government Documents

Bachelder, John. Map of the Battle Field of Gettysburg, July 2-3, 1863. Washington, D.C.: Office of the Chief of Engineers US Army, 1876.

Connecticut Adjutant General's Office. *Catalogue of Connecticut Volunteer Organizations (Infantry, Cavalry and Artillery)*. Hartford, CT: Brown & Gross, 1869.

Hammond, Schuyler A. Map of the Battlefield of Gettysburg. Washington, D.C.: Gettysburg National Park Commission, 1903.

Heitman, Francis R. *Heitman's Register and Dictionary of the US Army* on Fold3. Washington, D.C.: Government Printing Office, 1903.

Hopkins, G. M. Map of Adams County, Pennsylvania. Philadelphia, PA: M. S. & E. Converse, 1858.

Janes, Henry. Camp Letterman General Hospital Orders and Correspondence Journal, July 26-September 9, 1863. Burlington, VT: University of Vermont.

New York Monuments Commission for the Battlefields of Gettysburg and Chattanooga. "Final Report on the Battlefield of Gettysburg." Albany, NY: J. B. Lyon Co., 1902.

United States Congress. Elliott's Map of the Battlefield of Gettysburg, Pennsylvania. Philadelphia, PA: S. G. Elliott & Co., 1864.

United States House of Representatives. *The Miscellaneous Documents of the House of Representatives for the First Session of the Fifty-first Congress, 1889-90*. Washington, D.C.: Government Printing Office, 1891.

United States Sanitary Commission. "Report on the Operations of the Sanitary Commission During and After the Battles at Gettysburg" in *Documents of the US Sanitary Commission*, vol. 2, nos. 61-95. New York, NY, 1866.

United States Surgeon General's Office. *The Medical and Surgical History of the War of the Rebellion (1861-65)*. Washington, D.C.: Government Printing Office, 1875.

United States War Department. *War of the Rebellion: Official Records of the Union and Confederate Armies*. Washington, D.C.: Government Printing Office, 1880-1901.

Autobiographies, Biographies, Published Personal Papers

Becker, Carl M. and Ritchie Thomas, eds. *Hearth and Knapsack: The Ladley Letters, 1857-1880*. Athens, OH: Ohio University Press, 1988.

Bell, Raymond Martin. "From James to Richard: The Nixon Line." Washington, PA: Washington & Jefferson College, 1957.

Brinton, Daniel G. "From Chancellorsville to Gettysburg, a Doctor's Diary" in *The Pennsylvania Magazine of History and Biography*. Harrisburg, PA: University of Pennsylvania Press, 1965.

Broadhead, Sarah M. *The Diary of a Lady of Gettysburg, Pennsylvania, June 15 to July 15, 1863*. Gettysburg, PA: Adams County Historical Society, 1863.

Butterfield, Daniel. *The Union Generals Speak*. Baton Rouge, LA: Louisiana State University Press, 2003.

Campbell, Eric A., ed. *A Grand Terrible Dramma: From Gettysburg to Petersburg: The Civil War Letters of Charles Wellington Reed*. New York, NY: Fordham University Press, 2000.

Dunkelman, Mark H. *Brothers, Heroes, Martyrs: The Civil War Service of Lewis and George Bishop, Color Bearers of the 154th New York Volunteer Infantry*. Allegany, NY: Allegany Area Historical Association, 1994.

———. *Brothers One and All*. Baton Rouge, LA: Louisiana State University Press, 2004.

Favill, Josiah Marshall. *The Diary of a Young Officer*. Chicago, IL: R. R. Donnelley & Sons Company, 1909.

Fuller, Charles A. *Personal Recollections of the War of 1861*. Sherburne, NY: News Job Printing House, 1906.

Hancock, Almira. *Reminiscences of Winfield Scott Hancock by His Wife*. New York, NY: C. L. Webster & Co., 1887.

Harold Earl, ed. *Diary of a Union Lady, 1861-1865*. New York, NY: Funk & Wagnalls Co., 1962.

Hedrick, David T. and Gordon Barry Davis Jr., eds. *I'm Surrounded by Methodists: Diary of John H. W. Stuckenberg Chaplain of the 145th Pennsylvania Volunteer Infantry*. Gettysburg, PA: Thomas Publications, 1995.

Holland, Mary A. Gardner. *Our Army Nurses: Interesting Sketches, Addresses and Photographs*. Boston, MA: B. Wilkins & Co., 1895.

Howard, Oliver. *Autobiography of Oliver Otis Howard, Major General United States Army*. New York: The Baker & Taylor Company, 1907.

Howard, Rowland B. "At Gettysburg." American Peace Society. Boston, MA, 1887.

Jaquette, Henrietta Stratton, ed. *Letters of a Civil War Nurse: Cornelia Hancock, 1863-1865*. Lincoln, NE: University of Nebraska Press, 1998.

Kamphoefner, Walter D., and Wolfgang Helbich, eds. *Germans in the Civil War: The Letters They Wrote Home*. Chapel Hill, NC: The University of North Carolina Press, 2006.

Leale, Charles A. "Memoir of Dr. Charles S. Wood, M.D." in *Transactions of the New York State Medical Association for the Year 1884-1899*. New York, NY: New York State Medical Association, 1891.

Letterman, Jonathan. *Medical Recollections of the Army of the Potomac.* New York, NY: D. Appleton and Company, 1866.

Livermore, Thomas L. *Days and Events, 1860-1866.* Boston, MA, and New York, NY: Houghton, Mifflin and Company, 1920.

Meade, George G. *The Life and Letters of George Gordon Meade.* New York, NY: Charles Scribner's Sons, 1913.

Merrill, Catharine. *The Soldier of Indiana in the War for the Union.* Indianapolis, IN: Merrill and Company, 1869.

Morrison, James L., ed. *The Memoirs of Henry Heth.* Westport, CT: Greenwood Press Inc., 1974.

Ryder, John J. *Reminiscences of Three Years' Service in the Civil War.* New Bedford, MA: 1928.

Schurz, Carl. *The Reminiscences of Carl Schurz.* New York, NY: The McClure Company, 1908.

Shaffer, Duane E. *Men of Granite: New Hampshire's Soldiers in the Civil War.* Columbia, SC: University of South Carolina Press, 2008.

Silliman, Justus M. *A New Canaan Private in the Civil War: Letters of Justus M. Silliman, 17th Connecticut Volunteers.* New Canaan, CT: New Canaan Historical Society, 1984.

Skelly, Daniel Alexander. *A Boy's Experiences During the Battles of Gettysburg* (1932). Ann Arbor, MI: University Microfilms, 1973.

Smith, Henry Perry, ed. "The Cortland County Medical Society" in *History of Cortland County.* Syracuse, NY: D. Mason & Co., 1885.

Souder, Mrs. Edmund A. *Leaves From the Battle-field of Gettysburg. A Series of Letters From a Field Hospital and National Poems.* Philadelphia, PA: C. Sherman, Son & Company, 1864.

Spangler, Lee. *Jacob Thomas Zehrung Civil War Personal Diary.* Canal Winchester, OH: 2001.

Sparks, David S., ed. *Inside Lincoln's Army: The Diary of Marsena Rudolph Patrick, Provost Marshal General, Army of the Potomac.* New York, NY: T. Yoseloff, 1964.

Stowe, Charles Edward and Harriet Beecher Stowe. *Life of Harriet Beecher Stowe: Compiled From Her Letters and Journals.* London: Sampson Low, Marston, Searle & Rivington Limited, 1889.

Stuart, George H. *The Life of George H. Stuart.* Philadelphia, PA: J. M. Stoddart & Co., 1890.

Tagg, Larry. *The Generals of Gettysburg: The Leaders of America's Greatest Battle.* El Dorado Hills, CA: Savas Publishing, 1998.

Tucker, Glenn. *Hancock the Superb.* Indianapolis, IN: Bobbs-Merrill Co., 1960.

"Tyler, Robert Ogden: A Memorial." Philadelphia, PA: J. B. Lippincott & Co., 1878.

Underwood, Robert Johnson and Clarence Clough Buel, eds. *Battles and Leaders of the Civil War.* New York, NY: The Century Company, 1888.

Wittenmyer, Mrs. Annie. *Under the Guns: A Woman's Reminiscences of the Civil War*. Boston, MA: E. B. Stillings & Company, 1895.

Campaigns and Battles

Baumgartner, Richard A. *Buckeye Blood: Ohio at Gettysburg*. Huntington, WV: Blue Acorn Press, 2003.

Bigelow, John. *The Peach Orchard: Gettysburg*. Minneapolis, MN: Kimball-Storer, 1910.

Busey, John W. and David G. Martin. *Regimental Strengths and Losses at Gettysburg, Fourth Edition*. Hightstown, NJ: Longstreet House, 2005.

Busey, John W. and Travis Busey. *Union Casualties at Gettysburg: A Comprehensive Record*. Jefferson, NC: McFarland & Company Inc., 2011.

Hessler, James A. and Wayne Motts, *Pickett's Charge at Gettysburg: A Guide to the Most Famous Attack in American History*. Eldorado Hills, CA: Savas Beatie, 2015.

Jacobs, Michael. *Notes on the Rebel Invasion of Maryland and Pennsylvania and the Battle of Gettysburg*. Philadelphia, PA: J. B. Lippincott & Co., 1864.

Ladd, David L. and Audrey J. Ladd. *The Bachelder Papers*, 3 vols. Dayton, OH: Morningside Press, 1994.

McIntosh, David Gregg. *The Campaign of Chancellorsville*. Richmond, VA: W. E. Jones' Sons Inc., 1915.

Moore, Frank, ed. "The Battles of Gettysburg. Cincinnati Gazette Account" in *The Rebellion Record: A Diary of American Events*. New York, NY: Van Nostrand, 1864.

Nicholson, John P., ed. *Pennsylvania at Gettysburg*. Harrisburg, PA: Commonwealth of Pennsylvania, 1914.

Sauers, Richard, ed. *Fighting Them Over: How the Veterans Remembered Gettysburg in the Pages of The National Tribune*. Baltimore, MD: Butternut and Blue, 1998.

Shay, Ralph S., ed. *Reflections on the Battle of Gettysburg*. Lebanon, PA: Lebanon County, PA, Historical Society, 1890.

Tenney, W. J. *The Military and Naval History of the Rebellion in the United States*. New York: D. Appleton & Company, 1866.

Unit Histories

Baker, Levi Wood. *History of the Ninth Massachusetts Battery*. Fort Mitchell, KY: Ironclad Publishing, 1996.

Child, William. *History of the 5th New Hampshire Volunteers*. Bristol, NH: R. W. Musgrove, 1893.

Culp, Edward C. *Raising the Banner of Freedom: The 25th Ohio Volunteer Infantry in the War of the Union.* Bloomington, IN: iUniverse, 2003.

Haskin, William L., ed. *The History of the First Regiment of Artillery From its Organization in 1821, to January 1st, 1876.* Portland, ME: B. Thurston and Company, 1879.

Hurst, Samuel H. *Journal-history of the Seventy-third Ohio Volunteer Infantry.* Chillicothe, OH: 1866.

Hyde, Thomas W. *Following the Greek Cross Or, Memories of the Sixth Army Corps.* New York, NY: Houghton, Mifflin and Company, 1894.

Kiefer, William R. *History of the One Hundred and Fifty-Third Regiment Pennsylvania Volunteers Infantry: Which Was Recruited in Northampton County, Pa., 1862-1863.* Easton, PA: The Chemical Publishing Co., 1909.

Meyer, Thomas P. "The Pioneer's Story." J. W. Muffly, ed., in *The Story of Our Regiment: A History of the 148th Pennsylvania Volunteers.* Des Moines, IA: Kenyon Printing & Manufacturing Co., 1904.

Morse, Charles F. "The Twelfth Corps at Gettysburg." Boston: Military Historical Society of Massachusetts, 1917.

Nichols, G. W. *A Soldier's Story of His Regiment (61st Georgia).* Ithaca, NY: Cornell University, 1898.

Osborn, Hartwell. *Trials and Triumphs: The Record of the 55th Ohio Volunteer Infantry.* Chicago, IL: A. C. McClurg & Co., 1904.

Pula, James S. *Under the Crescent Moon with the XI Corps in the Civil War. Vol. 1: From the Defenses of Washington to Chancellorsville, 1862-1863.* El Dorado Hills, CA: Savas Beatie, 2017, and *Vol. 2: From Gettysburg to Victory, 1863-1865.* Savas Beatie, 2018.

Reinhart, Joseph R., ed., *Yankee Dutchmen Under Fire: Civil War Letters From the 82nd Illinois Infantry.* Kent, OH: Kent State University Press, 2013.

Saxton, William. *A Regiment Remembered: The 157th New York Volunteers.* Cortland, NY: Cortland County Historical Society, 1996.

Smith, Jacob. *Camps and Campaigns of the 107th Regiment Ohio Volunteer Infantry, From August, 1862, to July, 1865.* Navarre, OH: Indian River Graphics, 2000.

Sturtevant, Ralph Orson and Carmi Lathrop Marsh, *History of the 13th Regiment Vermont Volunteers.* Newport, VT: 1910.

Warner, George H. *Military Records of Schoharie County Veterans of Four Wars.* Albany, NY: Weed, Parsons and Company, 1891.

Other Publications

"A Company Officer." *Lippincott's Magazine of Popular Literature and Science.* Philadelphia: J. B. Lippincott & Company, 1883.

Adams County Historical Society. *History of Adams County Pennsylvania.* Gettysburg, PA: 1992.

American Medical Association. *The Journal of the American Medical Association.* Chicago, IL: 1883, 1905.

American Tract Society. Pamphlets "I'm Too Young," No. 62, and "To the Sick, Who are Without Hope in Christ," No. 110. Boston, MA.

Baker, Albert R. and Samuel W. Kelley, eds. *Cleveland Medical Gazette.* Cleveland, OH: 1895.

Biographical Record of the City of Rochester and Monroe County, New York, The. New York, NY: S. J. Clarke, 1902.

Brockett, Linus Pierpoint and Mary C. Vaughan. *Woman's Work in the Civil War: A Record of Heroism, Patriotism and Patience.* Philadelphia, PA: Edgewood Publishing Co., 1867.

Clegg, Miriam. "Secrets of Old Houses: Their Hidden Passageways." Historical Society of the Phoenixville Area newsletter. Phoenixville, PA: 1988.

Coco, Gregory A. *On the Bloodstained Field.* Gettysburg, PA: Thomas Publications, 1987.

——. *A Strange and Blighted Land—Gettysburg: The Aftermath of a Battle.* El Dorado Hills, Savas Beatie, 2017.

Connecticut Medical Society. *Proceedings of the Connecticut Medical Society, 1898.* Bridgeport, CT.

Cooper, William and George Suckley. *The Natural History of Washington Territory and Oregon; With Much Relating to Minnesota, Nebraska, Kansas, Utah, and California . . . Being Those Parts . . . Northern Pacific Railroad Route. . . .* New York, NY: 1859.

Cranmer, Gibson Lamb. *History of the Upper Ohio Valley.* Madison, WI: Brant & Fuller, 1891.

Crocker, James F. *Gettysburg – Pickett's Charge and Other War Addresses.* Portsmouth, VA: W. A. Fiske, 1915.

Cross, Andrew B. "The Battle of Gettysburg" in *The War and the Christian Commission.* Baltimore, MD, 1865.

Dickinson County, Kansas, Historical Society & Museum. Dickinson County Cemetery Survey, Center Township, Mount Hope Cemetery. Abilene, KS: 1982.

Duncan, Louis C. *The Medical Department of the United States Army in the Civil War.* Cornell University Library.

Dyer, Frederick H. *A Compendium of the War of the Rebellion.* Des Moines, IA: The Dyer Publishing Company, 1908.

Ellis, Franklin, ed. *History of Cattaraugus County, New York.* Philadelphia, PA: L. H. Everts, 1879.

Fee, William I. *Bringing the Sheaves: Gleanings From Harvest Fields in Ohio, Kentucky and West Virginia.* Cincinnati, OH: Cranston & Curts, 1896.

Fox, George Benson, in Christine Dee, ed., *Ohio's War, the Civil War in Documents.* Athens, OH: Ohio University Press, 2006.

Gettysburg Foundation. George Spangler Farmstead Historic Structure Report. Gettysburg, PA, 2011.

Glassie, Henry. "Eighteenth Century Cultural Process in Delaware Valley Folk Building" in *Common Places: Readings in American Vernacular Architecture.* Athens, GA: The University of Georgia Press, 1986.

Grand Army of the Republic. *Journal of the Forty-ninth National Encampment Grand Army of the Republic.* Washington, D.C., 1916.

Green, Frank B. "History of the Medical Profession of the City of Brooklyn, 1822-1884" in *History of Kings County, Including Brooklyn, N.Y.* New York, NY: W. W. Munsell & Co., 1884.

Harris, Ellen. "Fifth Semi-annual Report of the Ladies' Aid Society of Philadelphia." Philadelphia, PA: Ladies Aid Society of Philadelphia, 1863.

Hewett, Janet B. *The Roster of Confederate Soldiers, 1861-1865.* Wilmington, NC: Broadfoot Publishing Co., 1996.

——. *The Roster of Union Soldiers, 1861-1865.* Wilmington, NC: Broadfoot Publishing Co., 1998.

Lowry, Thomas and Terry Reimer, *Bad Doctors: Military Justice Proceedings Against 622 Civil War Surgeons,* Frederick, MD: National Museum of Civil War Medicine Press, 2010.

Military Service Institution. *Journal of the Military Service Institution of the United States.* New York, NY: 1883.

Mitchell, Mary H. *Hollywood Cemetery: The History of a Southern Shrine.* Richmond, VA: Library of Virginia, 1999.

Philadelphia College of Pharmacy. "Twenty-second Annual Report of the Alumni Association." Philadelphia, PA: 1886.

Poerner, J. B. "United States Christian Commission: Third Report of the Committee of Maryland." Baltimore, MD: James Young, 1864.

Reid, Whitelaw. *Two Witnesses at Gettysburg,* Malden, MA: Wiley-Blackwell, 2009.

Stanton, Samuel Cecil, ed. *The Military Surgeon: Journal of the Association of Military Surgeons of the United States,* vol. 32. Chicago, IL: The Association of Military Surgeons, 1913.

The Medical and Surgical History of the War of the Civil War. Wilmington, NC: Broadfoot Publishing Company, 1990.

United States Christian Commission. "United States Christian Commission for the Army and Navy, for the Year 1863, Second Annual Report." Philadelphia, PA, 1864.

Waldo Jr., George Curtis, ed. *History of Bridgeport and Vicinity,* vol. 2. New York, NY, and Chicago, IL: S. J. Clarke Publishing Company, 1917.

Articles

"Causes of Lee's Defeat at Gettysburg," *Southern Historical Society Papers*, vol. 4, no. 1. Richmond, VA, 1877.

Chamberlain, Joshua Lawrence. "Through Blood and Fire at Gettysburg," *Hearst's Magzine*, vol. 23, January 1913.

Dodge, Theodore Ayrault. "Left Wounded on the Field," *Putnam's Magazine*, vol. 4, July-December, 1869.

Easley, D. B. "With Armistead When He Was Killed," *Confederate Veteran*, vol. 20, no. 1, 1912.

Farinholt, B. L. "Battle of Gettysburg – Johnson's Island," *Confederate Veteran*, vol. 5, no. 1, 1897.

"General Pickett at Gettysburg," Confederate Veteran, vol. 21, no. 1, 1913.

Harding, Milton. "Where General Armistead Fell," *Confederate Veteran*, vol. 19, no. 1, 1911.

Holland, T. C. "With Armistead at Gettysburg," *Confederate Veteran*, vol. 29, no. 1, 1921.

Kuykendall, Rhea. "Surgeons of the Confederacy," *Confederate Veteran*, vol. 34, no. 1, 1926.

Lewis, Mrs. H. F. "General Armistead at Gettysburg," *Confederate Veteran*, vol. 28, no. 1, 1920.

Martin, R. W. "Armistead at the Battle of Gettysburg," *Southern Historical Society Papers*, vol. 39, no. 39. Richmond, VA, 1914.

Medical School of the Western Reserve University. "A War Letter From Dr. Himes," *The Western Reserve Medical Journal*. Cleveland, OH: 1895.

Musselman, Curt. "McAllister's Mill and the Underground Railroad," *The Sentinel*, National Park Service at Gettysburg, 2013.

"Notes and Queries," *Southern Historical Society Papers*, vol. 10, nos. 1 and 2. Richmond, VA: 1882.

"Notes and Queries," *Southern Historical Society Papers*, vol. 11, no. 1. Richmond, VA: 1883.

Potter, William Warren. "Field Hospital Service With the Army of the Potomac," vol. 29, *Buffalo Medical Journal*. Buffalo, NY: 1889, 1912.

——. "Three Years With the Army of the Potomac: A Personal Military History," vol. 67, *Buffalo Medical Journal*. Buffalo, NY: 1889, 1912.

"Reminiscences of the Gettysburg Battle," *Lippincott's Magazine of Popular Literature and Science*, vol. 32, 1883.

Schurz, Carl. "The Battle of Gettysburg," *McClure's Magazine*, vol. 29, May to October, 1907.

"War Songs and Sonnets of the South," *Confederate Veteran*, vol. 3, no. 1, 1895.

Dissertations

Harman, Troy D. "In Defense of Henry Slocum on July 1." Seminar Papers, Gettysburg National Military Park.

Websites

www.1stminnesota.net

www.achs-pa.org

www.ancestry.com

www.arlingtoncemetery.net

www.bergencountyhistory.org

www.brotherswar.com

www.civilwardata.com

www.civilwarindex.com

www.dmna.ny.gov

www.famousamericans.net

www.findagrave.com

www.fold3.com

www.gdg.org

www.harrietbeecherstowecenter.org

www.history.army.mil

www.in2013dollars.com

www.jstor.org

www.newspapers.com

www.npshistory.com

www.russscott.com

www.soldierstudies.org

www.unionveterans.wordpress.com

www.usgenweb.info

www.vermontcivilwar.org

www.warfarehistorynetwork.com

Index

Acknowledgments

National-caliber historian Wayne Motts could have written a great book about the Spanglers if he had the time.

His books on Confederate Brig. Gen. Lewis A. Armistead and Pickett's Charge were well-written and well-received, and Wayne was interested in George and Elizabeth Spangler's farm before most of the rest of us even knew it existed. He wanted to see the farm so badly that he got permission from the owners—the Andrew family—to visit when he was 21 years old. I can envision this history buff college kid looking around in awe and reverence and knocking down spider webs while paying respect to the places where the limbs came off and the wounded and dying men lay and cried.

And when the Gettysburg Foundation purchased the farm in 2008, you can guess who it turned to for a lot of its research and information. But Wayne is busy as CEO of The National Civil War Museum in Harrisburg, PA, leading tours on the battlefield, with speaking engagements, and with being one of the widely accepted experts on Gettysburg and the go-to guy with questions. So instead of writing this book, Wayne graciously helped me do so by answering questions and providing me with information, guidance, suggestions, and, most importantly, his precious time. This book is better because of Wayne Motts' expertise on and passion for the Spangler property.

Historians have been unsuccessfully looking for the lost records of this XI Corps hospital at the National Archives and Records Administration in Washington, D.C., since the late 1800s. I, too, tried and failed. What was lost were the names of the wounded men treated there, their regiment, rank, company, wound, and treatment. We had this information for other Gettysburg hospitals but not Spangler. History lost, and a source of great frustration. And then Jim Fielden of Cleveland came across something in 2018 while searching for information on great-grandfather Roland E. Perry of the 75th Ohio, who had a finger amputated at Spangler. He didn't find the actual lost register written by surgeons at Spangler in 1863, but he found an obscure, dusty register with the names of wounded men from multiple corps at Gettysburg that was hand-written in the 1880s. And he was kind enough to share this discovery with me as well as introduce me to the world of carded medical service records. With Jim's discovery, I could piece together one by one the names of most of the wounded who were at the XI Corps hospital. Jim single-handedly unlocked the hidden history of the George Spangler farm, and because of that we have the names of more than 1,400 Spangler wounded in this book. World, please say a big thank-you to Jim Fielden of Cleveland.

George Rapp is descended from Spangler nurse Rebecca Lane Pennypacker Price, whom I didn't know about until George walked up to me outside the summer kitchen on a sunny summer day at the farm. He provided important photos and information on Nurse Price that resulted in two chapters in this book. I look forward to the tour of the Phoenixville, PA, area that George has promised me.

Likewise, Rex Hovey contributed greatly with his guidance and actual materials from 1863 to the chapter on his ancestors—Dr. Bleecker Lansing Hovey, Marilla Hovey, and their son, Frank. Rex has portrayed Dr. Hovey at the farm for years and is the proud owner of his great-uncle's surgical kit.

Helping me from beginning to end on this project from the Gettysburg Foundation were Mike Shealer, Ray Matlock, Cindy Small, Brian Shaffer, and Paul Semanek. Mike grew up on Powers Hill on the former Nathaniel Lightner property and spent time as a child playing on the former Spangler land, so this ground is personal to him. He was this book's first editor. Cindy and Brian were involved with the Spangler farm since its purchase by the Gettysburg Foundation and this book does not happen without their help, nor does the public get to visit the farm today without their vision. Ray offered his photo skills and overall guidance and was the one who trusted me enough despite my inexperience in 2013 to allow me to begin as a volunteer guide at the farm. Paul and I have had many discussions about and at Spangler over the years as he advanced from volunteer there to running the place for the Foundation. When he opens the farm's gates and doors in the summer he is also opening the public's eyes to the world of Civil War medicine and the lives of George and Elizabeth Spangler.

The Gettysburg Foundation's small group of volunteer Spangler docents has a passion for the property, and these folks show it by leading tours and putting on informative and entertaining programs there. The Foundation knows it's a better organization because of these dedicated volunteers, just as I know this book was improved because of their caring and interest in seeing that this project was done right. Volunteer Randy Grimsley knows so much about the Spangler family that he has portrayed George at events; Mary Ellen King, as did George Rapp, did extensive research and handed me information on Nurse Price that was invaluable in this book; and Dave Shackleton offered support and helped round up old photos of the farm that I didn't know existed. Their help was crucial.

From the National Park Service, I went to Historian John Heiser when things didn't make sense and I got stuck, and he always calmly cleared things up for me. And each time I thanked him he came back with a reassuring and friendly "Any time, Ron." Eric A. Campbell has done a great deal of research on the 9th Massachusetts Battery, and he and *Gettysburg Magazine* were the sources of that unit's route into action from Spangler on July 2, 1863. Additional crucial expertise and time from the Park Service came from Bert Barnett, Christopher Gwinn, Troy Harmon, and Curt Musselman.

Also providing invaluable information and time were noted author and historian James Pula on the XI Corps; Andy Gelfert on the Rev. John B. Poerner and the United States Christian Commission; Katja Sirrenberg on the Germans; Sister Betty Ann McNeil, D.C., Vincentian Scholar-in-Residence, DePaul University, on the Daughters of Charity; author William Thomas Venner on Confederate casualties; Dr. Spencer Annabel and Dr. Jon Willen on Civil War medicine; author Jeffrey Stocker of "We Fought Desperate" on the 153rd Pennsylvania; David Maclay on barn preservation; Ken Rich on Powers Hill; Thomas Palmer on his ancestor, Dr. Jay Kling; Jack Craig with his tour of Mount Hope Cemetery in Enterprise, Kansas; Christopher Philip DiElsi of Ridgefield, CT, and Carolyn Ivanoff of Seymour, CT, for leading me to and helping me with Pvt. James R. Middlebrook of the 17th Connecticut Infantry; and Terry Reimer of the National Museum of Civil War Medicine in Frederick, MD. The high quality of the National Museum of Civil War Medicine cannot be overstated. Several visits to its main facility in Frederick and to its satellite Pry House near Sharpsburg, MD, during early research yielded a bounty of useful information that was used throughout this book. Both museums are highly recommended.

Tim Smith and Rodger Rex of the Adams County Historical Society enthusiastically spent hours with me poring over 1800s deeds, tax records, notebooks, and old photos and stories. Tim and Rodger seem to know where every piece of paper and photo is located in the society, even if it's in a long-forgotten book in the deepest, darkest corner of the society's historic and stately Wolf House on the campus of the Lutheran Theological Seminary.

Joyce Peters of the Vinton County (Ohio) Historical and Genealogical Society spent weeks exploring Pvt. George Nixon III in his home county for this book. She was tenacious in researching Nixon in the library, courthouse, and historical society in the town of McArthur in addition to finding and interviewing a Nixon relative because, as she said, "I just don't want to leave any stone unturned." The work of Joyce and the society is of great service to history and the readers of the Nixon chapter.

Gettysburg and Little Bighorn enthusiast William Kane of Harrisburg accompanied me on research trips and gave me lists of questions that he didn't want me to forget to ask. He also climbed through mud, thorns, poison ivy, and weeds to help me locate and measure the buried foundation of the former Granite Schoolhouse, retraced with me the steps of the 9th Massachusetts, served as research trip photographer, and edited and commented on early text.

Graphic designer Derek Wachter is a friend and former co-worker from Harrisburg whose talent is obvious with the eight maps he created for this book. What is not so obvious is his kindness and superhuman patience, which were needed as I constantly changed my mind on what I wanted placed where on the maps. Any map errors are mine. Design excellence may be credited to Derek.

Managing Director Theodore P. Savas, Marketing Director Sarah Keeney, and Media Specialist Sarah Closson from my publisher Savas Beatie took my hand and ushered me through my first book. Ted is a writing and editing expert, and he filled holes in the book that I didn't know existed. Sarah and Sarah are teaching me as they spread the much-needed word on this farm. All three have a love for Spangler that I will forever appreciate.

Finally and especially, my loving thanks to my wife, Barbara, who traveled with me on research trips to libraries, small-town city halls, historical societies, cemeteries, battlefields, museums, and archives all over the East Coast and as far west as Kansas. She asked important questions that I hadn't thought of and encouraged me when writing or research stalled. A one-week trip to Cornell University for searches through 19 boxes of brittle 1800s papers and three weeks at the National Archives each would have taken twice that time without Barb's help. And this book would have been completed two years earlier if only I had started it when she suggested.

Ronald D. Kirkwood is retired after a 40-year career as an editor and writer in newspapers and magazines including *USA TODAY*, the *Baltimore Sun*, the *Harrisburg* (PA) *Patriot-News*, and the *York* (PA) *Daily Record*. Ron edited national magazines for *USA TODAY Sports* and was NFL editor for *USA TODAY Sports Weekly*. He won numerous state, regional, and national awards during his career and managed the copy desk in Harrisburg when the newspaper won a Pulitzer Prize in 2012.

Ron has been a Gettysburg Foundation docent at the George Spangler Farm Civil War Field Hospital Site since it opened in 2013. He is a native of Dowagiac/Sister Lakes, MI, and a graduate of Central Michigan University, where he has returned as guest speaker to journalism classes as part of the school's Hearst Visiting Professionals series. Ron and his wife, Barbara, live in York. They have two daughters, two sons-in-law, and five grandchildren.